Fairness and Division of Labor in Market Societies

FAIRNESS AND DIVISION OF LABOR IN MARKET SOCIETIES

A Comparison of the U.S. and German
Automotive Industries

Hyeong-ki Kwon

Berghahn Books
NEW YORK · OXFORD

Published in 2004 by
Berghahn Books

www.berghahnbooks.com

© 2004 Hyeong-ki Kwon

Library of Congress Cataloging-in-Publication Data

Kwon, Hyeong-ki
    Fairness and division of labor in market societies : a comparison of the
U.S. and German automotive industries / Hyeong-ki Kwon.
    p. cm.
Includes bibliographical references.
ISBN 1-57181-671-2 (alk. paper)
    1. Automotive supplies industry—Employees—Supply and
demand—United States. 2. Automobile supplies industry—Employees—
Supply and demand—Germany. 3. Automobile supplies industry—
Subcontracting—United States. 4. Automobile supplies industry—Sub-
contracting—Germany. 5. Labor market—United States. 6. Labor mar-
ket—Germany. 7. International division of labor. 8. Fairness. I. Title.

HD5718.A82U637 2004
331.7'6292'0943—dc22

                                                            2003062930

British Library Cataloguing in Publication Data

A catalogue record for this book is available from
the British Library.

Printed in the United States on acid-free paper

CONTENTS

TABLES

PREFACE

This book studies divergent ways of constituting social norms and efficiency in market societies by investigating the ways in which the U.S. and German automotive (parts) industries adjusted and changed during the 1990s. Based on intensive and extensive empirical study, this book critically reconsiders the prevalent paradigms of political economy, proposing an alternative "reflexive" model.

Recent changes in the U.S. and German automotive parts industries present major challenges to the prevalent paradigms of political economic literature, especially those produced by the neoliberal and the Varieties of Capitalism schools of thought, which lead one to expect a particular line of adjustment (such as the convergence of national economies toward liberal markets or the path-dependent divergence). Contrary to the explanations offered by the Varieties of Capitalism literature, the U.S. and the German automotive industries undertook strikingly similar patterns of industry modification under tough international competition, departing from their traditional national patterns. The U.S. and German automotive companies deintegrated their vertically integrated in-house production, contracted out with independent suppliers, adopted new, flexible-production systems, and developed new forms of long-term and closely interactive market relations.

Despite the similar patterns of adjustments in the U.S. and Germany, however, the neoliberal paradigm is not confirmed by this research. The apparent revival of contractual relations has not involved a neoclassical market of discrete exchange based on the anonymity principle; rather, both national markets share a common departure from the logic of the neoclassical understanding of market governance. Furthermore, the new form of long-term and closely interactive contractual relations, in which prior institutional arrangements about contracts and contractual relations do not produce stable governance, caused new problems in market governance, leaving room for creatively new divergent paths in resolving conflicts and establishing stable regimes.

In order to better account for this recomposition of the market relations, which I have termed "converging but non-liberal" and "diverging but not predetermined," I propose an alternative model of "politics among reflexive agents," emphasizing different kinds of problem-solving practices among those reflexive agents. First, I claim a new conception of "politics of multiple rationalities" in the market. An ideal type of market rationality is not the apparent single necessity that the neoliberal paradigm assumes. Rather, multiple types of market rationality are in play, as are the politics that constitute them. Secondly, the form and pace of successful industry adjustment toward collaborative markets varies tremendously, as in the U.S. and German automotive parts industries. Keeping in mind the contingencies of national difference, I criticize the rigid, nonreflexive, and path-dependent institutionalism prevalent in theories produced by the Varieties of Capitalism group, instead emphasizing agents' reflexivity and methods of organizing deliberations. I argue that different forms and regimes of market are established in the process of recomposition, in which agents reflect upon not only market rationality but also their own institutions. Different regimes, resulting from the recomposition process, are closely related to the different ways agents deliberate their problems and create new norms.

In the course of preparing this book, I have accumulated many debts of thanks. First and foremost, I would like to express my deepest appreciation to my committee, Gary Herrigel, William Sewell, and Michael Geyer. In particular, Professor Herrigel guided me through the murky and turbulent process of this project with tremendous encouragement, tough and insightful criticism, and soul-caring advice. Regarding the intensive and extensive field research on which this book is based on, I will never forget the indispensable help offered by interview and survey participants in the U.S. and Germany: managers of supplier companies, automakers (Mercedes, BMW, VW, and Audi), associations, and regional institutes. In particular, I would like to give special thanks to the Soziologischesforschung Institut (SOFI) in Göttingen, Germany, and Professor Volker Wittke and numerous friends at Universität Göttingen who supported my research in Germany. I am also grateful for the generous financial support of the Deutscher Akademischer Austauschdienst (DAAD), the Mellon Foundation Dissertation Fellowship, the Seoul National University Alumni Fellowship, and the University of Chicago scholarship.

Some parts of this book, particularly parts of chapter 1, were first published as "Divergent Constitution of Liberal Regimes" in *Politics & Society* (March 2003), and "Markets, Institutions, and Politics under Globalization" in *Comparative Political Studies* (February 2004). I would like to thank Mary-Ann Twist, editor of *Politics & Society,* and Janet Wilt, editor of *Comparative Political Studies*. And above all, special thanks are due to Marion

Berghahn, publisher and editor of Berghahn Books, for her generous offer to publish this volume.

Finally, I would like to thank my family for their endless sacrifice, love, and encouragement. I owe special thanks to my wife Jung-Hee Choi, who always stands by me with speechless love and sacrifice, without which I could not have finished my project. I dedicate this book to my parents, Taek-Yong Kwon and Youngja Ko, who taught me how to live a meaningful life by their own example.

ABBREVIATIONS

AIAG   Automotive Industry Action Group
ArGeZ   German Supplier Confederation (Arbeitsgemeinschaft Zulieferindustrie)
BAIKA   Automobile Supplier Initiative for Innovation and Cooperation in Bavaria (Bayerischen Innovations- und Kooperationsinitiative- Automobilzulieferindustrie)
BDA   Federal Association of German Employers (Bundesvereinigung der Deutschen Arbeitgeberverbände)
BDI   German Federal Industry Association (Bundesverband der Deutschen Industrie e.V)
BMW   Bayerischen Motoren Werke
DGV   German Foundry Association (Deutscher Gießereiverband e.V)
DQP   Diversified Quality Production
EBM   The Trade Association of Iron, Plate, Metal Industries (Wirtschaftsverband Eisen, Blech und Metall verarbeitende Industrie e.V)
FAW   Research Center of Automobile Economics in Bamberg University (Forschungstelle Automobilwirtschaft at the Universität Bamberg)
GKV   General Association of Synthetic Industry (Gesamtverband kunststoffverarbeitende Industrie e.V)
NAM   National Association of Manufacturers
NBER   National Bureau of Economic Research
NTMA   National Tooling and Machine Association
OEMs   Original Equipment Manufacturers
OESA   Original Equipment Supplier Association
PMA   Precision Metal Forming Association
PMPA   Precision Machine Product Association
SCORE   Chrysler's "Supplier Cost Reduction Effort" Program
TMA   The Tooling and Manufacturing Association

VDA   German Automobile Association (Verband der Automobilin-
       dustrie e.V)
VDI   German Engineer Association (Verein Deutscher Ingenieure e.V)
VDMA   German Machine Tool Industry Association (Verband
       Deutscher Maschinen- und Anlagenbau).
VIA   Automobile Industry Initiative (Verbundinitiative Automobil
       Nordrheinwestfalen)
VW   Volkswagen AG
WdK   German Rubber Association (Wirtschaftsverband der
       deutschen Kautschukindustrie)
WMDC   Wisconsin Manufacturers' Development Consortium
WSI   Economic and Social Science Institute (Wirtschafts- und
       Sozialwissenschaftliches Institut)
WSU   German Steel Forging Association (Wirtschaftsverband
       Stahlumformung e.V)
WVM   Trade Association of Metal Industry (Wirtschaftsvereiningung
       Metalle e.V)
WZB   Berlin Science Center (Wissenschaftszentrum Berlin)
ZVEI   German Electro- and Electrics Association (Zentralverband
       Elektrotechnik- und Elektronikindustrie e.V)

INTRODUCTION

Recent industrial adjustments under globalization challenge prevalent paradigms of political economy. Although hierarchical governance (Keynesian state regulation and vertically integrated corporation) has been replaced by the growth of market relations, the neoclassical paradigm has been called into question. Institutionalists propose alternatives to the universal relevance of the neoclassical market, but many institutionalist approaches are too rigid to explain the dynamic transformation of market economies. This book suggests alternative conceptions of the market and politics by focusing on two advanced market societies, particularly on the dynamic process of transformation in the U.S. and German automotive parts markets.

The process of industrial adjustments in the U.S. and German automotive industries in the 1980s and 1990s showed strikingly similar patterns under severe global competition. For example, agents in both the U.S. and German automobile industries deintegrated their hierarchical, in-house mass production. Almost all companies in both the American and German automobile industries adopted a new, flexible production system, cross-functional team structure, and long-term, closely interactive contractual relations with independent suppliers. The similar pattern of adjustments challenges the institutionalist view of rigid national trajectory, which dictates that "a pattern of national production and market system is very path-dependent."

Furthermore, the similar pattern of markets in the U.S. and Germany also challenges the neoclassical paradigm. The last two decades of the twentieth century were characterized by the triumph of market relations as the hierarchical production system was decentralized, which contrasts with the retreat of market relations in the first half of the twentieth century. Contrary to prevalent belief, however, the apparent revival of contracts in society has not rejuvenated a neoclassical market of discrete exchange based on the anonymity principle. Instead, agents in the new

---

Notes for this section begin on page 21.

markets pursue collaborative relations based on the long-term contract. The new form of long-term and closely interactive markets challenges the neoclassical paradigm of market governance, which causes many new problems for market governance. Strikingly, these long-term contracts are not as free of opportunism as the neoclassical paradigm would predict; for instance, the neoclassical belief based on the repeated game theory states that a long-term business contract generates a partnership reducing opportunism.[1] On the contrary, the long-term contracts are plagued by opportunism. Long-term and collaborative contractual relations make the existing market governance more incomplete and leave more space for divergence, as shall be seen in the U.S. and German automotive parts markets. However, the divergent orders of market governance are not predetermined by the "national trajectories" that institutionalists argue for based on the distinct institutions and cultures in the process of rebutting the neoclassical paradigm. Although the domain of the market in society has increased, the existing models of market governance are not sufficient for understanding the new market relations.

This book asks: Do market economies of nation-states converge toward American-led, liberal markets? How can we understand the complicated process of industrial adjustments that reveals "converging but non-liberal" and "diverging but not predetermined" markets? What makes market regimes different? If the existing institutions and models of market governance, such as liberal contract law, are less relevant, how are the new market relations constituted and, more importantly, sustained? A central claim of this book is that the market rationality and market governance are not predetermined by abstract, universally relevant market rationality, or by cultural and institutional heritage; rather, market rationality and its governance are continuously constituted by agents' discursive politics. This book suggests a new conception of "politics of multiple rationalities." Moreover, conceptions of meaningful fairness for market governance play a decisive role in the constitution of market relations. These conceptions of fairness differ across societies, giving rise to systemic differences in the way in which the new forms of market regimes are constructed in different societies. Meaningful fairness is neither a product of abstract universal reason nor a "natural fact" of cultural heritage. Meaningful fairness is continuously being constituted by the politics of reflexive agents in a novel context related to the division of labor. The conceptions of meaningful fairness mainly depend on how agents in society deliberate and adjudicate conflicts. This book investigates the different ways market regimes are constituted by looking at two market societies.

In order to investigate the manner of adjustments in market societies, this book examines the way in which the American and German automotive industries and their parts markets were transformed in the 1980s and 1990s. The automobile industry was selected for this study chiefly because the automobile industry has a large impact on each nation's economy.

One in seven jobs in the U.S., and one in eight jobs in Germany, are directly or indirectly related to the automobile industry. There are, of course, variations in industrial adjustments among industrial sectors in each country. For example, machinery, chemicals, and electronics in the U.S. and Germany show different patterns of industrial adjustments. The machinery industry in Germany still maintains a traditional form of functionally oriented structure, instead of a cross-functional team structure, because of their customer-oriented production and strong tradition of craftsmanship.[2] German companies in the chemical industry have also lagged in abandoning their traditional sources of strength, such as functional specialization and hierarchical structure.[3] In the U.S., consumer electronics, specifically the television industry, is lagging in adopting the flexible, lean production model of the automobile industry because television assembly is highly standardized and simplified, and because assembly lines have been relocated to countries with lower labor costs, making the restructuring of domestic production lines unnecessary.[4] Many non-auto industries in the U.S. still maintain many elements of Taylorist characteristics, although the U.S. auto industry has adopted Japanese-style lean production successfully.[5] Specific features of the automobile industry, such as high volumes, multinational companies of Original Equipment Manufacturers (OEMs), and concentrated OEM structure, as well as politics in different contexts of production and industrial relations, generated variations in restructuring during the last two decades.

Nonetheless, in the recent restructuring of industries in both the U.S. and Germany, lean production initiated by the automobile industry has been proposed as the leading model among alternatives to traditional, Taylorist mass production. Non-auto industries in both the U.S. and Germany, such as electronics, machinery, biotechnology, textiles, steel, semiconductors, computers, and chemicals, are also undertaking lean production policies such as just-in-time delivery, decentralized planning, and close relationships with suppliers.[6] An automobile contains approximately 20,000 parts that work together as an integrated unit; thus, the impact of the automobile industry on various national industries such as electronics, chemical, and steel is significant. For example, many German machinery companies began to change as the automobile companies that are their customers requested that they adopt new production practices such as just-in-time delivery. As the Lancashire cotton mills did in the nineteenth century, the automobile industry has played the role of trend-setter in the organization of modern production, shaping a new division of labor in the twentieth century.[7] Just as the traditional market relations were established in the division of labor under the principle of mass production, the new collaborative market comes up with new ideas on the division of labor, called "post-Fordism," "Toyotaism," or "lean production."

Furthermore, the automobile industry represents general characteristics of a national economy. For example, general characteristics in the German industry system, such the emphasis on high quality, deep-skilling, vocational training, strong unions, and strong *Mittelstand* (small and medium sized companies) among suppliers—which many institutionalists note as national characteristics of the German political economy—are nicely represented in the automobile industry. This is why many industrial sociologists and political economists point to the example of the automobile industry when dealing with a national pattern of industrial systems. In addition, owing to the structure of multinational OEMs and their participation in intense global competition, the automobile industry has been used as a strong *prima facie* case for testing market-driven convergence.[8] Germany and the U.S. were chosen for this investigation because they are both advanced market societies with very strong automobile industries. Both have experienced a transformation of market relations from neoclassical to the new long-term and collaborative markets. Furthermore, the American and German markets differ systematically from each other in creating a new market order.

For example, although contractual relations in society have increased by replacing traditional in-house production, they do not confirm the revival of the neoclassical market. The market rationality of the neoclassical market is not universal, but it is contextualized, particularly by the division of labor. The traditional markets under the mass production system in the U.S. and Germany were similar to the neoclassical market. In mass production, tasks are separate in detail, and a worker performs only one simple task; in a similar fashion, suppliers receive simple tasks developed by the customer. Standardization in mass production enabled customers to switch vendors in a short period based on the anonymity principle, as the neoclassical market assumes. However, as the development of technology became rapid and the market for end-products became more volatile, agents in the American and German markets needed more flexible collaboration to take advantage of the specialties of trading partners. Even Germans who had been praised for their flexible systems could not avoid having to reorganize their production and market systems in the face of tough international competition. The traditional German system based on functional specialization had become too rigid to meet the volatility of the market and the rapid changes in technology.

The new markets emerging in the novel context of this new division of labor were fundamentally different from traditional, neoclassical markets under the mass production system. In the new collaborative markets, customers and suppliers tried to collaborate with each other throughout the entire process of value creation, from the early stages of development to production and on through delivery, by taking advantage of partners' specialties. Under the rationality of collaboration and flexible application engineering, new market relations were created in both the U.S. and Germany, challenging the neoliberal market governance. To benefit from collaborative and flexible application engineering, customers and suppliers developed long-term contractual relations instead of relying on the traditional short-term (normally less than one year) contracts. In order to closely interact with each other, customers in the U.S. and German markets reduced the number of vendors that they were dealing with, and thus, they tried to share proprietary information such as production techniques and costs. Contrary to the rationality of anonymity or the impersonal relationships of the neoclassical market, agents in the new long-term and collaborative markets began to emphasize the partners' capability for development, willingness to cooperate, and the history of relations. In the new long-term collaborative markets, which the U.S. and German markets took on similarly, neoliberal devices to govern market relations, such as the threat of exit and liberal contract law, are being challenged. In the long-term and mutually committed contracts, it is not easy to switch contract-partners. In addition, long-term and collaborative market relations are too incomplete for liberal contract law to govern.

Although the American and German markets adopted similar patterns of industrial adjustments and market relations, new divergent regimes emerged due to the unclear governance of the new market. Contrary to the conventional belief, the long-term and closely interactive market relations themselves did not automatically generate trustful and stable relationships. Instead, the powerful party in the contract took advantage of incomplete and unclear conditions of the contract, such as price, volume, and distribution of common benefits. Many suppliers in both the U.S. and Germany complained of customers violating confidentiality and dictating prices arbitrarily. The closer the relations became, the higher was the risk of partners hurting each other. In the American markets, powerful customers such as GM, Ford, and first-tier suppliers took advantage of unclear and incomplete contractual relations, redefining the price and terms of the contract in arbitrary ways. In contrast, German automotive parts markets have established "fair and trustful" partnerships. Americans in the automotive parts markets have developed an extremely power-dominated and formal conception of fairness, whereas Germans in the markets have established a substance-oriented conception of fairness and a stable market regime.

However, this divergence of market regimes is not predetermined by institutions and cultural heritage. The new conceptions of fairness and market regimes were created by agents in a novel context related to the new division of labor. In actuality, the relationships in the German market were similar to those of American markets in the first half of the 1990s. Powerful German customers such as Volkswagen caused distrust through their opportunistic and unfair behaviors. Traditional norms for market governance in Germany no longer held true in the new, long-term, closely interactive markets. The main problems that German suppliers faced were similar to those of American markets, such as the arbitrary revision of contracts and confidential issues. Germans in the automotive parts market have successfully established stable and fair relationships through collectively deliberating and adjudicating conflicts in the public realm.

This book endeavors to explain the similarities and differences between the American and German cases. They hold in common a departure from the logic of the neoclassical understanding of market governance between firms. Yet, in a novel context related to the division of labor and the new rationality of market economy, the cases diverge in the manner in which fundamental understandings of relationships are constituted—in particular, in the way in which fairness and social order for legitimate governance of market relations are constituted.

Methodology

The primary empirical methodology of this book is in-depth interviews for qualitative data and a mail survey for quantitative data in the American and German automobile industry from 1999 to 2001. The personal interviews were conducted with main actors in the U.S. and German automobile industry such as automakers, suppliers, and members of associations, regional institutes, and regional governments. In each firm, I carried out interviews with managers in charge of production and marketing. I conducted interviews two times for each country. The first field research of in-depth interviews with Germans was carried out in the second half of 1999, and the first field research with Americans was conducted in the winter of 1999–2000. Based on the preliminary research on both U.S. and German society, I developed further questions. The second set of interviews was carried out in the spring and summer of 2000 for the German case, and in the summer of 2001 for the American case. Through the entire process of field research from 1999 to 2001, I conducted 45 personal interviews for the U.S. market and 62 interviews for the German market. Most of the 45 U.S. personal interviews were with representatives of supplier companies; three were with chiefs of associations. Of the 62 German personal interviews, 56 were with presidents or vice presidents of supplier companies, 4 with purchasing and production managers of automakers, and 2 with chiefs of associations. The personal interviews lasted between 90 and 120 minutes, on average. The in-depth interviews were supplemented by interviews conducted via e-mail. The e-mail interviews in the U.S. were held with 71 automotive suppliers, 5 trade associations, and 1 legal association. For the German market, I carried out e-mail interviews with 18 suppliers and 2 associations.

Meanwhile, I also conducted mail surveys in both the U.S. and Germany in 1999 and 2000 in order to obtain reliable quantitative data. Based on the most popular directories of American and German automotive parts suppliers that are mainly first- and second-tier suppliers, I sent 1,481 mail surveys to members of the U.S. market and 1,034 mail surveys to members of the German market.[9] Because the 1996 and 1997 American directories are outdated, many surveys were returned as undeliverable. Thus, to the 1,216 mail surveys delivered in the U.S. market, I received 186 responses, a response rate of 15 percent.[10] Of these, only 173 answers were relevant because ten companies are no longer automotive suppliers and three companies refused to give detailed information. For the German case, I received 190 responses to the 1,034 mail surveys sent, a response rate of 18 percent. Of the 190 responses, 147 answers were relevant because 43 companies are no longer automotive suppliers and thus were not relevant for this survey.[11] The mail-survey questionnaires were developed on the basis of the initial field research in the German and American markets. I also consulted many earlier survey questionnaires, such as Susan Helper's survey of the automotive parts markets, *Industrielle Netwerke* (1996) by Markus Pohlmann et al., and the like. These questionnaires were written in English and German, and proofread by native American and German speakers.

The empirical evidence is also supplemented by secondary writings in economics, sociology, and business studies. In particular, in order to trace the development of market governance in time sequences, I used many American and German newspapers and periodicals such as *Ward's Auto World, Automotive News, Handelsblatt and Frankfurter Allgemeinezeitung (FAZ)*, and other, similar sources.

Review of Literature

Three main paradigms dominate the debate on market regimes. Each contains a specific view of how markets actually function and of the grounds for the normative evaluation of the fairness of these institutions. The neoliberal paradigm emphasizes universal relevance of market rationality and a strictly market-based concept of justice; institutionalists focus on conventions and cultural heritage as shapers of both the way markets work and their norms of fairness; power theorists argue that market processes are inherently structured around power inequalities and conflict, and that since justice requires at least rough equality of power, it is generally absent from market processes. Before presenting the theoretical framework of this book, this section explores prevalent theoretical views on market societies.

While the 1930s and 1940s were characterized by consensus on the "failure of market economy," the 1980s and 1990s are depicted as a period of "government failure" or "rejuvenated classical liberalism (or market liberalism)" based on neoclassical economics.[12] In particular, many social scientists in the 1990s emphasized the dominance of market forces in a society. The traditional solution of Keynesian demand management resulted simply in a vicious circle of capital flight, foreign debt, and devaluation. As the state regulation that had been one of the main alternatives to the market became discredited, many social scientists and political economists argued for the convergence of national economies toward the liberal market.[13] In particular, the market liberals emphasized the high speed of technological change, the growth of the global financial market, and the high fluidity of capital and knowledge as driving forces of market dominance. Furthermore, in the 1990s, as the American economy, which had been regarded as a representative of the liberal market economy, achieved great success while the so-called institutional economies such as Japan and Germany receded, market liberalism based on the neoclassical paradigm gained credence. Even some strong proponents of divergent capitalism based on the German model, such as Wolfgang Streeck, argued for the convergence of institutionally embedded economies toward an American-led liberal market. Streeck says:

> Globalization, by increasing the mobility of capital and labour across national borders, extricates the labour supply from national control and enables the financial sector to refuse doing service as a national utility. By internationalizing, and thereby disorganizing, capital and labour markets, globalization dissolves whatever negotiated coordination may have been nationally accomplished between them and replaces it with global hierarchical dominance of the former over the latter.[14]

This is in contrast to the 1980s, when institutionalists emphasized the state and its capacity as an alternative to the free market on the basis of the successes of the German and Japanese economies.[15] However, with the retreat of the state, the emergence of globalization, and the success of the U.S. economy, even some institutionalists and culturalists such as Crouch and Streeck (1997) and Schmitter (1997), who had been strong proponents of diversity of national economies, came to concede that national economies would converge toward a liberal market economy in imitation of the U.S.[16]

The "market," in the parlance of market liberals as well as some institutionalists, refers to the neoclassical market characterized by arms-length bargaining, vigorous pursuit of self-interests, impersonal and anonymous relations, and comprehensive, short-term contracting. The neoliberal governance of market society is based on the assumption that voluntary exchange for self-interest maximization is the most efficient way. The so-called perfect competition in an ideal market provides a guideline for the best efficiency.[17] To the extent that a real market deviates from the perfect competition, the real market is less efficient. Therefore, politics, social identity, and morality should only minimally intrude on market processes. Justice in the neoclassical market is derived by universal "natural reason"; thus, so long as one has a well-functioning market, its outcomes will necessarily be just. In the period between 1770 and 1870, when classical market liberalism emerged, a uniform body of general principles tended to replace the local and customary law.[18] Recently, the market liberals of comparative legal systems have argued that legal systems of nation-states are converging due to the development of the market.[19] The market liberals assumed that justice (law) should be applied to any cases in the market. The liberal law is formal justice in which substance distribution is determined by market forces. The market is governed by liberal contract law and "the threat of exit" within the free market.

Strikingly, the revival of contractual relations in the 1990s did not lead to the rejuvenation of market liberalism based on the neoclassical economics, as will be highlighted in the first chapter of this book. The new market relations are in contrast to the neoclassical market. In the new market, agents favor long-term contracts over short-term mobility and emphasize the identity or history of their transactions instead of anonymous relations. Buyers prefer the reduction of vendors instead of competition among multiples in order to conduct efficient collaborative works. In the long-term and collaborative markets, it is not so easy to change a contract-partner.[20] On the other hand, liberal contract law based on the neoclassical market has difficulty in governing incomplete long-term contracts. Liberal contract law that is based on the freedom of contracts in modern liberal thought—"all the sources of rights and duties of the parties to the contracts are exclusively the voluntary will"—requires that a contract as a promise is comprehensive. In liberal contract law, not all promises are enforceable; only the "perfect contract" in the "perfect competition" is strictly enforceable. The perfect contract assumes almost perfect information, which enables contractors to present a future situation.[21] This assumption of perfect information might have few problems in snapshot transactions of perfect competition. But as the contracts become longer, they hardly complete because long-term contracts are open-ended in many items, including price and volume. Furthermore, contrary to the neoclassical expectation that "the long-term contracts will generate self-enforcing and trustful partnerships,"[22] the long-term contracts are plagued by opportunism. The incompleteness of long-term contracts leaves room for divergence. As the U.S. and German cases will show, contrary to the neoliberals' expectation, market societies are not simply converging due to the necessity of market forces. The rationality of economic efficiency in market relations is not as apparent as the neoclassical economist assumes. Rationality even in a market is contextualized, particularly by the division of labor. In addition, market rationality is subject to conflicting interpretation. Market societies have a tendency toward divergence by the politics among multiple ideal types of market rationality.

Meanwhile, in providing alternatives to the neoclassical paradigm, institutionalists emphasize varieties of capitalist societies based on varieties of formal and informal institutions and cultures.[23] Unlike the neoclassical thinkers, the institutionalists hold that the rationality of the market is embedded in an institutional context and, thus, market societies are systematically different and diverging. The institutions that constrain agents' rationality include a set of formal and informal rules, whether they are normative, cognitive, or material. According to institutionalists, institutions as a matrix of sanctions and incentives constrain the agents' strategy; or institutions as cognitive frameworks that are seldom explicitly articulated reproduce a persistent pattern of practices.[24] Institutionalists hold that although market forces prevail under globalization, societies are systematically different due to the constraints of institutions such as associations, financial system, formal laws, and informal cultures. Institutionalists argue that national economies have their own trajectories or national patterns and are difficult to redirect into other patterns. Institutionalists such as Hollingsworth argue that "forms of economic coordination and governance cannot easily be transferred from one society to another, for they are embedded in social production distinctive to their particular society." Hollingsworth continues, "a society's social system of production is very path dependent and system specific."[25] For example, the U.S. and U.K. economies are mainly presented by many institutionalists as liberal market economies or Anglo-Saxon market economies. These liberal market economies are mainly characterized by "high vertical integration," "standardized mass production," "absence of long-term contracts with suppliers as well as with employees," "short-term and formal contracts," "arms-length market relations," and "priority of shareholder values." By contrast, institutionally embedded markets such as those in Germany and Japan are mainly characterized by "flexible production system," "long-term contractual relations with suppliers as well as with employees," "relational contracts instead of complete formal contracts," "high trust," and "long-term finance." According to the institutionalists, the American national trajectory of its economic system is embedded in a particular institutional environment that includes pervasive market mentality, sparse associations, and a liquid financial market. By contrast, the German and Japanese national patterns of flexible production are embedded in a particular institutional environment in which a communitarian culture, dense networks of associations, regulatory courts, and bank-based finance deter opportunism.[26] Because agents gravitate toward strategies that are constrained by institutional sanctions and incentives, or because agents take their practices for granted due to unreflective cognitive frameworks, institutionalists hold that once institutions are established, they persist even though they are collectively suboptimal.

The reasons for the persistence of national trajectories are diverse even among institutionalists. First, many institutionalists, such as Ronald Dore, Charles Hill, and Philippe D'Iribarne, emphasize that a historically and cognitively locked-in informal norm or culture has great power in "resisting incorporation into American-led global capitalism and preserving its own distinctiveness."[27] According to Dore, the "behavioral dispositions" nourished in education and social relations have a tendency to avoid dissonance in cognition and practices. Due to these behavioral dispositions, the Japanese developed long-term cooperation whereas the Anglo-Saxons became oriented toward short-term interests; the Japanese are more altruistic while the Anglo-Saxons are more selfish.[28] Hill also argues that, due to cultural norms such as group identification and reciprocal obligations that were developed in the Tokugawa era, Japanese firms are able to develop self-managing work teams and decentralized flexible systems. By contrast, Hill emphasizes individual culture over the high vertical integration of American companies.[29] D'Iribarne and Hollingsworth maintain that the American political culture, which values the priority of free will, freedom of contracts between equals, and resistance against an arbitrary master, deters trustful cooperation in subcontracting relations; American contractual relations tend to be neoclassical and short-term.[30] Moreover, noticing the differences between the Japanese and German flexible systems, many institutionalists like Streeck and Lane have argued that German companies would not adopt the Japanese lean production and collaborative systems due to the differences between Japanese authoritarian culture and German democratic pluralism and professional specialization.[31]

In addition to the tendency of historically locked-in informal cultures to resist convergence, institutionalists also emphasize the complementarity of institutions for the persistence of national patterns.[32] According to institutionalists, the institutions in a society, such as formal laws, informal culture, associations, and financial systems, are closely interconnected and thus difficult to transform. Although a component of institutions in a society may be changed, it will ultimately not work if its goals are contradictory to the entire social system. For example, Hollingsworth, Porter, and Robert Putnam argue that communitarian norms and long-term contracts emerge in dense networks of associations and patient financial markets. Casper argues for institutional complementarity between national systems of contract law and modes of interfirm collaboration—German regulatory law and long-term contracts versus American liberal contract law and short-term, arms-length relations. Ronald Dore holds that lifetime employment, patient stock, and long-term trustful relations are mutually interlocked in Japan, while short-term contacts and individualism are interlocked in the U.S. Orru, Biggart, and Hamilton (1997) argue for institutional isomorphism—that institutions tend to resemble each other in an entire configuration of institutions.

Finally, institutionalists such as Soskice, Hall, and Vitols have proposed "comparative institutional advantage" as a more proactive incentive for the persistence of national patterns instead of passive resistance against convergence of market regimes. They argue that even under the effects of globalization, market regimes diverge because agents try to take advantage of comparative institutional advantages. Hall and Soskice hold that due to the comparative institutional advantages of corporatism, German firms show a national pattern of better performance in medium technology sectors through high quality incremental innovation (HQII) or by taking a strategy of "diversified quality production (DQP)"; in contrast, firms in the liberal markets of the U.S. show a national pattern of better performance in high technology through radical innovation.[33] Furthermore, institutionalists in favor of "comparative institutional advantage" argue that agents should not move to another pattern of activities because of the disadvantages in the international competition. For example, Hall and Soskice suggest that coordinated economies should not deregulate their economy, saying that "[a]lthough there will be some calls for deregulation even in such settings, the business community is likely to provide less support for it, because many firms draw competitive advantage from systems of relational contracting that depend on the presence of supportive regulatory regimes."[34] Even in the crisis of the German system during the 1990s, when many political economists worried about the backwardness of high technology and its effects on other sectors, Carlin and Soskice argued that "it makes little sense to engage in costly policies to promote companies in the high technology sector; it makes more sense to wait for the time when the high technologies eventually become established ones."[35] Even when most political economists and industrial experts thought that the existing German model of production had no hope and needed restructuring, institutionalists promoting comparative institutional advantage argued that firms in Germany should stick to the old pattern of production in order to realize the comparative institutional advantages.

However, in actuality, market regimes in Germany and the U.S. have not continued their national patterns. They have undergone tremendous transformation, as shall be examined in the first chapter of this book.[36] American companies have successfully adopted Japanese-style flexible production, including features such as deintegration of parts production, decentralized team work, and collaborative market relations, contrary to the institutionalist expectation that American neoclassical markets would not change into long-term and collaborative markets due to their institutional characteristics. By adopting the methods of lean production and collaborative markets, American firms performed better in medium technology sectors such as the automobile and machine tool industries. Americans have constructed untraditional institutions such as new social networks and training systems instead of passively sticking to the comparative institutional advantages of traditional institutions or taking existing production and market relations for granted.[37]

Similarly, Germans have also undergone intensive restructuring of existing production and market relations. The German flexible system based on "professional specialization," or the so-called craft system, which had been praised for its better performance over the American and British strict mass production systems in the 1980s, revealed rigidity and other obstacles to innovation in comparison with the lean production system in the 1990s. In the 1980s, the German model was decentralized production based on highly specialized and skilled workers.[38] The craft system could perform "fast retooling" and "incremental innovation" by combining and recombining the specialists within a vocation. In particular, the German model of the 1980s was praised for its strong small- and medium-sized companies, which boasted of the agility of small batches, highly skilled labor, and highly niche-oriented specialties. Advanced vocational training systems, associational cooperation for vocational training, cooperation between labor and management by corporatist arrangements, and long-term financial systems were regarded as necessary ingredients for the German craft-based flexible system.

However, the German craft-based system turned out to be rigid compared with lean production systems in the first half of the 1990s. The model industries of German craft-based production, such as the automobile and machine tool industries, suffered from lower productivity and slower innovation than even the American firms that institutionalists expected to perform poorly in these medium technology sectors. Industrialists and industrial experts did not believe that the existing model of the German craft-based system had any hope; they held that the upgrading of skill in existing craft-based production would not provide a solution. Germany needed to reorganize the division of labor in the production process.[39] The professional specialization (*fachliche Spezialierung*) and vocational training for the craft system deterred the development of cross-functional coordination and communication, causing many problems around collaboration of interfaces (*Schnittsstellenproblematik*), which meant not only between functional departments within a company but also between companies in markets.[40] For example, electricians had difficulty working with mechanical specialists due to deep specialization based on vocational training and the craft order of production. In the process of development, workers in production and marketing did not interact. A job was carried out through different departments sequentially instead of them interacting simultaneously. By the same token, external suppliers were isolated from the development process. Although institutionalists such as Casper, Hall, and Soskice argue that agents in the German market traditionally developed long-term and relational contracts, unlike in the U.S., this book posits that this is not the case.[41] As in the U.S. case, contractual relations in the traditional German markets were short-term and distant until the late 1980s; they underwent intensive transformation toward collaborative markets in the 1990s, as shall be seen in chapter 1.

Due to the rigidity in interfaces, German companies suffered from over-engineering, over-complexity, and slow innovation. Facing tough international competition, German companies carried out intensive restructuring of their production and market relations in the 1990s. German companies also deintegrated their vertical in-house production to the extent that they competed for flexibility with Japanese and American lean producers. The interfaces between specialties were reorganized. Germans adopted process-oriented and cross-functional teams while revising their vocational training toward more general skilling. Instead of traditional distant markets in which customers hesitated to involve suppliers in the early stages of development due to fear of them leaking their specialties, German markets have changed into collaborative markets in which customers interact closely with suppliers, sharing proprietary information from the very early stages of development to the final stage of delivery. Like the Americans, Germans have struggled to reconstruct the norms that had governed their traditional markets.

Agents in market societies are not completely determined by institutional and cultural heritages. On the contrary, agents in the American and German markets reflect and reinterpret the meanings of the institutions. Although institutionalists argued that firms in Germany would not adopt lean production and collaborative market relations due to the cultural differences between German and Japanese society, firms on German soil have successfully adopted cross-functional team structure and collaborative market relations. Moreover, in order to govern the new market relations, they have reconstituted the existing norms that had prevailed in the traditional market. Instead of sticking to the comparative advantages of the existing institutions, Germans in the crisis of the 1990s reflected on the meanings of their institutions, disengaging banks from manufacturing firms, weakening corporatist arrangements, and encouraging stock markets. Furthermore, not all agents in a society evaluate the advantages of institutions in the same way. For example, although instititutionalists in favor of comparative institutional advantage argue that "the comprehensive wages negotiations in Germany contribute to the German high performance based on the diversified quality production," employers and employees differ in the evaluation of the tight corporatist arrangements.[42] Institutions do not socialize or constrain all agents in the same way. Although institutionalists correctly point out the variety of market rationality based on different institutional contexts, they fail to see the dynamic changes of market relations. The institutions do not have the same meanings to all agents in a society. Agents contest the meaning of institutions in the process of an ongoing interpretation of institutions.

In the sense of focusing on the conflicts in a society, power approaches based on the Marxist tradition might be right.[43] According to Marxists, institutions do not have the same meaning to all agents in a society. Theorists of power approaches always raise the question "Who benefits?" rather than concentrating on "beneficial constraints of institutions" that are assumed to substitute for market sub-optimality. Power approaches contend that the seemingly neutral institutions are not neutral but mainly beneficial to the powerful party; the powerful and the weak parties conflict in the distribution of benefits. In the same vein, power approaches contest the neoliberal paradigm of universal justice and market rationality. The scholars of power approaches regard the contract as a representation of asymmetrical power relations in which the weak parties are dominated by the powerful. For example, Sauer (1992), Bieber and Sauer (1991), Bennett, Jr.

(1994), and Semlinger (1991) argue that the recently developed long-term contractual relations between automakers and suppliers have resulted in the automakers' domination and fundamental injustice.[44] In the contracting relations of parts markets, they argue, the suppliers are almost always dominated by powerful customers. There is no justice in market societies. Contract law and shared norms are not relevant in correcting the injustice of contractual relations. The solution to these power approaches is that the relations should be transformed into more egalitarian ones or that, as Bennett (1994) argues, a court or the state should intervene in the market to reverse the domination.

Although theorists of power approaches correctly point out the conflicts in markets, they fail to explain why a new form of market emerges, how differently authorities are distributed and justified in the diverse forms of markets, and why some markets develop fair partnerships while others do not. As shall be highlighted later, agents in the U.S. and German markets preferred to construct shared norms for new markets rather than go without clear norms and rules. Many suppliers in both the U.S. and Germany needed to establish shared ethical codes in the unclear governance of long-term contractual relations instead of despising shared norms. Market regimes are tremendously different in the sense of how an authority is legitimated and on what basis it is justified. The reason why Daimler-Chrysler has developed fair partnerships is not that it has less power than Ford. The reason Germans have improved their relationships in the markets while Americans suffer from rancorous conflicts is not that German suppliers are more powerful than Americans. The manner of exercising power is continuously constrained and guided by shared rules that agents can create by adjusting their differing ideas of rationality and fair norms.

Theoretical Framework

This book makes a number of presuppositions based on a critical review of the existing theories. First, an ideal type of market rationality is not as apparent as the neoclassical paradigm assumes. Although international competition drives agents to consider their existing rationality and to sometimes try to imitate the rationality of competitors' strategy, the types of market rationality are diverse. In this book, the conception of "politics of multiple rationalities" is proposed. Even in the sense of Weber's ideal type, there are many different ideal types of rationality for economic efficiency.[45] For example, economies of scale are sometimes emphasized while economies of scope are more important at other times. From the viewpoint of production processes, standardization is rational, whereas if innovation of products is the goal, standardization becomes burdensome. From the perspective of transaction costs, high vertical integration might be an optimal solution, whereas vertical integration becomes problematic within a structure of flexible production. Regarding market relations, the rationality of profit maximization in transactions also varies. An ideal type of rationality in transactions is to see transactions as simply transferring the given value. From this perspective, the rationality of market relations is to minimize the partner's bargaining power. In this market, a buyer puts as many vendors as possible in severe competition with one another. This is the ideal type of market rationality in the neoclassical paradigm. Another ideal type of rationality in the market is to see transactions not as transferring the already given value but as a joint–value–creating activity. From this perspective, the same slice of the pie is not transacted in a repeated way; rather, the amount of the pie varies according to contractors' commitments. By sharing information and using partners' specialties mutually, the benefits of collaborative engineering are increased. This is an ideal type of rationality in long-term and collaborative markets. The ideal types of rationality in markets are neither apparent nor single-minded. As reference points and perspectives vary, the ideal types of market rationality revealed are diverse and sometimes conflicting.

The multiple types of rationality in a market mean that politics occurs among different perspectives inside a market. This is in contrast to the idea of the neoclassical market and some institutionalist theories, which assume that politics is external to the market. Market liberals who adhere to the neoclassical economics believe that politics distorts the rationality of the market; thus, politics and other external constraints should be kept to a minimum. Corporatist institutionalists such as Schmitter (1997) and Crouch and Streeck (1997) expect that market societies will converge due to market forces because they believe the politics of state retreats.[46] They assume that the market is driven by iron necessity or a single universal rationality that exists beyond agents' interpretation of the world and their strategies. By contrast, this book assumes that market rationality is continuously constituted by politics within a market. The problem in a market is not whether agents misunderstand (or well understand) the "objective" real constraints of a market or an institution, but that ideal types of market rationality themselves are diverse, based as they are on agents' perspectives and their accentuation. Various forces with different perspectives of market rationality compete with each other, or varieties of market rationality compromise with each other and constitute a new rationality instead of replacing the "misunderstood rationality" with a "well understood" one.

While this book is in agreement with institutionalism on the point that the rationality of an action in a market is not free of institutional contexts—market rationality varies in different institutional contexts—it argues that agents are not completely constrained by institutions. Institutionalism is too rigid to explain the endogenous changes and transformations of national patterns of markets. The institutionalists' logic of path dependence, in which agents reproduce the same pattern of practices, is contradicted by the argument of this book, which underlines agents' reflexivity. Agents continuously reflect on the practices and meanings of institutions.[47] This does not mean that institutions are not important in explaining different market regimes; quite to the contrary, institutions can constrain agents' strategy and provide agents with a repertoire of solutions. What is being refuted is not the fact that institutions influence upon agents' activities, but the rigid view of path-dependent institutionalism that disregards agents' reflexivity. A market regime is not predetermined by institutions; more fundamentally, institutions, which, institutionalists believe, generate path-dependent regimes and encourage the repetition of the same patterns of behavior, do not have constant meaning and characteristics independent of agents' reflection and reinterpretation. Rather, institutions and cultural heritages are continuously reinterpreted and contested by reflexive agents; thus the meaning, way of functioning, and effects of institutions and cultural heritages, which influence agents, vary based on the politics of reflexive agents.

On the other hand, agents' reflexivity does not mean that agents can do anything beyond institutional contexts. On the contrary, agents are influenced by cognitive norms and external institutional constraints. The social conditions in the process of action and the consequences of practices are frightfully objective; thus an actor continuously reflects on the gap between her or his habitus (internally represented institutions) and the consequences of practices. The tensions between habitus and social reality outside the actor enable an actor to reflect on the practices and consider new strategies. The existing institutions may persist. But this does not mean institutional path dependence; instead, institutions are reconfirmed by agents' reflection. Furthermore, agents reflect on their actions collectively and discursively. The manner of deliberation among reflexive agents can constrain the agents' reflexivity. One of the main arguments of this book is that the ways of deliberating practices and social norms can foster important differences in market regimes. Market regimes are continuously constituted and sustained by the politics of how to deliberate the varieties of market rationality and fairness, instead of misunderstanding agents being defeated by those who well understand.

In the theoretical vein of the "politics of multiple rationalities" among reflexive agents, this book investigates the different ways market regimes are constituted. Why do market governance and conceptions of fairness matter? The market needs governance of stable transactions because opportunism is an essential element of the market itself, in which agents pursue self-interests. Moreover, in a world in which market rationality varies according to perspectives, and in which new market relations generate new forms of opportunism and new problems in market governance, the ongoing constitution of market governance matters. The "meaningful fairness" that agents believe effective and legitimate in the justification and adjudication of current transactions is constantly attracting attention and is always contested in the market. Meaningful and currently effective justice in a market society is not driven by universal natural reason, but is continuously being constituted by differentiating "opportunistic" from "legitimate" or "fair" behavior in everyday practices, and by adjusting personal views in order to create mutual grounds for adjudication. More specifically, as new long-term and collaborative markets develop and existing market governance becomes unclear, agents need to constitute new norms for market governance. In a situation in which few agents in the markets bring the opportunistic partner to court and traditional norms do not work, agents try to create self-governing norms in the market. This is why meaningful fairness requires more attention in the long-term and collaborative markets. If there are no fair rules equally shared between trading partners, or if there is no legitimacy in the actions of those who distribute risks and responsibility, the collaborative markets in which agents work together from the early stages of development to the end stage of delivery may lead to dysfunction and pathologies. As many empirical studies reveal, for instance, the same suppliers perform differently according to their relationships with customers in the same form of long-term collaborative markets. Fair rules and legitimate governance in the collaborative markets are closely related to economic performance.

In order to better understand the different constitution of two advanced market regimes, this book differentiates between forms of markets (short-term, distant markets vs. long-term, interactive markets) and governance of relationships (adversarial vs. trustful relationships). In this sense, the prevalent but false dichotomy between short-term, adversarial markets and long-term, trustful markets is contradicted. The prevalent belief in the analysis of markets is that the long-term and collaborative form of market is trustful while short-term, contractual relations are adversarial or distrustful. For example, many studies of supplier markets argue that the Japanese long-term contracts represent trustful cooperation while short-term contracts in Western societies are adversarial and distrustful. But even the traditional forms of markets based on short-term contracts were not always plagued by distrust. Agents could enjoy trustful relationships even in short-term and not-so-closely interactive (distant) contractual relations.[48] Furthermore, my own research as well as many other empirical studies on the supplier markets in the 1990s reveals that rancorous conflict and distrust exist even in long-term and collaborative markets. For example, although in both the American and German automotive parts markets agents transformed their traditional, short-term and distant contractual relations into a new form of long-term and collaborative markets in the 1990s, they suffered from unfair behaviors and distrust.

"Collaborative markets" refer to the form of working in the market. In collaborative markets, agents share more information and interact more closely than those in the traditional distant market. In the traditional markets, suppliers received the customer-developed blueprints; it was up to each individual agent to decide how to create profit. But in collaborative markets, agents interact with each other very closely through the entire process of value creation: suppliers participate in the early stages of development with a customer; customers and suppliers deliberate the innovation of products and production by sharing their specialties. Long-term and collaborative (or closely interactive) markets do not automatically generate trustful relationships. On the contrary, there are more risks, such as confidentiality of information, which agents have to govern. The closer the relations are, the higher the risks of hurting one another. Many suppliers in interviews with me complained that they had more difficulty governing the relationships of the collaborative markets than they did the simple relationships of old, distant markets—e.g., "customers want to know too much"; "partners abuse my know-how that I gave for collaborative works"; "customers revise the price arbitrarily by using the incompleteness of long-term contracts." As this book will highlight, although the American and German markets took on the new form of long-term and collaborative markets, they diverged in the governance of relationships. Both Americans and Germans suffered unfair and opportunistic behaviors in the late 1980s and the first half of the 1990s. But thereafter, Germans have improved their relationships while Americans have not. This book will examine why Germans have developed fair partnerships while Americans still suffer from distrustful relationships even in long-term and collaborative markets.

The divergent consequences of market regimes mainly stem from differences in organizing discourse among reflexive agents. This book will focus on the *different practices of norm-creation*, instead of *prior norms of contracts and contractual relations* as such, in order to explain divergent constitutions of market regimes. The repertoire of *norms of norm-creation*, rather than norms of contracts and contractual relations, influences the manner of agents' deliberation, which in turn generates different market regimes, although the norms of norm-creation are also subject to agents' reflection. Participatory reflection in the public realm is more likely to generate society-wide effective norms and substance-oriented fairness than deliberation in the individual dyadic relations between two private contractors, as this book will show.

The hypotheses for divergent governance of liberal markets are as follows. First, trustful relationships are more likely to emerge when there exist shared norms of meaningful fairness. Shared norms of fairness provide agents with stable expectations of their transactions. In particular, in long-term and collaborative markets, meaningful fairness, in the sense of substantive justice governing distribution of risks and responsibilities in the process of collaborative works, enables agents to identify their interests with the common benefits resulting from collaborative engineering.

Second, the method of constituting fairness matters for the society-wide establishment of fair partnerships. Meaningful fairness in markets is neither derived from formal justice based on universal reason nor given as a "natural fact" by cultural heritages. "Civic norms" do not arise automatically out of institutional environments such as associational networks or long-term financing systems. The shared conceptions of meaningful fairness are constituted through reflection on market rationality and deliberation of conflicts. Agents create the common ground for adjudication of conflicts by adjusting formal and substantive criteria and contesting varieties of market rationality. However, agents constitute their conceptions of meaningful fairness in different ways. For example, in one way, many social agents participate alongside the two contractors in the deliberation of conflicts and fairness in the "public" realm. In another, individual and dyadic way, only the two parties to a contract determine the relationships. The second hypothesis of this book is that the public way is more likely than the individual way to build society-wide fair partnerships.

This book's investigation of the similarities and differences of the American and German market regimes is constituted as follows. Chapter 1 highlights the consequences of transformation in the U.S. and German markets in the 1990s—"converging but not neoliberal" and "diverging but not predetermined" markets. First, chapter 1 investigates the American and German automotive parts markets' common departure from the traditional markets. Although huge bureaucratic corporations in both the U.S. and Germany have deintegrated their previously vertically integrated in-house production systems and contracted out to external vendors in the market, the revival of markets did not lead to the rejuvenation of the neoclassical market; rather, both the American and the German markets in the 1990s have commonly departed from their traditional, neoclassical form of markets. This transformation of markets contradicts not only the neoclassical paradigm but also the institutionalism that is too rigid to explain the transformation of national market patterns. In addition, chapter 1 addresses the extent to which American and German markets differ from each other in the sense of governance of relationships, even in the similar form of long-term and collaborative markets. The new, long-term and collaborative markets have raised new problems of market governance in both the U.S. and Germany. But despite their similar form, the American and German automotive parts markets produced systematically different results in their market relationships. The differences in market governance between the American and German markets are analyzed based on the results of the mail survey. Regarding formal and substantive fairness, American automotive parts markets show low levels of trust and formal fairness, while German counterparts reveal high levels of trust and substantive fairness.

Chapters 2 and 3 investigate why these differences came into being. Chapter 2 addresses why American automotive parts markets failed to establish society-wide fair partnerships. This failure was not due to the absence of associational networks or long-term financing systems. On the contrary, Americans maintain and develop dense social networks. In addition, it is not impossible for Americans to build fair partnerships; the case of Chrysler will be examined as an example of the American version of fair partnerships. Nevertheless, Americans in the automotive parts markets cannot be said to have achieved society-wide fair partnerships. To investigate this failure, this book examines the American processes of deliberating conflicts and market rationality. On the whole, Americans tried to adjudicate their conflicts in individual, dyadic relations between two parties to a contract, although recently the dominant way of dyadic solutions has been contested by a new experiment of "publicly mediated deliberation."

Chapter 3 addresses how Germans have succeeded in establishing society-wide fair partnerships. The Germans' ways of adjudicating conflicts and deliberating fair norms are contrasted with those of their American counterparts. The public process of deliberation of market governance in the German markets generates effectively meaningful fairness and society-wide fair partnerships. Finally, in conclusion, this book considers the theoretical implications of the varieties of market regimes and the way social norms are constituted in market society.

Notes

1. Robert Cooter and Thomas Ulen, *Law and Economics* (Reading, Mass.: HarperCollins, 1988), 244–245; Gary J. Miller, *Managerial Dilemmas: The Political Economy of Hierarchy* (Cambridge: Cambridge University Press, 1995), chap. 10; Joseph Farrell and Eric Maskin, "Renegotiation in Repeated Games," *Games and Economic Behavior* 1, no. 4 (1989): 327–360; James D. Morrow, *Game Theory for Political Scientists* (Princeton: Princeton University Press, 1994), 260–314; Gary S. Becker and George J. Stigler, "Law Enforcement, Malfeasance, and Compensation of Enforcers," *Journal of Legal Studies* 3, no. 1 (January 1974): 1–18; B. Douglas Bernheim and Debraj Ray, "Collective Dynamic Consistency in Repeated Games," *Games and Economic Behavior* 1, no. 4 (1989): 295–326.
2. Gary Herrigel, "The Limits of German Manufacturing Flexibility," in Lowell Turner, ed., *Negotiating the New Germany: Can Social Partnership Survive?* (Ithaca: Cornell University Press, 1997), 177–205; Ulrich Jürgens, "Communication and Cooperation in the New Product and Process Development Networks: An International Comparison of Country- and Industry-Specific Patterns," in Ulrich Jürgens, ed., *New Product Development and Production Networks: Global Industrial Experience* (Heidelberg: Springer Verlag, 2000), 107–148; Hartmut Hirsch-Kreinsen, "The Machine Tool Industry: New Market Challenges and the Crisis of the Traditional German Pattern of Innovation," in Jürgens, *New Product Development and Production Networks*, 55–66; Inge Lippert, "Reorganizing Process Chains in the German and American Machine Tool Industry," in Jürgens, *New Product Development and Production Networks*, 149–180.
3. Kirsten S. Wever, "Renegotiating the German Model: Labor-Management Relations in the New Germany," in Lowell Turner, *Negotiating the New Germany*, 207–226.
4. Martin Kenney, "Transplantation? A Comparison of Japanese Television Assembly Plants in Japan and the United States," in Jeffrey K. Liker, W. Mark Fruin, and Paul S. Adler, eds., *Remade in America: Transplanting and Transforming Japanese Management Systems* (New York: Oxford University Press, 1999), 256–293.
5. Davis Jenkins and Richard Florida, "Work System Innovation among Japanese Transplants in the United States," in Liker, Fruin, and Adler, *Remade in America*, 331–360.

6. Horst Wildemann, *Entwicklungs- und Vertriebsnetzwerke in der Zulieferindustrie* (Munich: Transfer-Centrum GmbH, 1998); Richard K. Lester, *The Productive Edge: How U.S. Industries Are Pointing the Way to a New Era of Economic Growth* (New York: W.W. Norton & Company, 1998); J. Reese and R. Geisel, "JIT Procurement: A Comparison of Current Practices in German Manufacturing Industries," *European Journal of Purchasing & Supply Management* 3, no. 3 (1997): 147–154; Masao Nakamura, Sadao Sakakibara, and Roger G. Schroeder, "Just-In-Time and Other Manufacturing Practices: Implications for U.S. Manufacturing Performance," in Liker, Fruin, and Adler, *Remade in America*, 361–384; Walter W. Powell and Peter Brantley, "Magic Bullets and Patent Wars: New Product Development and the Evolution of the Biotechnology Industry," in Toshihiro Nishiguchi, ed., *Managing Product Development* (New York: Oxford University Press, 1996), 233–260; Wever, "Renegotiating the German Model," 207–226; Jürgens, "Communication and Cooperation in the New Product and Process Development Networks," 107–148; Gary Herrigel, "Varieties of Collective Regeneration: Comparisons of the German, Japanese and American Steel Industries since the Mid 1970s," Research Paper, University of Chicago (2002); Arnoud de Meyer, "Product Development in the Textile Machinery Industry," in Nishiguchi, *Managing Product Development*, 280–292; Peter Berg, Eileen Appelbaum, Thomas Bailey, and Arne Kalleberg, "The Performance Effects of Modular Production in the Apparel Industry," *Industrial Relations* 35, no. 3 (1995): 356–374. Other countries also adopted the new form of collaborative markets. For British firms' adoption of the Japanese-style collaborative markets, see Mari Sako, Richard Lamming, and Susan R. Helper, "Supplier Relations in the Multinational Automotive Industry," in Ram Mudambi and Martin Ricketts, eds., *The Organization of the Firm: International Business Perspectives* (London: Routledge, 1998), 178–194; Nick Oliver and Barry Wilkinson, *The Japanization of British Industry* (New York: Basil Blackwell, 1988).
7. James P. Womack, Daniel T. Jones, and Daniel Roos, *The Machine that Changed the World: The Story of Lean Production* (New York: Harper Perennial, 1990); Peter Drucker, *The Concept of the Corporation* (New York: John Day Company, 1946).
8. Wolfgang Streeck, "Lean Production in the German Automobile Industry: A Test Case for Convergence Theory," in Suzanne Berger and Ronald Dore, eds., *National Diversity and Global Capitalism* (Ithaca: Cornell University Press, 1996).
9. The three directories of the U.S. and German suppliers are: *The ELM Guide to U.S. Automotive Sourcing* (1997 edition); *Automobil-Zulieferer in Deutschland* (1997/1998 edition); and *World Wide Automotive Supplier Directory* (1996 edition).
10. Later I traced the "undeliverable" companies via recent editions of books and the Internet. Of these 265 companies, 148 companies (56 percent) were dissolved; 74 companies (28 percent) had moved their location.
11. Actually, most of the non-auto suppliers did not provide detailed information in the survey.
12. See John L. Kelley, *Bringing the Market Back In: The Political Revitalization of Market Liberalism* (New York: New York University Press, 1997); David Boaz and Edward H. Crane, eds., *Market Liberalism: A Paradigm for the 21st Century* (Washington, D.C.: Cato Institute, 1993); Andrew Gamble, *The Free Economy and the Strong State*, 2nd ed. (Basingstoke: Macmillan, 1994).
13. For the convergence toward market economy and market liberalism, see Susan Strange, "The Future of Global Capitalism: Or, Will Divergence Persist Forever?" in Colin Crouch and Wolfgang Streeck, eds., *Political Economy of Modern Capitalism* (Thousand Oaks, Calif.: Sage Publications, 1997), 182–191; idem, *The Retreat of the State: The Diffusion of Power in the World Economy* (New York: Cambridge University Press, 1996); Joseph A. Camilleri and Jim Falk, *The End of Sovereignty? The Politics of a Shrinking and Fragmenting World* (Brookfield, Vt.: Edward Elgar, 1992); Kenichi Ohmae, *The Borderless World: Power and Strategy in the Interlinked Economy* (New York: Harper Business, 1991); Richard B. McKenzie and Dwight R. Lee, *Quicksilver Capital: How the Rapid Movement of Wealth Has Changed the World* (New York: The Free Press, 1991); Lowell Bryan and Diana Farrell,

Market Unbound: Unleashing Global Capitalism (New York: John Wiley & Sons, 1996); Richard O'Brien, *Global Financial Integration: The End of Geography* (London: Printer, 1992); World Bank, *World Development Report: The State in a Changing World* (New York: Oxford University Press, 1997); Walter B. Wriston, *The Twilight of Sovereignty: How the Information Revolution Is Transforming Our World* (New York: Scribner, 1992); Daniel Yergin and Joseph Stanislaw, *The Commanding Heights: The Battle Between Government and the Market Place That Is Remaking the Modern World* (New York: Simon & Schuster, 1998); David M. Andrews, "Capital Mobility and State Autonomy: Toward a Structural Theory of International Monetary Relations," *International Studies Quarterly* 38, no. 2 (1994): 193–218; Jonathon W. Moses, "Abdication from National Policy Autonomy: What's Left to Leave?" *Politics & Society* 22, no. 2 (1994): 125–148.

14. Wolfgang Streeck, "German Capitalism: Does It Exist? Can It Survive?" in Crouch and Streeck, *Political Economy of Modern Capitalism*, 49.

15. In the 1980s, institutionalists emphasized the diversity of capitalism and the efficiency of political regulation as an alternative to markets. Most of them underlined the capability of the state to regulate markets. For the theories of the 1970s and 1980s, see Stephen Cohen, *Modern Capitalist Planning* (Berkeley: University of California Press, 1977); John Zysman, *Governments, Markets and Growth* (Ithaca: Cornell University Press, 1983); Andrew Cox, *State, Finance and Industry: A Comparative Analysis of Post-War Trends in Six Advanced Industrial Economies* (Sussex: Wheatsheaf Books, 1986); Chalmers Johnson, *MITI and the Japanese Miracle: The Growth of Industrial Policy, 1925–1975* (Stanford: Stanford University Press, 1982). Even in the 1990s, there were still many state-centered institutionalists. See Linda Weiss and John M. Hobson, *States and Economic Development: A Comparative Historical Analysis* (Oxford: Polity Press, 1995); Robert Boyer and Daniel Drache, eds., *States Against Markets: The Limits of Globalization* (London: Routledge, 1996); Geoffrey Garrett, *Partisan Politics in the Global Economy* (New York: Cambridge University Press, 1998). Geoffrey Garrett argues that left-wing politics is still a decisive factor based on the experiences of 1980s, but at the end of his book Garrett also accepts that the traditional labor movement receded in the 1990s.

16. See Colin Crouch and Wolfgang Streeck, "Introduction: The Future of Capitalist Diversity," in Crouch and Streeck, *Political Economy of Modern Capitalism*, 1–18; Philippe C. Schmitter, "Levels of Spatial Coordination and The Embeddedness of Institutions," in J. Rogers Hollingsworth and Robert Boyer, eds., *Contemporary Capitalism: The Embeddedness of Institutions* (Cambridge: Cambridge University Press, 1997), 311–317.

17. For the neoclassical market, see George J. Stigler, *The Theory of Price* (New York: Macmillan Company, 1946); idem, "Perfect Competition, Historically Contemplated," *The Journal of Political Economy* 65, no. 1 (1957): 1–17; idem, "Competition," in David L. Sills, ed., *International Encyclopedia of the Social Science* (New York: Macmillan Company & Free Press, 1968), 181–186; Frank H. Knight, *Risk, Uncertainty and Profit* (Chicago: University of Chicago Press, 1971). For the criticism of the neoclassical market within the liberal tradition, see Friedrich A. Hayek, *Individualism and Economic Order* (London: Routledge & Kegan Paul Ltd., 1949); idem, *New Studies in Philosophy, Politics, Economics and the History of Ideas* (London: Routledge & Kegan Paul, 1968), particularly the chapter "Competition as a Discovery Procedure."

18. For the history of classical or market liberalism, see P. S. Atiyah, *The Rise and Fall of Freedom of Contract* (Oxford: Clarendon Press, 1979); idem, *An Introduction to the Law of Contract*, 4th ed. (Oxford: Clarendon Press, 1989), 1–39; A. W. B. Simpson, "Innovation in Nineteenth Century Contract Law," *The Law Quarterly Review* 91, no. 362 (1975): 247–278.

19. For the convergence of legal systems, see Konrad Zweigert and Hein Kötz, *An Introduction to Comparative Law* (Oxford: Clarendon Press, 1992); Michael Bogdan, *Comparative Law* (Deventer: Kluwer, 1994); Ann Glendon, Michael W. Gordon, and Christopher Osakwe, *Comparative Legal Traditions* (St. Paul, Minn.: West, 1994), 12ff.; Basil S. Markesinis, "Learning from Europe and Learning in Europe," in B. S. Markesinis, ed., *The Gradual Convergence: Foreign Ideas, Foreign Influences, and English Law on the Eve of the 21st*

Century (Oxford: Oxford University Press, 1994), 1–32; Richard Helmholz, "Continental Law and Common Law: Historical Strangers of Companions," *Duke Law Journal* 39 (December 1990): 1207–1268.

20. For example, Ford suffered a loss of DM 200 million due to the delay of delivery of parts from its supplier Kiekert in 1998, but Ford could not easily go to the open market because the exchange of contract partners in the short-term period was too dangerous to secure quality and, more importantly, it was too expensive, compared with the price based on their long-term relations. See "Latch Maker Closes Ford Plants," *Automotive Industries* 178, no. 8 (August 1998): 10; "Ford fehlen Türschösser: Weil ein Zulieferer nicht liefert," *Die Tageszeitung*, 17 June 1998; "Kiekert hat den Bogen überspannt," *Süddeutsche Zeitung*, 14 October 1998, 28.

21. For the liberal market governance and contract law, see Jack Beatson and Daniel Friedmann, "From 'Classical' to Modern Contract Law," in Jack Beatson and Daniel Friedmann, eds., *Good Faith and Fault in Contract Law* (Oxford: Clarendon Press, 1995), 3–21; Charles Fried, *Contract as Promise: A Theory of Contractual Obligation* (Cambridge, Mass.: Harvard University Press, 1981); Morris R. Cohen, "The Basis of Contract," *Harvard Law Review* 46, no. 4 (1933): 553–592; Cooter and Ulen, *Law and Economics*; Charles J. Goetz and Robert E. Scott, "Enforcing Promises: An Examination of the Basis of Contract," *Yale Law Journal* 89, no. 7 (1980): 1261–1322; P. S. Atiyah, "Contract as Promise," *Harvard Law Review* 95 (1981): 509–528; Anthony T. Kronman and Richard A. Posner, eds., *The Economics of Contract Law* (Boston and Toronto: Little, Brown and Company, 1979); Richard A. Posner, *Economic Analysis of Law*, 4th ed. (Boston: Little Brown and Company, 1992); Victor P. Goldberg, "Toward an Expanded Economic Theory of Contract," *Journal of Economic Issues* 10, no. 1 (1976): 45–61; Daniel A. Farber, "Contract Law and Modern Economic Theory," *Northwestern University Law Review* 78, no. 2 (1983): 303–339.

22. Cooter and Ulen, *Law and Economics*, 244–245; Miller, *Managerial Dilemmas*, in particular chap. 10.

23. For the institutionalists' writings, see Peter A. Hall and David Soskice, eds., *Varieties of Capitalism: The Institutional Foundations of Comparative Advantage* (New York: Oxford University Press, 2001); Ronald Dore, *Stock Market Capitalism: Welfare Capitalism—Japan and Germany vs. the Anglo-Saxons* (New York: Oxford University Press, 2000); Herbert Kitschelt, Peter Lange, Gary Marks, and John D. Stephens, eds., *Continuity and Change in Contemporary Capitalism* (Cambridge: Cambridge University Press, 1999); Crouch and Streeck, *Political Economy of Modern Capitalism*; Hollingsworth and Boyer, *Contemporary Capitalism*; Berger and Dore, *National Diversity and Global Capitalism*; Boyer and Drache, *States Against Markets*; Richard Whitley and Peer Hull Kristensen, eds., *The Changing European Firm: Limits to Convergence* (London: Routledge, 1996); J. Rogers Hollingsworth, Philippe C. Schmitter, and Wolfgang Streeck, eds., *Governing Capitalist Economies: Performance and Control of Economic Sectors* (New York: Oxford University Press, 1994); Michel Albert, *Capitalism versus Capitalism* (New York: Four Walls Eight Windows, 1993); Wolfgang Streeck, *Social Institutions and Economic Performance* (London: Sage Publishers, 1992); John L. Campbell, J. Rogers Hollingsworth, and Leon N. Lindberg, eds., *Governance of the American Economy* (New York: Cambridge University Press, 1991).

24. Recently, many streams of institutionalism have developed. The new institutionalism varies according to the different fields. In political science, the old institutionalism refers to the formal and legal approaches that existed before World War II. The new institutionalism in political science emphasizes informal norms and culture. In economics, new institutionalism refers to the writings of Oliver E. Williamson and D. C. North, while the old institutionalism means social norms and culture as Veblen's writings show. In sociology, new institutionalism emphasizes the "cognitive revolution," while old institutionalism means the Parsonsian ideas of institutions that emphasize the assimilation of norms and evaluation of culture. For the various streams of old and new institutionalism in different fields, see B. Guy Peters, *Institutional Theory in Political Science: The New*

Institutionalism (New York: Printer, 1999); Geoffrey M. Hodgson, "The Return of Institutional Economics," in Neil J. Smelser and Richard Swedberg, eds., *The Handbook of Economic Sociology*, (Princeton: Princeton University Press, 1994), 58–76; Victor Nee, "Sources of the New Institutionalism," in Mary C. Brinton and Victor Nee, eds., *The New Institutionalism in Sociology* (New York: Russell Sage Foundation, 1998), 1–16; Paul J. DiMaggio and Walter W. Powell, eds., *The New Institutionalism in Organizational Analysis* (Chicago: University of Chicago Press, 1991), particularly the introduction; Paul J. DiMaggio, "Culture and Economy," in Smelser and Swedberg, *The Handbook of Economic Sociology*, 27–57; Arthur L. Stinchcombe, "On Virtues of the Old Institutionalism," *Annual Review of Sociology* 13 (1997): 1–18; Paul M. Hirsch and Michael Lounsbury, "Ending the Family Quarrel: Toward a Reconciliation of 'Old' and 'New' Institutionalism," *American Behavioral Scientist* 40, no. 4 (1997): 406–418.

25. J. Rogers Hollingsworth, "Continuities and Changes in Social Systems of Production: The Cases of Japan, Germany, and the United States," in Hollingsworth and Boyer, *Contemporary Capitalism*, 265–266.

26. See Hollingsworth, "Continuities and Changes in Social Systems of Production," 265–310; Michael E. Porter, "Capital Disadvantage: America's Failing Capital Investment System," *Harvard Business Review* 70, no. 5 (1992): 65–82; David Soskice, "The Institutional Infrastructure for International Competitiveness: A Comparative Analysis of the U.K. and Germany," in Anthony B. Atkinson and Renato Brunetta, eds., *Economics for New Europe* (New York: New York University Press, 1991), 45–66; Steven Wayne Casper, "The Legal Framework for Corporate Governance: The Influence of Contract Law on Company Strategies in Germany and the United States," in Hall and Soskice, *Varieties of Capitalism*, 387–416; Peter A. Hall and David Soskice, introduction to *Varieties of Capitalism*, 1–68.

27. Dore, *Stock Market Capitalism: Welfare Capitalism*, 222.

28. Ronald Dore, "The Distinctiveness of Japan," in Crouch and Streeck, *Political Economy of Modern Capitalism*, 27–29; idem, *Stock Market Capitalism*, 38, 47–48, 57.

29. Charles W. Hill, "National Institutional Structures, Transaction Cost Economizing and Competitive Advantage: The Case of Japan," *Organization Science* 6, no. 1 (1995): 119–131.

30. Philippe D'Iribarne, "A Check to Enlightened Capitalism," in Crouch and Streeck, *Political Economy of Modern Capitalism*, 161–172; Hollingsworth, "Continuities and Changes in Social Systems of Production," 265–310; idem, "The Institutional Embeddedness of American Capitalism," in Crouch and Streeck, *Political Economy of Modern Capitalism*, 133–147; idem, "The Logic of Coordinating American Manufacturing Sectors," in John Campbell, Hollingsworth, and Lindberg, *Governance of the American Economy*, 35–73.

31. Streeck, "Lean Production in the German Automobile Industry," 138–170; Christel Lane, "The Social Constitution of Supplier Relations in Britain and Germany," in Whitley and Kristensen, *The Changing European Firm*.

32. For the complementarity of institutions, see Hall and Soskice, introduction to *Varieties of Capitalism*, 1–68; Casper, "The Legal Framework for Corporate Governance," 387–416; Dore, "The Distinctiveness of Japan," 19–32; Hollingsworth, "The Institutional Embeddedness of American Capitalism," 133–147; J. Rogers Hollingsworth and Robert Boyer, "Coordination of Economic Actors and Social Systems of Production," in Hollingsworth and Boyer, *Contemporary Capitalism*, 1–47; Marco Orru, Nicole Woosley Biggart, and Gary G. Hamilton, *The Economic Organization of East Asian Capitalism* (Thousand Oaks, Calif.: Sage Publications, 1997).

33. Hall and Soskice, introduction to *Varieties of Capitalism*, 1–68.

34. Ibid., 58.

35. Wendy Carlin and David Soskice, "Shocks to the System: The German Political Economy Under Stress," *National Institute Economic Review* 57, no. 159 (January 1997): 68.

36. There have been numerous empirical studies that show the transferability of Japanese-style lean production and collaborative markets even in the different cultural and institutional backgrounds such as those in the U.K, U.S., and Germany. See Liker, Fruin, and

Adler, *Remade in America*; Lester, *The Productive Edge*, particularly parts 2 and 3; Oliver and Wilkinson, *The Japanization of British Industry*; Martin Kenney and Richard Florida, "Beyond Mass Production: Production and the Labor Process in Japan," *Politics & Society* 16, no. 1 (March 1988): 121–158; Richard Florida and Martin Kenney, "Transplanted Organizations: The Transfer of Japanese Industrial Organization to the U.S.," *American Sociological Review* 56, no. 3 (June 1991), 381–398; Wever, "Renegotiating the German Model." For the intensive international surveys about the spread of lean production in the automobile industry, see Susan Helper's and Mari Sako's writings.

37. Americans have collaborated for the public good such as training systems by using existing associations or by building new social networks instead of "enjoying" American comparative institutional advantages such as "liberal markets." For the creation of new social networks, see Paul Osterman, Thomas A. Kochan, Richard Locke, and Michael J. Piore, *Working in America: A Blueprint for the New Labor Market* (Cambridge, Mass.: MIT Press, 2001); Charles F. Sabel, "Experimental Regionalism and the Dilemma of Regional Economic Policy," paper presented to Conference on Socio-Economic Systems of Japan, the United States, the United Kingdom, Germany and France (1996).

38. For the German model of political economy, see Streeck, *Social Institutions and Economic Performance*; Michael J. Piore and Charles F. Sabel, *The Second Industrial Divide* (New York: Basic Books, 1984); Andrei S. Markovits, ed., *Political Economy of West Germany: The Model of Deutschland* (New York: Praeger, 1982); Gary Herrigel, *Industrial Constructions: The Sources of German Industrial Power* (New York: Cambridge University Press, 1996); Soskice, "The Institutional Infrastructure for International Competitiveness," 45–66; Horst Kern and Michael Schumann, "Kontinuität oder Pfadwechsel? Das deutsche Productionsmodell am Scheideweg," in Bruno Cattero, ed., *Modell Deutschland, Modell Europa, Problems Perspectiven* (Opladen: Leske + Budrich, 1998), 85–97; Carlin and Soskice, "Shocks to the System," 57–76; Sigurt Vitols, "Globalization: A Fundamental Challenge to the German Model?" in Richard Stubbs and Geoffrey R. D. Underhill, eds., *Political Economy and the Changing Global Order* (Oxford: Oxford University Press, 2000), 373–381.

39. There have been many diagnoses of the crisis of the German model in the 1990s. Except for the institutionalists who argue for the theory of comparative institutional advantages, such as Carlin and Soskice (1997) and Vitols (2000), most agree that the crisis was not cyclical; the problems were structural. For example, industrialists and trade unionists themselves tried to restructure their existing pattern of practices although the directions and ways of organizational reform were different. See Wolfgang Streeck, "German Capitalism: Does It Exist? Can it Survive?" in Crouch and Streeck, *Political Economy of Modern Capitalism*, 46–47; Kurt J. Lauk, "Germany at the Crossroads: On the Efficiency of the German Economy," *Daedalus* 123, no. 1 (January 1994): 57–83. For the history of restructuring in the German production system, in particular in the automobile industry, see Roland Springer, *Rückkehr zum Taylorismus? Arbeitspolitik in der Automobilindustrie am Scheideweg* (Frankfurt: Campus Verlag, 1999).

40. For a more detailed analysis of the German crisis, see chapter 1 of this book.

41. See chapter 1 of this book.

42. Employers and trade unionists differed on the maintenance of corporatist arrangements and the introduction of Japanese lean production. But this does not mean that workers stuck to the old model of production. The workers offered their own restructuring programs, which were more "humanized" group works than employers' programs. See Roland Springer, *Rückkehr zum Taylorismus?*; Lauk, "Germany at the Crossroads," 57–83; Siegfried Roth, "Germany: Labor's Perspective on Lean Production," in Thomas A. Kochan, Russel D. Lansbury, and John Paul MacDuffie, eds., *After Lean Production* (Ithaca: ILR Press, 1997), 117–136; idem, "Automobilhersteller und ihre Zulieferer in Deutschland und Japan" in Klaus Zwickel, ed., *Vorbild Japan? Stärken und Schwächen der Industriestandorte Deutschland und Japan* (Frankfurt am Main: Otto Brenner Stiftung, 1996).

43. For the power approaches, see Markus Pohlmann, Maja Apelt, Karsten Buroh, and Henning Martens, *Industrielle Netzwerke: Antagonistische Kooperationen an der Schnittstelle Beschaffung-Zulieferung* (Munich and Mering: Rainer Hampp Verlag, 1995); Markus Pohlmann, Maja Apelt, and Henning Martens, "Autonomie und Abhängigkeit—Die Voraussetzungen der kooperation an der Schnittstelle Beschaffung-Zulieferung," in Manfred Deiß and Volker Döhl, eds., *Vernetzte Produktion: Automobilzulieferer zwischen Kontrolle und Autonomie* (Frankfurt: Campus Verlag, 1992), 177–208; Markus Pohlmann, "Antagoistiche Kooperation und distributive Macht: Anmerkungen zur Produktion in Netzwerken," *Soziale Welt* 47, no. 1 (1996): 44–67; Heinz-Rudolf Meißner, Klaus Peter Kisker, Ulrich Bochum, and Jörg Assmann, *Die Teil und die Herrschaft: Die Reorganisation der Automobilproduktion und der Zulieferbeziehungen* (Berlin: Ed. Sigma, 1994); Erich Hecker, "Neue Abhängigkeiten—neue Belastungen," in Hans Gerhard Mendius and Ulrike Wendeling-Schröder, eds., *Zulieferer im Netz—Zwischen Abhängigkeit und Part-nerschaft: Neustrukturierung der Logistik am Beispiel der Automobilzulieferung* (Cologne: Bund-Verlag GmbH, 1991), 113–116; Daniel Bieber and Dieter Sauer, "Kontrolle ist gut! Ist Vertrauen besser?: Autonomie und Beherrschung in Abnehmer-Zulieferbeziehun-gen," in Mendius and Wendeling-Schröder, *Zulieferer im Netz*, 228–254; Dieter Sauer, "Auf dem Weg in die flexible Massenproduktion," in Deiß and Döhl, *Vernetzte Produk-tion*, 49–80; Robert B. Bennett, Jr., "Just-In-Time Purchasing and the Problem of Conse-quential Damages," *Uniform Commercial Code Law Journal* 26 (spring 1994): 332–358; Robert W. Gordon, "Macaulay, MacNeil and the Discovery of Solidarity and Power in Contract Law," *Wisconsin Law Review* 54, no. 3 (1985): 565–580; Klaus Semlinger, "Stel-lung und Probleme kleinbetrieblicher Zulieferer im Verhältnis zu großen Abnehmern," in Norbert Altmann and Dieter Sauer, eds., *Systemische Rationalisierung und Zuliefer-industrie* (Frankfurt: Campus Verlag, 1989), 89–118; idem, "New Developments in Sub-contracting: Mixing Market and Hierarchy," in Ash Amin and Michael Dietrich, eds., *Towards a New Europe? Structural Change in the European Economy* (Brookfield, Vt.: Edward Elgar, 1991), 96–115.

44. Sauer, "Aufdem Weg in die flexible Massenproduktion"; Bieber and Sauer, "Kontrolle ist gut! Ist Vertruen besser?"; Bennett, Jr., "Just-In-Time Purchasing and the Problem of Consequential Damages"; Semlinger, "New Developments in Subcontracting."

45. The conception of an "ideal type" refers to neither the accumulation and combination of an empirical world nor the consensus of agents with diverse motives in the real world, but is an analytical tool produced through an "analytical accentuation of certain elements of reality."

46. Crouch and Streeck, "Introduction: The Future of Capitalist Diversity," 1–18; Philippe C. Schmitter, "Levels of Spatial Coordination and the Embeddedness of Institutions," in Hollingsworth and Boyer, *Contemporary Capitalism*, 311–317.

47. For agents' reflexivity in the debate on political economy, see Charles F. Sabel, "Consti-tutional Orders: Trust Building and Response to Change," in Hollingsworth and Boyer, *Contemporary Capitalism*, 154–188; idem, "Experimental Regionalism and the Dilemmas of Regional Economic Policy"; idem, "Learning by Monitoring: The Institutions of Eco-nomic Development," in Smelser and Swedberg, *The Handbook of Economic Sociology*, 137–165; Charles F. Sabel and Jonathan Zeitlin, "Stories, Strategies, Structures: Rethink-ing Historical Alternatives to Mass Production," in Charles F. Sabel and Jonathan Zeitlin, eds., *World of Possibilities: Flexibility and Mass Production in Western Industrializa-tion* (New York: Cambridge University Press, 1997), 1–33. For general theories of reflex-ivity and habitus, see Pierre Bourdieu, *Outline of a Theory of Practice* (Cambridge: Cambridge University Press, 1998); idem, *The Logic of Practice* (Stanford, Calif.: Stanford University Press, 1992).

48. This book defines trust as "the mutual confidence that no party to a contract will exploit the trading partner's vulnerability whether it arises out of self-interest or out of social norms." A party is trustworthy if she or he chooses to refrain from opportunism, that is, if she or he does not act for her or his immediate self-interest at the expense of a trading

partner. The problem is that collaborative markets need a higher level of trust than the traditional distant markets because they contain high risks of opportunism. For a similar definition of trust, see Charles F. Sabel, "Studied Trust: Building New Forms of Cooperation in a Volatile Economy," in F. Pyke and W. Sengenberger, eds., *Industrial Districts and Local Economic Regeneration* (Geneva: International Institute for Labour Studies, 1992), 215; Bruce Lyons and Judith Mehta, "Private Sector Business Contracts: The Text Between the Lines," in Simon Deakin and Jonathan Michie, eds., *Contract, Cooperation, and Competition* (Oxford: Oxford University Press, 1997), 52.

Chapter One

SIMILARITIES AND DIFFERENCES IN THE TRANSFORMATION

In the mid 1980s, Western manufacturers and automakers in particular began to reflect on the rationality of their existing manufacturing and market systems against the background of the wave of international competition and apparent success of the Japanese automobile industry. Huge bureaucratic corporations dismantled existing vertically integrated organizations by favoring market relations. A new rationality of division of labor generated a reorganization of market relations. Just as Fordism in the early twentieth century made significant impacts not only on the process of production but also on the entire society, so-called lean production has contributed to the reorganization of societies by backfiring against the old division of labor. Mass production created huge, vertically integrated in-house production and neoclassical markets, while the lean production system is characterized by low vertical integration and flexible interaction between market partners.

The complicated processes of restructuring in the U.S. and German automotive industries—"converging but not neoliberal" and "diverging but not predetermined" markets—challenge prevalent paradigms of political economy. Contrary to neoliberal belief, the apparent revival of market relations did not confirm the rejuvenation of neoliberal market governance. On the other hand, rigid institutionalists promoting a theory of path dependence also failed to explain the dynamic process of transformation of national economies. In contrast to those institutionalist expectations, both the American and German automotive parts markets successfully adopted a new form of flexible lean production and collaborative markets in which agents share their know-how and work together through the entire process of value creation. In addition, the varying consequences of market regimes are not predetermined by particular institutions and cultures.

This chapter investigates the similarities and differences in the process of industrial adjustments in both the U.S. and German automobile industries.

Notes for this chapter begin on page 75.

First, this chapter explores in detail why market relations became prevalent in both the U.S. and Germany in the last decade of the twentieth century; then it examines the complicated process of adjustments, illustrating the "converging but not neoliberal" and "diverging but not predetermined" markets. Finally, before subsequent chapters studying in more detail what caused the differences in both the U.S. and German markets, this chapter analyzes how the American and German market regimes differ from each other regarding market governance.

Similarities in Transformation

Contrary to many institutionalists' expectations that the lean production and collaborative markets initiated in Japan would not take root in Western societies, Americans and Germans have in fact undergone tremendous transformation by deintegrating their hierarchical governance and reorganizing current market relations. This section examines why large U.S. and German corporations in the automobile industry came to rely on market relations instead of their existing hierarchical governance; furthermore, it highlights how the new markets in both countries commonly depart from neoclassical or traditional markets.

Creation of the Market

Most observers of the automobile industry agree that the recent trend in the industry is deintegration. It is very difficult, however, to accurately measure the extent of vertical integration. This is not simply because the automakers, considering their company images, hesitate to reveal the degree of outsourcing. Although the companies provide data on purchasing costs, the composites of the purchasing costs are different. The different methods of calculation also contribute to the difficulty of obtaining comprehensive and accurate data.[1] Nevertheless, almost all experts agree that the basic trend in the manufacturing industry, particularly in the automotive industry, is deintegration and outsourcing (contracting out with external suppliers in the market).

Throughout the 1990s, it was very easy to find cases of automakers' deintegration. Automakers liquidated their parts-making operations. In November of 1993, Ford sold its seat assembly operation to a supplier, Lear Seating. In 1999, Ford spun off one of its biggest suppliers, Visteon. Chrysler also followed the trend, selling two operations for leather and fabric seat covers to Johnson Controls in May 1994. Also in 1994, Chrysler sold eight operations for making wiring assemblies to Yazaki, a Japanese supplier. General Motors was one of the fastest companies to spin off parts plants. From 1993 to 1994, GM disposed of radiator caps, vacuum pumps, and forty one other lines of business operations worth $25 billion per year. In

April 1994, GM sold 80 percent of its electronic motors units to ITT Automotive. GM also sold its Delco-Remy operation of three plants and spun off its biggest parts-making operation, Delphi, in 1998.[2] GM deintegrated its in-house production from 80–85 percent in the 1960s and 70 percent in the late 1980s to 47 percent in 1993; Ford also reduced its vertical integration from 60–50 percent in the 1960s to 50 percent in 1988 and 38 percent in 1993. Chrysler maintained a relatively lower level of vertical integration, dropping from 40 percent in 1983 to 34 percent in 1993 and 22 percent in 2001.[3]

German automakers also followed the trend of deintegration. Traditionally, German automakers, with the exception of Volkswagen, maintained lower levels of vertical integration compared with American automakers. During the zenith of vertical integration in the 1960s and 1970s, VW had about 80 percent vertical integration in the value of an automobile while BMW and Porsche maintained levels of approximately 35 percent to 40 percent. German companies reduced their vertical integration by approximately 30 percent in 1996.[4] Dismantling the hierarchical governance of in-house production, VW increased its outsourcing from DM 40 billion in 1994 to DM 100 billion in 1999. Now, VW depends on outsourcing for two-thirds of a car's value.[5] Mercedes-Benz AG also started to spin off its parts-making operation in the 1990s. For example, Mercedes-Benz AG sold its plants for seat production to Keiper Recaro and plants for valve-making to Mahle.[6] According to a 1993 study by Deutsche Bank, from 1985 to 1992 automakers increased their outsourcing, doubling the volume of purchasing by almost DM 22 billion.[7] Employment is also an indicator of the trend of vertical integration. As automakers contract out more, the number of employees in the automaker companies declines, while their counterparts in the supplier companies grow. From 1994 to 1996, employment in the German automakers dropped by 3 percent, whereas the employment in the supplier companies increased by 6 percent. The turnover of supplier companies in this period grew by about 20 percent.[8] The outsourcing of all German automakers on average increased from about 32 percent in 1985 to 53.7 percent in 1987, 62.2 percent in 1993, and 70.7 percent in 1999.[9] First-tier system suppliers in Germany also reduced their in-house production. According to the calculations of Reinhard Schmitt in the Siemens SGP Verkehrstechnik GmbH in Graz, Germany, first-tier suppliers of the automotive industry increased their outsourcing from about 40 percent in 1980 to 70 percent in 2000.[10]

The revival of contracts through deintegration in the last two decades of the twentieth century stands in opposition to the trend of vertical integration initiated in the early decades of the century. In early automobile industry history, automakers simply assembled parts purchased from outside suppliers. Most automakers purchased parts, assembled them, and sent the car to market.[11] With the rise of mass production, automakers tried to integrate parts production to realize economy of scale and secure the production process of mass production. In the second and third decades of the twentieth century, American automakers internalized parts production. General Motors bought companies like AC Spark Plug, Dayton Engineering Laboratories (Delco), and Charles Kettering, which were spun off later in the 1990s. Ford's method of vertical integration was to expand internal operations instead of buying out independent companies. The automakers in the early decades of the twentieth century tried to build complete vertical integration in which all stages—from design and engineering to production—were owned and controlled by the automakers.[12] The outsourcing percentage, the value of purchased components of the finished vehicle values, had declined from 55 percent in 1922 to 26 percent in 1926 with the establishment of mass production and the rise of vertical integration.[13] Vertical integration, set by Ford and GM, continued in the succeeding four decades. Chrysler, established in 1924, followed the same trajectory. American automakers reached the zenith of vertical integration in the mid 1960s.

German automakers took on a pattern similar to that of U.S. automakers, although German automakers' adaptation to mass production was relatively delayed up to the 1950s.[14] During and after World War II, massive vertical integration took place in Germany. In this period, many automakers took over parts, assistance, and additional production due to a shortage of parts. Automakers tried to internalize the parts suppliers to avoid the interruption of production.[15] In the 1960s, German companies understood the rationalization of their production as the realization of economies of scale and vertical integration. The major German automakers integrated the production of parts such as the piston, gear joint-shaft, clutch, and the like.[16] Through continuing vertical integration, the major German automakers produced an average of 60—65 percent of parts in-house by the late 1960s.

The deintegration of manufacturing companies—in particular, the deintegration and establishment of a flexible system in the U.S. automobile industry—contradicts existing theories based on transactions costs theory or institutionalism.[17] Transaction costs theorists hold that different countries take on different types of governance because their cultures and institutions contribute to the reduction of opportunism to different degrees; due to opportunism, American corporations tend to internalize parts production in the form of highly vertical integration. Institutionalists such as Hollingsworth and Boyer argue that American corporations reproduce the national pattern of standardized mass production based on high vertical integration due to specific American institutional environments such as low trust, sparse social networks, and market mentality. But the transaction costs theorists fail to explain why American automakers deintegrated their hierarchical governance while parts suppliers increased asset specificity. Through reflection upon the drawbacks of current production system, Americans transformed their economic system toward a pattern opposite from institutionalists' expectations.

Just as Fordism generated a new rationality of the division of labor, lean production or "Toyotaism," based on the apparent success of Japanese manufacturers under tough global competition, encouraged Western manufacturers to reflect on their existing production system. As changes in technology became more rapid and the market for end-products became more volatile, the highly vertically integrated in-house production that had emerged under the rationality of mass production proved too rigid to catch up to the turbulent changes. From the viewpoint of the production process, standardization was rational, whereas from the perspective of flexible innovation of products, standardization had become burdensome. From the perspective of transaction costs, high vertical integration might be an optimal solution, whereas from the perspective of flexible production, vertical integration was problematic. Economic rationality is neither as universal nor as apparent as the neoclassical paradigm assumes. On the contrary, the ideal types of economic rationality are multiple and contested. In particular, market rationality has been relativized by the division of labor. With new opinions on the rationality of the division of labor, agents in the U.S. and Germany deintegrated hierarchical governance.

It is noteworthy that the rejuvenated markets created by deintegration in the 1980s and 1990s are not simply an extension of the traditional markets. Rather, agents in both the American and German markets reorganized their market relations by creating more closely interactive relations based on long-term contracts. The next section will investigate how the newly emerging market is different from the traditional mass production markets in both the U.S. and Germany.

Neoclassical Market vs. Collaborative Market

Although the U.S. and German markets show strikingly similar patterns of adjustments under globalization, the similarities do not confirm the neoclassical paradigm. To the contrary, the newly emerging markets depart from the neoclassical market, challenging neoliberal market governance. Just as vertical integration and the distant form of market came to being with the rationality of mass production, a new form of market and production system emerged when producers began to reflect on the drawbacks of mass production. This section examines how the similar patterns of transformation in both the American and German markets depart from both traditional markets. The following subsection begins by delving into the traditional markets of the U.S. and Germany.

Neoclassical market in mass production. The traditional markets in both the U.S. and Germany were similar to the neoclassical markets. Neoclassical markets had been fully realized with mass production, which ironically reduced the portion of the market in society. This subsection argues that the traditional markets in both the U.S. and Germany were closely related to the rationality of mass production, and that, under the rationality of mass production, the traditional markets were similar to the neoclassical markets. Furthermore, it explains that those markets shifted as the rationality of the existing division of labor was altered.

The development of markets is closely related to the division of labor, as Adam Smith points out in the famous story of the pin-making process.

> One man draws out the wire, another straights it, a third cuts it, a fourth points it, a fifth grinds it at the top for receiving the head; to make the head requires two or three distinct operations;… the important business of making a pin is, in this manner, divided into about eighteen distinct operations, which, in some manufactories, are all performed by distinct hands, though in others the same man will sometimes perform two or three of them.[18]

A market comes into being with the division of labor. Whether in a factory, a community, or a family, exchanges between discrete agents (individuals or collective units) occur based on the division of labor. The free exchanges between independent agents, who pursue self-interests by determining their own strategies of operation, are in contrast to the relations under hierarchy.[19] Agent A, in the process of pin-making, might cover the process from purchasing the metal to drawing the wire; agent B buys the drawn wire from agent A and straightens it; agent C cuts the straightened wire and sells it to agent D, and so on. The number of stages in the entire value creation process covered by agent A depends not just on the transaction costs, but, more importantly, on the rationality of organizing the value creation process. In addition, the way of doing business is influenced by the rationality of how to organize the process of value creation.

The markets are reorganized as the rationality of division of labor in value creation changes. Neoclassical market relations based on the anonymity principle were realized as mass production came into being. Mass production seems to contradict the free market held by the neoclassical economists because it encourages vertical integration of large corporations and thus reduces the portion of market exchanges. However, the market that remains after vertical integration in the period of mass production resembles the neoclassical market. The ideal type of neoclassical market assumes the homogeneity of products in industry to facilitate switching between contracting partners. Standardization of products and the simplification of tasks because of mass production have paralleled development of the neoclassical market.

Perfect competition in the neoclassical market is not a "real market." Neoclassical economists hold that the so-called perfect competition provides the best market efficiency, and that, to the extent that a real market deviates from perfect competition, it is undesirable and inefficient. Perfect competition is an ideal type of market free from restraints imposed by institutions or customs.[20] In a perfectly competitive market, there are no restraints on the movement of price and resources. For the free movement of resources and prices, a homogeneous commodity should be offered by a large number of vendors; thus, there should be little difficulty in switching to another market partner. For the free movement of resources or for the freedom of contracts, the market should be free from institutional constraints that arise from governmental restraints, customs, and associations; agents should not take care of identity, but move following the price indications. A neoclassical economist argues that "[the market's] essential feature is that all economic relations are impersonal"; "anyone will exchange with anyone else upon the slightest advantage appearing."[21] The market should be easily recontracting; thus, contracts should be short-term. Finally, the neoclassical market assumes complete knowledge with which agents can make error-free adjustment to the optimality of using resources by detecting who offers the cheapest goods.

However, the rationality of the neoclassical market is not universally valid but contextualized, particularly by a specific form of division of labor. The neoclassical market was more similar to the markets in the period of mass production than in the era of the craft system. Specifically, the automobile parts markets that were reshaped with the initiation of mass production were similar to the neoclassical market. In the 1910s and 1920s, as sales of automobiles grew rapidly, American automakers consolidated their market power and reshaped market relations with parts suppliers. To realize a stable process of mass production, American automakers internalized the production of specialized components, but left the simple and standardized parts to other vendors in the market. Automakers could easily switch suppliers by searching for the lowest price. This market differed from the market under the craft system, in which automakers benefited from suppliers' technical expertise and design capability.

The standardization in mass production enabled customers to reorganize the closely interactive markets based on the old craft system toward the neoclassical, distant markets. American automakers and suppliers made efforts to standardize parts in recognition of the rationality of mass production. Through the efforts of the Society of Automobile Engineers (SAE) around 1910, for example, the number of different lock washers was reduced from 800 to 16. The models of steel tubing also fell from 1,600 to 210. Standardization makes commodities more homogeneous and facilitates agents switching to another partner, as neoclassical economists hold. Before standardization, if an automaker wanted to switch its supplier of carburetors or spark plugs, the automaker often needed to redesign its engine because the carburetor or spark plug was specific to the engine. This made it difficult to find another supplier. Suppliers experienced similar difficulties: if an automaker collapsed, the supplier had to file a huge inventory of parts because they would not work for other automakers.[22] The homogeneity created by standardization facilitated the buyer's movement between the vendors.

Conception and execution in mass production were separate not only within in-house production but also between a customer and a supplier. In the process of vertical integration, American automakers increased the number of engineering staff and produced detailed designs of components for independent suppliers. Automakers were reluctant to permit outside suppliers to maintain special engineering skills and capabilities because automakers were worried that the suppliers' opportunism might disturb the smooth flow of the production process for an economy of scale. In the 1920s, the suppliers' role in technical improvement and innovation in the automobile industry declined significantly.[23] In the old craft system, tasks of craftsmen were complicated: gathering all the necessary parts, planning the jobs, performing complex fitting jobs, and checking over their work. By contrast, in mass production, the tasks became very simple: a worker performed just one simple task, for example, put two nuts on two bolts. Likewise, suppliers received simple tasks developed by a customer, based on standardization and separation between conception and execution. The customers broke down each system used on the vehicle into small and separate parts. The in-house engineers of the automaker companies developed the detailed specifications and drawings for each small part. Suppliers made the simple and standardized parts following the customer's blueprint. Then the customers assembled the system in-house using the parts purchased from the separate suppliers.[24] The customers in mass production did not intend to hand over development capability to the suppliers because it might increase the switching costs. Simple tasks and customer-developed drawings reduced switching costs among parts vendors.

Another characteristic of the markets during the period of mass production was that automakers and suppliers exchanged little information. Automakers did not need to utilize the suppliers' design and engineering capability after giving them simple and standardized tasks. Only price mattered. Without knowing the costs of supplier production, customers required supply-side competition in order to secure a lower price. Carrying their own blueprint, the buyers for the automaker could move to this or that supplier quickly. Until the early 1980s, the role of buyers was relatively simple. They considered only the price of parts, and offered a contract to the vendor that offered the lowest price. By contrast, in the old craft system and in current collaborative markets, buyers have to consider suppliers' capability for design, willingness to cooperate, and history of relations in order to achieve the benefits of collaborative application engineering. In neoclassical, distant markets, suppliers tried to hide information from the customer, such as how to make the parts and their internal efficiency, in order to secure a better position in negotiations. The only information shared between a buyer and a seller was price. Suppliers brought few ideas for improvement of design and cost efficiency.[25] The separation between conception (by the customer) and execution (by a supplier) under mass production made it possible for the remaining market relations to be reorganized according to the neoclassical model.

The neoclassical market worked in the period of mass production in which, paradoxically, "hierarchical governance" prevailed not only through vertically integrated corporations, but also through governmental involvement in the market to secure the operation of mass production, for example, by supporting mass consumption. Homogeneous products by standardization, simple tasks, and customer-developed blueprints based on the separation of conception and execution under the rationality of mass production enabled customers to switch between vendors easily while considering only prices.

German market relations during the period of mass production also took on the form of neoclassical, distant markets, as their American counterparts did. But the adoption of mass production in Germany did not mirror exactly the American process. The legacy of the craft system survived through the era of mass production in Germany. American automakers integrated major suppliers in the 1920s and 1930s, while German automakers contracted out with independent suppliers continuously for a long time.[26] Until the late 1940s, German suppliers maintained their capacity for development. Up that point, only the products that suppliers developed were in the category of original supply (*Zulieferung*); otherwise, they were in the category of sub-supply (*Unterlieferung*). The German production system did not undergo de-skilled Taylorism as much as the U.S. system did. German blue- and white-collar workers received extensive occupational training. German training policy and the legacy of craftsmanship reversed the fragmentation of work.[27] Workers maintained high levels of discretion rather than receiving fragmented and simple tasks. Likewise, German suppliers were production specialists in most cases. German automakers maintained a relatively small batch system compared with that in place in the U.S. In the early decades of the twentieth century, German automakers followed the trend of standardization slowly, but it did not lead to the introduction of complete mass production. German automakers like Daimler boasted of careful hand work for their high-quality cars. Although Daimler started to use American machine tools because of their greater precision and changed the organization from a confederation of mostly independent shops, the firm was still anchored in the craft system, in which specialist teams did jobs on a series of stationary chassis during the first half of the twentieth century.[28] Although Volkswagen was built for mass production based on Fordism, it lay idle until 1940 due to massive start-up costs. Between 1945 and 1950, VW could not operate its plants fully due to a shortage of materials. It was in 1955 that VW installed a new, special-purpose machine, replacing older multi-purpose tools. Not until the early 1960s did VW fully realize mass production.[29]

In spite of the delay, the German automobile industry adopted more or less the rationality of mass production after World War II. German automakers began to reshape supplier relations by integrating parts production in-house. In the late 1940s, automakers were concerned with vertical integration of the parts production because of the shortage of parts supply.[30] Through the late 1940s and 1950s, German automakers internalized many special parts suppliers. VW made significant investments in 1958 and 1960 focusing on the in-house production of components.[31] In the mid 1960s, the increase of in-house production of parts was a tendency not only in Germany, but also in other European countries like France and Italy.[32] The tendency toward vertical integration continued through the 1970s.

With internalization of parts production and an increased capacity for development and engineering, automakers developed the blueprints while suppliers became simple producers following the customer-developed drawings. As benefits resulting from a supplier's special know-how and flexible application engineering decreased, German automakers could easily move the business for parts in-house or switch to another supplier. Suppliers' position became more precarious in vertical integration because parts suppliers were in competition with their customers.[33] Under the threat of vertical integration, German suppliers were less likely to offer their information to automakers. Although German suppliers had been praised for their cooperation for the public good, such as vocational training, market relations with customers became neoclassical and distant, as in the American markets.

Standardization increased the number of business partners for both customers and vendors. To protect themselves from automakers' power under the threat of vertical integration, German suppliers undertook the diversification of markets by reducing models and standardizing products. Until the 1960s, German suppliers maintained a variety of products under the legacy of the craft system. For example, the Fichtel & Sachs company added about 300 variations to the existing five basic types of clutches (*Kupplungen*) until the 1960s. This practice of producing numerous variations was prevalent in Germany, while American companies achieved success based on strong standardization in mass production. But from the 1960s on, most German suppliers in the automobile industry developed standardization, considering the diversification of the market.[34] On the other hand, the adoption of mass production enabled German automakers to increase the number of suppliers because entry to the market for the simple and standardized parts was easy. For example, the number of suppliers for Daimler-Benz increased from 13,856 in 1954 to 16,558 in 1960 and 17,760 in 1961.[35] The competition among suppliers was severe. The number of suppliers was between two and twenty, although two suppliers were normally chosen.[36] The price for a part decreased as the number of suppliers increased.

Although German companies had relatively more flexibility than strict mass producers in the U.S. until the 1980s, market relations in Germany were similar to those of the U.S. in the sense that short-term and distant contractual relations prevailed with the adoption of the rationality of mass production. Until the late 1980s, the German production system, which had maintained the legacy of the craft system, was praised for its high quality products and incremental innovation based on decentralized production by high-quality labor. The German model, termed "flexible specialization," "diversified quality production" (DQP), or "craft system," in comparison with American strict mass production, was characterized by highly skilled workers and professional specialization instead of Tayloristic de-skilling of labor.[37] The German flexible system based on some elements of the craft system could perform "fast retooling" and incremental innovation better than the American mass producers until the 1980s. In particular, the German production system was praised for its strong small- and medium-sized companies (*Mittelständer*). The strength of small- and medium-sized companies was based on agility of small batches, highly skilled labor, and high niche-oriented specialty. The small- and medium-sized companies were praised for their cooperation in building public infrastructure like the vocational training that supported the craft system. The small- and medium-sized companies, given their interactive combination of small batch shops, enabled the German production system to be more flexible and incrementally innovative than the highly vertically integrated mass producers in the U.S.

Nevertheless, market relations in Germany were similar to those in the U.S. during the era of mass production.[38] Some institutionalists, such as Lane (1996), Casper (2001), Teubner (2001), and Hall and Soskice (2001), argue that German institutions such as regulatory contract law/court, dense networks of associations, and bank-based finance generate long-term and cooperative contractual relations, while American institutions such as liberal contract law/court, loose networks of associations, and fluid finance engender short-term and arms-length contractual relations. But it is not true that German markets were traditionally characterized by long-term and cooperative relations, while American relations were short-term and arms-length. As shall be investigated later, the German markets up to the early 1990s were dominated by neither long-term nor relational contracts. Most contracts in the traditional German markets were for less than one year, as they were in the U.S. It was not until the 1990s that Germans adopted long-term contractual relations. In addition, in the 1990s, Americans employed long-term and collaborative markets earlier than the Germans did.

Until the late 1980s, market relations in Germany were similar to the neoclassical and distant ones in America. Although German suppliers were production specialists reliant on highly skilled workers, they did not have design and development capacity in most cases. Although the existence of strong *Mittelständer* enabled the German production system to be more flexible than the strict mass producers in the U.S., collaboration between suppliers and automakers was not systematic but irregular. Most suppliers served as a kind of buffer zone (*Verlängerte Werkbank*) for the big corporation, absorbing the shocks from fluctuating market demands, rather than as a partner for flexible application engineering through the entire process of value creation. Under the threat of vertical integration, suppliers could not make relation-specific investments. Also, suppliers and customers in the traditional markets shared little information, compared to the new form of collaborative markets in the 1990s. Although some special suppliers like Bosch and Fichtel & Sachs had strong competence for development, they tended to practice individual development rather than systematic collaboration with customers. Until the early 1990s, most customers in the German automobile industry believed that every supplier should be substitutable. Suppliers were reluctant to open their production because they were afraid that customers might take advantage of the information.[39] In spite of the remaining legacy of craftsmanship, German automotive parts markets, like those in the U.S., were neoclassical and distant under mass production.

During the period of mass production, American and German supplier markets moved toward neoclassical markets. Mass production, which created huge corporations and reduced the portion of market in society, paradoxically realigned the remaining market relations based on the rationality of the neoclassical market in both the U.S. and German supplier markets. During the old craft period, automakers and suppliers developed relational-specific products and skills, so they could hardly switch trading partners in a market. By contrast, standardization and simplification of work in mass production enabled market relations to be more substitutable. The homogeneity of products and the simplification of tasks reduced not only switching costs but also barriers to the supplier's entry into the market. After internalizing their development and engineering capability, customers could easily switch vendors with the blueprint they had developed by themselves. Not focusing on the suppliers' potential capability for application engineering, buyers just searched for the lowest price while recontracting in the short term among numerous vendors.

Transformation to the collaborative market. In the 1980s, Western automakers began to consider their existing manufacturing systems and purchasing policies against the background of a strong wave of international competition and the apparent success of the Japanese automobile industry. Industry experts criticized the rigidity of the mass production system and distant market relations. Agents in the U.S. and Germany made tremendous efforts to transform their existing market and production systems. The successful reorganization of both the U.S. and German markets in the 1990s contradicts existing views of institutionalists as well as of market liberals. The fact that the U.S. and German markets adopted strikingly similar patterns of adjustments even under different institutional environments contradicts the rigid institutionalist view of path-dependent divergence. Although the reorganization of market relations was similar in the U.S. and Germany, the similarities depart from the neoclassical market. This section illustrates how much the American and German markets have been transformed from their traditional markets, and why they changed.

Reflecting on the problems of mass production and neoclassical market relations, as well as the apparent success of Japanese competitors, Western automobile makers began to restructure their market and production systems in the 1980s. In the late 1970s and early 1980s, American experts tried to understand the causes of the apparent Japanese economic success. The American automobile industry suffered tough competition from foreign competitors, particularly Japanese automakers, at that time. The first three years of the 1980s were the worst years on record for the American automotive industry. The American Big Three (GM, Ford, and Chrysler) lost a total of $4.73 billion. Chrysler would have collapsed without the government's bailout.[40] By contrast, the success of Japanese automakers was obvious. During the 1980s, Japanese automakers encroached on the American market by 25 to 30 percent.[41] While trying to explain Japanese success, American industrial experts focused on transient factors such as oil shocks, low Japanese labor costs, and automation.[42] Soon, however, people began to pay attention to the Japanese flexible manufacturing and supplier management system when comparing the international automotive (parts) industries.[43] Japanese production and customer-supplier relations were regarded as the "best practice" in comparison with American and European suppliers.

American automakers began to restructure their organization by deintegrating the mass production system. The fundamental organizational change was to reverse the extreme separation between conception and execution, which was a rationality of mass production. In mass production, workers performed only one or two simple and standardized tasks, using a single-purpose machine that produced standard products in high volume. A foreman did not perform production work but made sure that the production workers followed the instructions devised by the industrial engineers. The production workers were totally separate from planning their jobs. They kept their heads down while they worked. The jobs were also very narrowly defined for specific tasks such as arrangement of parts, assembling on conveyor belts, house cleaning, checking quality, repair, and the like. People followed narrowly defined professional careers. Companies were organized in the form of functional departments.[44]

By contrast, in the lean production system initiated by the Japanese automakers, a team integrates separate jobs. For example, workers on the shop floor integrate various jobs, like assembling and performing quality management at the same time. Workers in the team plan their jobs and learn skills by doing more than one job on the team. In new development, design engineers, process engineers, and production operators interact in a team structure. A plant manager in a U.S. company says, "When they [specialists from different areas] put them all together and they share their ideas, you have a truly dynamic system which gives you very, very good results."[45] In the early 1990s, U.S. automakers realigned the existing functional departments into the radical form of platform teams. A platform team for an automobile consists of about 500 people. The platform team is subdivided into "product action teams," and further, into small teams for subsystems, such as the instrument panel or climate control team.[46] Through the cross-functional team, automakers reduce over-engineering. Design engineers become less likely to develop a design not favorable to manufacturing.

In similar fashion, external suppliers are integrated in customers' teams at different levels. People from supplier and customer companies closely collaborate with each other, sharing information. Suppliers participate in the customers' teams from a very early stage of development. Automakers and suppliers improved production through closely interactive application engineering. For example, in mass production, customers simply returned the defective parts after detecting them. By contrast, in new, collaborative markets, both the supplier and customer trace back every stage at which a defect occurs. They interact closely to find and solve problems together.[47] In addition, automakers and suppliers bring their specialties not only to quality management, but more importantly, to improvement of products and production. Many different suppliers in the development team of a module, say, a door system, consider various issues such as cost-saving, technical performance, and the like. This is called "simultaneous engineering." In "value engineering," a customer and suppliers break down the costs of each stage of production to find a way of reducing costs together.[48] This is a significant departure from past practices in which suppliers received just the customer-developed blueprint and the parties hid their information from each other. An American supplier compares the traditional and recent working styles:

> In the past, customers came to us, just took a look at general production and ordered what they wanted. They did not get involved in the details, machine-setting and the process of our production. But, nowadays the customers have access to every detail of whatever we do in a very intimate way. They visit the shop and they get whatever information they want to get.[49]

The fundamental departure from past practices is that agents in the collaborative markets share much more proprietary information regarding production techniques and costs. Agents in the U.S. automotive parts markets have reorganized their relations, changing from distant relations to more closely interactive relations and thereby correcting some problems of the former market and production systems.

Meanwhile, the German automotive industry has also undergone tremendous changes, though German transformation toward collaborative markets was relatively delayed because of reunification. Several empirical studies about informal collaboration between customers and suppliers reveal that in the early 1990s, American automotive parts markets had more collaborative relations than their German counterparts.[50] This is a surprising divergence from the conventional wisdom that Germans are more cooperative than Americans. In particular, this fact contradicts the institutionalist view that Germans developed long-term and cooperative contractual relations because of their institutional environments, such as regulatory contract law/court, dense networks of associations, and long-term financial system. The traditional markets in Germany were not long-term, collaborative markets. It was not until the 1990s that German automotive parts markets began to develop new forms of long-term and collaborative markets. Thus, it must be investigated in detail why Germans had to transform their existing production system and how the new markets differ from the old ones.

The reason Americans were more cooperative than Germans in the early 1990s is that the traditional merits of the German craft-based system turned out to be too rigid to assimilate the new flexible and collaborative system in the early 1990s. Until the early 1990s, most German companies did not develop cross-functional teams and collaborative market relations. They still maintained traditional distant relations. The German model based on professional specialization and highly qualified labor became problematic in the late 1980s and early 1990s.[51] The strictly functional specialization in Germany deterred cross-functional team structure. For example, German automakers separated prototype design and prototype building in time and space. The designer of a prototype had little knowledge of the actual conditions of production plants, while the manufacturing staff received little information on the experiences and ideas that the designers of a prototype had. The jobs for development followed sequentially different functional departments. Many empirical studies in the 1990s revealed that German companies exhibited major weaknesses in the process of product development, particularly in terms of collaboration and communication across functional specialties. The functional, department-oriented structure of German companies caused delays in time-to-market as well as huge costs from double engineering. The strong functional-specialty orientation or professional specialization deterred the development of flexibly interactive teams across functional departments.

By the same token, collaboration between suppliers and customers was also less developed in comparison with lean producers. Many independent observations confirm that by the early 1990s Americans had developed more a collaborative and lean system than their European counterparts.[52] In comparison with suppliers in other countries like the U.S., the U.K., and Japan, German automakers and suppliers in the early 1990s were less efficient in flexible development. The product life cycle of the German supplier companies in the early 1990s (84 months) was longer than that of Japanese suppliers (48 months) and that of U.S. suppliers (76 months). In quality management, German suppliers indicated 885 defects of one million on average, while U.S. suppliers indicated 253 defects.[53] To produce higher quality, German companies needed an abundance of rework at the end of the production line. The empirical studies on German suppliers in the early 1990s, such as research by Die Roland-Berger, A.T. Kearney GmbH, and Bamberg University (the Forschungsstelle Automobilwirtschaft an der Universität Bamberg), revealed that German suppliers were just at the beginning stages of restructuring in the early 1990s, and that German suppliers and customers had not developed collaborative relations.[54] Another study of the Velbert region of Germany shows that cooperation between suppliers and customers was rare through the late 1980s. The new form of collaborative work, such as just-in-time delivery, had attracted less attention among suppliers.[55] According to the Bamberg University study, German parts suppliers and customers in the automotive industry met together every 19 months (on average) to talk about development or quality. Other empirical studies for international comparison such as Schrader and Sattler (1993) and Birou and Fawcett (1994) reveal that Americans were more cooperative than Germans in the early 1990s; American suppliers participated in the early stages of development while few German suppliers did.

Contrary to the institutionalists' description of German markets, the traditional markets in Germany did not feature long-term and cooperative contractual relations. A president of a German supplier company describes his experience of the traditional market:

> In about 1985, customers and suppliers did not need so much communication. A customer provided their drawings and asked price. Suppliers took the drawings and offered price. That's it. There was little discussion. We, as a stamping producer, did not know anything about sheet metal parts. Recently we meet with customers and other suppliers to discuss how to make and improve the products. Recently, customers and suppliers open more information to each other.[56]

In traditional market relations, German agents focused on just their narrow specialty and simple tasks. Without close interaction in "simultaneous engineering," German automakers and suppliers suffered from "double engineering" until the early 1990s.[57] In particular, the German professional specialization that had been highly praised for diversified quality production until the late 1980s aggravated problems between different professions as well as between customers and suppliers owing to the strict demarcation between professions.

However, through the crisis in the first half of the 1990s, German companies also began to make tremendous efforts to restructure their intrafirm as well as interfirm structure. German companies struggled to improve their productivity, adopting process-oriented team work. According to the research of the German trade union (IG Metall), only 4 percent of employees in the automotive industry participated in team work in 1990. But the figure grew rapidly after the crisis of 1992 and 1993. The share of employees in team work was 9 percent in 1993, 22 percent in 1994. And recent studies reveal that about 80 percent of German automotive suppliers overcame difficulties expected in the process of adopting team work.[58] For the interfirm collaboration, for example, collaborative quality management in the early 1990s was just a pilot experiment by a few companies in Germany. But between 1995 and 1997, many German automotive suppliers adopted collaborative quality management. According to a Fraunhofer Institute study on German automotive suppliers conducted in 1997, German automotive suppliers had also adopted just-in-time delivery by 76 percent, and simultaneous engineering by 54 percent.[59] According to my own survey conducted in 2000, a majority of German suppliers (79 percent) take part in the early stages of development while sharing information and discussing technology and economic efficiency with customers.

The agents in the German automotive parts markets have developed a new form of collaborative markets in a relatively short time although they began the process relatively late. A bearing supplier describes clearly the recent changes in comparison with past market relations in Germany:

> Fifteen years ago, companies focused on only their specialties. But people started to think that it might not be the best way. Fifteen years ago, it was sufficient to state what is the loading capacity for a bearing and what will be the calculated life-time for the bearing and what grease has to be used. But, recently, you know, bearings for a wheel are assembled in knuckles. Knuckles are screwed to an accelerator. Sometimes the knuckle is not properly made to endure the load coming from bearings. Sometimes the knuckle has a bad impact on bearings. Recently we have to look at how other brakes are properly designed and whether they are properly located because they create lots of heat, and the heat can cause problems with grease. If the grease does not work, the bearing fails.[60]

German agents overcame the traditional culture of narrow-minded specialty and established ways of cross-functional and collaborative interaction, contrary to the expectation of rigid institutionalists such as Streeck (1996) that cross-functional teams and collaborative markets would not take root on German soil due to the German culture of professional specialization. Through reflecting on the rigidity of their existing model of professional specialization, Germans tried to adopt cross-functional teams and collaborative market relations. In particular, it is noteworthy that almost all German suppliers want to participate in the process of development earlier if possible, instead of hesitating to be involved in the process of collaborative works.[61] The reason for the preference for early involvement in the development process is that they believe they can reap an abundance of benefits by making the conditions favorable to them. For example, if a customer changes an engine design slightly, the engine spring maker can save money on the different design. But if the supplier has to revise the given design after the customer has already fixed the model of engine system, it is very costly to change the given model.[62]

Both the American and German automotive parts markets have largely transformed from traditional neoclassical markets to a new form of collaborative markets. How much have they changed?

First, suppliers in both the U.S. and German markets developed a capability for design and development by which they work together with a customer from the early stages of development. In the 1980s, about 81 percent of U.S. suppliers received detailed drawings developed by customers, while about 62 percent of Japanese suppliers conducted their own engineering based on automakers' rough functional descriptions.[63] It can be said that competition between U.S. and Japanese automobile industries until the late 1980s was between mass producers and collaborative lean producers. But through continuous restructuring, only 22 percent of U.S. suppliers in 1996 received the customer-developed blueprint.[64] But at the end of the 1990s, as is shown in table 1, only 15 percent of American suppliers went by the traditional activity of just receiving the final drawing. A majority of suppliers participate in the early stage of development or in the prototype stage, sharing information for the collaborative work.

In addition, as table 1 shows, a majority of suppliers (79 percent) in Germany are also actively involved in the early stages of development, which is a sharp departure from the past practice in which few suppliers in the German automotive parts markets took part in the early stages of development of a new automobile. The table shows that in both the U.S. and German markets, collaborative engineering and development between a customer and suppliers had became normal by the late 1990s.

TABLE 1 Way of Doing Business (multiple entries)

Style of Business	U.S.	Germany
(a) Our company participates in the development stage of the process of production and discusses with our customers how to develop the product.	65%	79%
(b) Our company participates in the prototype stage and discusses the prototype product with our customers.	34%	41%
(c) Our company receives a detailed pre-description on the product and how to produce it, but we discuss it with our customers for 2–3 months before starting serial production.	23%	28%
(d) We receive a fixed and detailed pre-description on the product, and we produce the product only according to our customer's description.	15%	22%

Source: My own survey conducted in 1999–2000.

The practice of information disclosure between customers and suppliers has spread in both the U.S. and European countries as a new form of collaborative markets develops. This is a sharp departure from the traditional, distant market relations that prevailed through the clear separation of conception (by a customer) and execution (by a supplier) in the period of mass production. According to an extensive international survey on automotive suppliers conducted by Sako, Lamming, and Helper in 1993 and 1994, both the U.S. and European countries had begun to adopt the new form of collaborative markets and share more information.[65] The proportion of suppliers that provide customers with detailed information on their production increased between 1989–90 and 1993–94 in almost all Western countries: from 50 to 80 percent in the U.S., from 51 to 90 percent in the U.K., from 42 to 69 percent in the rest of Europe, and from 81 to 80 percent in Japan in the same period.

On the other hand, long-term contracts began to prevail in order to realize the rationality of collaborative markets. Customers offer suppliers long-term contracts in order to encourage suppliers to develop their specialties for collaborative development and relational specific investments. This practice is also a sharp departure from the neoclassical market. In the 1970s, about 99 percent of American automotive parts markets were based on short-term contracts of less than one year.[66] American suppliers conducted annual competitive bidding based on customer-developed blueprints.

German suppliers were not different from their American counterparts. As table 2 shows, German contracts until the late 1980s were short-term. This directly contradicts what many institutionalists argue. Institutionalists such as Lane (1996), Casper (1997; 2001), Teubner (2001), and Hall and Soskice (2001), who rely on the German model, hold that German contracts were long-term and relational due to particular German institutions, whereas Americans developed neoclassical, short-term contracts in the absence of such institutions. But as table 2 shows, and many other empirical studies confirm, most contracts in the German (automotive) parts markets were for less than one year, like American contracts, until the late 1980s.[67] In particular, about 40 percent of the suppliers in German parts

TABLE 2 Duration of Contract in the Old German Market

Year	1973		1982/83		1988/89	
	absolute	%	absolute	%	absolute	%
Up to 3 months	—	—	—	—	75	40.1
Up to 6 months	—	—	—	—	33	17.6
Up to 1 year	115	88.4	—	—	44	23.5
Less than 1 year	—	—	209	81.0	—	—
Over 1 year	15	11.6	49	19.0	35	18.7
Total	130	100.0	258	100.0	187	100.0

Source: Von Kubota and Witte (1990: 393), table 12.

markets were contracted for less than three months. Like the Americans, the Germans conducted annual bidding based on customer-developed blueprints. One might mention the duration of business relations instead of contracts in order to compare the German and American markets. But Americans had also maintained long-term business relationships, contrary to the conventional wisdom.[68] My own research conducted in 1999 and 2000 reveals that Americans maintain business relations longer (17.3 years on average) than Germans (12.8 years) in the automotive parts markets. To sum up, in the traditional automotive supplier markets, both Germans and Americans conducted short-term and annual bidding based on short-term contracts in the era of mass production, when customers and suppliers were less concerned with collaborative engineering.

Table 3 shows that the recent trend of long-term contracts in both the U.S. and German automotive parts markets departs from the previous trend of traditional contracts, which lasted until the late 1980s. Until the late 1980s, about 40 percent of contracts were for less than three months, whereas at the end of the 1990s, 44 percent of German contracts were for more than five years. German and American contracts in the automotive supplier markets became longer at the end of the 1990s. About 62 percent of American suppliers and 68 percent of German suppliers now make multi-year contracts. In particular, five-year contracts have increased.[69]

TABLE 3 Length of Contract in the U.S. and Germany

Years of Contract	U.S. (N=172)	Germany (N=144)
Less than 1 year	38%	33%
2–3 years	36%	24%
4–6 years	24%	38%
More than 7 years	2%	6%

Source: My own survey conducted in 1999–2000.

Another characteristic of the new markets is reduction of the number of vendors. As customers in the new form of collaborative market have tried to develop close interactions and mutual commitments with a few suppliers, they have reduced the number of suppliers. This is also in sharp contrast to the traditional, neoclassical markets. In the neoclassical market, competition among numerous vendors is believed to be the best way to achieve optimal efficiency in a market. In the period of mass production, customers lowered the level of a supplier's entrance to a market by standardizing and simplifying parts.[70] By contrast, as collaborative markets emphasized close interaction between a customer and a supplier, customers began to consider the costs of managing interaction with suppliers, e.g., costs in keeping records and logistics management. Automakers in both the U.S. and German parts markets have gradually replaced many small direct suppliers with a few large system suppliers who take care of the subassembly of small parts.

For example, in 1988, Ford changed its existing purchasing policy of buying small parts from numerous suppliers. Ford called all the suppliers of parts for a door system to announce that it would not receive individual parts any more, then asked one supplier to supply a complete door system. Ford used about 700 suppliers for the 1994 Tempo and Mercury Topaz. But for their successors, the 1995 Contour and Mercury Mystique, Ford used only 227 suppliers. GM has also reduced the number of suppliers for each platform. GM's Cadillac Motor cut the number of suppliers for its Fleetwood line from 800 in 1986 to 600 in 1987. The average number of competitors producing the same product for a given customer fell from 2 in 1984 to 1.5 in 1989 in the U.S. automotive parts markets. The average number of rivals producing a similar product fell from 2.3 in 1984 to 1.9 in 1989. This is a sharp departure from traditional markets, where up until the late 1970s automakers maintained a pool of suppliers, with six to eight suppliers often supplying a single part, and dozens delivering a simple and general class of parts. First-tier suppliers in the U.S. automotive parts markets have also followed the trend. According to research conducted by the Center for Automotive Research at the Environment Research Institute of Michigan, in 2001 about 77 percent of American first-tier automotive suppliers anticipated reducing the number of their suppliers over the next year.[71]

German automakers have also reduced the number of suppliers since the late 1980s, changing their traditional policy of maintaining many suppliers. Some customers announced single sourcing. For example, the VW purchasing chief said in 1987 that "about 70 percent of the purchased Golf parts are single sourced." Volkswagen reduced its suppliers from 2,500 in 1989 to 1,500 in 1993, and planned to reduce further. Audi reduced the number of suppliers from 1,100 in 1989 to 900 in 1993, while BMW also went from 1,000 in 1989 to 900 in 1993. General Motors in Europe tried to cut the number of suppliers by 20 percent. Ford in Germany reduced the number of its suppliers from 2,100 in the early 1980s to 1,100 in 1990, and 900 in 1993.[72] In the process of restructuring in the early 1990s, almost all automakers were planning to reduce the number of suppliers. Dieter Hundt, president of the Federal Association of German Employers (Bundesvereinigung der Deutschen Arbeitgeberverbände: BDA) said that in many new automobile plants, there would be fewer than 50 system suppliers by the end of the 1990s, replacing the existing 1,000 direct suppliers.[73]

When international competition became tough and the markets for end-products became volatile, agents in the both the U.S. and German markets reflected on their existing pattern of production and market relations. Contrary to the institutionalist contention of path-dependent divergence, the American and German automotive parts markets have more or less undergone a similar pattern of transformation toward the new form of long-term and collaborative markets. Customers in the new markets in the U.S. and Germany involve suppliers in the entire process of value creation with long-term contracts. Contrary to the institutionalists' anticipation, Germans as well as Americans transformed their so-called national trajectory, adopting new flexible production systems and market relations.

On the other hand, the similar pattern of markets in the U.S. and Germany, particularly the apparent revival of contracts in the 1980s and 1990s, did not confirm the rejuvenation of the neoliberal paradigm. The new form of markets in both the U.S. and Germany systematically differs from the neoclassical paradigm. The neoclassical market is not universal but contextualized, particularly by the rationality of the division of labor. The anonymity principle and short-term mobility were rational in the neoclassical market, and were realized in the period of mass production. However, from the perspective of flexible collaboration between market partners, the anonymity principle and short-term mobility become sub-optimal. Furthermore, the new long-term and closely interactive contractual relations, which both the U.S. and Germany adopted in the last decade of the twentieth century, are challenging the neoliberal paradigm of market governance based on the neoclassical market. The new long-term and closely interactive markets cause an abundance of problems for governance due to the incompleteness of long-term contracts and the unclear governance of collaborative works. The unclear governance of long-term and collaborative markets leaves room for divergence in the sense of governance. The next section investigates how different the American and German automotive parts markets are in governing long-term and collaborative markets, before studying what makes the differences.

Differences of Governance

As the interfaces for collaborative work between customers and suppliers become more important, the way of governing the relations attracts more attention. Long-term and collaborative contractual relations have proven too unclear and incomplete for the existing devices to govern. When incomplete governance engenders an abundance of opportunism—in particular, when a powerful customer can easily take advantage of the incompleteness in coordinating contractual relations and distributing risks and benefits—a new way of governance is urgently needed. The ways of governing new problems that emerge with the departure from traditional markets leave room for systemic differences even given the same form of long-term and collaborative markets. Some markets, like the American automotive parts market, suffer from rancorous conflicts and distrust, while other markets, like the German automotive parts market, establish "fair and trustful partnerships" through painful adjustments. One possible explanation of these different outcomes might be that they simply

reflect long-standing cultural differences in norms about appropriate contract behavior and market practices. This book argues against this view.
These divergent patterns of market governance are not predetermined by
prior norms about contracts and contractual relations. On the contrary,
fair norms and partnerships have been newly created, and the divergent
market regimes come from the different ways of deliberating on norms
and mutual adjustments, or what might be called different practices of
norm-creation. Before examining in later chapters the reasons why the
new markets in the U.S. and Germany diverge in governance of relationships, this section investigates whether the American and German market
regimes really differ from each other in governance of relationships and
how different they are even in the same types of long-term and collaborative markets. The next subsection first investigates why fairness and governance matter in markets, particularly in long-term and collaborative
markets; then the kinds of problems that occur in the new form of long-
term and collaborative markets will be outlined; finally, the extent to
which the U.S. and German automotive parts markets differ from each
other in addressing frequent unfair problems will be explored.

New Market and Governance Problems

Before delving into the explanation of differences in market governance
between the U.S. and German automotive parts markets, one must clarify
in what dimension they differ and why fair norms matter. In order to better understand the differences of market regimes, this book differentiates
between *forms of markets* (short-term, distant market vs. long-term, closely
interactive market) and *governance of relationships* (adversarial vs. trustful
relationships) and contradicts the prevalent but false dichotomy between
short-term, distrustful and long-term, trustful relations. The prevalent
belief in the analysis of markets is that the long-term and closely interactive form of market is trustful, while short-term contractual relations are
adversarial or distrustful. But even the traditional forms of markets based
on short-term contracts were not always plagued by distrust. Trustful
relationships existed even in the form of short-term and not so closely
interactive contractual relations. In contrast, the form of long-term and
collaborative (or closely interactive) markets does not automatically generate trustful relationships. On the contrary, agents have more risks to
consider, such as confidentiality of information. The closer the relations
are, the higher the risks of hurting one another. Furthermore, as it shall be
examined later, long-term and closely interactive markets generated many
new problems in the sense of how to govern their interaction and how to
distribute the common benefits and responsibilities. New problems and
unclear governance have left room for divergence of governance.

Fair norms matter in a market, particularly in the new form of collaborative market. Fair norms in the new collaborative market matter not

only because the interfaces between a customer and a supplier become more essential, but more importantly, because existing market governance comes to be more unclear and unstable—neither neoliberal contract law and short-term exit nor existing norms based on Durkheimian non-contractual norms work well for governance of the new problems. Furthermore, bad governance of relations causes not only distrust but also an abundance of pathology in economic performance. This subsection investigates why fair norms matter in the new form of long-term and collaborative market. In particular, it highlights why neoliberal contract law and alternatives do not work for governance of long-term and collaborative markets.

Historically, liberal contract law and liberalism paralleled the development of markets. However, the revival of contracts in the 1980s and 1990s has not generated a rejuvenation of neoliberal governance. On the contrary, a new form of long-term and collaborative market is challenging market liberalism. Liberal contract law defines a contract as a promise in a model of bargaining.[74] In liberal governance, there is no contractual solidarity except enforcement of voluntary promises. This liberal contract law of defining contract as a voluntary promise is based on the modern liberalism of "priority of free will" and "freedom of contract" in social thought. Modern liberalism holds that "all the sources of rights and duties of the parties to a contract come from exclusively voluntary promise or free will of the promisor to bind oneself."[75] The supremacy of the individual agent's autonomous will means that if it is vitiated by such elements as mistake, misapprehension, or duress, a contract should not be enforceable.

Not all promises are enforceable. Liberal contract law holds that the "perfect contract" is strictly enforceable. The perfect contract is a contract made in the situation of neoclassical economic conception, the "perfect competition" market. Liberal contract law maintains that "[c]ontract formed under perfectly competitive conditions should be strictly enforceable."[76] The reason for the strict enforceability of the perfect contract is first that the promise of the perfect contract is strictly based on the individual's "free will" independent of social constraints such as customs and governmental involvement. The freedom of contract in liberalism means not only the restricted role of the state but also freedom from morality and external supervision. Neoliberal contract law assumes the discrete transaction is, like the contract in the spot market, based on the anonymity principle.[77] In the sense that liberal contract law assumes freedom from morality and customs, liberal contract law is concerned with strictly formal justice, not substantive morality; thus, so long as one has a well-functioning market, its outcomes will necessarily be just. Except for some cases, such as agreements to restrain the freedom of market competition, almost all contracts are free of moral and ethical norms.[78] Another reason for strict enforceability of perfect contract is that market liberals believe that, based on neoclassical economics, voluntary agreement under perfect competition leads to an optimal result. Based on Benthamite utilitarianism, market liberalism assumes that every person knows his own interest best; free choice of every individual leads to the Pareto optimal condition. Over-regulation by external forces is discouraged because it can generate sub-optimality in the market.[79]

This liberal contract law faces an abundance of problems in the new form of long-term and collaborative market.[80] Liberal contract law based on the promise model and the priority of individual free will assumes that a voluntary promise or contract should be complete in its presentation of the future situation. As contracts become longer, however, gaps between presentation at the time of contracting and real conditions at the time of execution often become too large for liberal law to fill, because long-term contracts are open-ended in items such as price and volume. A supplier compares past contracts with recent long-term ones: "In the past, agreements were very clear and customers kept the contracts. But recently agreements are not so clear and customers change their promise easily. In the past, say 1980s, contracts kept clear contents."[81] It is hard to figure out the changes in price over period of five years. Clearly specified prices in the short-term contracts of the traditional markets were easy to observe. An empirical survey shows that about 98.8 percent of traditional, short-term contracts were not transgressed.[82] Even though there was power asymmetry between a customer and a supplier in traditional markets, there were few cases in which a powerful customer changed price arbitrarily. In traditional markets, the relationships tended to be stable even though they were distant.[83] By contrast, in the recent long-term contracts there are many complaints about the insecurity of price and volume. In long-term contracts, it is hard to completely calculate total costs of a project stretching over five years. Costs and prices fluctuate due to technological and design changes over several years. Furthermore, close collaboration between a customer and a supplier makes it more difficult to predict the costs and prices accurately because costs, prices, and volume depend in many cases on the consequences of collaborative engineering between the customer and a supplier.[84] Long-term and collaborative contracts do not generate trustful relationships automatically. On the contrary, they cause more problems for governance due to their unclear and incomplete terms.

These incomplete and unclear contracts challenge liberal justice. Liberal contract law based on the priority of "free will" can hardly enforce the conditions that voluntary promises did not specify. The problems of long-term contracts have been continuously repressed in liberal contract law, or sometimes dealt with by *ad hoc* deviations rather than by clear principles. In liberal contract law, as Beatson and Friedmann say, "there is no room for a specific category of long-term contracts to which specific rules will apply" because liberal contract law is based on the neoclassical market in which short-term, discrete, and arms-length contractual relations prevail.[85]

An easy alternative to liberal contract law is an activist state. This view believes that a regulatory state can fill the gaps of contracts between presentation at contracting and conditions at execution.[86] The activist state view emphasizes the institutional arrangements such as regulation or active judicial discretion in contract law. In particular, Casper (1997, 2001) and Teubner (2001) argue that German markets developed long-term and cooperative contracts due to regulatory contract law and courts, while American contracts represent neoclassical, short-term, and arms-length relations because of liberal contract law and court.[87] According to Casper, the German contract laws with "Good Faith" clauses enable courts to wield active discretion in the disputes of long-term contracts. The regulatory courts in Germany deter firms from choosing opportunistic behaviors because courts punish price competition and opportunistic behaviors.

However, German regulatory courts do not punish price competition in markets, where companies are encouraged to compete over price even in Germany. It was not until the 1990s that long-term and collaborative markets prevailed in German markets. So it is hard to say that German firms developed long-term and relational contracts because of courts' regulatory policies. On the other hand, long-term and relational contracts were also widespread in the U.S. in the late 1980s and early 1990s, earlier than in Germany. The Good Faith clause that has been prevalent in Continental law has also been adopted in the U.S. Under the prevailing view of U.S. jurisdictions, American courts can also intervene in the terms of contracts in cases of grossly excessive price change and in cases in which the terms are extremely unfair in their content.[88] However, it is not because of the Good Faith clause or regulatory policy that American firms were able to develop long-term and relational contracts in the 1990s. As we have seen in the former subsections, firms in the U.S. and Germany realigned their market relations by reflecting upon the drawbacks of their existing division of labor under tough competition of international markets.

In addition, the incompleteness and unclearness of long-term and collaborative contractual relations are hard for courts to rule. It is not clear how to define illegality in the conflicts of long-term and collaborative markets. For example, although industry frameworks developed by associations recommend that prices not be changed, it is still hard for a court to judge whether the revision of prices is illegal, a tolerable strategy in a market, or a fair deal. In some cases, private parties in a contract agree to a tradeoff between price revision and future business, or between a price cut and informal service. In these cases, agents do not believe the revision of prices unfair. Another ambiguous case is property right of information: despite the stipulations of court law, it is in many cases unclear to a third party what kinds of sharing information in the process of collaborative works are illegal. In fact, few suppliers bring their "opportunistic" customers to courts at all, not only because they are not sure whether the "opportunistic" behaviors are illegal or tolerable, but also because they are concerned about their own reputation and future business in the market. Agents in both the American and German markets rarely refer to courts to solve problems arising from customers' unfairness.

Social norms gain importance for self-governance within a civil society in a situation in which agents are reluctant to go back to the old solution of vertical integration, and in which, due to the incompleteness and unclearness of long-term and collaborative contracts, the state only barely regulates opportunism. The problem is, however, that social norms do not automatically emerge from dense networks of associations, nor are they determined by cultural heritages or non-contractual customs. Furthermore, as a new form of market relations comes into being, old norms begin not to work for new relations. In the early 1990s, when the American and German automotive parts markets were undergoing transformation toward the new form of collaborative markets, agents in both the U.S. and Germany complained of unclear norms for market governance. A chief of a German supplier company said that in the turbulent period of the early 1990s, "consensus of business norms in this market was, to a high degree, endangered."[89] People in both the American and German markets repeatedly argued that they needed new ethical standards for governance of new relations.

For instance, one of the traditional norms in the German automotive parts markets is *Leben und leben lassen* (Live and let live); people should allow other people to live in their own way, the way they want to live according to their own freedom. In other words, people should not interfere in the affairs of others. This norm is based on neoclassical market relations. Agents in the neoclassical market calculate and take care of their own costs of inputs and margins. Hiding information on real costs and their true bargaining position, they compromise on a price assuming that the price is satisfactory to a trading partner; otherwise, the trading partner will exit the deal. The traditional norm *Leben und leben lassen* worked for the neoclassical market, in which one takes care of only one's own business for survival (*Einzelkämpferdasein*). But it no longer worked in the new collaborative market, where automakers and suppliers collaborate by sharing proprietary information.[90] Indeed, the extent and manner of a customer and a supplier's exchange of information proved highly problematic in a collaborative market, creating totally new problems for governance of market relations. The "fair" norms in the German automotive parts market are not the legacy of cultural heritage but consequences of practices of norm-creation.

Similarly, Americans in the automotive parts market needed to create new norms once existing norms ceased to work. As many empirical studies conducted by Durkheimian sociologists have shown, non-contractual norms prevailed even in the U.S., which has been regarded as representative of the neoliberal market. This contradicts the institutionalist contention that American contracts are complete and formal contracts. Rather, many Americans also developed "handshake agreements" and informal norms in traditional, short-term markets, as was the case in the German traditional markets.[91] But as the new long-term and collaborative market develops, the existing norms, such as "keeping agreements," do not work because agreements themselves are incomplete and sometimes unclear. In addition, customers' commitments to a specific supplier, or customers' appreciation of a current relationship with a supplier for a collaborative market, conflicted with traditional American conceptions of fairness that dictated that "everyone should have an equal opportunity to compete for business at each point in time." Formal fairness based on equal chance was emphasized, particularly when there was public outcry against favoritism, such as when in 1960 the president of Chrysler placed large orders with a company in which Chrysler had a significant interest.[92] But the existing formal fairness not only was insufficient for distribution of risks and benefits in a collaborative market, but also needed some revision to support for the development of long-term and cooperative relations.

Furthermore, in the early period of transformation toward collaborative markets, American suppliers had expectations of substantive fairness regarding distribution of risks and benefits. This expectation of substantive fairness caused many problems with existing conceptions of formal fairness and revealed many unclear points in the definition of fairness. For example, the division of benefits and risks for a collaborative work was a problem totally at odds with the formal norms such as "freedom for survival alone" and "keeping agreements." It was traditionally permissible and normally expected by both suppliers and automakers in the U.S. (and Germany) that suppliers would bid at a very low price to get business and then raise the price by a moderate amount. However, in the collaborative markets of the 1990s, these norms did not work. Customers in a collaborative market expect that prices will fall as time goes on because collaborative efforts between a customer and a supplier increase productivity and benefits in the supplier company.[93] If the old norms are no longer at work, the question of how to divide benefits and how to share responsibility for collaborative work becomes problematic because powerful customers can easily take advantage of unclear norms and incomplete contracts by using their market power.

Another reason why fairness matters in collaborative markets is that fair norms and trustful relations are closely related to economic performance. In other words, unfairness generates many pathologies in economic performance by causing distrust and deterring voluntary cooperation even in closely interactive markets. As many empirical studies reveal, the question of how to organize and govern the interfaces between customers and suppliers influences economic performance in a collaborative market.[94] The form of collaborative work itself does not automatically improve economic performance. Many empirical studies, whether in the automobile industry or in non-auto sectors, conclude that fair partnership facilitates faster communication and hence improves adaptability and flexibility in production; suppliers' willingness to cooperate is more important for successful product development than an individual supplier's technical competence alone.[95] In particular, the empirical study conducted by Liker and Wu is very instructive in describing how the same supplier performs differently depending on relationships with customers. After investigating the performance of 91 U.S. suppliers who deliver similar products to both American and Japanese customers on U.S. soil, Liker and Wu conclude that "U.S. suppliers perform at much higher levels when they are supplying Japanese automakers than when working with U.S. automakers."[96] The same U.S. suppliers are much leaner and more flexible in almost all aspects of production when they work with Japanese customers on U.S. soil than when they work with U.S. customers.

The different performance by the same supplier is mainly attributable to its varying relationships with customers. Both German and American automotive suppliers confirm in my personal interviews that "fair governance" of contractual relations creates trustful relationships between a customer and a supplier, which in turn generates more voluntary cooperation for common benefits. Karl Werner Armbruster, chief of purchasing of BMW, argues that "[how to build trustful cooperation] is a matter of fairness, fair sharing of benefits, and working together."[97] Many suppliers in my personal interviews report that they do not hide new ideas for improving the product and production from a "fair" customer who appreciates "fairly" the supplier's honest cooperation.[98] Without "fair" sharing of the benefits, suppliers in both the U.S. and German markets are unwilling to announce genuine benefits resulting from application engineering, or hesitate to share their know-how for application engineering honestly. An American supplier says, "We give some concessions to GM to get permission for engineering and design change. But, in this case, we do not tell more than the concession." If suppliers in the U.S. and Germany have an innovative idea for technology or the production process, they go first to a "fair" customer to get business rather than an "unfair" customer who they believe might transfer the information to their competitors to get a better price.[99] Many suppliers say that they play numbers when customers force them to open cost structure without "fair" sharing benefits.[100] Few agents disagree that "fair" governance is one of main factors in the establishment of trustful cooperation. In the U.S., according to the research conducted by the Office for the Study of Automotive Transportation (OSAT) and A.T. Kearney in 1995 and 1996, almost all respondents report that they need "more formalized rules or ethical standards to govern these new and developing relationships."[101] Most Germans in the new collaborative markets also agreed that the great obstacle to innovation was customers' unfair behaviors.[102]

As collaborative markets develop, fairness calls for more attention. Long-term and collaborative markets do not automatically generate trustful cooperation and stable market relations. On the contrary, they cause an abundance of governance problems. Under unclear and unstable governance, unfairness by the powerful party causes distrust, thus engendering pathologies in economic performance. The problem is that neither liberal justice nor traditional social norms work well for governance of contracts in long-term and collaborative markets. Since current norms have no hold over the new practices of collaborative markets, new fair norms should be constituted. These new norms emerge from ongoing interpretations of everyday practices by distinguishing "fair" from "opportunistic" behavior. Before investigating how agents in both the U.S. and German markets have constituted fair norms and stabilized their market relations, the next subsection highlights the kinds of unfair problems that prevail in the U.S. and German markets.

Frequent Cases of So-Called Unfair Behavior

Leading up to the investigation of how the American and German market regimes differ with regard to governance of relationships, this subsection investigates frequent "unfair" cases in the new long-term and collaborative markets of both the U.S. and Germany. Let it be noted that while this book calls opportunistic behavior "unfairness," some agents in the markets might not agree with the definition; they would term this behavior not "unfair" but "unethical" or "inhumane." But although not all agents in the U.S. and German automotive parts markets agree with this definition of fairness, almost all of them agree that this so-called opportunistic behavior is distasteful. This book defines "unfairness" in a broad sense that includes concepts ranging from illegality to distasteful and opportunistic behavior. The so-called unfair cases are easy to find in my personal interviews with 45 American suppliers and 56 German suppliers, and e-mail interviews with about 80 agents in both the U.S. and German markets. In addition, this book refers to documents published by German associations such as the VDA (Automobile Association), the BDI (Federal Industry Association), and the ArGeZ (Supplier Confederation), concerning unfair cases in the process of social adjustments.[103]

One of the most frequent main causes of distrust is a customer's transfer of a supplier's information to competitors. The information that a customer might share with a supplier's competitors ranges from cost structure and new ideas on product and production to official blueprints of a new product. In the neoclassical market under mass production, in which a customer developed a blueprint and a supplier followed it, a supplier and a customer rarely experienced the "unfair" transfer of a supplier's information because they exchanged little information. Distasteful behavior among suppliers is not limited to cases in which customers disregard suppliers' commitments in development of a new product. Still more distasteful is customers' abuse of suppliers' information, which is intended to be used for collaborative engineering. After a supplier and a customer make a new print and prototype, the customer frequently threatens to move the business if the supplier does not reduce the price. Sometimes a customer hands over the blueprint and prototype directly to the supplier's competitors, asking whether they can make the product at a lower price. Suppliers cannot make a confidential contract on all information, although suppliers expect confidentiality of their information based on the practices of traditional business. Some suppliers think that a customer might also have a right to the blueprint and prototype because the customer also worked on it. Many suppliers do not have clear criteria for fairness or legality.

Another cause for distrust is an asymmetrical exchange of information between a customer and a supplier. Customers frequently talk about transparency and partnership in exchange of information. But in many cases, suppliers do not believe that they exchange information with customers in a "fair" way. Customers provide suppliers with little information, yet they request an abundance of detailed information from suppliers. The problem is not just the asymmetrical exchange of information but the opportunistic usage of the supplier's information. Even to unfair customers who abuse suppliers' information, suppliers have to send a detailed information sheet by fax or e-mail to maintain business. To counter this opportunism, suppliers in many cases play with numbers when unfair customers request detailed cost information. When the unfair customer's team visits suppliers under the pretext of helping the supplier improve product and production, the supplier runs production very slowly while the customer is present; the normal speed of production is resumed after the customer's team has gone, in anticipation of the customer's future request for price reduction or improvement of productivity. Many suppliers describe the situation as "a game of hide-and-seek."[104] Such unfair behavior causes much dysfunction in the collaborative market.

Another frequent case that violates the sense of "fairness" is when customers disregard their agreement in a unilateral way. Breaches of agreements range from breaking small promises to redefining contracts in an arbitrary way. This is a sharp departure from past practices in neoclassical short-term contractual relations, in which contracts specified conditions so clearly that few agents in either the German or American markets revised and broke agreements unilaterally. As late as the 1960s, there were few cases in which customers revised contracts in an arbitrary way.[105] Only in a few exceptional cases did customers and suppliers change prices in order to adjust to fluctuations of volume and changes of employment. However, as contracts become open-ended, customers and suppliers began to revise contents frequently. Most stressful is revision of price and volume in an arbitrary way. Powerful agents sometimes redefine prices and volume unilaterally. As one supplier says, "If a competitor offers a lower price, a customer reduces the volume of an order to almost zero."[106]

In order to govern an open-ended volume, a customer and a supplier use an index of sales of the end-product (a car). In another case, they use an index of correlation between quantity and price of a delivered product. But customers frequently disregard such indices. Very few suppliers in the early 1990s believed that the terms of a contract would continue without any change.

However, revision of a contract is not in itself unfair. For example, when a customer provides a supplier with future business in exchange for a price reduction, the revision does not indicate unfairness. Nor do suppliers believe it unfair when a customer and a supplier revise an existing price to reflect the results of collaborative application engineering.[107] Conversely, if collaborative application engineering changes the original costs, the formal rule of "keeping agreement" (e.g., price) is regarded as unfair because the existing price does not reflect the contract partners' efforts. The elements of formal fairness, such as "keeping contract," are closely related to those of substantive fairness, such as "sharing benefits."

Another prevalent type of unfairness is asymmetric distribution of benefits. Many suppliers believe it unfair that price revisions move only downward, coming from customers in almost all cases. It is very difficult for suppliers to reopen negotiations to increase a component price. If suppliers try to reopen negotiations because of the growth of engineering and material costs, customers can move the business and tooling to another supplier. The most frequent scenario is that customers demand frequent price reduction, disregarding the contracts already signed. For example, American and German customers frequently use a fixed rate of price reduction in long-term contracts—e.g., a 3 percent discount for the first year, 5 percent for the second, 4 percent for the third and the fourth, and 3 percent for the fifth; or 6 percent, 2 percent, 2 percent for three-year contracts. But unfair customers can disregard the fixed rate of price reduction and demand greater discounts in the middle of contracts.

There are some extreme cases in which customers disregard contracts in an arbitrary way. Some customers request that suppliers make new investments in a new project for a long-term contract; then, after suppliers make huge investments following customers' promise of long-term business, customers sometimes reopen the contracts in order to cut the price. This unfairness can occur not only between an automaker and a supplier but also between a high- and a sub-tier supplier.[108] For example, when I visited a second-tier supplier, the director of the company showed me a new plant, still uncommisioned, beside an old one. The new plant had been built according to a first-tier customer's new order. The supplier and the first-tier customer signed a long-term contract for a new bumper that would be used for a new truck coming in 2001. But the customer moved the business to someone else after requesting a huge (15 percent) price cut.

One of the most stressful scenarios for suppliers is when customers press prices down in an "dictatorial" way and to an "unreasonable" extent. Customers sometimes dictate their own target price regardless of the existing relationships and suppliers' conditions. Suppliers do not believe the fairest solution to be simply an even division of benefits. It is hard to calculate an even division of common benefits because reference points for division can be different. In addition, many suppliers accept the relative power of companies in a market, believing that power relations should be reflected in distribution of benefits; thus, some suppliers believe fair a distribution of 30:70 in which a powerful customer takes 70 percent.[109] What suppliers complain of is the way prices and "unreasonable" price cuts are pressed. In some cases, a customer dictates a target price, having defined it unilaterally after analyzing detailed elements of costs provided by suppliers, by combining the cheapest elements from all bidders. Sometimes suppliers have to bid against companies that do not have the competence to perform a job, yet are responsible for setting the target price. Sometimes the target price is lower than raw material and labor costs. Suppliers complain that their customers do not share benefits resulting from collaborative works even after the customers transfer a large share of responsibility to, and request many services from, suppliers. Suppliers believe it unfair that customers' margins go up while they lower suppliers' margins continuously, although customers often pay lip service to "partnership."

Recently, suppliers have been under stress from the issue of liability and warranty. The problem is not simply that customers increase the length of warranty and liability by taking advantage of competition among suppliers, but also that it is unclear how to determine who is responsible for a defect in the process of collaborative interactions. In traditional markets, a supplier was responsible for only the defect that the supplier caused after matching a customer's blueprint with the supplier's product. But nowadays it is unclear what is whose job and who is responsible for a defect because the final design is a result of collaborative work between a customer and many suppliers. In the recent form of collaborative market, a customer does not specify in detail what a final product looks like. Although a supplier designs a component with a customer and receives approval from the customer, the customer can complain about the product—e.g., the customer can claim that "this is not what we want." Sometimes a supplier is charged for the disruptions in an entire system that its defective part might cause. The responsibility for a defect goes back down through supply chains. Some customers push their own responsibility on suppliers. Sometimes a dealer of cars charges an automaker for a defect; the automaker passes the responsibility for a defect to a first-tier supplier; the first-tier supplier then passes it to a sub-tier supplier, and so on. Sometimes a sub-tier supplier has to bear responsibility for a defect that the supplier cannot control.

In sum, it is clear that the practice of signing long-term contracts did not automatically engender trustful relationships. On the contrary, long-term contracts caused new problems that neither liberal justice nor traditional social norms could govern. Agents in the new, long-term, and collaborative markets needed new ethical standards to stabilize their relationships for cooperation. But in the process of establishing new norms and governing systems, the U.S. and German markets diverged in their conceptions of fairness and ways of governance. Americans in the market developed an extremely formal conception of fairness and failed to develop trustful partnerships, while Germans in the market developed a substantive conception of fairness and have successfully improved their trustful relationships. Before the causes of differences between market regimes are investigated, the next section examines whether the American and German market regimes are actually different, and how different they are.

Differences between the American and German Markets

As market governance becomes unclear, opportunistic behavior frequently occurs, causing distrust between a customer and a supplier. It is not surprising that agents in both the U.S. and German markets have sought new ethical standards to provide stability in the governance of new market relations. However, the U.S. and German automotive parts markets showed systematic differences in stabilizing relationships, although they both changed into long-term, collaborative markets in the 1990s. American automotive parts markets suffered rancorous conflicts, and the so-called unfair behavior did not abate during the 1990s. By contrast, German agents improved their relationships; the unfair cases in the German automotive parts markets tapered off through the 1990s. The conception of fairness in the American automotive supplier markets is oriented to an extreme formalism. By contrast, in German markets, expectations of "fair" sharing of substantive benefits prevail. The belief that fair and trustful cooperation works better than a vicious cycle of confrontation and bad performance dominates the German automotive parts market. This section investigates how different the U.S. and German automotive parts markets are in the establishment of stable relationships.

In order to estimate the levels of trust and fairness in the U.S. and German automotive parts markets, I conducted mail surveys in both countries between 1999 and 2000. Because the same questionnaires, proofread by native Americans and Germans, were sent to all suppliers in the well-known directories in each country, and all responses are based on voluntary participation, there is little possibility for bias caused by favorable selection in comparison between two countries. There might be bias between respondents and non-participants in the survey. However, the non-response bias is not significantly large, considering that the test for non-response bias shows no significance at any variable, based on comparison between the responses of the first comprehensive survey and the responses of the second, follow-up survey—at the significance level of 0.1.[110] Furthermore, many other empirical studies in each country confirm my findings. My intensive and extensive personal and e-mail interviews with 110 American suppliers and 74 German suppliers also confirm the result of the mail survey: that Americans in the market suffer from distrust and unfairness while Germans have substantively improved their relationships.

In order to estimate the levels of fairness and trust in the U.S. and German automotive parts markets, participants in the survey were asked to evaluate each statement with five categories on a Likkert scale: strongly agree = 2; agree = 1; neither agree nor disagree = 0; disagree = -1; strongly disagree = -2. This method could create a problem in estimating the degree of agreement or disagreement because the distance between categories, e.g., the distance between "strongly agree" and "agree," and between "agree" and "neither," does not mean the same degree of agreement (scale 1). To ascertain the clear difference between the two market regimes, I also tested for the differences by collapsing five categories into three categories (yes, neither, no). But the results of this dyadic form of test were the same as those of the Likkert scales.

Table 4, "Comparison of Trust and Fairness in the U.S. and Germany," shows the results of my mail survey. I tested three indices of trust and five indices of fairness. In order to measure the levels of trust in the U.S. and German markets, I first tested the general estimation of trust. In the survey, participants evaluated the sentence "We believe that we trust our customers and they trust us" (item 1 in table 4). This question gauges the mutual trust between a supplier and a customer. Participants in both the American and German markets answered positively, perhaps because they might not want to answer negatively about their relationships. But there is a significant difference in the trust level between the American and German markets. A dominant majority of Germans (63.1 percent) believed there is mutual trust in their relations with customers. But a much smaller portion of Americans (32.9 percent) agreed that they have trustful relationships with customers. The difference of means between the U.S. and Germany is significant at the level of p=.001.

To measure the level of trust more accurately, I developed two more operational indices of trust. I asked two questions about detailed behavior showing the level of trust. In a collaborative market, a supplier and a customer are required to share much information. In many cases, however, they seem to share their information while actually hiding it for fear that a trading partner might take advantage of their information. In the survey, participants evaluated the sentence "Given the chance, our customers might try to take unfair advantage of our business" (item 2, table 4). A majority of Americans agreed or strongly agreed that their customers might take unfair advantage of their business, while a majority of Germans disagreed or strongly disagreed with this statement. I calculated one sample test, that is, I tested each country independently on whether it is trustful or not. The statistical results show that American suppliers

TABLE 4 Comparison of Trust and Fairness in the U.S. and Germany

Question	Distribution of Responses					Mean	Significance of mean (difference from 0)	Significance of difference of means in U.S. and Germany
	Strongly agree (2)%	Agree (1)%	Neither (0)%	Disagree (-1)%	Strongly disagree (-2)%			
1. *General Evaluation of Trust:* "We believe that we trust our customers and they trust us."								
United States	6.9	26.0	48.6	16.2	2.3	.19	p=.005	p<.001
Germany	12.9	50.3	32.0	3.4	1.4	.70	p<.001	
2. *Possibility for Customer Abuse:* "Given the chance, our customers might try to take unfair advantage of our business"								
United States	13.9	46.8	18.5	15.6	5.2	.49	p<.001	p<.001
Germany	3.4	12.2	33.3	38.1	12.9	-.45	p<.001	
3. *Openness and Transparency:* "We believe that the exchange of information between our firm and customers is open and transparent"								
United States	5.2	17.3	30.6	42.8	4.0	-.23	p=.002	p<.001
Germany	10.2	49.0	29.9	9.5	1.4	.57	p<.001	
4. *Violation of Confidentiality:* "If we give information on our product and production to our customers in collaborative work, our customers often transfer it to our competitors in order to increase competition and reduce price."								
United States	9.8	38.2	20.8	24.3	6.9	.20	p=.023	p<.001
Germany	4.1	14.3	32.7	36.1	12.9	-.39	p<.001	
5. *Abuse of Information:* "Our Customers often use the information we give to check up on us rather than to solve problems."								
United States	9.2	43.9	19.7	24.9	2.3	.33	p<.001	p<.001
Germany	4.1	17.0	34.7	36.7	7.5	-.27	p<.001	

Item							Mean	p	p
6. *Disregarding Contracts:* "Our customers disregard the contract and move to another supplier when a favorable alternative in market emerges."									$p<.001$
United States	11.1	18.7	29.2	33.3	7.6	-.08	p=.379	
Germany	3.4	13.6	21.8	48.3	12.9	-.54	p<.001	
7a. *Supplier to Customer Information Exchange:* "We believe that our firm gives our customers new ideas for improvement of quality and reduction of costs."									
United States	32.9	54.9	10.4	1.7	0.0	1.19	p<.001	
Germany	30.6	56.5	12.2	0.7	0.0	1.17	p<.001	
7b. *Customer to Supplier Information Exchange:* "We believe that our customers give our firm new ideas for improvement of quality and reduction of costs."									
United States	6.9	19.7	40.5	28.3	4.6	-.04	p=.585	
Germany	2.7	38.1	41.5	15.6	2.0	.24	p<.001	
7c. *Asymmetry of Information Exchange:* (mean of 7a—mean of 7b)									$p<.001$
United States						1.23		
Germany						.93		
8. *Price Pressure:* "Our customers press the price to the degree of 'zero-profit' or 'minus-profit' without considering the cost conditions of suppliers or without considering the conditions of our production."									$p<.001$
United States	21.4	35.3	25.4	14.5	3.5	.57	p<.001	
Germany	11.6	23.1	35.4	25.9	4.1	.12	P=.161	
9. *General Appreciation of Fairness:* "We believe that our relations with customers are fair."									$p<.001$
United States	7.6	44.2	34.9	10.5	2.9	.43	p<.001	
Germany	13.7	52.7	29.5	4.1	0.0	.76	p<.001	

Source: My own survey in 1999–2000.

worry considerably that their customers might abuse their information and know-how if a chance to do so arises (p < .001 at one sample test for the possibility of abuse in the test value = 0). By contrast, German suppliers are less likely to believe that their customers might take unfair advantage of their information and know-how (p = 0.000 at one sample test for the possibility of abuse in the test value = 0). Surely, the difference between countries in the level of trust is significant at the p < .001 level. American suppliers worry that their customers might abuse their information and know-how if given the chance, whereas German suppliers are less likely to believe this might happen.

Another question inquired about the openness and transparency of the information exchange. Participants evaluated the sentence "We believe that the exchange of information between our firm and customers is open and transparent" (item 3, table 4). As the distribution of responses shows, a small portion of Americans (22.5 percent) agreed that their relationships are open and transparent, whereas a majority of Germans (59.2 percent) agreed that their information exchange is open and transparent. The test of significance of mean in each country confirms statistically that American suppliers believe that the exchange of information between their firms and customers is neither open nor transparent (p = 0.002 at one sample test of test value = 0); by contrast, German suppliers believe the exchange of information between their firms and customers is open and transparent (p < .000 at the test value = 0). The countries differ at the p < .001 significance level. This test shows clearly that American suppliers worry about exchanging information with their customers, whereas Germans show high levels of trust in the exchange of information with their customers.

As the three above indices of trust reveal, distrustful relationships are prevalent in the American automotive parts market, while trustful relationships dominate the German market. Each index of trust shows significant difference between the American and German markets. German suppliers in the automotive parts markets are less likely to worry about the risk of customers' opportunistic behaviors than Americans are. German suppliers are more open and transparent in the exchange of information with their customers than Americans are. The American automotive parts markets have transformed toward a form of collaborative market in which agents are required to provide one another with more information than in traditional markets. But American agents in the automotive parts market suffer pathologies resulting from distrust.

The main reason for suppliers' distrust in the new form of collaborative market is customers' unfair behavior. As we saw above, long-term and collaborative contractual relations are so incomplete and unclear in governance that powerful customers can easily take advantage of the incompleteness and unclearness of the contractual relations. Although almost all agents in both the U.S. and German markets requested new standards of ethics, criteria for "fairness" and the ways of governance often diverge.

After conducting an intensive study in the automotive parts markets, OSAT and A.T. Kearney emphasized the importance of fair norms:

> The ethical concerns are a core area of relationships and go right to the heart of the industry's attempts to establish more effective "partner-like" relationships. Until some agreement or shared beliefs about general codes of behavior (ethical rules) are established, it is difficult to imagine that the industry will make much progress in changing these relationships.[111]

As many suppliers hold in my interviews, and as other studies in the automotive supplier markets confirm, shared norms of fairness are a key factor in the development of trustful relations.

In order to assess different regimes of long-term and collaborative markets, I assessed five indices of fairness in a formal as well as a substantive sense. I asked first about the issue of confidentiality. Powerful customers often transfer the information that suppliers provide for collaborative works to the suppliers' competitors in order to increase competition. First, the participants in the U.S. and Germany evaluated the sentence "If we give information on our product and production to our customers in collaborative work, our customers often transfer it to our competitors in order to increase competition and reduce the price" (item 4, table 4). While 48 percent of the American suppliers feel that they face this risk, only 28 percent of Germans do. The test of "significance of mean" in each country shows that German suppliers are less likely to suffer from a customer's violation of confidentiality ($p < 0.001$ at the test value $= 0$); by contrast, the American suppliers are more likely to suffer from customers' opportunistic behavior in the confidentiality issue ($p = 0.023$ at test value $= 0$). The difference between the two market regimes is significant at the $p < .001$ level. An American supplier describes the process in which customers normally take the information.

> [In the bidding process], we also enclose various design enhancements that will improve the product and lessen the cost. Typically these ideas are transferred to the competitors to quote in the secondary rounds of bidding against us. Obviously, after this occurred repeatedly, we now include only vague, nonspecific ideas during quoting but are frequently pressured to clarify.[112]

The fact that German suppliers have more trust and more transparency in information exchange than Americans is closely related to the fact that German customers are less likely to violate their suppliers' confidentiality than their American counterparts; the regression analysis between trust and the violation of confidentiality shows a significant correlation ($p < .001$ in both the U.S. and Germany).

Suppliers also evaluated the sentence "Our customers often use the information we give to check up on us rather than to solve problems" (item 5, table 4). A majority of Americans (53.1 percent) agreed that customers abused suppliers' information, while a much smaller portion of Germans (21.1 percent) agreed with the statement (the difference between the countries is significant at the p < .001 level). In an e-mail interview, one American supplier describes clearly prevalent unfair cases, saying that "customers use the information provided as a stick to beat us with, so we are careful not to give the customers a very large stick."[113] By contrast, few Germans interviewed made similar comments. The results of this survey suggest that German markets tend to be fair while American counterparts suffer from unfairness.

Another index for fairness is the frequency of switching contracts. This might not be unfair at all in the neoclassical market; on the contrary, easy recontracting itself is an ideal feature of the neoclassical market. But it can be a problem in long-term and collaborative markets, where it is unfair for a customer to revise a given contract unilaterally. In particular, after a customer has requested that a supplier invest heavily in development and production for collaborative work by offering long-term contracts, it would be unfair for the customer to give the business to another supplier who offered a lower price, or to dictate a price cut by threatening to move the business or reduce expected volume unilaterally.

In the mail survey, suppliers evaluated the sentence "Our customers disregard the contract and move to another supplier when a favorable alternative in the market emerges" (item 6, table 4). Again, the two regimes of the American and German long-term and collaborative markets are significantly different (p < .001). American suppliers are more likely than their German counterparts to believe that their customers disregard given contracts in order to search for a lower price. In the first half of the 1990s, particularly in 1993 when purchasing executive Lopez moved from GM to Volkswagen, many German customers also tore down current contracts while dictating huge price cuts unilaterally. But in the current German automotive parts market, such unfair cases of disregarding contracts have tapered off following painful social adjustments.

For the indices of fairness, three main indices have been tested so far: the violation of confidentiality, the abuse of information to control, and disregarding contracts. In these indices of fairness, American markets show significantly higher levels of unfairness while their German counterparts reveal higher levels of fairness, and the differences between the two market regimes are significant (all p-value < .001). It is noteworthy that the three main indices are related to formal definitions of fairness such as "keeping confidentiality" and "keeping contracts." Formal criteria are in many cases good yardsticks to judge whether a behavior is a violation of fairness or not, but they may not suffice to generate a sense of fairness that would enable two parties to cooperate. For example, a customer may keep the original contract, yet may arouse a sense of unfairness on the part of supplier companies if the customer does not consider that the cost of materials has skyrocketed. On the other hand, a customer may revise a fixed rate of price reduction, but the supplier can feel that this is a fair tradeoff between an immediate price discount and future business. Furthermore, substantive fairness between a customer and a supplier often generates trustful cooperation because it enables the agents in collaborative markets to identify common benefits with their self-interests.

I have tested two issues to attain an index of substantive (rather than simply formal) fairness. One is asymmetry in exchange of information; the other is price pressure. For the asymmetry of information exchange, I assume that as the asymmetry of information exchange between a customer and a supplier decreases, it more closely approaches fairness. To ascertain the degree of asymmetry of information, participants in this survey were requested to evaluate two sentences (items 7a and 7b, table 4) using the Likkert scale: (a) "We believe that our firm gives our customers new ideas for improvement of quality and reduction of costs" (supplier to customer information transfer—s-c info); and (b) "We believe that our customers give our firm new ideas for improvement of quality and reduction of costs" (customer to supplier information—c-s info).[114] For the index of fairness, I first measured the difference between s-c info and c-s info in each country; then I tested the difference between the two countries to ascertain the extent of the asymmetry of information exchange. These measures indicate that the asymmetry of information exchange between a supplier and a customer in Germany is significantly smaller than that in the U.S. market ($p < .001$). In the German automotive parts market, customers and suppliers are more likely to exchange information in a fair way than their American counterparts are. A regression analysis between trust and "asymmetry of information exchange" shows the significance of the correlation in both countries: as the asymmetry of information exchange between a customer and supplier becomes larger, the level of trust falls in both countries ($p = 0.005$ in Germany and $p = 0.005$ in the U.S.).

Another index for substantive fairness concerns the degree of price pressure, which indicates how a customer and a supplier distribute the common benefits resulting from collaborative works. In my interviews, almost all suppliers in both the U.S. and Germany admitted that price pressure has been growing. And many suppliers understand that because automakers are also under international competition, suppliers themselves should reduce the price. But in some cases, there is too much pressure on suppliers. Many suppliers complain that customers' profits go up while suppliers' profits go down. Sometimes suppliers consider the price pressure "unreasonable."

For the index of price pressure, participants in the survey evaluated the sentence "Our customers press the price to the degree of 'zero-profit' or 'minus-profit' without considering the cost conditions of suppliers or without considering the conditions of our production" (item 8, table 4). In this question, I assume that as the one-sided pressure becomes higher, it is less fair in the sense of sharing collaborative benefits. The difference between the U.S. and German markets in sharing benefits is significant (p < .001). American customers are more likely than their German counterparts to press prices without considering suppliers' conditions. This result suggests that German markets are more fair than American markets in the substantive justice of sharing collaborative benefits.

All five indices of fairness tested above reveal the significant differences between the American and German automotive parts markets. The German automotive parts market clearly shows a prevalence of "fair" relationships between customers and suppliers, whereas "unfair" relationships dominate the American automotive parts market. This is important because American customers' unfair behavior deters trustful cooperation, which is counterproductive to economic performance. As an American supplier says:

> [Due to customers' power], we accept their unfair practices but have found ways to protect ourselves; we frequently do not give improvements or design enhancements to the customers until after we have the business locked down. This is actually counterproductive to the reduction of development lead-time.[115]

American suppliers are very cautious about giving genuine information to customers who might abuse the information to control the suppliers themselves or share it with the suppliers' competitors. By contrast, German suppliers and customers have developed fair and trustful relationships. German suppliers and customers obtain more benefits resulting from flexible application engineering.

Many empirical studies confirm my finding that the U.S. automotive supplier market has problems in the interfaces between customers and suppliers. Susan Helper's extensive survey, the survey conducted by OSAT and A.T. Kearney, Inc., and Jenet Hartley's survey conclude similarly that fair and trustful relationships between automakers and suppliers in the U.S. automotive parts market are exceptions rather than the rule.[116] In particular, extensive research conducted by the Berlin Science Center (Wissenschaftzentrum Berlin: WZB) from 1993 to 1996 shows that American automobile companies suffer dysfunction in the interfaces with suppliers more than German companies do. According to the WZB research, American automakers suffered from distrustful relationships with their suppliers to an "extraordinarily serious" extent, although they had adopted a new, flexible organization. Andreas Bartelt's empirical research, conducted in 1999, which gathered data from 283 German suppliers, also confirms my finding that German suppliers have improved their relationships. According to Bartelt's research, about 80 percent of German suppliers evaluate their relationships as "very successful"; German suppliers are less worried about the risk of customers' opportunistic behavior, such as violation of confidentiality.[117]

Regardless of companies' tier position and size, German markets have established fair and trustful relationships, whereas American markets are unfair and distrustful. This runs counter to power theorists' expectation that small companies could not build fair partnerships and would collapse under high pressure from customers.[118] I conducted regression analyses between company size, represented by the number of employees, and all indices of trust; and regression analyses between tier position and trust in both the U.S. and Germany. The regression analyses do not show any significance of correlation between trust and company size, or between trust and tier position; all the p-values in these regression analyses are larger than 0.05. Through personal interviews and e-mail interviews, I also conducted another mini-survey on the relationships between first-tier suppliers and sub-tier suppliers.[119] Worrying about a respondent's bias (i.e., that a first-tier supplier might deny its own unfairness toward sub-tier suppliers), I raised questions with sub-tier suppliers about the relationships with their customers (first-tier suppliers) only after identifying the interviewee as a sub-tier supplier. To the question of whether first-tier suppliers treat sub-tier suppliers in a manner commensurate to their own unfair treatment from automakers, 90 percent of American sub-tier suppliers agreed that first-tier suppliers "pass the buck" directly down to sub-tier suppliers; only 4 percent of respondents disagreed with the statement. By contrast, only 11 percent of German sub-tier suppliers agreed that the first-tier suppliers passed on unfair behavior, while 89 percent of German sub-tier suppliers answered that they had better relationships with first-tier suppliers. A survey conducted by the automotive journal *Ward's Auto World* in 2000 confirms that American first-tier suppliers are confrontational. Bartelt's extensive 1999 survey concluded that there is little difference between big and small suppliers in the fairness and trust indices.[120] These data indicate that fair and trustful relationships have spread throughout the German automotive parts markets while unfair and distrustful relationships prevail in the American automotive parts markets regardless of tier position and power. The information also reveals that the reason that Germans established fair and trustful partnerships is not that German suppliers are more powerful than their American counterparts.

It is also noteworthy that fair partnerships are not predetermined by prior norms about contracts and contractual relations, but are consequences of the actors' tremendous efforts. In the first half of the 1990s, the German automotive parts market suffered from unfair behavior by powerful customers. According to empirical research by Mittelstandsinstituts Niedersachsen based on 437 suppliers, 87.7 percent of German suppliers stated in the early 1990s that they felt discriminated against and pressed by their powerful customers. In addition, 84 percent of the suppliers held that they had had to concede to unfair requests by customers.[121] But after a painful process of society-wide adjustments, the unfair cases began to taper off around 1995. By contrast, Americans in the automotive parts market have made little progress in establishing fairer relationships. Helper's research on the American automotive parts market, conducted in 1984, 1989, and 1993, reveals that Americans in the early stages of transformation to a new market suffered from distrust and unfairness. Many independent research projects, such as those conducted by Jürgens, Chotangada, Maloni, and *Ward's Auto World* in the second half of the 1990s, show that relationships in the U.S. markets had not improved; agents still suffered from distrust and opportunism. This will be analyzed in detail in the subsequent chapters.

I must note before concluding this section that the conception of fairness is not identical in American and German automotive supplier markets, although I have used it neutrally in this research. To ascertain the difference, I asked suppliers to evaluate the sentence "We believe that our relations with customers are fair" (item 9, table 4). As the test of mean difference on the issue of "General Appreciation of Fairness" shows, there is significant difference between the American and German estimation of fairness (p < .001). Nevertheless, it is noteworthy that a majority of American suppliers (52 percent) believe that their relationships with customers are fair, and only about 13 percent believe they are unfair. The reason why American suppliers agree with the above statement, even though they have experienced such opportunistic behaviors as customers' violation of confidentiality and arbitrary revision of contracts, is not only that participants tend to answer positively to an abstract question. Through my personal interviews and e-mail interviews, I came to know that fairness in the American automotive parts market is judged differently than in the German market.

Plentiful cynicism regarding partnership and fairness hangs over the U.S. automotive parts market because of long-lasting distrustful relationships and conflicts. By the late 1990s, although they felt distaste for the usual relationships, few people in the American automotive parts markets expected the fair sharing of substantive benefits between a customer and a supplier. Many American suppliers complain of the extreme pressure of price cuts, but they do not think that it is unfair. Although they feel that customers' opportunistic behavior is very distasteful, many suppliers believe that it is a customer's job to press prices down, while it is a supplier's job to try to endure. An American supplier paraphrases: "I do not think our customers would be dishonest; they would use any other advantages to reduce the price of our product, and they should; it is our obligation to preserve profits for our shareholders."[122] An American supplier who declines to define customers' opportunistic behaviors as unfair says, "They approach it as war or survival; we have the same approach."[123] Many suppliers define fairness as "all's fair in love and war." American conceptions of fairness are extremely formal in the sense that few agents in the American automotive parts markets refer to substantive fairness. The criteria for distribution of benefits resulting from collaborative work totally depend on personal taste and individual power. The fair rules in the American automotive supplier market are not simply formal, but are determined by power to an extreme. One supplier defines the rules as "the law of the jungle—perform or perish." Survival is justified.

But this conception of fairness is not predetermined by prior norms about market relations. In the early period of transformation toward the collaborative market, people in the U.S. markets also had expectations of substantive fairness.[124] However, by the end of the 1990s, Americans in the markets believed that the so-called unfair behavior was a kind of "given rule" in their markets. The reason many are reluctant to call it unfair is that customers' opportunistic behaviors are a part of everyday life. American suppliers believe that opportunism is given conditions in their markets. After suppliers accept the opportunism as having been given rules in the market, the remaining issue is not whether to reform the rules toward better ones, but whether to accept them as a form of individual choice. Another reason for why customers' opportunistic behavior is not thought of as unfair is that the extremely power-conditioned rules are justified by liberal ideas of justice. Although suppliers' freedom of contracts is limited by customers' power, the formal rules distorted by power are justified by an abstract idea of "individual freedom of choice." Many suppliers say that "it is up to a supplier's own free will to accept the customers' rules or not." A supplier explains a typical reason for fairness: "Unfair treatments are fairly common…. No matter what, it is still your right as a supplier to end the relationship."[125] Another supplier says that "complaining is not only useless but also absurd, because a supplier already knows the customers' rules, and it is up to suppliers themselves whether to play by the customers' rules."[126] Customers' opportunistic behavior is not unfair because the acceptance of it depends on a supplier's own free choice. To many American suppliers, customers' opportunistic behavior might be distasteful and unethical, but it is not unfair since every supplier is playing by the same rules. While many American suppliers refer to affirmative action, such as awarding contracts to minority business groups, as unfair cases, they are reluctant to define customers' opportunistic behavior as unfair because they believe customers' opportunistic behavior is the given rule; the rules are fair, at least in the sense that they treat all suppliers in the same way.[127]

By contrast, in addition to criteria of formal fairness such as "keeping contract and confidentiality," many German suppliers mentioned substantive aspects of fairness such as a "fair" balance between quality and price; a fair trade between price concession and future business; and a reciprocity of openness and benefits between the customer and the supplier.[128] Many German suppliers said "without fairness, no partnership" (*Ohne Fairness, Keine Partnerschaft*). Many suppliers reported that Opel (GM) and Ford in Germany were unfair because they talked of partnership while taking away entire benefits. But this does not mean that only an even distribution of benefits is thought fair. Many suppliers consider the power of big customers and accept that powerful customers can take a bigger part of the pie.[129] Sometimes it is hard to calculate what an even distribution of risks and benefits is.

To sum up, American and German automotive parts markets underwent tremendous changes in their market relations in the 1980s and 1990s. The revival of contracts challenged not only the neoliberal paradigm but also institutionalism. Contrary to the institutionalists' expectations of national patterns of production and market systems, both the American and German automotive industries went through a strikingly similar transformation toward lean production and collaborative markets in the 1980s and 1990s. On the other hand, the similar adjustments in both the U.S. and German markets do not confirm the neoliberal paradigm. The economic rationality of the neoclassical market is not universally relevant. Rather, it is contextualized, particularly by the division of labor. Just as the neoclassical market prevailed with the establishment of mass production, a new rationality of flexible lean production has generated new market relations. The new form of long-term and collaborative markets that German as well as American markets have commonly taken on is a sharp departure from the traditional, neoclassical form of markets. In the collaborative markets, the rationality of the neoclassical market turned out to be suboptimal. In addition, in the new long-term and collaborative markets, the neoliberal paradigm of market governance, such as short-term exit and liberal contract law, did not work. Long-term and collaborative markets caused an abundance of new problems for governance due to their incompleteness and unclearness.

The unclear governance of long-term and collaborative markets leaves more room for divergence in governance. In a situation in which the interfaces between a customer and a supplier become more important, the regimes of long-term collaborative markets are not the same in how they create new ethical norms and stabilize the relationships. The U.S. and German markets differ significantly from each other. Germans in the automotive parts markets have developed a conception of substantive fairness and trustful market regimes through painful adjustments. By contrast, distrust still prevails in the U.S. automotive parts market and an extremely power-driven conception of formal fairness has prevailed as the argument of substantive fairness has receded with time. However, the differences between the U.S. and German regimes are not predetermined by the countries' cultural heritages. On the contrary, when traditional norms for governance failed to work, agents in both the American and German automotive supplier markets had to redefine their relationships and establish new ethical standards. In the coming chapters—chapter 2 for the American market and chapter 3 for the German market—it will be investigated why and how American and German agents developed their governance differently.

Notes

1. The methods of calculating vertical integration are very different, depending on the researchers. The prevalent ways in Germany are also different from those of the U.S. For the three prevalent ways of calculating vertical integration in Germany, see Ulrich Jürgens and Werner Reutter, "Verringerung der Fertigungstiefe und betriebliche Interessenvertretung in der deutschen Automobilindustrie," in Norbert Altmann and Dieter Sauer, eds., *Systemische Rationalisierung und Zulieferindustrie* (Frankfurt: Campus Verlag, 1989), 122–124; Reinhard Doleschal, "Just-in-time-Strategien und betriebliche Interessenvertretung in Autombil-Zulieferbetrieben," Altmann and Sauer, *Systemische Rationalisierung und Zulieferindustrie*, 157. For the prevalent ways of calculating in the U.S., see Susan Osborn Griffin, "Two Hypotheses Accounting for the Different Levels of Vertical Integration in the U.S. and Japanese Auto Industries" (Ph.D. diss., Emory University, 1994), appendix B, 109–114. Although the calculations are not the same, the results of numerous independent researches indicate the decline of vertical integration.
2. "The Auto Industry Meets the New Economy," *Fortune* 130 (5 September 1994): 52–60.
3. See Christoph Scherrer, "Governance of the Automobile Industry: The Transformation of Labor and Supplier Relations," in John L. Campbell, J. Rogers Hollingsworth, and Leon N. Lindberg, eds., *Governance of the American Economy* (New York: Cambridge University Press, 1991), 217, 220; Paul D. Ballew and Robert H. Schnorbus, "Realignment in the Auto Supplier Industry: The Rippling Effects of Big Three Restructuring," *Economic Perspectives* 18, no. 1 (1994): 7; Jeffrey Robert Yost, "Components of the Past and Vehicles of Change: Parts Manufacturers and Supplier Relations in the U.S. Automotive Industry" (Ph.D. diss., Case Western Reserve University, 1998), 354; Robert E. Cole and Taizo Yakushiji, "The American and Japanese Auto Industries in Transition," report of the Joint US-Japan Automotive Study (Ann Arbor: Center for Japanese Studies, University of Michigan, 1984).
4. Dirk Riesselmann, "Entwicklung der Automobilzulieferindustrie: Strukturen, Lieferantentypen und Erfolg" (Ph.D. diss., Universität Bundeswehr, Hamburg, 1998), 41.
5. Interview with VW on 22 June 2000; Volkswagen AG, "Der Volkswagen Konzern," pamphlet of Beschaffung (Volkswagen, 2000).
6. "Schwere Zeiten für die Zulieferindustrie," *Die Welt,* 16 September 1996, A3.
7. "Japan-Autos nur durch Kooperation zu kontern," *Handelsblatt,* 10 May 1993, 15.
8. "Erfolgreich im globalen Wettbewerb," *Frankfurter Allgemeine Zeitung* (hereafter *FAZ*), 8 September 1997, B2.
9. See Horst Wildemann, *Die deutsche Zulieferindustrie im europäischen Markt—ein Blick die Zukunft: Ergebnisse einer Delphi Studie* (Technische Universität Munich, 1993); IKB Deutsche Industriebank, "Automobilzulieferer 1996: Differenzierte Ertragsergebnisse," *IKB Branchenbericht* (December 1997); "1997—ein erfolgreiches Jahr für die deutschen Automobilzulieferer," *IKB Branchenbericht* (December 1998); "Die Automobilzulieferer 1998—Kräftiges Umsatzwachstum, differenzierte Ertragsentwicklung," *IKB Branchenbericht* (December 1999).
10. "Die Fähigkeit zur perfekten Abstimmung ist oft noch all zu schwach ausgeprägt," *FAZ,* 24 May 2000, 22.
11. For the early history of the automobile industry, see Susan Helper and David Hochfelder, "Japanese-Style Supplier Relationships in the American Auto Industry," in Takao Shiba and Masahiro Shimotani, eds., *Beyond the Firm: Business Groups in International and Historical Perspective* (Oxford: Oxford University Press, 1997), 187–214; Yost, "Components of the Past and Vehicles of Change"; James M. Laux, *The European Automobile Industry* (New York: Twayne Publishers, 1992); Susan Helper, "Strategy and Irreversibility in Supplier Relations: The Case of the U.S. Automobile Industry," *Business History Review* 65 (winter 1991): 781–824; Lawrence H. Seltzer, *A Financial History of the American Automobile Industry* (Boston, Mass.: Houghton Mifflin Company, 1928); George

V. Thompson, "Inter-Company Technical Standardization in the Early Automobile Industry" *Journal of Economic History* 14 (winter 1954): 1–20.

12. Yost, "Components of the Past and Vehicles of Change," 12, 26, 138; "GM Plans to Spin Off Delphi Car Parts Unit," *Los Angels Times*, 4 August 1998; "Can Detroit Outsource Its Way Back to the Top?" *Machine Design*, 21 March 1991, 139–140; James P. Womack, Daniel T. Jones, and Daniel Roos, *The Machine That Changed the World* (New York: HarperPerennial, 1990), 39.

13. Seltzer, *A Financial History of The American Automobile Industry*, 59.

14. The diffusion of mass production was delayed in Europe until the second half of the 1940s although Ford had established complete mass production in 1915. From the 1920s to the 1940s, economic chaos, narrow nationalism, wars, and strong attachment to the craft system traditions deterred the development of mass production. In particular, the German automobile industry developed slowly compared with those of other countries like France and the U.S. due to its limited market. For example, the percentage of inhabitants per car in 1929 was 237 in Germany, 45 in Britain, and 44 in France. Although VW was designed to produce through mass production, it was mainly idle during wartime. From 1945 to 1948, VW could not make full use of its operations due to the shortage of raw materials and disruption by the division of Germany. It was not until the early 1960s that VW could realize full and visible mass production. See Womack, Jones, and Roos, *The Machine That Changed the World*, 45; Steven Tolliday, "Enterprise and State in the West German Wirtschaftswunder: Volkswagen and the Automobile Industry, 1939–1962," *Business History Review* 69 (autumn 1995): 277–338.

15. Hans Roeper, "Teile- und Montage-Industrie," *Betriebswirtschaftliche Forschung und Praxis* 1, no. 9 (1949): 560–561.

16. Inge Petzold, "Die Zulieferindustrie: Eine Betriebswirtschaftliche Untersuchung unter Besonderer Berücksichtigung der industriellen Zulieferbetriebe zur Automobilindustrie" (Ph.D. diss., Wirtschaftswissenschaft, Düsseldorf, 1968), 30, 39, 121; Johann Heinrich von Brunn, *Wettbewerbsproblem der Automobilindustrie* (Cologne: Carl Heymanns Verlag KG, 1979), 12, 64–65, 95; Bruno Hake and Philip M. Lynch, *The Market for Automotive Parts in Germany, France, and Italy*, Michigan International Commerce Reports, no. 2 (Ann Arbor: University of Michigan, 1970), 31; "Ein Auto besteht nicht allein aus dem Motor," *Blick durch die Wirtschaft*, 19 February 1964, 5.; "Die stummen Diener der Automobilindustrie," *Blick durch die Wirtschaft*, 17 February 1964, 3; "Für über sieben Milliarden DM Autozubehör," *Blick durch die Wirtschaft*, 28 September 1964, 5.

17. See Oliver E. Williamson, "Transaction-Cost Economics: The Governance of Contractual Relations," *Journal of Law and Economics* 22, no. 2 (1979): 233–261; idem, *The Economic Institutions of Capitalism* (New York: Free Press, 1985), 15–102; idem, "Strategizing, Economizing and Economic Organization," *Strategic Management Journal* 12 (1991): 75–94; Kirk Monteverde and David J. Teece, "Supplier Switching Costs and Vertical Integration in the Automobile Industry," *The Bell Journal of Economics* 19, no. 1 (1982): 206–213; Sharon Novak and Steven D. Eppinger, "Sourcing by Design: Product Complexity and the Supply Chain," *Management Science* 47, no. 1 (2001): 189–204; Thomas Hübner, "Vertikale Integration in der Automobilindustrie—Anreizsystem und wettbewerbspolitische Beurteilung" (Ph.D. diss., Technischen Universität Berlin, 1987), 69–88; Jürgen Hanke, *Hybride Koordinations-strukturen: Liefer- und Leistungsbeziehungen kleiner und mittlerer Unternehmen der Automobilzulieferindustrie* (Cologne: Verlag Josef Eul, 1993); Martina Hempfling-Wendelken, *Vertikale Beziehungenstrukturen in der deutschen Automobilindustrie: Theoretischer Aufbau von zwischenbetrieblichen Beziehungsumstern und empirische Ergebnisse zu Beurteilungsverfahren* (Frankfurt am Main: Peter Lang GmbH, 1997).

18. Adam Smith, *The Wealth of Nations*, ed. Edwin Cannan (New York: Modern Library, 1937), 4–5.

19. In this sense, this book differs from the networks or institutionalist theories of "neither market nor hierarchy." The theorists of "neither market nor hierarchy" rightly point out a third type of coordination of transactions in the situation in which the transaction

costs theory and neoclassical economists call attention only to the market and hierarchy for coordination of transactions. Even though the transactions costs theory provides theoretical ground for the rationality of non-market institutions, it tends to blank out hybrid types of transactions between market and hierarchy. In this theoretical terrain, some institutionalists posited a third type of transaction by naming it "neither market nor hierarchy." But this category includes not only long-term markets but also associations and social networks. In other words, they do not differentiate the long-term contracts made by voluntary agreement in a market from associations that do not pursue the maximization of their profits in a market. See Walter W. Powell, "Neither Market Nor Hierarchy: Network Forms of Organization," *Research in Organization Behavior* 12 (1990): 295–336.

20. For the neoclassical market, see endnote 16 in the introduction of this book. On the other hand, Friedrich Hayek criticizes the method and assumptions of the neoclassical economics although he is also one of the main proponents of liberalism based on the market principle. Hayek does not assume perfect information or apparent equilibrium. Instead, he emphasizes the process of searching for order through decentralized activities among bounded rational agents. See Friedrich A. Hayek, *New Studies in Philosophy, Politics, Economics, and the History of Ideas* (London: Routledge & Kegan Paul, 1968), particularly the chapter "Competition as a Discovery Procedure."

21. George J. Stigler, "Perfect Competition, Historically Contemplated," *Journal of Political Economy* 65, no. 1 (1957): 6–7, 18, 24.

22. Helper and Hochfelder, "Japanese-Style Supplier Relationships in the American Auto Industry," 203–204; Ralph Epstein, *The Automobile Industry* (Chicago: A. W. Saw Company, 1928), 41, 184; John Bell Rae, *American Automobile Manufacturers: The First Forty Years* (Philadelphia: Chilton, 1959), 79–80; Thompson, "Inter-Company Technical Standardization in the Early American Automobile Industry," 1–20.

23. Yost, "Components of the Past and Vehicles of Change," 25–26.

24. Michael E. Porter, *Cases in Comparative Strategy* (New York: Free Press, 1983), 278–279; Susan Helper, "Supplier Relations and Technical Change: Theory and Application to the US Automobile Industry" (Ph.D. diss., Harvard University, 1987), chap. 4; Yost, "Components of the Past and Vehicles of Change," 3–12, 138, 344; Womack, Jones, and Roos, *The Machine That Changed the World*, 59, 142–144.

25. Womack, Jones, and Roos, *The Machine That Changed the World*, 60, 141–145; Cole and Yakushiji, "The American and Japanese Auto Industries in Transition," 156; Helper, "Supplier Relations and Technical Change," 11–19, 56 in chap. 4.

26. Helper, "Supplier Relations and Technical Change," iv-83.

27. See Wolfgang Littek and Ulrich Heisig, "Taylorism Never Got Hold of Skilled White-Collar Work in Germany," in Wolfgang Littek and Tony Charles, eds., *The New Division of Labour: Emerging Forms of Work Organization in International Perspective* (Berlin: Wlafter de Gruyter, 1995), 373–396; Michael J. Piore and Charles F. Sabel, *The Second Industrial Divide* (New York: Basic Books, 1984); Horst Kern and Michael Schumann, *Ende der Arbeitsteilung?* (Munich: Beck, 1984).

28. Laux, *The European Automobile Industry*, 51–60.

29. Tolliday, "Enterprise and State in the West German Wirtschaftswunder," 273–350.

30. Roeper, "Teile- und Montage-Industrie," 558–563.

31. Tolliday, "Enterprise and State in the West German Wirtschaftswunder," 331–338.

32. "Für über sieben Milliarden DM Autozubehör," *Blick durch die Wirtschaft*, 28 September 1964, 5.

33. von Brunn, *Wettbewerbsprobleme der Automobilindustrie*, 64–65.

34. Petzold, "Die Zulieferindustrie," 84; "Für über sieben Milliarden DM Autozubehör" *Blick durch die Wirtschaft*, 28 September 1964, 5.

35. Daimler-Benz AG, *Das Großunternehmen und der industrielle Mittelstand: Eine Untersuchung über die klein- und mittelbetrieblichen Zulieferer der Daimler-Benz AG* (Stuttgart-Untertürkheim: Daimler-Benz AG, 1962), 17; Petzold, "Die Zulieferindustrie," 113.

36. Annerose Iber-Schade, "Auswirkungen des Strukturwandels in der Automobilindustrie auf Kfz-Zulievererunternehmen," in Burkhardt Röper, ed., *Strukturpolitische Probleme der Automobil-Industrie unter dem Aspekt des Wettwerbs* (Berlin: Duncker & Humbolt GmbH, 1985), 95–127.

37. For the German model of production systems, see Piore and Sabel, *The Second Industrial Divide*; Kern and Schumann, *Das Ende der Arbeisteilung?*; Wolfgang Streeck, *Social Institutions and Economic Performance* (London: Sage Publishers, 1992); Gary Herrigel, *Industrial Constructions: The Sources of German Industrial Power* (New York: Cambridge University Press, 1996).

38. Traditional market relations in Germany were neither long-term nor relational contracts. Most contracts in traditional markets were for less than one year. Relations between customers and suppliers were distant; suppliers were understood as extended plants (*verlängerte Werkbank*) for in-house production as absorbers of shock from the business cycle. See Hideo von Kubota and Herman Witte, "Strukturvergleich des Zulieferwesens in Japan und in der Bundesrepublik Deutschland," *Zeitschrift für Betriebswirtschaft* 60, no. 4 (1990): 383–406; Petzold, "Die Zulieferindustrie," 62–63, 69, 127–129; Kurt Döring, "Die ungleichen Partner," *Zeit*, 9 April 1965, 39; K. Klinger, "Zulieferungen und Zulieferer in betriebswirtschaftlicher Sicht," *Der Betrieb* 12, no. 45 (1959): 1229–1232; Kurt Kaiser, *Vor- und Zulieferungen des Metall Verarbeitenden Handwerks an die Industrie im Regierungsbezirk Düsseldorf* (Essen: Rheinisch-Westfälisches Institut für Wirtschaftsforschung, 1964); Norbert Marahrens, *Struktur und Angebot von Klein- und Mittelbetrieben im Zulieferbereich* (Göttingen: Verlag Otto Schwartz & Co., 1973); Monopolkomission, *Mißbräuche der Nachfragemacht und Möglichkeiten zu ihrer Kontrolle im Rahmen des Gesetzes gegen Wettbewerbsbeschränkungen* (Baden-Baden: Nomos Verlagsgesellschaft, 1979); Hinrich-Mattias Geck and Günther Petry, *Nachfragermacht gegenüber Zulieferern: Eine Untersuchung am Beispiel der Automobil- und der elektro-technischen Industrie* (Cologne: Carl Heymanns Verlag KG, 1983); Iber-Schade, "Auswirkungen des Strukturwandels in der Automobilindustrie auf Kfz-Zulieferunternehmen," 95–127; Hans Gerhard Mendius and Stefanie Weimer, "Betriebsübergreifende Zusammenarbeit bei der Delegschaftsqualifizierung in kleinen Zulieferunternehmen," in Hans Gerhard Mendius and Ulrike Wendeling-Schröder, eds., *Zulieferer im Netz—zwischen Abhängigkeit und Partnerschaft: Neustrukturierung der Logistik am Beispiel der Automobilzulieferung* (Cologne: Bund-Verlag GmbH, 1991), 274–303.

39. Petzold, "Die Zulieferindustrie," 110.

40. Yost, "Components of the Past and Vehicles of Change," 378.

41. Helper, "Supplier Relations and Technical Change," v-2.

42. See William J. Abernathy, Kim B. Clark, and Alan M. Kantrow, "The New Industrial Competition," *Harvard Business Review* 59, no. 5 (1981): 68–81; Yost, "Components of the Past and Vehicles of Change," 380.

43. For research of international comparison, see Toshihiro Nishiguchi, *Strategic Industrial Sourcing: The Japanese Advantage* (New York: Oxford University Press, 1994); Womack, Jones, and Roos, *The Machine That Changed the World*, 54–80, 111–133, 146–158; Michael A. Cusumano and Akira Takeishi, "Supplier Relations and Management: A Survey of Japanese, Japanese-Transplant, and U.S. Auto Plants," *Strategic Management Journal* 12, no. 7 (October 1991): 563–588; M. N. Baily and H. Gerbach, "Efficiency in Manufacturing and the Need for Global Competition" (Brookings Papers on Economic Activity: Microeconomics, 1995); Jeffrey H. Dyer and W. G. Ouchi, "Japanese-Style Partnerships: Giving Companies a Competitive Edge," *Sloan Management Review* 35, no. 1 (fall 1993): 51–63.

44. Womack, Jones, and Roos, *The Machine That Changed the World*, 28–37, 55, 63, 106–115.

45. Carol J. Haddad, "Involving Manufacturing Employees in the Early Stages of Product Development: A Case Study from the U.S. Automobile Industry," in Ulrich Jürgens, ed., *New Product Development and Production Networks: Global Industrial Experience* (Heidelberg: Springer-Verlag, 2000), 302.

46. Ibid., 293–294.

47. Womack, Jones, and Roos, *The Machine That Changed the World*, 150–152.

48. Interview with A22 on 9 December 1999; interview with A12 on 1 December 1999.

49. Interview with A2 on 16 December 1999.

50. See Stephan Schrader and Henrik Sattler, "Zwischenbetriebliche Kooperation: Informaler Informationsaustausch in den USA und Deutschland," *Die Betriebswirtschaft* 53, no. 5 (1993): 589–608; Laura M. Birou and Stanley E. Fawcett, "Supplier Involvement in Integrated Product Development: A Comparison of US and European Practices," *International Journal of Physical Distribution & Logistics Management* 24, no. 5 (1994): 4–14.

51. The core of the German crisis in the 1990s was the crisis of the German production system, which had supported high wages and high competitiveness until the late 1980s. For the rigidity of the craft system in the 1990s, see Horst Kern and Charles Sabel, "Verblaßte Tugend: Die Krise des deutschen Produktionsmodells," in *Soziale Welt* (special edition, 1993): 605–624; Gary Herrigel, "The Limits of German Manufacturing Flexibility," in Lowell Turner, ed., *Negotiating the New Germany: Can Social Partnership Survive?* (Ithaca: Cornell University Press, 1997), 177–205; Gary Herrigel and Charles F. Sabel, "Craft Production in Crisis: Industrial Restructuring in Germany during the 1990s," in Pepper D. Culpepper and David Finegold, eds., *The German Skills Machine: Sustaining Comparative Advantage in a Global Economy* (New York: Berghahn Books, 1999), 77–114; Andreas Genter, *Entwurf einer Kennzahlensystems zur Effektivitäts- und Effizienzsteigerung von Entwicklungsprojekten, dargestellt am Beispiel der Entwicklungs- und Anlaufphase in der Automobilindustrie* (Munich: Franz Vahlen, 1994); Hans Grabowski and Kerstin Geiger, eds., *Neue Wege zur Produktentwicklung* (Stuttgart: Raabe Verlag, 1997); Bruno Cattero, *Lavorare alla Fiat: Arbeiten bei VW: Technologie, Arbeit und soziale Regulierung in der Automobilindustrie* (Münster: Westfälisches Dampfboot, 1998); idem, "Beruf und Berufausbildung—Mythen und Widersprürche im 'deutsche Modell,'" in Bruno Cattero, ed., *Modell Deutschland, Modell Europa, Problems Perspectiven* (Opladen: Leske + Budrich, 1998), 225–246; Ulrich Jürgens and Inge Lippert, "Schnittstellen des deutschen Produktionsregimes: Innovationshemmnisse im Produktentstehungsprozess," in Frieder Naschold et al., eds., *Ökonomische Leistungsfähigkeit und institutionelle Innovation: Das deutsche Produktions- und Politikregime im globalen Wettbewerb* (Berlin: Sigma, 1997), 65–94; Ulrich Jürgens, "Communication and Cooperation in the New Product and Process Development Networks—an International Comparison of Country- and Industry-Specific Patterns," and "Toward New Product and Process Development Networks: The Case of the German Car Industry," in Ulrich Jürgens, ed., *New Product Development and Production Networks* (Heidelberg: Springer-Verlag, 2000), 107–148, 259–288.

52. Womack, Jones, and Roos, *The Machine That Changed the World*; Schrader and Sattler, "Zwischenbetriebliche Kooperation," 589–608; Birou and Fawcett, "Supplier Involvement in Integrated Product Development," 4–14. For the Boston Consulting Group research, see Hendrik Heinze, "Ein virtuell-flexibles Zuliefermodell—Neue Positionen für Automobilzulieferunternehmen" (Ph.D. diss., St. Gallen University, 1996); for Arthur Andersen Consulting's research in 1991 and 1993, "Eine Herausforderung für die deutsche Automobilindustrie," *Handelsblatt*, 9 June 1994, B7.

53. This is based on an international study by the Arthur Andersen consulting group. See "Eine Herausforderung für die deutsche Automobile," *Handelsblatt*, 9 June 1994, B7; "Deutsche Automobilzulieferer schneiden schlecht ab," *FAZ*, 8 November 1994, 26; "Keine Spitzennoten für deutsche Autozulieferer," *VDI nachrichten*, 2 December 1994, 7.

54. The consulting company Roland-Berger studied the forty four Niedersachsen auto suppliers. A.T. Kearney GmbH collaborated with the European Logistics Association and the Bundesvereinigung Logistik (BVL) to investigate the just-in-time system of twelve European countries. The research center for automotive economics at Bamberg University also conducted a survey of more than eighty German supplier companies in 1993, concluding that German suppliers and automakers had not developed collaborative relations sufficiently. See "Schlechte Noten für Zulieferer," *Süddeutsche Zeitung*, 2 November 1993, 29; "Die Verbesserung der Qualität ist meistens nur eine Reaktion auf

Reklamationen," *Handelsblatt*, 10 December 1992, 23; "Die Zulieferer befinden sich im Stimmungstief," *Handelsblatt*, 23/24 July 1993, 12; "Niedersachsen fördert Fahrzeug-Zulieferer," *FAZ*, 1 September 1994, 12.

55. Karlheinz Hopfeld, "Gewerkschaftliche Interessenvertretung in einer klein- und mittelbetrieblich geprägten Zulierferregion," in Mendius and Wendeling-Schröder, *Zulieferer im Netz*, 148–153.

56. Interview with G24 on 3 April 2000.

57. Professor Bullinger of Stuttgarter *Fraunhofer-Institut für Arbeitswirtschaft und Organiza-tion* concluded, based on empirical data in the early 1990s, that too little information was shared between customers and suppliers in Germany; they suffered from double engineering. See "Zulieferer suchen die Zusammenarbeit," *VDI nachrichten*, 11 December 1992, 6.

58. Michael Schumann, "The German Automobile Industry in Transition," *The Economic and Labour Relations Review* 8, no. 2 (1997): 230–231; Stefan Zischka, "Gestaltung der Kunden- und Marketorientierung und Andwendung des Quality Function Deployment in Entwicklungsprojekten der deutschen Automobilzulieferindustrie: Ergebnisse einer Umfrage," Institute Newsletter on Quality Management (Institut für Qualitätsicherung, Hanover University, 1998), 20–24.

59. Gunter Lay and Werner Wallmeier, "Stand und Entwicklungstendenzen der Produktionsmodernisierung," Research Paper of Production Innovation Improvement (Karlsruhe: Fraunhofer Institut für Systemtechnik und Innovationsforschung, 1999), 17.

60. Interview with G44 on 5 May 2000.

61. Interview with G48 on 10 May 2000; interview with G53 on 22 May 2000; interview with G24 on 3 April 2000; interview with G26 on 5 April 2000.

62. Interview with G41 on 28 April 2000.

63. Cusumano and Takeishi, "Supplier Relations and Management," 565.

64. See Rati Apana Chotangada, "Governance Systems that Facilitate Innovation: Changing Perspectives of Supplier Customer Relationships. The Case of the Automotive Industry" (Ph.D. diss., University of Cincinnati, 2000), 80.

65. See Mari Sako, Richard Lamming, and Susan R. Helper, "Supplier Relations in the Multinational Automotive Industry," in Ram Mudambi and Martin Ricketts, eds., *The Organization of the Firm: International Business Perspectives* (London: Routledge, 1998), 178–194. The empirical data of this study are from an extensive survey of first-tier suppliers in 1993 and 1994. In the U.S., 675 responses (55 percent response rate) were received from independent U.S.–owned firms in 1993; in Japan, 472 responses (30 percent response rate) were received from independent Japanese-owned firms in July 1993; in Europe, 262 responses (16 percent) were received from European suppliers in 1994. Of the European suppliers, 44 percent were U.K.–based suppliers, 24 percent were from Germany, 9 percent from France, 10 percent from Italy.

66. Susan Helper, "Strategy and Irreversibility in Supplier Relations," 799–800; Yost, "Components of the Past and Vehicles of Changes," 344.

67. Other empirical studies confirm von Kubota and Witte's conclusion that German contracts in the manufacturing markets were short-term, less than one year. See Petzold, "Die Zulieferindustrie," 50, 113, 134; Monopolkommission, *Mißbräuche der Nachfragemacht und Möglichkeiten zu ihrer Kontrolle im Rahmen des Gesetzes gegen Wettbewerbsbeschränkungen*, 71; Geck and Petry, *Nachfrafermacht gegenüber Zulieferern*, 40, 74; Iber-Schade, "Auswirkungen des Strukturwandels in der Automobilindustrie auf Kfz-Zulieferunternehmen," 104. According to studies conducted by Arthur Andersen and Horst Wildemann, 84.4 percent of contracts in 1987 were for less than one year, 11.8 percent were for two years, and 3.4 percent were for more than three years. See Hanke, *Hybride Koordinationsstrukuten*, 162, 166; Marcus Reeg, *Liefer- und Leistungsbeziehungen in der deutschen Automobilindustrie: Strukturelle Veränderungen aus unternehmerischer und wirtschaftpolitischer Sicht* (Berlin: Duncker & Humbolt, 1998), 92–93.

68. See Cusumano and Takeishi, "Supplier Relations and Management," 570.

69. The duration of German contracts increased rapidly in the 1990s, as tables 2 and 3 show. By contrast, American long-term contracts developed quickly in the late 1980s but slowly throughout the 1990s. American automakers introduced long-term contracts relatively earlier than Germans. Ford had already adopted multi-year contracts by 70 percent in 1985; GM had adopted long-term contracts by 30 percent in 1984. But the growth slackened: in the U.S. automotive parts markets, the average length of contracts grew from 1.2 years in 1984 to 1.7 years in 1990, 2.4 years in 1993, and 2.424 years in 2000. By contrast, the average length of German contracts was just around 1 year in the late 1980s, but 3.2 years in 2000. The development of length of contracts in both the American and German supplier markets shows that as American customers abused the incompleteness of long-term contracts, suppliers tried to avoid long-term contracts in the second half of the 1990s. For the historical trajectory of contact terms, see Helper, "Supplier Relations and Technical Change," v-5, v-15; "Strategy and Irreversibility in Supplier Relations," 812; Christoph Scherrer, "Governance of the Automobile Industry," 218; Cusumano and Takeishi, "Supplier Relations and Management," 564, 570; Susan R. Helper and Mari Sako, "Supplier Relations in Japan and the United States: Are They Converging?" *Sloan Management Review* 36, no. 3 (spring 1995): 79.

70. Yost, "Components of the Past and Vehicles of Change," 64; Richard N. Langlois and Paul L. Robertson, "Explaining Vertical Integration: Lessons from the American Automobile Industry," *The Journal of Economic History* 49, no. 2 (1989): 369; Seltzer, *A Financial History of the American Automobile Industry*, 50.

71. Dennis L. Marler, "The Post Japanese Model of Automotive Component Supply: Selected North American Case Studies," (IMVP International Policy Forum, MIT, 1989), 12; Alex Taylor III and Robert A. Miller, "The Auto Industry Meets the New Economy," *Fortune* 130, no. 5 (5 September 1994): 52–57; Helper, "Supplier Relations and Technical Change," iv-17, v-31; idem, "How Much Has Really Changed between US Automakers and Their Suppliers?" *Sloan Management Review* 32, no. 4 (summer 1991): 19; "New Research Indicates 77% of North American Tier-1 Automotive Suppliers Will Reduce Supplier Base," *PR Newswire*, 6 August 2001.

72. Hanke, *Hybride Koordinationsstrukturen*, 94; "Autohersteller," *VDI nachrichten*, 16 July 1993, 8; "Eine organizatiorische Innovation in Zulieferketten," *Handelsblatt*, 3 July 1990, 14; "Verhältnis zwischen Automobilkonzernen und Lieferanten wird immer 'japanischer,'" *Handelsblatt*, 7 June 1990, 5.

73. "Zulieferer vor Konzentrationswelle," *Handelsblatt*, 23 September 1999, 16.

74. In American contract law, the Restatement (Second) defines the contract as a promise: "A contract is a promise or a set of promises for the breach of which the law gives a remedy, or the performance of which the law in some way recognizes as a duty" (§ 1 of American Law Institute [1973)] Restatement [2nd] Contracts); quoted in Ian R. Macneil, *The New Social Contract: An Inquiry into Modern Contractual Relations* (New Haven: Yale University Press, 1980), 4–5. See also Charles Fried, *Contract as Promise: A Theory of Contractual Obligation* (Cambridge, Mass.: Harvard University Press, 1981).

75. Morris R. Cohen, "The Basis of Contract," *Harvard Law Review* 46, no. 4 (1933): 553–592.

76. Robert Cooter and Thomas Ulen, *Law and Economics* (Reading, Mass.: HarperCollins, 1988), 230.

77. Victor P. Goldberg, "Toward an Expanded Economic Theory of Contract," *Journal of Economic Issues* 10, no. 1 (1976): 49.

78. There are some cases in which the voluntary agreements are restricted. For example, agreement detrimental to the institution of marriage, agreement related to sexual immorality, agreement to restrain the freedom of contract itself, and the like are regulated by the public power.

79. P. S. Atiyah, "Contract as Promise," *Harvard Law Review* 95 (1981): 509–528; Cooter and Ulen, *Law and Economics*, 230, 233–241.

80. Liberal contract law faces not only the problem of long-term contracts but also many other problems, and has filled the gaps with many variations and exceptions. In the

early liberal era, almost all cases in a liberal society were regarded as branches of a unified contract theory. But many cases, such as family law, labor law, antitrust law, corporate law, and even international law, came to be regarded as inassimilable to contract theory. The bodies of law and social practices such as fiduciary relationships were classified in an anomalous set of principles within the contract theory. But the problems of long-term contracts have been continuously repressed by the neoclassical economic model. See Robert Mangabeira Unger, *The Critical Legal Studies Movement* (Cambridge, Mass: Harvard University Press, 1983), 57–90.

81. Interview with G22 on 21 March 2000.
82. Markus Pohlman, Maja Apelt, Karsten Buroh and Henning Martens, *Industrielle Netzwerke: Antagonistische Kooperationen an der Schnittstelle Beschaffung-Zulieferung* (Munich: Rainer Hampp Verlag, 1995), 160–161.
83. "Der selbständige Zulieferer muss erhalten bleiben," *Handelsblatt*, 15 June 1966, 3; Geck and Petry, *Nachfragermacht gegenüber Zulieferern*, 38–39, 43, 52, 58–59; Monopolkommission, *Missbräuche der Nachfragemacht und Möglichkeit zu ihrer Kontrolle im Rahmen des Gesetzes gegen Wettbewerbsbeschränkungen*, 71–74.
84. Interview with G26 on 5 April 2000; interview with G48 on 10 May 2000.
85. Jack Beatson and Daniel Friedmann, "From 'Classical' to Modern Contract Law," in Jack Beatson and Daniel Friedmann, eds., *Good Faith and Fault in Contract Law* (Oxford: Clarendon Press, 1995), 7–17; Unger, *The Critical Legal Studies Movement*, 57–90.
86. Goldberg, "Toward an Expanded Economic Theory of Contract," 54–55.
87. Steven Wayne Casper, "The Legal Framework for Corporate Governance: The Influence of Contract Law on Company Strategies in Germany and the United States," in Peter Hall and David Soskice, eds., *Varieties of Capitalism* (New York: Oxford University Press, 2001), 387–416; idem, "Reconfiguring Institutions: The Political Economy of Legal Development in Germany and the United States" (Ph.D. diss., Cornell University, 1997); Gunther Teubner, "Legal Irritants: How Unifying Law Ends Up in New Divergences" in Hall and Soskice, *Varieties of Capitalism*, 417–441.
88. Beatson and Friedmann, "From 'Classical' to Modern Contract Law," 14–20; Melvin Eisenberg, "The Bargain Principle and its Limits," *Harvard Law Review* 95, no. 4 (1982): 741–801; John D. Calamari and Joseph M. Perillo, *The Law of Contracts*, 3rd ed. (St. Paul: West Publication, 1987), 406. For the development of Good Faith in the U.S., see E. Allan Farnsworth, "Good Faith and Contract Performance," in Beatson and Friedmann, *Good Faith and Fault in Contract Law*, 153–170. For the German case of Good Faith, see Werner F. Ebke and Bettina M. Steinhauer, "The Doctrine of Good Faith in German Contract Law," in Beatson and Friedmann, *Good Faith and Fault in Contract Law*, 171–190.
89. "Autoindustrie gefährdet industriellen Konsens," *Handelsblatt*, 25/26 June 1993, 19.
90. "Autohersteller brauchen die Zulieferer," *FAZ*, 5 March 1993, 15; Horst Wildemann, *Entwicklungs- und Vertriebsnetzwerke in der Zulieferindustrie* (Munich: Transfer-Centrum GmbH, 1998), 6–8; interview with G51 on 12 May 2000; interview with G44 on 5 May 2000.
91. Hall and Soskice argue that American contracts are "sharp in by clear agreement, sharp out by clear performance" due to their liberal market economy and liberal courts. See Hall and Soskice, introduction to *Varieties of Capitalism*, 30–31. But many sociologists' empirical studies have revealed the prevalence of non-contractual, informal norms even in U.S. markets. See Stewart Macaulay, "Non-Contractual Relations in Business: A Preliminary Study," *American Sociological Review* 28 (February 1963): 55–67; Hugh Beale and Tony Dugdale, "Contracts Between Businessmen: Planning and the Use of Contractual Remedies," *British Journal of Law and Society* 2 (summer 1975): 45–60; John Livermore, "Exemption Clauses in Inter-Business Contracts," *The Journal of Business Law* (March 1986): 90–102; Richard Lewis, "Contracts between Businessmen: Reform of the Law of Firm Offers and an Empirical Study of Tendering Practices in the Building Industry," *Journal of Law and Society* 9, no. 2 (winter 1982): 153–175; Peter Vincent-Jones, "Contract and Business Transactions: A Socio-Legal Analysis," *Journal of Law and Society* 16, no. 2 (1989): 166–186.

92. Helper, "Supplier Relations and Technical Change," iv-39.
93. Womack, Jones, and Roos, *The Machine That Changed the World*, 141, 145; Helper, "Supplier Relations and Technical Change," iv-45.
94. See K. B. Clark, "Project Scope and Project Performance: The Effect of Parts Strategy and Supplier Involvement on Product Development," *Management Science* 35, no. 10 (1989): 1247–1263; B. J. Zirger and J. L. Hartley, "A Conceptual Model of Product Development Cycle Time," *Journal of Engineering and Technology Management* 11, no. 3–4 (1994): 229–251.
95. For example, Eisenhardt and Tabrizi (1995) and Zirger and Hartley (1996) conclude based on their empirical study in the electronics industry market that suppliers' early involvement does not automatically reduce development time. See K. M. Eisenhardt and B. N. Tabrizi, "Accelerating Adaptive Process: Product Innovation in the Global Computer Industry," *Administrative Science Quarterly* 40, no. 1 (1995): 84–110; B. J. Zirger and J. L. Hartley, "The Effect of Acceleration Techniques on Product Development Time," *IEEE Transactions on Engineering Management* 43, no. 2 (1996): 143–152; D. L. Blenkhorn and A. H. Noori, "What It Takes to Supply Japanese OEMs," *Industrial Marketing Management* 19, no. 1 (1991): 21–30.
96. Jeffrey K. Liker and Yen-Chun Wu, "Japanese Automakers, U.S. Suppliers and Supply-Chain Superiority," *Sloan Management Review* 42, no. 1 (2000): 82.
97. Interview with BMW on 18 May 2000.
98. Interview with G21 on 20 March 2000.
99. Interview with A45 on 13 August 2001.
100. Interview with G35 on 19 April 2000; interview with G46 on 9 May 2000; interview with G48 on 10 May 2000; interview with A23 on 9 December 1999; interview with A22 on 9 December 1999.
101. OSAT and A.T. Kearney, Inc., *The 21st Century Supply Chain: The Changing Roles, Responsibilities and Relationships in the Automotive Industry* (Southfield, Mich.: A.T. Kearney, Inc., 1996), v, 3.
102. Wildemann, *Entwicklungs-, und vertriebsnetzwerke in der Zulieferindustrie*, 85.
103. In the process of social adjustments, German associations such as the VDA, BDI, and ArGeZ published unfair cases and recommendations for fair rules, which shall be examined in chapter 3 in detail. As for the U.S., it is easy to find unfair cases through my personal interviews and in periodicals.
104. Interview with A26 on 5 January 2000.
105. For German markets, see Petzold, *Die Zulieferindustrie*, 108–109, 139. Empirical studies in the U.S. also confirmed the fact that agents normally abided by the contracts. In the U.S., even "handshake agreements" were normally observed. See Macaulay, "Non-Contractual Relations in Business," 55–66; Otto Gandenberger, *Die Ausschreibung* (Heidelberg: Quelle & Meyer, 1961).
106. Interview with G22 on 21 March 2000.
107. Interview with G25 on 4 April 2000; interview with G26 on 5 April 2000.
108. Interview with A4 on 18 November 1999; interview with A8 on 24 November 1999; interview with A15 on 3 December 1999.
109. Interview with G26 on 5 April 2000; interview with G15 on 21 September 1999.
110. See appendix at the end of this volume.
111. OSAT and A.T. Kearney, Inc., *The 21st Century Supply Chain*, 31.
112. E-mail interview with US51 on 23 November 1999.
113. E-mail interview with US18 on 4 November 1999.
114. Suppliers in both the U.S. and Germany answered similarly, indicating that they give more information to their customers than their customers give to them. The reason for this apparent asymmetry might be respondents' biases—e.g., "I give more information than my customer"—or might be due to the fact that suppliers are required to hand over more information to their customers.
115. E-mail interview with US51 on 23 November 1999.

116. Susan R. Helper and Mari Sako, "Supplier Relations in Japan and the United States: Are They Converging?" *Sloan Management Review* 36, no. 3 (spring 1995): 77–84; Ram Mudambi and Susan Helper, "The 'Close but Adversarial' Model of Supplier Relations in the U.S. Auto Industry," *Strategic Management Journal* 19, no. 8 (1998): 775–792; OSAT and A.T. Kearney, Inc., *The 21st Century Supply Chain*, 30–31; Janet L. Hartley, "Collaborative Value Analysis: Experiences from the Automotive Industry," *The Journal of Supply Chain Management* 36, no. 4 (fall 2000): 27–32.

117. Ulrich Jürgens, "Communication and Cooperation in the New Product and Process Development Networks," 133–135; Andreas Bartelt, "Vertrauen in Zulieferbeziehungen der Automobilindustrie: Ergebnisse einer empirischen Untersuchung," Summary of Research Paper (Würzburg, Germany: Julius-Maximilians-Universität, 2000), 16 and table 7, 32. This is a summary pamphlet of Bartelt's research. Bartelt corrected some misprints in a personal meeting with me, particularly the figure of fairness-trust on page 26, which should be reversed.

118. For the explanation of power approaches, see Daniel Bieber and Dieter Sauer, "Kontrolle ist gut! Ist Vertrauen besser? Autonomie und Beherrschung in Abnehmer-Zulieferbeziehungen," in Mendius and Wendeling-Schröder, *Zulieferer im Netz*, 249–251; Dirk Riesselmann, "Entwicklung der Automobilzulieferindustrie," 177–181; Thomas Klebe and Siegfried Roth, "Autonome Zulieferer oder Diktat der Marktmacht?" in Mendius and Wendeling-Schröder, *Zulieferer im Netz*, 180–199; "Mittelstand wehrt sich gegen Preisdiktate aus den Reihen der Automobilindustrie," *Handelsblatt*, 22 July 1993, 3. The Economist Intelligence Unit in London predicted that only a fourth of German suppliers would survive to the end of the decade. See "Auto-Zulieferer stehen vor einer Revolution," FAZ, 6 September 1993, 16; "Suche nach Wegen für Kooperation," *Handelsblatt*, 31 August 1993, 13.

119. In order to avoid the respondents' bias, I raised this question only after identifying whether an interviewee was a sub-tier supplier. I asked the questions of 46 sub-tier suppliers in the U.S., while in Germany, I identified 28 sub-tier suppliers. Even in this small sample, the difference between the U.S. and German markets is significant.

120. The *Ward's Auto World* research team also tested similar questions in the U.S., asking whether first-tier suppliers are as aggressive as the automakers. Only 20 percent of respondents (automakers and suppliers) denied it. A majority of respondents (56 percent) answered yes. See Ward's Auto World, *Ward's Auto World 22nd Supplier Survey*, Supplement to Ward's Auto World (August 2000), 19; Andreas Bartelt, "Vertrauen in Zulieferbeziehungen der Automobilindustrie," 16 and table 7, 32.

121. Eberhard Hamer, "Zuliefererdiskriminierung: Machtwirtschaft statt Marktwirtschaft?" in Mendius and Wendeling-Schröder, *Zulieferer im Netz*, 75–76.

122. E-mail interview with US16 on 3 November 1999.

123. E-mail interview with US41 on 16 November 1999; e-mail interview with US44 on 17 November 1999.

124. "Risky Business in Detroit," *Industry Week*, 4 March 1991.

125. E-mail interview with US42 on 17 November 1999.

126. Interview with A30 on 21 January 2000.

127. E-mail interview with US20 on 7 November 1999; e-mail interview with US35 on 12 November 1999.

128. Interview with G29 on 12 April 2000; interview with G30 on 13 April 2000.

129. Interview with G41 on 28 April 2000; interview with G38 on 26 April 2000.

Chapter Two

TRANSFORMATION IN THE
AMERICAN SUPPLIER MARKET

The American automotive parts market has, like the German market, moved toward a new long-term and collaborative market system. Actually, many culturalists and institutionalists at the beginning of this transformation doubted that agents in the American supplier market would be able to build Japanese-style long-term and collaborative markets because of the individualistic American culture, the long tradition of the spot-market, and the fluid financial system. However, American agents in the automotive parts market have successfully adopted lean production and collaborative market relations. But contrary to prevalent belief, the adoption of long-term and collaborative markets did not automatically build trustful and stable relationships. Americans in the new collaborative market suffered from an abundance of opportunistism and distrust.

This chapter examines why American agents in the automotive parts markets have not made progress in their relationships, unlike the Germans. Why have Americans not developed a fair and trustful model as an alternative to the confrontational model? Why does an extreme form of formal fairness prevail in the U.S. market, while a conception of substantive fairness works in the German market? The basic explanation for the differences between the U.S. and German markets is that the manners of deliberation—the kinds of interactions and the ways of adjudicating conflicts—generate a specific form of market regime. In the absence of socially shared norms, and in the absence of democratic, participatory practices of creating norms in the public realm, powerful customers easily take advantage of incomplete contracts. In the final section of this chapter, I try to explain why American agents in the automotive parts market have not developed a public way of deliberating fair norms even though they have dense networks of associations similar to those of the Germans. Before examining the types of interactions and adjudication in the main sections,

---

Notes for this chapter begin on page 130.

I begin by giving a general overview of the characteristics of the U.S. automotive (parts) industry.

Although many industrial experts and observers hold that the organization of interfaces between customers and suppliers critically influences the performance of product and production improvement, agents in the U.S. automotive industry have failed to establish society-wide trustful partnerships. Toward the end of the 1990s and at the beginning of the twenty-first century, competition occurred in a different manner than in the 1980s, when competition was largely between American mass producers and Japanese lean producers. Recently, competition has arisen among all lean producers, since the traditional mass producers have adopted the Japanese-style lean production. Although the Americans have adopted lean production and collaborative markets, American automakers are losing their market share in almost all segments due to bad quality and the pathology of supplier relationships in the collaborative market.

Although American automakers have improved the quality of their vehicles significantly in the last decade compared with the 1980s, the quality of the vehicles built by U.S. companies has continuously lagged behind that of the Japanese transplants and German automakers, as illustrated in table 5.[1] Because they had more quality problems than their foreign competitors, American automakers were losing their market share at the turn of century. BMW, Lexus, and Mercedes have already surpassed American luxury cars like Cadillac and Lincoln. According to a survey of sales from late 2000 and early 2001, such key segments for the U.S. automakers as SUVs, minivans, and pickups, in which they enjoyed the highest percentage of sales during the past decade, began to show weaknesses. Automobile analyst Susan G. Jacobs, president of Jacobs & Associates, says: "I don't see a single segment where I think [the Big Three] will be gaining shares."[2] While the American Big Three lag behind, German and Japanese car makers are faring very well. As many experts point out, one of the main causes of quality problems is distrustful relationships all over the

TABLE 5 Share of the Blame

	Total vehicles recalled (U.S.)		Share of total vehicles recalled		Share of total vehicles sold	
	1999	2000[1]	1999	2000	1999	2000
DCC	5,719,804	6,590,052	29.7	28.2	15.6	14.5
Ford	6,398,883	7,485,466	33.3	32.1	24.5	23.9
GM	3,557,662	5,806,857	18.8	13.6	29.4	28.3
Toyota	589,190	8,379	3.1	0.03	8.7	9.3
VW	277,571	191,418	1.5	0.9	2.2	2.8

[1]Potential total.

Source: National Highway Traffic Safety Administration; Mayne et al., "Quality Crunch," *Ward's Auto World* 37, no. 7 (July 2001): 33.

entire chain of parts supply. According to the 2001 North American Automotive Supply Survey conducted by Birmingham-based Planning Perspectives, the reason the quality of the American Big Three's vehicles still lags behind that of Japanese vehicles is that the American automakers are putting too much pressure on the suppliers.[3] John Henke, Jr., president of Planning Perspectives, who has conducted similar surveys in the American automotive industry for eleven years, holds that two things have not changed in the last decade: first, the quality of U.S. vehicles has continuously lagged behind that of the vehicles made by the Japanese transplants; second, U.S. automakers consistently put far more emphasis on price than quality. In response to unfair treatment and unreasonable pressure, American suppliers skimp on quality, though without jeopardizing safety. As the research team of Planning Perspectives reports, suppliers believe that "If the Big Three will only give lip service to higher quality, why should they incur the cost to provide it, especially when they won't be paid for it, and it won't help them win new business?"[4] Suppliers are cutting services to the automakers, withholding the adoption of new technology and extra testing. As the research conducted by Liker and Wu in 2000 shows, the same U.S. suppliers perform better when they supply to Japanese automakers than when working with U.S. automakers.[5] Suppliers are less likely to provide important information to distrustful customers. American suppliers make fewer relational specific investments in business with U.S. automakers. At the turn of the century, Americans in the automotive parts markets suffered from distrust between customers and suppliers in the new environment of international competition between all of the lean producers.

Distrust and cynicism regarding "partnership" dominate relations in the U.S. automotive parts markets. The unfairness and distrust are not restricted to small suppliers in the American market. Contrary to the contention of power approaches that big system suppliers might develop trustful cooperation with automakers while small and non-system suppliers will not, as my survey shows and many other studies confirm, unfairness and distrust are not limited to lower-tier suppliers. In the U.S., the suppliers through all tiers are in distress due to customers' opportunism. Although first-tier suppliers feel distaste at automakers' unfair behavior, they put pressure on lower-tier suppliers in the same way that they are pressured by the automakers as chapter 1 of this book shows. Unfair and dictatorial approaches are adopted throughout the supplier chain of the U.S. automotive parts market. This is in contrast to the German market. German suppliers develop close cooperation with lower-tier suppliers. Regardless of the tier position and the size of the company, suppliers in the German automotive parts market build fair partnerships, as will be discussed in detail in chapter 3.

Another characteristic of the American automotive parts market is that customers and suppliers in the U.S. market have made little progress in relationships while agents in the German markets have ameliorated their relationships. This does not mean that the unfair regime in the U.S. and fair regime in Germany are predetermined by the traditional cultural heritages and institutions. Table 6 shows that Americans in the automotive supplier market have failed to establish fair partnerships despite long-lasting suffering from distrustful relationships. The massive research conducted by Helper in 1984, 1989, and 1993 on the American automotive

TABLE 6 Trajectory of Relationships in the U.S. Automotive Parts Market

Year[1]	Researchers (year)[2]	Evaluation of Relationships
1988	Arthur Anderson[3]	A dominant number of suppliers believe that trust is extremely necessary for the collaborative market.
1989	Helper (1991)	The 1984 and 1989 research conducted by Helper reveals that suppliers did not believe in 1989 that relationships with customers had improved compared with those of 1984.
1992	Dyer, Cho, and Chu (1998); Nishiguchi (1992)	The relationships in the U.S. automotive supplier market are characterized as confrontational and arms-length relationships. This is so even with the *"keiretsu*-like" suppliers in the U.S.
1993	Helper and Sako (1995)	The American automotive parts market converges toward the Japanese market in the sense that American agents develop long-term and closely linked relations as the Japanese do. However, even in the closely linked relations, suppliers feel a lack of trust.
1995	OSAT/A.T. Kearney (1996)	American automakers and suppliers experience tremendous changes in the form of working relations, but they fail to build sound partnerships.
1993–1996	Jürgens (2000)	American automobile companies are in distress in the interfaces with external suppliers to an extremely serious extent, although they have adopted new, flexible organization.
1996	Chotangada (2000)	American customers in the automotive parts market are engaged in confrontational relations even in long-term and collaborative work.
1997	Maloni (1997)	American automakers, in particular GM and Ford, undermine relationships with suppliers by using coercive power.
1999	Hartley (2000)	Trustful relationships between automakers and suppliers in the U.S. automotive industry are an exception rather than the rule.
2000	WAW (2000)[4]	The fair sharing of cost saving is rare in the American automotive supplier market. American suppliers are cynical about partnership

[1]Refers to the year when the empirical research was conducted.
[2]Refers to the publication year.
[3]Anderson research is quoted in Yost, "Components of the Past and Vehicles of Change," 386–387.
[4]"Ward's Auto World 22nd Supplier Survey," *Ward's Auto World* (August 2000).

parts market reveals that there has been no improvement in trustful relationships, although since the mid 1980s American automotive supplier
markets have converged toward the Japanese-style long-term and collaborative markets. According to the two independent research projects
of Nishiguchi (1992) and Dyer, Cho, and Chu (1998), most advanced relationships with the *keiretsu*-like suppliers in the U.S. parts market in the
early 1990s were still distrustful. Until the late 1990s and 2000, as studies
by Maloni (1997), Chotangada (2000), and *Ward's Auto World* show, agents
in the U.S. automotive parts markets did not make progress in their relationships, even though they developed a collaborative form of market. In
particular, according to the international research of WZB (Wissenschaftzentrum Berlin) led by Ulrich Jürgens, American automakers suffered
more with external suppliers than did the Germans,[6] whose agents in the
automotive supplier markets made progress toward fair and trustful relationships in the mid 1990s while their counterparts in the American market did not.

The long-lasting distrustful relationships and conflicts have led cynicism over partnerships and an extreme form of formal fairness to dominate
the U.S. automotive parts market. In the early period of transformation
toward a collaborative market, people in the U.S. markets also had expectations of substantive fairness. Many suppliers expected that it would be
fair if automakers and suppliers shared risks as well as benefits.[7] However, by the late 1990s there were few people who believed that it would
be unfair for a customer to push the price down, though the idea did
arouse distaste. People in the U.S. automotive parts market at the end of
the 1990s seldom expected the fair sharing of substantive benefits between a customer and a supplier; rather, they believed that so-called
unfair behavior was a part of life. In sum, fairness in the U.S. automotive
parts market has receded to extreme formalism. The rules of fairness are
just "rules of war" in which any attempt to survive is justified if it does
not apparently contravene the law. However, when the legality of a situation is unclear, the rules of the game become "the rules of the jungle."
Suppliers in the U.S. market accept customers' opportunistic behavior
as a given rule. The customers' behavior is fair if they treat competing
vendors equally, whether the customers' rules are distasteful or not.
Likewise, suppliers in the U.S. markets do not believe that customers'
violations of confidentiality and arbitrary revisions of contracts are
unfair if they treat all suppliers the same way. In the American markets,
the expectation of substantive fairness has receded to an extremely cyn-
ical formalism of fairness in which suppliers are excluded from the process of rule-making.

Why do distrust and cynicism over partnership prevail in the U.S. automotive supplier market even as it is transforming into a long-term and
collaborative market? Why have American agents not made progress in
their relationships while the Germans have? Why have Americans not

developed substantive fairness and trust as an alternative to the confrontational model?

Many cultural and institutional approaches emphasize cultural and institutional peculiarities to explain the differences of market governance. For example, some institutionalists, such as Casper and Teubner, hold that due to liberal contract law and courts, arms-length and complete contractual relations prevail as the national pattern of U.S. markets, whereas regulatory contract law and courts in Germany developed long-term and relational contracts. On the other hand, many institutionalists emphasize non-contractual norms and culture. The traditionally strong dependence on market forces and a Western legal philosophy emphasizing the value of autonomy in the U.S. contribute to the prevalence of the arms-length contractual relations. Many cultural approaches also stress that differences between German and Anglo-American culture account for economic governance and its performance. The strong tradition of *Technik* and the weak culture of business thinking in Germany account for the decrease in sensitivity to costs and the increase in managers' long-term cooperative commitments, whereas the business thinking and individualism in the U.S. create short-termism.[8] Meanwhile, many institutional and network approaches also call attention to institutional environments such as finance and associations—American companies were not expected to build long-term relationships due to their dependence on the stock market for finance.[9]

However, institutionalism is too rigid to understand the significant changes that occurred in the 1980s and 1990s. Even with the American peculiarity of culture and institutions such as liberal courts and individualism, Americans developed long-term and relational contracts in the 1990s. Trustful relations are not determined by culture and social institutions. American suppliers also developed trustful relationships with Chrysler and Japanese transplants on U.S. soil, even without Japanese-style culture and *keiretsu*-like institutions. In addition, the reason that Germans developed long-term contracts was not their courts' regulatory policy, which did not prevent German market relations from being short-term and distant until the late 1980s; moreover, Germans suffered from customers' unfair behavior in the first half of the 1990s as Americans did.

Institutions themselves—for example, the meaning, way of functioning, and effects of financial institutions—are subject to agents' reflection. Germans tried to disconnect their traditional ties between banks and industrial companies, and to deconstruct corporatist coordination, contrary to rigid institutionalist expectation. Also contrary to institutionalist explanation, the U.S. financial system did not cause paralyzing disruptions in developing long-term relations in the 1980s and 1990s. In the U.S. financial system, the board of directors became insiders, as opposed to outsiders, who only represent shareholders. They are more involved in scrutinizing corporate strategy and CEO selection. This contrasts with their behavior from the 1930s to the 1970s, when board members were simply the "abject creature[s] of management."[10] A study commissioned by the Institutional Investor Project of Columbia University demonstrates the extent to which board members are no longer outsiders. A vast majority of those interviewed rejected the idea of separation between the office of board member and that of CEO. The ideal model for a director is very similar to that of the CEO. Even given the dependence on the stock market, the board members themselves appreciate long-term investments and finance decisions in the same way that inside managers do. In particular, in the 1970s and 1980s, when U.S. companies underwent an economic crisis and Japanese competitors apparently succeeded, board members considered the adoption of a production system that resembled the Japanese-style system.

On the other hand, many institutional approaches and network theories also focus on associations for prevalence of trust. They argue that associations contribute to the stability of assembler-supplier relations, which are a major source of superior performance.[11] In particular, neo-Tocquevillian Robert Putnam maintains that dense networks of associations contribute to the emergence of cooperative "civic norms" and high economic performance. However, American association networks are almost as dense as those of German associations. Most American suppliers participate in one or two specific associations, as will be outlined later in this chapter. In each specific industry sector (such as metal forming, plastics, and machine tools) whose companies supply automobile manufacturers, American companies build dense associational networks at national and regional levels. In addition, contrary to the expectations of the institutionalists of Comparative Institutional Advantages, Americans have built new social networks to promote aspects of the public good such as social training, instead of enjoying the comparative advantages resulting from less embeddedness in social networks. What engenders the differences in governance between the U.S. and German markets is not the number of associations, but the way agents interact in associations in which the agents reinterpret existing institutions and deliberate norms. The Japanese supplier associations and close networks like *keiretsu*, which used to be frequently praised for their contribution to the development of trustful relationships, were reevaluated during the severe recession of the 1990s because of their rigid structure. Associational networks in Germany could not deter automakers' unfair behavior in the early 1990s, although they played an important role in establishing fair partnerships later in the 1990s. Again, what makes the difference in market governance is not the *number* of associations, but *the way that agents interact in associations*.

Although many cultural and institutional approaches focus on the fact that economic activities take place within a broad institutional and cultural framework, rigid institutionalists fail to explain the dynamic development of market governance, in which agents in the market make ongoing interpretations of the culture and institutions themselves and develop new strategies. This does not mean that institutions are not important in generating market regimes. Quite to the contrary, institutions can constrain agents' strategy and provide agents with a repertoire of solutions. This is not to refute the fact that institutions influence agents' activities, but to renounce a rigid view of path-dependent institutionalism that disregards agents' reflexivity. The view that institutions have constant meaning and characteristics independent of agents' reflection and reinterpretation is an erroneous result of the institutionalists' belief that they generate path dependent regimes and a persistent pattern of behavior. Institutions and cultural heritages are continuously reinterpreted and contested by reflexive agents; thus the meaning, way of functioning, and effects of institutions and culture that influence agents vary based on the politics of reflexive agents. In order to explain what makes for different consequences of market governance, this book focuses on the *manner of deliberation* in which agents reflect upon their institutions and strategies; institutions contested by agents influence different practices of norm-creation. The following section examines first what strategies the American customers and suppliers have developed in the process of establishing a collaborative market, and then how they interact and adjudicate the conflicts. This chapter will also illustrate why Americans do not deliberate conflicts in a public way, despite having sufficient networks for public deliberation.

Automakers and Suppliers in the American Market

Neither distrustful relationships nor short-term contracts are a predetermined national trajectory, contrary to path-dependent institutionalists' explanation. Chrysler and Japanese transplants on U.S. soil have developed trustful partnerships with suppliers. Even within the same national institutions and cultural heritages, reflexive agents develop different relationships: some trustful, while others not. The consequences are mainly related to agents' strategies and their interactions. In this section, two different paths in the American automotive parts market are initially investigated—the "fair partnership" versus the "adversarial and confrontational" model. The question is raised as to how Chrysler developed trustful relationships whereas GM and Ford damaged their relationships in the long-term and collaborative markets. These contrasting cases show, as I have stated, not only that the U.S. market is not predetermined by institutions and culture, but also that there exists the possibility of an alternative model to the confrontational relationships in the U.S., although Americans at the turn of the century had failed to develop further the burgeoning prospects for society-wide fair partnerships, while their German counterparts did.

The American Way of Partnership: The Chrysler Corporation

Chrysler and the Japanese transplants on U.S. soil have developed trustful relationships with suppliers, although relationships like theirs are not prevalent in the U.S. automotive parts market. Before Chrysler damaged relationships with suppliers by requesting comprehensive price cuts at the end of 2000, almost all suppliers agreed that for the last ten years Chrysler had been the best customer in the U.S. automotive parts market. Chrysler and the Japanese transplants are a benchmark for trustful relationships in the American automotive parts market. In this subsection, the manner in which Chrysler developed relationships with suppliers is investigated. One of the main reasons for the success of these partnerships is fairness in the sense of not only formal agreement but also substantive fairness. Chrysler made suppliers believe in the principle of fair distribution as it pertains to substantive issues, such as benefits and responsibilities for collaborative work. The case of Chrysler shows not only a way to establish fair partnerships on U.S. soil but also their limitations.

How was Chrysler able to change from its traditional and adversarial relationships to trustful partnerships with suppliers? Until the mid 1980s, Chrysler, like other automakers in the U.S., had made traditional neoclassical contracts in the parts market under the rationality of mass production, where the automakers' in-house engineers designed all components and then simply ordered the customer-designed parts from suppliers. Chrysler, like other American automakers, got the lowest price in the market by switching suppliers in the short term, providing customer-developed blueprints. Historically, Chrysler set the price through a competitive-bidding process and then put constant pressure on suppliers to reduce prices regardless of whether the supplier could reduce the costs. This led to the suppliers' minimal capital investment and involvement in the relation-specific production.[12]

During the financial crisis of the 1980s, Chrysler, like other American automakers, tried to learn lean production and collaborative supply chain management from Japanese companies. In the midst of this difficult period, Chrysler reflected on its existing practices and rationality of efficiency. During the crisis, Chrysler had had difficulty adopting Japanese production rationality: like other American automakers, it could reduce the number of suppliers and make long-term contracts, but it was not easy to build flexible and cooperative relations. Chrysler studied Honda, which had expanded its sales in the U.S. faster than Toyota in the mid 1980s. However, Honda's practices were "completely foreign" to Chrysler. It was after Chrysler acquired the American Motors Corporation (AMC) in 1987 that Chrysler became familiar with Japanese supplier relations. AMC had conducted a Japanese-style supplier relationship, involving suppliers in engineering and design of components because AMC had neither the capability to design all of its own parts nor the economic power to dictate the prices.[13]

AMC's experiment helped Chrysler's executives to change their viewpoint on economic efficiency and also introduced them to the process of forming a core group of people who could carry out the new idea of collaborative market relations.

Suppliers maintained close contacts with Chrysler because they were eager to offer the corporation innovative ideas for collaborative works when Robert Lutz, president of Chrysler, asked the suppliers for their assistance. Why didn't suppliers react cynically to Chrysler's request for help in the given tradition of adversarial relationships with the automobile company? At the time of Chrysler's crisis in the late 1980s, suppliers knew that "Chrysler was on the ropes."[14] In addition, Chrysler's new leaders changed their policies. Chrysler's senior executives visited key suppliers in order to get ideas from them. These unusual visits impressed suppliers, contrasting as they did with GM's tough bargaining and authoritarian attitude. Suppliers preferred a democratic method to traditional authoritarian relations. In keeping with its history, Chrysler, like other automakers in the U.S., had turned down suggestions from its suppliers earlier in the 1980s. However, Chrysler's new policy tried to induce suppliers' innovative participation in the process of development and production. Beyond their profitability, suppliers appreciated being listened to in the process of development and production. Through new policies, Chrysler encouraged, reviewed, and acted on suppliers' ideas quickly.

The process of forming fair partnerships in the new collaborative market was carried out not simply by changing outside relations with suppliers, but also by making inside alterations. In order to encourage suppliers' commitments, people inside Chrysler had to change their attitude, becoming more democratic and open. Considering suppliers' complaints that customers did not respond to or disregarded suppliers' new ideas for reduction of costs, it was very important to respond to suppliers' proposals in an agile and open way. As many suppliers point out, one of the main reasons for distrust is that customers' engineers do not respond to suppliers' proposals.[15] At the inception of the adoption of the new collaborative relations, there was resistance to the introduction of collaborative market relations inside Chrysler. Chrysler's engineers refused to consider suppliers' suggestions because reviewing and applying suppliers' proposals increased engineers' workloads. Pacifying the engineers, Francois Castaing, the head of vehicle engineering, encouraged engineers to simply give the new ideas a try. Chrysler's practices convinced suppliers that Chrysler had changed and become open to suppliers. Soon, the suppliers' proposals broke down the engineers' reluctance.[16] Chrysler's managers also helped suppliers make proposals, serving as the suppliers' advocates for Chrysler.

In addition, Chrysler changed the existing incentive system for buyers in the purchasing department. The traditional incentive system for purchasers in U.S. companies deterred the development of trustful and cooperative relationships between a customer and a supplier. Purchasers received bonuses and awards based on their individual achievements in cutting prices. Since they were concerned only with price cuts and did not focus on collaborative benefits, buyers were distrusted by suppliers. In contrast, Chrysler developed a new incentive system and evaluation process for purchasers, who began to be evaluated by the people (including suppliers) with whom they deal.[17] With a stake in their satisfaction, Chrysler's buyers became more open-minded toward suppliers.

The most important aspect of building trustful relationships at Chrysler was that the corporation developed fairness in the formal as well as the substantive sense in conducting business with suppliers. The formal fairness in Chrysler's practices contrasted with that of other automakers. For example, Ignacio Lopez, the purchasing director of GM in the early 1990s, negated contracts and reopened negotiations on price, taking advantage of the incompleteness of long-term contracts. By contrast, Chrysler convinced suppliers to believe their agreements; in addition, Chrysler was very cautious not to abuse the information provided.[18]

However, the most important element in building partnerships is not formal fairness but substantive fairness, which Chrysler showed toward suppliers. Chrysler tried to be fair not only in the process of setting goals for price reduction, but also in the distribution of risks, responsibility, and benefits resulting from collaborative work. Fairness in the substantive sense enabled suppliers to identify the common benefits with their own interests. A supplier describes Chrysler's fair way of doing business succinctly: "They [Chrysler] came to us and proposed that we share the benefits of cost reduction; I don't hear suppliers bellyaching about the way they did it. That's a reasonable approach—'Let's take cost out of the system and share the gains'; that sits better in the stomach of the supplier."[19] The main reason for suppliers' willingness to participate in collaborative work is that suppliers were convinced of the Chrysler program's substantive fairness. The next step is to observe Chrysler's substantive fairness in detail.

First, Chrysler creates a reasonable target together with suppliers, a process that they prefer over the "dictatorial way" of other customers. GM, for example, puts forth a target price that combines the cheapest elements of proposals GM has received from all suppliers in the market, repeating the rounds of bidding; thus, sometimes the price is ridiculously low. By contrast, Chrysler's target is a negotiated one. Chrysler first calculates the market price that will be paid for a vehicle by the end-customer; then, the allowable costs are offered to a component supplier. Instead of dictating the price, Chrysler and the supplier strive to find ways to reduce costs together. If the supplier has problems with reaching the target, Chrysler discusses the problems with them, supporting the suppliers in order to meet the target.[20]

Chrysler also appreciates suppliers' commitments. In other words, Chrysler evaluates the history of relationships with existing suppliers.

Unlike other American customers, Chrysler selects the best suppliers and tries to develop a long-term relationship. GM and Ford do not pay attention to the history of relationships with suppliers.[21] By contrast, if another supplier comes up with a lower price, Chrysler gives the existing supplier a chance to justify better points in quality, delivery time, and capability.

Chrysler shares the responsibility for collaborative work with suppliers. Although customers and suppliers develop a closely interactive working style, the way of carrying out collaborative work varies. Some share responsibility while others do not. Although almost all automakers organize customers' teams to visit suppliers, ostensibly to provide assistance, they differ in their use of the teams. Chrysler and Japanese transplants in the U.S. spend much time and energy cultivating competitive suppliers, while other American automakers simply insist on cost reduction; furthermore, they penalize suppliers for not following their requests.[22] Most suppliers believe that Chrysler's engineering teams help the supplier to be competitive and respect suppliers' innovative ideas. Many suppliers say that they address Chrysler more honestly and give more information to Chrysler than to any other customer.

Chrysler shares the savings in a fair way. When a supplier's proposal is accepted by Chrysler, the supplier has two options. One is that the supplier can claim its half of the benefits. Another is that it can deposit the savings for its performance rating and obtain more business from the automaker. Chrysler records the number of proposals each supplier has made and the total savings that the supplier has generated.[23] Chrysler and suppliers agree that fairness in distribution of cost-saving is key to the partnership. Bryan Zvileman, a Chrysler spokesman, says that "what makes the program [SCORE] so successful is that suppliers share the savings they bring to us and their profit margins are left alone."[24] Herb Haggard, president of Haggard & Stocking Associates, Inc., Indianapolis, Indiana, represents the suppliers' opinion, saying that "Chrysler works with you trying to retain your profits, and recognizes your need to make a profit in order to survive. GM and Ford don't concern themselves with the longevity of the supplier—they just care how cheap they can get it today."[25] Fairness in the distribution of savings enables suppliers to match the common benefits of collaborative work with their own interests.

Chrysler has greatly improved efficiency through trustful partnerships with suppliers by shortening product development, reducing the cost of development, and reducing defects.[26] The trust of suppliers facilitates the increase of their voluntary commitments in collaborative activities such as investigating cost reduction and investing in dedicated assets to serve Chrysler's needs.[27] The time it takes a new model of vehicle to be developed was reduced from an average of 234 weeks in the 1980s to 160 weeks, on average, in the 1990s. The total savings resulting from the SCORE program was $3.7 billion between 1989 and 1997. The overall cost to develop a new vehicle at Chrysler is much lower than at GM and Ford.

For example, Chrysler's Neon is similar to GM's Saturn and Ford's Escort. However, Chrysler's development of the Neon cost $1.2 billion, whereas GM's Saturn cost $3.5 billion and Ford's Escort $2.5 billion. Chrysler's Cirrus/Stratus is similar to Ford's Mondeo/Contour, but the Cirrus/Stratus cost less than $1 billion to develop, whereas the Mondeo/Contour cost $6 billion. Chrysler's profit per vehicle, which was lower than other automakers' throughout the 1980s, jumped from an average of $250 in the 1980s to $2,110 in 1994, the highest among the U.S. Big Three automakers, though it is true that Ford and GM also made a profit in the 1990s. What makes Chrysler different from Ford and GM is that Chrysler has increased efficiency through trustful relationships with suppliers.

Chrysler's partnerships illustrate the American way of partnership and its limitations. The case of Chrysler shows that customers and suppliers can develop long-term cooperative relationships even in a so-called individualistic culture, and in the fluid financial system. Fair governance in coordinating and distributing risks and benefits enables Chrysler and suppliers to establish stable and trustful cooperation. However, the case of Chrysler, as an ideal type of partnership in the U.S., also reveals the limitations of the development of partnerships in the U.S. Chrysler's partnerships are based on fair interactions in individual, dyadic relationships between a customer and a supplier. The fair norms that Chrysler developed have not become social criteria for governing long-term contracts. This is in contrast to the German case, in which the model of Mercedes' and BMW's relationships was articulated and spread society-wide by the suppliers and associations. The reason for the Americans' failure to build society-wide fair norms is that American suppliers and social agents such as associations did not deliberate fair norms in the public realm. It will be revealed later in this chapter that Americans considered Chrysler's fairness to fall within the sphere of personal and private relationships.

In the absence of society-wide fair norms, it is hard for a fair company to govern the decentralized supplier chains of the entire society. Even Chrysler's first-tier suppliers treated sub-tier suppliers in an unfair way, which caused quality problems for Chrysler. Chrysler's profits in 1997 declined for the first time since the introduction of new supplier relations. The main problem in Chrysler's supplier relations was the coordination of the supply chain. In 1997, Chrysler recalled many Cherokees because the fuel gauge still registered as full when they were running out of fuel. This led to customer dissatisfaction and decline of sales. A lower-tier supplier was identified as the source of the defect: the specification for the ink used on the register board in the fuel sender gauge had been changed.[28] In 1996, purchasing chief Thomas Stallkamp pointed out that "Most of our quality problems are not coming from the first-tier suppliers.... It's coming from the second and third tier, which do not have the same quality ethic yet."[29] Second- and third-tier suppliers can cause severe quality problems for the automaker. As the proportion of outsourcing increases and the collaborative form of market grows, it becomes more important to manage the entire supplier chain. However, because the whole supplier chain is too big for one automaker to manage, the dyadic way of establishing fair norms is limited in developing society-wide stable supply relationships, despite a potential need for democratic and decentralized self-governance through society-wide relations.

In addition, in the absence of socially shared norms, powerful customers can easily take advantage of an opportunistic policy. For example, Chrysler itself moved toward a confrontational policy by overruling existing trustful cooperation. At the turn of the twenty-first century, Chrysler damaged relationships with suppliers by forcing an aggressive price cut onto them. The problem for Chrysler was not just the size of the price cut, but the way it was implemented, considering the fact that other automakers requested similar price cuts in the same year. Chrysler's request for immediate price cuts by 5 percent in December 2000 was a turnabout from its old cooperative policy, a dictatorial way that contrasted with the existing fair method of cooperation.[30] Jeff Wincel, vice president of the Donnelly Corporation, says: "In the past, they [Chrysler] would say, 'let's work cooperatively'; now they are completely gone."[31] Just after Chrysler requested the "unreasonable" price cut, it lost its long-lasting top rank in the full use of suppliers' capability.[32]

The reason Chrysler adopted this confrontational policy might be that the crisis appeared too abruptly to expect a sudden sales downturn in 2000, as Chrysler managers emphasize.[33] The crisis of Chrysler mainly came from its failure to realize the expected synergy effects and from tougher international competition.[34] Nevertheless, crisis itself does not generate the confrontational policy automatically. Stallkamp, who founded the Chrysler partnership but left Chrysler in 1999 after clashing with its German owners, criticized Chrysler's current confrontational policy, saying: "It was at crisis that Chrysler founded the best supplier management."[35] It was also during a crisis period that Mercedes in Germany adopted fair partnerships with suppliers. As will be seen, Ford easily turned toward a confrontational policy in 1995, so it could not be denied that in the absence of society-wide fair norms and publicly mediated partnerships, it was easy for Chrysler to adopt the confrontational model. Lacking any society-wide model of fair governance, the powerful customers, including the higher-tier suppliers, easily take advantage of opportunistic policies and thus create distrust. The fair partnerships established in the individual, dyadic relations are hard to spread throughout society. As we see in the case of Chrysler's quality problem above, it is more difficult for one customer to maintain the cooperative partnership model in the absence of society-wide and publicly mediated self-governing norms, although fair partnerships in the U.S. are still an open possibility.[36]

The Confrontational Model in the Collaborative Market

Many people are confused about the differences between long-term contracts and trustful relationships or between closely interactive relations and trustful cooperation. Although the American automotive parts market has been transformed into long-term and closely interactive markets, relationships between automakers and suppliers are distrustful. Although Chrysler's relationships with suppliers demonstrate the possibility of the establishment of fair partnerships in the U.S., theirs are not a dominant style; instead, adversarial and distrustful relationships are prevalent in the U.S. automotive parts market. Ford and GM damaged relationships in the collaborative market by taking advantage of incompleteness and unclearness in the long-term, collaborative contractual relations. So-called unfair treatment and pressures were transferred down through the supplier chain. This section deals with why American customers and suppliers distrust each other even though long-term and collaborative contractual relations have been established. As the previous section revealed in the case of Chrysler, institutions such as the stock market do not predetermine the type of market governance. The ways of interactions between customers and suppliers generate the dynamic development of governance. The following subsections will examine first the case of GM, then Ford's relations with parts suppliers.

GM and suppliers. General Motors, ranked first among all U.S. automakers, formed a dominant type of transition toward long-term contracts in the American automobile parts market. By making the most of its huge economic power, rather than its mutual commitments, GM introduced long-term and collaborative contractual relations. J. Ignacio Lopez de Arriotua, chief of GM purchasing in the early 1990s, represents this type of strategy; in fact, people often use the name "Lopez" or "GM approach" to refer to distrustful relationships and unfair behavior. Although Lopez transferred to a German company (Volkswagen) in 1993, some of his methods are still prevalent in the American markets, while German companies do not use them anymore.

In 1992, when Lopez arrived from Europe, GM was in crisis, having sustained a $12 billion loss in 1990–1991. Lopez's strategy was to cut GM's bloated costs through rearranging the supplier relations.[37] This does not mean that the crisis itself automatically led to the confrontational model. On the contrary, the confrontational model was one of a number of possible methods of overcoming crisis. Lopez's approach built an archetype of the confrontational model in long-term and collaborative markets. The differences between GM's and Chrysler's relationships with suppliers resulted from their methods of adopting the collaborative market and of interacting with suppliers. GM's policy was characterized by the "use of bare power without fair governance," while Chrysler's was characterized by fair governance of interactions.[38] Like Chrysler, GM also sent assistant teams, called "efficiency teams," to its suppliers to rearrange equipment, material flow, and worker responsibilities. However, unlike Chrysler, GM's method of conducting jobs caused a great deal of distrust. Suppliers complained about GM's unfairness in the formal as well as the substantive sense. This subsection delves into GM's way of doing business.

The first thing suppliers complained of was that GM often violated the minimum criteria for business, that is, formal agreements. Although it was unclear whether arbitrary revision of contracts was illegal because the long-term contracts were incomplete, in the eyes of suppliers who were accustomed to keeping agreements, whether written contracts or handshakes, Lopez seemed not to honor contracts. This was a type of aggressive rule-making process by a powerful customer in a situation in which contract law did not work well due to its incompleteness and traditional norms for market governance needed reconsidering.

The first thing Lopez did after he came to Detroit in April 1992 was to make new long-term contracts while requesting organizational reforms and new investments. Long-term contracts are open-ended in terms of many items, including price and volume. One of the ways to govern incomplete long-term contracts was to use a fixed rate of price that reflected the future fluctuation of business and development of technology. GM requested a fixed rate of price reduction for the term of the contracts (e.g., a 5 percent discount in the first year, 5 percent in the second, 4 percent in the third, 4 percent in the fourth and 3 percent in the fifth). It is noteworthy that the price rate progresses in only one direction and plummets in comparison with traditional norms. Traditionally, suppliers could increase the price every year after making contracts. However, after Lopez's arrival, the direction of price adjustment violated the traditional norms. It is even more noteworthy that GM took advantage of the incompleteness of long-term contracts. Although GM and suppliers agreed upon the fixed rate of price reduction, it was not clear whether the agreement of percentage was legally binding or whether it was simply a type of guideline. Furthermore, there were many loopholes, so the fixed-rate agreement was hard to execute. With the frequent turnover of purchasing staff, buyers demanded more discounts, breaking the existing agreement of fixed-rate price reduction. To many suppliers, such unilateral revision constituted a breach of contract. However, if the existing suppliers did not accept a new buyer's demand for price reduction, GM's purchasers would threaten to reduce the volume of business with them or would sometimes transfer the business to another supplier in the middle of a contract by taking advantage of the unclear volume in the contract. Although suppliers followed the customer-revised price reduction, they did not receive any guarantee that GM would do business with them in the future. This arbitrary revision of long-term contracts occurred not only at GM, but also at Ford and other high-tier suppliers. GM reduced such cases of revision of contracts relatively at the end of the 1990s, while Ford and other high-tier suppliers continue to use such methods.

After repealing the current contracts, Lopez's next step was to nail down the price through multiple rounds of bidding. GM still uses such multiple or open-ended rounds of bidding.[39] An automaker normally has two or three potential and plausible suppliers for a component. However, when GM negotiates price, GM calls more than twelve smaller companies outside the normal and plausible suppliers, although the smaller suppliers cannot take full responsibility for the component. From all of the suppliers, GM gets extremely detailed information of broken-down costs for a component, such as material and labor costs. After GM gets the information on the costs of detailed elements, it combines the cheapest elements in each column of cost information and then offers a target price even lower than the sum of the cheapest elements. This is the first round of bidding. GM goes to multiple rounds (normally three) until a final supplier remains.

GM's strategy seemingly contradicts the form of collaborative markets. It chose the neoclassical principle of anonymity for the collaborative market. By using the incentive of long-term contracts, GM's strategy was to choose the "cheapest" product in the market instead of focusing on flexible application engineering with suppliers. Some suppliers described GM's purchasing process as "dehumanization." Purchasers become administrators rather than negotiators. The faceless committee of the central purchasing department determines the price for suppliers.[40] GM disregards the history of suppliers' commitments. For example, Bob Stevens, the president of Impact Forge, Inc., in Columbus, Indiana, was upset with GM's unfair actions. Impact Forge had received an award of the highest quality rating from GM. However, GM did not care about Forge's past assistance and award; only price mattered for GM. When Impact Forge suggested a 6 percent cost cut in response to GM's request of a 20 percent cost cut, GM pulled its $3 million in annual business.[41] This is in contrast to cases at Chrysler and the Japanese companies, where if a supplier gets an award from the customer, the supplier is fairly sure to get the business for the next project.

Another main reason for distrust is that GM transferred information provided by suppliers to their competitors. This violates the minimum and formal criteria for doing business in the sense of confidentiality, although it might not be illegal. In the process of bidding, GM copied designs and distributed them to other bidders in an attempt to increase competition among suppliers.[42] For example, suppliers would enclose in a bid various suggestions that would improve the product and lessen costs. Typically the ideas for improvement of a product and production were transferred to competitors to quote in the secondary rounds of bidding against the supplier. After repeated occurrences, suppliers became very cautious of their information. They now include only very vague ideas to meet GM's request.[43] The "confidential" problems occur not just in the process of bidding, but in the process of development and production. GM works with suppliers to develop a product and then transfers the prints and prototypes to other competitors of the suppliers. For instance, one supplier of plastic components worked with a customer to design and develop a product, investing a great deal of capital and energy in the process. However, before serial production, GM quoted under its own name the product that the supplier had actually developed, and then shared the prints with all competitors. Many suppliers lost the business even after they developed the product. These so-called confidential problems are now prevalent not only at GM, but also among other automakers and high-tier suppliers.[44] Such practices may not be illegal in a sense of positive law because the prints and prototypes are not patented in the process of collaborative work. However, suppliers believe such cases are unethical or unfair.

In the substantive sense of fairness, GM's practices are quite different from those of Chrysler and Japanese transplants in the U.S. The Japanese transplants and Chrysler try to share the burdens and responsibility for collaborative work with suppliers, while GM does not. For example, Japanese automakers in the U.S. invested time and energy to help suppliers improve their production and adopt lean production, whereas GM (along with many other American customers) threatened to stop business with suppliers who did not aggressively improve their production and quality. The result was a significant improvement of quality, but it occurred with little information exchange and mutual assistance. Suppliers had to solve the problems at higher costs for inspecting and reworking of the parts.[45] Even today, American automakers visit the suppliers for a one-day conference, whereas the people from the Japanese automakers spend a week or longer living with the people of the supplier company and thoroughly analyzing problems and inefficiency. My own experiences with American suppliers reveal that many American suppliers do not hesitate to mention Honda's and Toyota's cooperative approach as an example in contrast to U.S. customers' confrontational model.[46] Almost all of the suppliers who have worked with Japanese customers agree that the process is very painful but the results are beneficial. In the eyes of American suppliers, American customers request more proprietary information without giving any help. The proprietary information is used to cut the price in the next round of negotiation. American suppliers work in a mode in which they have to meet customers' formal requirements of providing information but must be very cautious not to give away their important information.

In the sharing of common benefits, GM looks like an unfair customer in comparison with Chrysler's fair sharing. GM tries to cut suppliers' margins for its own benefit. GM dictates a target price regardless of suppliers' production conditions, and sometimes requests that the price reduction be more than what a supplier can do. For example, one supplier reduced its price by more than 12 percent based on collaborative efforts with GM teams. However, GM teams requested a 20 percent discount in price. In the end, the supplier lost the business with GM. The collaborative efforts with GM resulted in the reduction of the supplier's margins.[47]

GM did not change the basic features of the Lopez approach much after he left GM in 1993. It was not until Harold Kutner took charge of GM's worldwide purchasing in July 1994 that GM began to consider partnerships with suppliers. The reason for the reconsideration of purchasing policy was that suppliers were reluctant to bring new ideas to GM for the improvement of products. Kutner described his policy as a "tough but fair" approach. Kutner tried to resolve cases of obvious unfairness.[48] However, GM is still backward in the realm of substantive issues such as distribution of risks and benefits. Although GM has softened its policies with suppliers, distrust still exists within its relationships with suppliers. The distrust is traceable not only to the after-effects of Lopez era, but also to GM's still maintaining so-called unfair policies in the formal and substantive sense.[49] GM does not share benefits and responsibilities for collaborative work. Some suppliers still feel betrayed because their ideas are abused by competitors and their contracts are revised arbitrarily although suppliers have invested in new infrastructure for GM production.

GM's strategy seems to be a somewhat awkward combination of the new collaborative market and the neoclassical policy. GM conducts business based on the neoclassical principle of anonymity in a situation in which they need trustful cooperation for flexible application engineering. This strategy aims mainly at getting the cheapest product among given products, rather than focusing on the collaborative application engineering with suppliers, although they have adopted the form of collaborative work. While GM requests that suppliers make a great deal of relation-specific investments of energy and capital, GM applies the anonymity principle of the neoclassical paradigm using its market power. This unbalanced policy has caused distrust among suppliers.

Ford and suppliers. Ford had relatively better relationships with suppliers than GM in the late 1980s and early 1990s, when Ford moved toward long-term and collaborative contracting. Until the first half of the 1990s, Ford was one of the most advanced automakers in the U.S. in adopting the new collaborative relations. However, in the mid 1990s Ford's relationships began to deteriorate. According to a survey by IRN, Inc., in the summer of 1999 Ford was the toughest customer in the American automotive parts market. Even while GM tried to reduce obvious unfair cases, considering the pathology of distrustful relationships, Ford took the confrontational policy. In this section, the reasons why Ford's relationships deteriorated are investigated.

The main cause for distrustful relationships at Ford is that Ford, like GM, wielded its power to redefine contracts in an arbitrary way and took advantage of the incompleteness of long-term and collaborative contractual relations. Ford, like GM, violated the minimum criteria for business norms through such practices as the arbitrary revision of contracts and the transfer of the provided information to competitors. Ford's method of collaboration was different from Chrysler's, although Ford has also adopted collaborative teams such as the VA/VE (value analysis/value added) team and SPECS (Supplier Purchasing Engineering Cost Suggestions), aiming to reduce costs through collaborative work with suppliers. However, many suppliers suspect that Ford teams are helpful in order to improve its competitiveness. A supplier compares Ford's teams with GM's infamous PICOS (supply management program) team: "It's difficult to smile [about Ford's VA team]; it's not exactly a PICOS, but the results could be equally devastating. They are getting closer to asking us to sacrifice our lives."[50] The reason for distrust is that Ford's teams search for price reductions rather than working together.

The relationship between Ford and Lear, one of Ford's key suppliers, illustrates the distrustful relationships between Ford teams and suppliers in collaborative work. Ford and Lear teams held regular meetings to collaborate on the development of the 1996 Taurus. However, engineers from Ford and Lear "could barely bring themselves to talk to each other, lest they inadvertently divulge proprietary information."[51] Ford teams did not trust suppliers, believing that suppliers would seize any opportunity to raise prices. In contrast, the Lear team knew that the Ford teams wanted to press prices down if there was a chance to do so. Many suppliers in my interviews reported that Ford VA/VE teams were not helpful to suppliers. For example, when a Ford VA/VE team visited a supplier of a fluid system, the supplier had to create thirty to forty new ideas about the production process and had to design to reduce costs. The supplier company spent four complete days developing new ideas. However, Ford purchasers and engineers did not allow the engineering to change because to approve a new design meant the failure of Ford engineers or increased workloads for Ford engineers.[52] Suppliers have learned through their experiences that Ford teams aim at taking as much information as they can from suppliers, with the objective of setting their own target price.[53]

It was in April 1995, when Ford was revising contracts arbitrarily and demanded a price cut of 5 percent each year over four years, that Ford's existing relationships started to deteriorate more severely. Actually, the arbitrary revision of contracts was inspired by the GM (Lopez) model in the early 1990s. Also, Ford sometimes used the policy of unilateral revision of contracts in the early 1990s. Meanwhile, Ford increased the number and frequency of requests for price reduction. The mood in April 1995, when Ford requested a comprehensive 5 percent price cut, was almost like a "supplier revolt." Suppliers charged the vice president of purchasing, Carlos Mazzorin, with tearing up contracts and demanding revisions even in hard times when the price of raw materials had risen.

Mazzorin's price-cut strategy came as Ford was downsizing its supply base through a global purchasing plan. In 1995, Ford tried to create a worldwide supplier network under the name Ford 2000. Ford was planning to reduce the supply base of the first-tier suppliers by up to fifty main suppliers on each continent; under each first-tier supplier, there would be ten sub-tier suppliers. This Ford 2000 plan placed suppliers in severe competition. Having fostered this competition among suppliers, Ford requested that they reduce costs by 25 percent over the next four years.[54] Ford's Mazzorin team thought that the remaining business was so big that the survivors would be able to work in a cooperative manner. Ford's expectation was correct in that the suppliers could not easily reject the customer's request. However, it was in error in that Ford expected that the suppliers would cooperate in a trustful way. One supplier of a special fastener reported its experiences.[55] In 1999, Ford called ten fastener suppliers among thirty to forty suppliers and requested a 5 percent price cut, saying that the ten suppliers were selected as long-term players for Ford. Although the supplier could not but concede to Ford, the supplier did not believe what Ford said about long-term business and cooperation. Paradoxically, Ford management regarded the process of building the collaborative market as a chance to take advantage of power imbalance instead of a way to establish trustful cooperation for better application engineering.

Based on the suppliers' evaluation, Ford is the customer that is most reluctant to share the benefits and costs of collaborative work. According to a survey by the consulting company IRN, Inc., in 1997 and 1999 Ford was the customer that asked for the biggest price reduction, 5.7 percent per year.[56] In addition, regarding the average length for which customers requested price reduction, Ford's time frame (1.8 years) was the shortest among American automakers. Ford has moved toward a year-by-year approach for price reduction. According to the IRN survey in 1999, suppliers gave Ford the highest score on the question of whether a supplier expected to be penalized in the future if the supplier did not grant a price reduction, indicating that Ford was the most punitive customer. This lack of substantive fairness caused distrust between Ford and suppliers.

In the absence of socially shared and publicly mediated fair norms, U.S. customers in the automotive parts market easily take advantage of unclear governance. In particular, in the absence of a participatory process of deliberation in the public realm, U.S. customers bear less of a burden to justify their unfair behaviors than Germans, who have to justify their position in formal and informal meetings. American suppliers and associations have not developed a public forum for deliberation of fair norms and adjudication of conflicts. At the turn of the century, most Americans in the automotive parts markets believed such unfair cases to be a matter of personal and private relationships, not a social problem, although there were some untraditional experiments with deliberation in the public realm. This will be discussed later in the section addressing the process of social adjustments.

Relationships between Suppliers

Relationships between high-tier and sub-tier suppliers in the American automotive parts market are also adversarial and distrustful although they have developed the new form of long-term and collaborative markets. Relationships between suppliers in the U.S. automotive parts market are in sharp contrast to those of the German market. German suppliers in the automotive industry have developed fair partnerships regardless of power and tier position, while Americans have not. German suppliers have developed a kind of solidarity among themselves in the process of adjudicating conflicts with automakers, while Americans have not. One of the main reasons for the prevalent distrust in the ranks of suppliers in the U.S. market is that American suppliers have not organized a method of society-wide adjudication of their conflicts with automakers. In a later section, the process of social adjustment will be analyzed in detail. In this section, an investigation is made as to how and why relationships between American suppliers have deteriorated. In particular, the strategies of American suppliers in the automotive parts market will be highlighted in order to show their ability to persevere in the midst of customers' unfair and tough pressure.

As chapter 1 of this book shows, my survey conducted in 1999 and 2000 reveals that distrust prevails among suppliers in the U.S. automotive parts market regardless of their size, power, or position in the tier structure. Many other empirical studies confirm that the relationships of American suppliers have deteriorated throughout the supply chain. The survey conduced by the Office for the Study of Automotive Transportation (OSAT) and A.T. Kearney in 1995 and 1996 demonstrates that American first-tier suppliers treat their own sub-tier suppliers in "unfair" ways while themselves complaining of automakers' unfair treatment and pressure.[57] According to the survey conducted in 1999 by the consulting company IRN, Inc., first-tier suppliers are the second toughest in the U.S., after Ford, in the realm of requesting annual price reductions (Ford: 5.7 percent; first-tier suppliers: 4.9 percent). In addition, first-tier suppliers are also the second most punitive customers in the question of whether suppliers expect to be penalized if they do not grant a price reduction—again, Ford is first.[58] Many sub-tier suppliers do not believe that their high-tier customers normally assist them in reducing costs. Another mini-survey, conducted through my personal interviews and e-mail interviews with U.S. and German suppliers, corroborates the observation that almost all sub-tier suppliers (about 90 percent) in the U.S. automotive parts market agree that the buck has been "unfairly" passed down through the supply chain; by contrast, most German sub-tier suppliers (89 percent) agree that they are not confronted by their customers, which are high-tier suppliers. *Ward's Auto World*'s 22nd survey in the U.S. and Andreas Bartelt's extensive survey in Germany confirm my finding that the relationships between German high-tier suppliers and sub-tier suppliers have not deteriorated as much as those of their American counterparts have.[59]

Why have relationships between American high-tier and sub-tier suppliers deteriorated? Why does distrust prevail? The main reason is that the high-tier suppliers in the U.S. automotive parts market choose the strategy of transferring the burdens to the sub-tier suppliers; Germans, on the other hand, are less likely to choose this strategy. American first-tier suppliers such as Delphi, Lear, Navistar, and Visteon transferred their burdens directly to sub-tier suppliers. As one supplier describes it, "like water running downhill," the pressure rolls down to the next tier level. For example, when Chrysler demanded a 5 percent price cut in 2000, suppliers transferred the request all the way down through the supply chain. Most first-tier suppliers placed similar demands on their sub-tier suppliers in the wake of Chrysler's 5 percent price cut.[60] Michael Heidingsfelder with Roland Berger, a consulting company, says that "The OEMs [automakers] are doing it, so [the high-tier suppliers] just kick the ball to the next level."[61] The aim of American suppliers is to easily and immediately recover the losses resulting from automakers' pressure. The problem is not just the intensity of the pressure rolling down on sub-tier suppliers, but the way they are treated. The high-tier suppliers treat the sub-tier suppliers in unfair ways that are similar to the ways they get treated by their customers.

The reason American suppliers so easily accept such opportunistic behavior is not the hierarchical structure between suppliers. Germany also developed tier structure in the 1990s, reducing the direct contact between automakers and suppliers. American suppliers failed to develop "fair partnerships" among themselves because of their market strategies and their preference for a process of adjudicating conflicts in an individual way. The suppliers' strategies and ways of responding to customers' tough treatment will be investigated before the process of adjudicating conflicts is illustrated in detail in a later section.

It is difficult to pinpoint a single and sweeping strategy among various companies. However, as many industry observers have pointed out, the volume-orientation mentality prevails in the U.S. automotive parts market.[62] To improve their competitiveness in the market, many American suppliers emphasize efficiency based on volume economy, whereas German suppliers focus on specialty orientation. Most, if not all American suppliers tried to make up for the lost profits that resulted from the automakers' high pressure with volume gains. American suppliers try to increase volume by making price concessions. American suppliers in the automotive parts market push their profit margins to near zero in order to win business, hoping to find profits later, or calculating that volume makes money. However, the large capacity for volume production forces the suppliers to concede more of their profit margin in the next round of negotiation to run the overcapacity.[63] At the same time, volume orientation reduces the complementarity between suppliers and increases the competition among them.

The reason that American suppliers in the automotive parts market emphasize price leadership and efficiency based on volume is that they focus on easy access to unskilled workers and the automakers' overemphasis on price, compared with German companies. It shall be discussed in chapter 3 how the prevalent strategy of German companies is different from that of U.S. companies. German suppliers pay more attention to product differentiation in the market in consideration of their expensive labor costs and highly skilled workers. As is shown in table 7, U.S. companies in the automotive industry have enjoyed relatively low levels of wages due to weak trade unions, while German companies have suffered from a high level of labor costs due to their strong trade unions.

TABLE 7 Labor Costs in the Automobile Industry (vehicle and parts industry)

	1980	1985	1990	1995[1]
Germany	100	100	100	100
France	98	102	68	71
Italy	92	95	82	79
Spain	87	118	72	79
U.K.	125	93	93	93
Japan	60	64	56	56
U.S.	86	85	66	55

[1]Estimation.
Note: The unit indicates a relative value under the assumption of labor costs of Germany = 100.
Source: Original source VDA (*Handelsblatt*, 15 March 1995, 21).

Proceeding contrary to institutionalist explanation, Americans have also tried to improve training systems by utilizing associations, and regional governments and various institutes recently have been supporting private companies in training workers. On the whole, though, many American companies still tend to focus on utilizing their easy access to cheap and unskilled workers in the labor market, rather than on differentiating their products based on skilled workers. In the absence of institutional constraints like the surveillance of layoffs by German trade unions and works councils, and against a background of relatively low wages and a large unskilled worker pool, American suppliers are oriented toward the so-called "volume economy" and price leadership in the market, whereas German companies in the automotive (parts) industry emphasize product differentiation and product innovation by well-paid, highly skilled workers. According to an empirical survey conducted by Birou and Fawcett, American companies are strongly oriented toward price leadership compared with

European companies, which focus on more product differentiation for the market, as table 8 shows.[64]

TABLE 8 Strategic Orientation—Low Cost vs. Product Differentiation

Characteristics	U.S. Rating	European Rating
Competitive pricing	6.10	5.52
Innovation in manufacturing Process	5.33	5.00
Innovation in marketing techniques	4.37	5.04
Low cost	5.53	5.34
Product differentiation	4.98	5.24

Note: Likkert Scale: 1=not important; 7=extremely important.
Source: Birou and Fawcett (1994, table 3).

In particular, as Lay and Wallmeier's empirical research reveals (see table 9, "Competition Strategy Following the Size of Company," in chapter 3 of this book), German companies in the automotive parts market focus on quality, innovation, and product differentiation, rather than prices, for their market competitiveness.[65]

American suppliers' strong orientation toward price leadership also stem from the fact that their automakers focus too much on price. According to an empirical study of 250 American first-tier suppliers conducted in 2001 by the consulting company Planning Perspectives, American automakers are focusing more than ever on price in the selection of suppliers, while Japanese transplants on U.S. soil are continuously balancing price with quality.[66] In response to automakers' high pressure and unfair treatment, many suppliers in the U.S. automotive parts market orient themselves toward low-cost strategies rather than focusing on product differentiation and flexible application engineering with their suppliers or customers. The prevalence of automakers' opportunistic behavior deters suppliers from investing energy and capital in a specific, collaborative work. As automakers cut prices in a given market, rather than saving through close application engineering with suppliers, suppliers in the U.S. automotive parts market are also less likely to involve the automakers in value engineering. Based on her empirical survey of American automotive suppliers, Janet Hartley holds that few first-tier suppliers have involved the automakers in value engineering in the past two years.[67]

U.S. suppliers in the automotive parts market have become oriented toward a volume economy because of reduced utilization of application engineering due to distrustful relationships, easy access to unskilled workers, and customers' tough pressure on prices. The dominant strategy in the U.S. automotive parts market has been to achieve economies of scale, with suppliers trying to increase the volume of sales for a given investment in research and development to meet the tough pressure of costs. Volume orientation increases competition rather than complementarity among suppliers, which has negative effects on the development of partnerships among them.

More importantly, as automakers request that suppliers take more responsibility for sub-assemblies like modules and systems, many American suppliers have tended to meet the demand by merger and acquisition of other supplier companies, rather than collaborating with other parts suppliers as Germans did. In the situation in which horizontal cooperation among suppliers has developed less, many American first-tier suppliers have opted for quick growth by acquisition, which reinforces the difficulty of horizontal cooperation. Many American suppliers believe that the complicated modules have enabled them not only to have room to adjust cost reductions but also to occupy the market share due to its newness. In addition, the fluid financial system based on the stock market facilitates easy takeovers of other companies, although contrary to institutionalist expectation, the stock market system did not deter American companies from developing long-term market relations.[68]

As the "Global Automotive Deal Survey" conducted by PricewaterhouseCoopers in 1998 reveals, the number of deals in the U.S. is greater than that in any other country.[69] For example, there was a total of 320 deals among automotive suppliers in the world in 1998. American companies were involved in 56.6 percent (180 deals). Although German suppliers also followed the trend, the deals with German companies comprised only 6.9 percent. American companies bought American in 108 deals (34 percent of world deals), whereas only 9 deals were between Germans (3 percent of world deals). The quick growth by acquisition that has occurred during the last five years in the calculation of volume economy as well as module production has caused economic inefficiency. Recently, for instance, large American first-tier suppliers such as Federal Mogul and TRW have suffered from economic inefficiency.

The quick expansion has also caused an overlapping of the main players' products, deterring trustful cooperation among suppliers in the U.S. market. In the round table of automakers' simultaneous engineering, components and module suppliers are very cautious about providing information on their own specialties because they are potential or current competitors.[70] For example, when an automaker and other suppliers in this environment ask a clutch supplier about the know-how and detailed information involved in clutch making, the clutch supplier does not want to reveal much. The reason for this reluctance is that one of the other suppliers also makes a clutch, although the company supplies only a clutch actuation for the current project. The clutch maker thinks that the clutch actuation maker will pass the information on to its clutch-making division. Although suppliers work together by being held responsible for different parts of a project, their product ranges overlap. Under the huge movement of consolidation in the U.S., this holds especially true for the big module and component suppliers. In the German automotive parts market, the dominant strategy of specialization generates complementarity among suppliers, whereas the dominant strategy of volume economy and quick expansion in the U.S. causes overlapping among suppliers' products. Thus, cooperation among suppliers in the U.S. automotive parts market is more likely to be deterred than in the German market.

The individual, dyadic way of deliberating conflicts and unfairness and the prevalence of a consolidation strategy reinforce each other in the U.S. automotive parts market. American suppliers try to solve unfair treatment through individual, dyadic relations with a customer: compromising with the customers or ignoring the problems in order to continue business relationships. In the absence of collective adjustments, the most popular response by American suppliers to so-called unfair treatment and pressure is that suppliers try to increase their own leverage, believing that power determines relationships in the market. The way to increase leverage is to become competitive or to consolidate a market by acquisition. Consolidation is one of the main strategies in response to pressure and the unfair treatment applied by customers. Neil de Koker, director of the Original Equipment Suppliers Association (OESA), succinctly points out one of main causes of consolidation: "Cost pressures are likely among the biggest forces behind consolidation, as companies merge in hopes of finding some sort of savings in the higher volume."[71] In the absence of society-wide adjudication and collective solutions, consolidation has become one of the dominant strategies in the U.S. automotive parts market. It is preferred not only because of the calculation of a volume economy, but also because of considerations of relative power in the supplier market. Consolidation diminishes the possibility of social adjustment and horizontal cooperation between suppliers, which further reinforces an individual, dyadic solution.

This individual, dyadic method of deliberation is one of the main reasons for American suppliers' failure to develop fair partnerships. In the absence of a public method of deliberation, Americans in the automotive parts market have failed to establish society-wide fair norms, unlike their German counterparts. American customers did not bear the burden of justifying their behavior in the civic public realm and thus easily took advantage of opportunistic policies, unlike the Germans. Lacking the opportunity for collective adjustments, American suppliers have resorted to individual solutions: a few strong suppliers rebuff all inquires into cost structure and let customers go to another supplier; however, most suppliers "grin and bear it" or "keep smiling even though they are bleeding inside" when they experience so-called unfairness. Without recourse to society-wide adjudication of conflicts, American suppliers simply hold their sales ground by tolerating unfairness in the hope that they might be stronger in the future. American suppliers try to solve problems with their own power relative to a customer's, and by increasing their individual leverage relative to their competitors'.

German suppliers, on the other hand, have created more stable market governance through formal and informal meetings. It is noteworthy that German suppliers objectify their position in the process in which they adjudicate conflicts in the public realm. German suppliers set their own fair rules in the public eye through the process of criticizing automakers' unfairness. And having criticized their customers' unfairness in the public realm, suppliers can hardly treat their sub-tier suppliers in the same way their customers treat them. By contrast, in the absence of such participation in public deliberation, American high-tier suppliers can easily treat their sub-tier suppliers in the same unfair way that they are treated by their customers. In the individual, dyadic way of adjudicating conflicts, American first-tier suppliers are less likely to objectify their relative position in the entire supply chain. According to the survey conducted by OSAT and A.T. Kearney in 1995 and 1996, "[American] suppliers focus primarily on their relationships with their customers and less on their relationships with their own suppliers, where they often still follow a selection model."[72] The selection model, which refers to the adversarial way of purchasing based on the principle of anonymity, contrasts with the development model, in which a customer commits itself to its suppliers by working with them to improve price, quality, and technology. Lacking a participatory process of public deliberation in which agents objectify their relative position and express their own rules, American high-tier suppliers easily transfer unfair treatment and pressure all of the way down through the supply chain. In the next section, the effects of the individual, dyadic way of deliberation in the U.S. automotive parts market will be illustrated in detail.

Social Adjustment in the U.S. Automotive Parts Market

Although agents in the U.S. automotive parts market are involved in many formal and informal networks, they have not developed a public way of deliberating conflict and thus have been unable to achieve the effects of the public way of adjudicating conflicts that German agents did. Society-wide shared norms established through conflicts and adjustments in view of the public are hard to violate without losing face. In particular, in the process of criticizing customers' unfair behavior, suppliers in the German automotive parts market not only set up their own fair criteria, but also created solidarity among suppliers. In contrast, American agents have not had a chance to express their own rules and articulate norms in the public realm. American associations have not organized a public way of adjudicating conflicts and elaborating ethical codes. Although American suppliers believe that other suppliers are suffering similar problems, they do not consider so-called unfair behavior to be a social issue that should be discussed from the perspective of making "rules of the game" for the market.

Why haven't American suppliers dealt with unfairness as a social issue in the public realm? Is it because Americans have fewer associations than Germans? In this section, the manner in which individual, dyadic ways of adjudicating conflicts affect governance and conceptions of fairness will be investigated, and the reasons the associations have not developed a public method of adjudication will be highlighted. The argument presented is that Americans have no fewer associations than do Germans; rather, the failure to organize public deliberations arises from different understandings of public versus private forms of jurisprudence. Utilitarian liberalism, the prevalence of which has been confirmed by practices in the U.S. automotive parts market, hinders the development of a public way of adjudicating conflicts in market society, although it is also being contested. Before highlighting the process of adjudicating conflicts, the networks of associations and the social fabric of the U.S. automotive parts market will be scrutinized.

Social Fabric

Many institutional approaches and network theories emphasize that associations contribute to the stability of assembler-supplier relations. In particular, neo-Tocquevillian Robert Putnam maintains that dense networks of associations contribute to the emergence of cooperative civic norms and high economic performance.[73] Many institutionalists believe that the reason for adversarial relationships in U.S. industries is their sparse networks of associations and pervasive individualism, whereas the dense networks of Japanese and German associations facilitate cooperation among companies.[74] However, contrary to these prevalent beliefs, U.S. companies in the automotive parts market are not playing alone. Agents in the U.S. automotive parts market are involved in as many associations as Germans are. People in the U.S. automotive parts market have also developed untraditional associational networks such as training centers, in defiance of rigid institutionalist expectations. Regional governments in the U.S. contribute to the formation of social capital as well. What makes the difference in market governance is not the *number* of associations, but *the way that agents interact* in associations. In this section, the ways that agents in the U.S. automotive parts market interlink to form a social fabric are investigated.

Contrary to institutionalist explanation, American associational networks are almost as dense as German associations. My research shows that most American suppliers in the automotive parts market take part in one or two specific associations in much the same way that Germans do in their automotive parts market. American associations do not number fewer than German associations in the automotive parts market. Not only do agents in the U.S. market take part in general associations such as the Motor Vehicle Manufacturers Association (MVMA), the Motor and Equipment

Manufacturers Association (MEMA), and the Society of Automotive Engineers (SAE); they also participate in specific functional associations, such as the Industrial Fastener Institute (IFI), the Rubber Manufacturing Association (RMA), the Precision Metal Forming Association (PMFA), the Gasket Manufacturer Association (GMA), the Precision Machined Production Association (PMPA), and the Spring Manufacturing Institute (SMI), among others. In each technical segment of the U.S. automotive parts market, there are specific associations at the regional as well as the national levels, just as in the German market. Approximately 160 associations work in areas related to the automotive industry.[75] American suppliers are linked not only by their technical specialties, but also by various identities, such as the Michigan Minority Business Development Committee (MMBDC), and by various interests such as the West Michigan Group and the West Michigan World Trade Association.

In addition, contrary to what the institutionalists of Comparative Institutional Advantages contend, American suppliers have built new organizations—such as the Automotive Original Equipment Suppliers Association (OESA), founded in 1998—to represent their own collective voice.[76] Comparative Institutional Advantages institutionalists such as Hall and Soskice argue that companies of a nation-state gravitate toward specific strategies that take advantage of the opportunities that the peculiar institutions of the national economy offer in comparison with other countries; thus, national economies are systematically different. According to the institutionalists, U.S. companies (should) take advantage of the opportunities that "liberal market systems" of free competition and weak social networks provide.[77] However, contrary to the expectation of the institutionalists of Comparative Institutional Advantages, U.S. companies did not stick to the strategy of enjoying the advantages determined by existing institutional frameworks. Instead, Americans reconstructed the institutions themselves. Americans have also collaborated for the public good, using the existing associations to promote training systems or building new social networks instead of sticking to the advantages of liberal markets framed by institutions. Throughout the U.S., new social networks of inter-firms, community colleges, and trade unions came into being in the 1980s and 1990s.[78] U.S. employers are interested in and have cooperated for the development of social networks that mainly focus on training programs, intermediation of job markets, and manufacturing extension services.

Recently, many regional business communities have been created for cooperative social programs in the U.S. For example, the Private Industry Councils and the Regional Employment Boards are community-based organizations constituted of employers, local government officials, educators, and labor representatives. The Regional Employment Boards were created by the recently enacted Workforce Investment Act. The Private Industry Councils and the Regional Employment Boards develop cooperative programs for upgrading skills and for continuous training of workers.

The community-based organizations also build national networks; for example, approximately forty community-based organizations representing one million families throughout the U.S. organized the Industrial Areas Foundation (IAF).

New social networks have sometimes been initiated by the current employer associations, or by trade unions, regional communities, and regional governments. For instance, one existing employer association, the National Tooling and Machining Association in Massachusetts, organized small machine shops into a network in order to train workers and share technical information. Trade unions have also initiated new social networks. For example, the UAW in the Detroit area initiated a Labor-Management Council for Economic Renewal, a kind of partnership among fifty five firms and their unions for the purpose of promoting organizational restructuring such as continuous improvement programs. The AFL-CIO has worked with local union leaders to build interfirm and industry-specific networks. Employers, trade unions, community institutes, and regional governments have cooperated for the establishment of new social networks such as consortiums, committees, working groups, and conferences to facilitate suppliers' rationalization of production. For example, the Wisconsin Manufacturing Extension Partnership organized a consortium for training between management and workers in about sixty metalworking companies that employ about 60,000 workers in the Milwaukee metropolitan area.[79] The state technical college organized a training consortium aimed at improving the management of quality and training of workers for small- and medium-sized supplier companies. Automakers like Ford are involved in the training and rationalization program. Ford operates a training program for quality improvement and inventory in collaboration with Cleveland's Manufacturing Technology Center (CAMP).

Many social networks have been supported by public authorities. According to one study, about twenty seven states in the U.S. were supporting 140 networks in 1994.[80] Some networks have been created by public authorities. Approximately 100 manufacturing extension service centers have been founded through a federal program called the National Institutes of Standards and Technology (NIST), housed under the Department of Commerce. Since 1998, the Department of Labor has funded a number of local partnerships. In addition, state governments in the U.S. facilitate the formation of social networks for industrial rationalization. For example, the Illinois Department of Commerce and Community Affairs (DCCA) funded a worker training system for small- and medium-sized suppliers. The DCCA has also funded associations and large customer companies such as Deere and Caterpillar to organize suppliers for training programs. In the training program, managers as well as workers from the supplier companies receive training for new organizational reform, learning such skills as statistical process control, short-cycle manufacturing techniques, and computer literacy. The state of Illinois has developed a concept of clustering in the training system, whereby a group of suppliers forms clusters around large customer companies. The Deere Company offers training courses at its own facilities as well as at other sites, including community colleges; about 100 supplier companies and their 6,000 employees take part in the program. Caterpillar conducts training at its in-house institute, including about 825 employees from 72 supplier companies.[81]

Existing associations have also actively worked for organizational reform and employee training programs, sometimes supported by the state government. For example, the Tooling & Manufacturing Association (TMA) of Illinois, an association of supplier companies, focuses on training programs in the same way that other regional associations in the U.S. do.[82] TMA offers about 100 courses and seminars related to tool- and die-making and precision sheetmetal and model-making. As other associations in the U.S. automotive parts market do, TMA organizes topics for training in which members are interested. Recently, TMA has been organizing lean production issues in collaboration with a consulting company called the Chicago Manufacturing Center. The state government supports such social activities through the associations. TMA gets support from state government programs called Prairie 2000 Assistance and the Industrial Training Program, which reimburse members 50 percent of the fees for some training programs.

Social networks might contribute to a stable community, which facilitates the sharing of common norms and makes social reprimands possible. However, social networks do not automatically generate cooperative civic norms. The reason for the failure to establish fair norms in the U.S. automotive parts market is not the absence of associations and social networks in which people can deliberate and adjudicate their conflicts; rather, it mainly lies in the *way of interacting* in the social networks and the *way of understanding social problems*. This topic will be addressed in more detail later; first, other aspects of the social fabric that might bring about different forms of governance from that of the German markets need to be explored: associational structure and personal relations.

With regard to associational structure, American associational networks are different from their German counterparts, although the number of associations in the U.S. and German markets is similar. German associations are comprehensive in their activities, while American associations are specialty-oriented and fragmented. American associations try to establish their own boundaries, and one specific goal is competing for memberships. This motive enables associations to fill a newly emerging vacancy as the industry and markets develop.[83] American associations have specialized their activities by limiting boundaries in order to maintain memberships within the association. For example, there are many associations of metal-working companies at the national level in the U.S.: the Precision Metal Forming Association (PMA), the National Tooling & Machine Association (NTMA), and the Precision Machine Product Association (PMPA), among others. There are also local associations such as the Tooling & Manufacturing Association (TMA) in Illinois and the Michigan Tooling Association (MTA) in Michigan. To compete for members, associations develop their own specialties. Different associations have different priorities and agendas.[84] For example, the PMA has a strong capability to support training and marketing but is not as strong in lobbying as the NTMA; the TMA and the PMPA are similar in the priority of education and training but specialize in different technical areas.

On the other hand, the relationships between national and regional associations are not hierarchical. They too occasionally compete with each other for members. Local associations like the TMA focus on the training of local companies, while the national associations call attention to lobbying in Washington, D.C., or have representatives in international organizations. On some issues, the local and national associations compete for members, while they do not on others. This is different from the structure of German associations. In Germany, regional associations conduct comprehensive activities in an industry, and the corresponding national association coordinates the local branches. By contrast, the structure of American associations is fragmented due to their specialty orientation. Also, the relations between associations are not stable but temporal. The existing associations cooperate with each other on a specific issue and then disperse after solving the problem. Many temporary coalitions have been formed to address tax relief, tariffs, health care, and the like. In representing the various interests of its members on many issues, sometimes one association (such as the TMA) makes coalitions with another (such as the NTMA, while it does not on other issues. In a coalition, different associations come together as if they have put their names on a petition list. After an issue is solved, the coalition dissolves and a new coalition is established to address a new issue.

These issue-oriented, ad hoc coalitions and the specialty-orientated fragmentation of the American associations might limit the capacity to create society-wide public norms. One reason that many American associations in the automotive supplier market have not initiated deliberation of fair norms in the public realm is that they are not interested in discussing "ethical issues" owing to their narrow specialty orientation in the competition over membership. Bruce Brake, president of the TMA, said, "If an association conducts a general and comprehensive thing, the service area of the association will be poached by other special associations." Many local associations like the TMA do not organize a public way of deliberating fair norms and adjudicating conflicts because such activities are not necessary for attracting members. In addition, American national associations, such as the National Association of Manufacturers (NAM) and the Chamber of Commerce, which might attempt to aggregate the various interests of diverse members as an encompassing association, do not have as much stable authority as the German BDI or the Japanese Keidanren.[85] This might influence the associations' capacity to organize deliberation of nationwide norms.

Nevertheless, the fragmented structure of American associations does not sufficiently answer why American associations have not organized a public process of deliberating unfair cases. Contrary to rigid institutionalist expectations, American associations and their newly established social networks have generated new public programs, such as training programs, as has already been examined. American associations might be able to initiate public deliberation of conflicts and fair norms, if they intended to do so. The reason that Germans in the automotive parts market developed fair regimes is not their traditional centralized structure of corporatism. As shall be examined in chapter 3 of this book, German associations became more decentralized in the 1990s through the process of agents' reflection upon the rigidity of corporatist resolutions. Fair norms in Germany were not produced by a centralized corporatist resolution that agents executed at the level of paralegal resolution. Fair norms in Germany became effective because of the agents' democratic participation in the deliberation itself, in which agents expressed their self-rules and formed social solidarity for fair norms.

It is noteworthy that even associations, which are very much concerned with suppliers' suffering from unfair treatment in the automotive parts market, hesitate to initiate deliberation of fair norms at the public level in the U.S. For example, the Original Equipment Suppliers Association (OESA) was founded to increase supplier bargaining power and to deal with hot issues in the collaborative markets. But the OESA did not organize public deliberation as German associations did. This also shows that the fragmented structure of associations is not a decisive factor in the different consequences of market regimes in the U.S. and Germany.

A more important factor in explaining why American associations are reluctant to initiate public deliberation is agents' understanding of private and public at the level of *norms about norm-creation*. Under the influence of utilitarian liberalism,[86] American associations have limited not only the problems they can address, but even more crucially, also the way in which they deal with issues. American associations evaluate unfair behaviors and conflicts as private affairs between two contractors in civil society; if two contractors need to resolve conflicts, they can refer to the public court. Conflicts within an American business community might produce temporary coalitions, but the process of resolving the conflicts typically occurs within governmental institutions. In this utilitarian liberalism, there is little room for a civic public realm in which agents in civil society deliberate common issues and act in concert. This will be examined in detail in the next subsection of this chapter.

Simultaneously, however, a new pattern of practices, not traditional but newly created in the process of transformation toward the collaborative market, changed the social fabric and thus influenced American market governance. As has been examined, the prevalent strategy of merger and acquisition by American suppliers has altered the social fabric, producing a negative impact on the development of horizontal cooperation among suppliers. In addition, changes in the level of personal relations in the 1990s, resulting from the adoption of cross-functional teams and new purchasing policies, have also had a negative impact on the development of stable relationships between buyers and suppliers in the U.S. automotive parts market. First, informal meetings that establish personal relationships between buyers and vendors have declined. Until the early 1990s, there were many interactions and informal meetings between buyers and suppliers, such as dinners and golf meetings. However, large companies in the U.S. automotive parts markets have recently been discouraging vendors and purchasers from maintaining informal personal contacts.

But more importantly, the reason for the instability of personal relations in the U.S. automotive parts market is that American companies frequently circulate their staffs as they adopt cross-functional teams and lean production. Some suppliers see four to six different buyers from a customer company in a year.[87] One supplier reports that buyers rotate every eight months on average. In particular, with the development of cross-functional team structures, American companies have adopted cross-functional training. In the past, American companies had strictly divided departments. In this structure, employees normally stayed in the same department and moved up through the hierarchy in the same department. From the 1980s through the early 1990s, however, American companies developed cross-functional teams and cross-functional training systems in order to increase flexibility in an organization. When young people with B.A. or M.A. degrees enter a company in the U.S., they switch between all different departments for the first three to five years. The American cross-functional training is different from that of German companies. Although German companies also adopted the cross-functional team system in the 1990s, people have relatively long-term personal relations due to different training systems and circulation, which will be investigated in the next chapter. Contrary to rigid institutionalist expectations, the cross-functional teams took priority in the organization of German companies in the 1990s, but employees were more likely to move within their occupational specialty. German suppliers in my survey estimated that they maintained contacts with current buyers for about five to ten years; moreover, most people in German supplier companies expected that they would meet with their buyers again in the future.

The frequent turnover of buyers makes American buyers and vendors unlikely to have stable personal relationships in which they might accumulate norms for governing their relationships.[88] If a new buyer comes up, she or he will set new issues and new rules by demanding more. Many of the German vendors in my interviews who have dealt with American buyers complain of frequent turnovers. A German supplier compares the short-term turnover of buyers in U.S. customer companies with German long-term personal relations: "To work with the American firm is very difficult because things and contracts are frequently changing. Although we agree to a certain point on the requirements this time, we have to discuss the point again next time. If you go there again, you meet new people. You have to start a new one."[89] Many American suppliers in the automotive parts market describe this kind of contact with their buyers as a "snapshot meeting." In these meetings, buyers are not interested in suppliers' specialties and conditions of production; they just take a look at the costs and prices rather than studying the benefits resulting from collaborative application engineering. If a supplier asks a customer to correct so-called unfair cases in reference to an existing contract, a new buyer often says that she or he does not know about predecessors. With rapid turnover, there is little space in which buyers and vendors can create their own norms and fair criteria for governing their own relationships.

In addition, the incentive system for buyers in American companies has a negative impact on the development of fair partnerships in the U.S. automotive parts market. The incentive system in U.S. companies tends to encourage the buyers to focus only on the price rather than considering the benefits of collaborative engineering. If a buyer's performance and subsequent compensation are evaluated according to the achievement of price cuts, the buyer becomes narrowly oriented toward price cuts in a short period. A supplier describes the mind set of her buyers: "The buyers are so narrow-minded. They consider only their personal bonus and salary. They don't consider the long-term benefits of their company. Their goal is to reduce the price in a short time." The reason for the obsession with price cuts is that, as many people put it, "The whole goal and measurement of the buyer's success are pricing; their success is measured by price reduction."[90] Richard Allen, CEO of the automotive sector at Freudenberg NOK, reports an interesting experience. He suggested to a purchaser a way of cost-saving through cooperation in the entire process of value creation. But the buyer from the OEM company said that if he did so, he could not get a record of how his job performance was measured. The benefits from value engineering are not counted as achievements for the buyer involved in a project.[91] Many industrial observers and empirical researchers confirm that the buyer's intense focus on price, which results from the incentive system, causes distrust and unfair behavior. Unlike the German incentive system, in which buyers do not have such personal bonus systems, the orientation toward buyers' personal achievement in U.S. companies, particularly through price-cutting, is more likely to discourage the development of fair partnerships for flexible application engineering.[92]

In summary, Americans do not have fewer associations and social networks than Germans, although the structure of American associations is more fragmented. The fragmented structure is not decisive in the failure to create fair social norms, however. Although the structure of associations is fragmented, Americans could deliberate and articulate fair norms by adjudicating conflicts in the public realm, if they wanted. Contrary to institutionalist belief, American associations and social networks in the automotive parts market are not significantly lacking in the development of collective solutions in a public way. American associations and regional governments have created common activities to promote companies' competitiveness in the market, which might be the resources with which stable and fair governance could be established. In contrast to institutionalist expectation, more negative effects upon the development of collaborative relationships came from untraditional and newly created patterns of practices in the process of adopting Japanese-style lean production. Frequent turnover of purchasers, along with customer companies' adoption of cross-functional training and an incentive system based on personal achievement, has had an adverse impact on the society-wide development of fair partnerships in the U.S. automotive parts market. However, the negative factors in the social fabric are not sufficient for understanding unfair regimes, considering that relationships at the personal level as well are influenced by companies' strategies and the environment that is continuously constituted by interfirm interactions and social governance. Again, the method of constituting a market regime and associations' roles in the process of deliberation deserve attention. It is noteworthy that in spite of an abundance of associations and common activities like training, Americans in the automotive parts market have not developed fair norms for stable governance through associational networks. Although Americans have no fewer associations than Germans, their different ideas about how to use associational networks create different consequences in governance. Different manners of problem-solving practices and different practices of norm-creation will be examined in the next subsection.

The American Way of Creating Norms

Americans in the automotive parts market are involved in as many associations or social networks as Germans are but have failed to develop fair norms and trustful cooperation. Although Americans are linked in formal and informal social networks, they have not created a public way of solving conflicts in which agents deliberate unfair behaviors and create society-wide norms for stable governance. While Americans in the automotive parts market believe that other people suffer from similar unfair cases, they do not treat the problems as social issues from the perspective of correcting the rules of market governance. This section investigates why the American automotive parts market has not developed a public way of deliberation in which agents try collectively to deliberate problems and build society-wide norms.

Contrary to the opinions of neo-Tocquevillians such as Robert Putnam, associations do not automatically generate civic norms. Even in the case of

Germany, which many institutionalists regard as an good example of associational governance, agents suffered unfair behavior in the late 1980s and the first half of the 1990s; few people expected that powerful customers would temper their opportunism. In the case of Japanese subcontracting, the dense networks of Japanese supplier associations that had been frequently praised for fostering cooperation in the 1980s began to be criticized as structures of domination and were subject to dissolution due to their rigidity as they resisted flexible innovation in the 1990s. Institutions like associations themselves are subject to agents' reflexivity.

More importantly, rigid institutionalists and neo-Tocquevillians, who focus on the number and formal structure of associations or on different norms for contracts and markets, have failed to explain why traditional civic norms do not work and how new norms are created. Traditional civic norms for contracts and contractual relations such as "live and let live," which had worked for the neoclassical market during the period of mass production, did not work in the new collaborative market. Agents in the German and American automotive parts markets needed new ethical codes in a new market. In this sense, rigid institutionalists such as Steven Casper, who focus on the norms and legal system that regulate contracts and contractual relations, failed to explain the dynamic process of norm-creation.[93] Casper holds that the regulatory approach of the German courts prohibits powerful customers from resorting to opportunistic behavior, while the liberal approach of U.S. courts does not; thus, Americans fail to build fair and stable regimes, while Germans succeed. However, few people in the U.S. or in the German markets bring to court so-called unfair cases, not only because unfairness in the long-term and collaborative market is hard to prove illegal—there are many loopholes in long-term contracts—but also because suppliers are concerned with their future business in the market. Although the German courts have a tradition of active intervention in private contracts based on the "Good Faith" clause, few people in the German market believe that active courts would stop opportunistic behavior by customers, a fact that contradicts Casper's explanation. The different consequences in the U.S. and German markets are not brought about by *norms* or *laws* about contracts and contractual relations, but by the different *practices of norm-creation*, i.e., the *ways of deliberating conflicts* and *ways of understanding politics* in social networks.

Different conceptions of fairness and different market regimes are mainly the result of different ways of deliberation, that is, deliberation in the civic public realm vs. the individual, dyadic method of deliberation. Agents engaged in public deliberation are more likely to generate substantive fairness than those engaged in isolated, dyadic deliberation, because the former generate rich neutral ground for adjudication through adjusting their differences. More importantly, as chapter 3 of this book will illustrate in detail, democratic participation in public deliberation is the process by which agents express their own rules—a process of legislation of self-rules—and form social forces to watch over violations of socially shared norms. The rules that agents deliberate through criticizing and justifying in the public realm are hard to violate because agents have difficulty overruling rules that they themselves have established in the public eye. In addition, in the public way of adjudicating conflicts powerful customers bear the burden of justifying their position in view of the public.

However, Americans in the automotive parts market have not developed such public deliberation, although the existing social networks and associations might be sufficient for the public realm, were they to begin to deal with conflicts in a public way. Americans in the automotive parts market have failed to build society-wide norms because they have tried instead to solve so-called unfair issues through individual, dyadic relations. In the absence of a process in which they may verbalize their own rules in the public eye by criticizing opportunism and justifying their own behavior, American first-tier suppliers have treated sub-tier suppliers as unfairly as automakers treated them. Lacking society-wide norms and free from having to justify their own behavior in public, American customers can easily transfer burdens to their own suppliers when they feel pressure in their own markets. Why have American associations not organized public ways of adjudicating conflicts? Why have Americans in the automotive parts market not deliberated so-called unfair problems in the civic public realm?

One might point out the influence of antitrust law on the activities of American associations. Traditionally, antitrust laws have been understood as anti-association. Since 1935, antitrust laws have swayed public policy in the U.S. Even during mobilization for World War II and later in the 1950s, the trade association approach in the U.S. did not emerge as a major policy alternative as it had during the 1920s and under the jurisdiction of the National Recovery Administration between 1933 and 1935. In order to promote economic progress, the American government has looked to large corporations rather than to the loose cooperation of the associative style.[94] Most activities of American associations are subject to the close scrutiny of antitrust law. Particular concerns are price fixing, information sharing, standard setting, defining memberships, and providing services to non-members. People in the American associations are nervous about keeping to antitrust law. A president of an automotive supplier association emphasized the observance of antitrust law in an interview with me, saying, "In order not to violate antitrust law, we make sure that lawyers are present in our meetings."[95] American associations are very cautious of any off-the-record sessions, secret meetings, or discussions of association business at social gatherings.

Nevertheless, antitrust law might not be decisive in explaining the differences in the U.S. and German regimes. As Louis Galambos rightly points out, "Trade associations remained important in the American political economy. Indeed, they were essential to businessmen in the postwar era." Galambos continues, "No significant industry can afford under current conditions in the United States not to be represented by effective associational representatives."[96] Furthermore, since the Reagan administration in the 1980s, American antitrust law has become less strict in order to encourage joint ventures and cooperation among companies.[97] On the other hand, the reason for the establishment of fair partnerships in the German automotive parts market is not that German antitrust law is weak. On the contrary, the German Cartel Office (Bundeskartellamt) has supported strong orientation toward a liberal market more than any other advanced capitalist country's antitrust institute. According to the results of a British study, the German Cartel Office received the highest record (a five-star grade) in an evaluation of world authorities for market competition—higher than the Justice Minister (a four-star grade) and the Federal Trade Commission (a three-star grade) in the U.S.; Japan and Portugal received the lowest ranking.[98] The strong antitrust laws of the U.S. might have some negative effects on the establishment of society-wide cooperative activities, but they are not a decisive factor in the failure to develop a public way of adjudicating conflicts in the U.S. automotive parts market. As many people in the U.S. market commented in my interviews, the activity of creating "ethical codes" or "codes of conduct" is not prohibited by antitrust law.[99] Actually, American associations such as automotive dealer associations have had experiences in which they developed ethical codes.

Why haven't American associations organized a public way of deliberating ethical codes? The fragmented structure of associations might impede associations' attempts to initiate public deliberation on the issues of unfairness, considering that some local associations, like the TMA, do not organize deliberations because such activities are not necessary for attracting members. However, as has already been examined, this fragmented structure is not a decisive factor in the American failure to organize public deliberation. A more important reason that American associations and suppliers have not addressed so-called unfair behaviors in a public way is that under the influence of *utilitarian liberalism*, agents in the U.S. automotive parts markets limit not only the problems they can address, but also the way in which they deal with issues. Under the understanding of a public/private dichotomy based on utilitarian liberalism, there is little room for a civic public realm in which agents in civil society deliberate social issues and act in concert. Americans in the automotive parts market believe that "[i]n order for there to be public rules, legal laws must already exist. Moreover, other issues should be personal and private issues within the public law; so-called 'unfair' cases ought to be problems between two private contractors; so-called 'unfair' cases shouldn't be problems which associations ought to deal with, but problems which the 'public' court should rule on only if the private contractors want."[100] American associations restrict the problems they should deal with to neutral issues, believing they should not be involved in political issues in civil society. In the American automotive parts market, utilitarian liberalism's influence on the adjudication of conflicts deters development of a public method of deliberation in market society.

Under the prevalence of utilitarian liberalism, based on neoclassical economics, the rules of the market are dealt with only in the public realm.[101] However, the usage of the term "public" in utilitarian liberalism refers to the government, while the term "private" refers to civil society. Within the utilitarian liberal paradigm, the whole society is constituted of: (a) individuals pursuing self-interests rationally; (b) voluntary, contractual relations between individuals; and (c) the public state. In practice, the distinction between public and private refers to the distinction between the governmental and non-governmental sectors. The non-governmental sphere is normally understood in terms of the market. The usage of the public/private distinction is preoccupied with questions of jurisdiction in liberal societies; thus, it tends to sharply demarcate the sphere of public authority of the state from the sphere of voluntary relations between private agents. These utilitarian liberal ideas totally blank out the civic public realm, which is not governmental. The civic public realm is a domain in which individuals discuss and actively deliberate their common activities.

Under the influence of utilitarian liberalism, American associations do not address customers' unfair behavior, even though such behavior is pervasive in society. What American associations address are common and neutral issues. However, this neutrality is very limited. Collective deliberations regarding the creation of neutral rules are avoided. American associations deal with technology and technical standards. Topics such as technology and instruments are seemingly beyond politics; in other words, they are value-neutral. American associations like the Automotive Industry Action Group (AIAG) focus on general, technical issues such as electronic commerce, bar coding, and standardization of products and production.[102] The OESA, which American suppliers in the automotive parts market founded in order to deal with new problems that were emerging in long-term and collaborative markets, could have developed a public way of deliberating governance problems in the same way that the German confederation of supplier associations (ArGeZ) did in the 1990s. The OESA, established in 1998, was created for the purpose of increasing the suppliers' own collective voice;[103] however, it did not organize a public way of deliberating and adjudicating so-called unfair cases. The way in which the OESA addresses problems is value-neutral and instrumental. For example, its deliberations on e-business have focused not on whether the customers in e-business behaved in an unfair way, but on how members implemented e-networks and what technology they used.

The way the OESA deals with controversial topics such as warranties is simply to provide the value-neutral facts about general trends of the customers' behavior.[104] The OESA refuses to organize public deliberation in which customers and suppliers criticize unfair behavior and justify their own behavior. The value judgement of customers' behavior depends entirely on an individual agent. Instead of organizing a legitimate way of responding to unfair treatment in a public realm and deliberating fair criteria collectively, the OESA leaves such responses and deliberations to the individual. The correct or legitimate way of responding to the behavior is decided by one's own personal resolution. For example, when Chrysler repealed existing contracts unilaterally by requesting a comprehensive price cut of 5 percent in December 2000, the OESA dealt with the problem not by organizing a collective discussion on the fairness of unilateral repeals, but by conducting a phone survey of value-neutral facts such as how many suppliers would accept them. The collected data on each individual resolution or market trend might help a supplier to consider its choice, but this is not a process of creating norms for market rules. American associations do not deliberate on value-related issues such as customers' unfair behavior and ethical codes. Agents in U.S. market society believe that politics should occur only in the "public" sphere as it is defined by utilitarian liberalism; in other words, the realm of the administrative government and its authority. The politics that American associations engage in consists mainly of lobbying the government, rather than self-government in civil society.

In contrast, Germans in the automotive parts market debate and deliberate their prevalent unfair cases in formal and informal meetings. They believe that they can address unethical issues because such issues are prevalent society-wide. German associations have articulated fair norms by organizing democratic participation in the public realm, as will be investigated in chapter 3 of this book. The German public way stands apart from the utilitarian liberalist conception of the public that facilitates the individual, dyadic way for adjudication of conflicts in the U.S. The civic public realm, which utilitarian liberalism disregards entirely, provides an alternative to market liberalism. This public realm, which stems from Aristotle's conception of politics—participation in collective self-determination—has been rediscovered in Tocqueville's conception of "political society," Hannah Arendt's conception of the "public realm," and Habermas's conception of the "public sphere." This public realm can be reduced neither to the state nor to the private (family and intimate relations) realm. However, despite its existence and availability, this civic public realm has not been utilized by agents in the U.S. automotive parts market. Americans in the automotive parts market who relied on the utilitarian liberalist conception of the public could not generate a public process for the establishment of fair norms as Germans did. This is why Americans did not develop civic norms even within dense networks of associations. To use Robert Putnam's metaphor, Americans in the automotive parts market do not bowl alone. They are bowling together but they do not talk about politics within their community.

Norms about norm-creation like utilitarian liberalism, rather than *norms about contracts and contractual relations*, strongly influenced the ways of deliberation in the U.S. automotive parts market; thus, they contributed to the prevalence of an extreme form of formal fairness and distrustful relationships. However, this does not mean that norms about norm-creation are not subject to agents' reflexivity, or that the distrustful regime is predetermined by the taken-for-granted culture. Utilitarian liberalism is one of the dominant interpretations of society and has been constantly contested. Actually, Americans in the automotive industry also have a tradition of self-government by associations.[105] Furthermore, Americans in the parts market have recently developed very "untraditional" and publicly mediated institutions, contradicting the tenets of relatively strongly utilitarian liberalism. For example, OEMs and suppliers in Wisconsin and Pennsylvania have developed public-private consortiums or partnerships, such as the Wisconsin Manufacturers' Development Consortium (WMDC).[106] These private-public consortiums, in which the state, the OEMs, the suppliers, and regional institutes took part, not only made tremendous efforts to upgrade supplier capabilities, but, more notably, tried to promote trustful relationships between the OEMs and the suppliers by elaborating a code of conduct for good behavior and by encouraging customers to develop good supplier relationship practices. This new model of publicly mediated coordination, which agents in the parts market built by reflecting upon their problems in collaborative markets, contests the existing utilitarian model. Publicly mediated coordination leaves open the possibility of whether Americans in the parts markets could develop genuinely trustful relationships in the collaborative market.

Despite the emergence of this new model of publicly mediated coordination, private-public consortiums are still at an early stage of evolution, and the utilitarian liberal model continues to prevail in the current U.S. automotive parts market. In particular, the utilitarian liberal model has been reinforced by the practices of individual solutions, such as quick growth of consolidation and reliance on individual power instead of horizontal cooperation and collective solutions. Particularly, formal associations are discouraged from organizing public deliberation by the members' reluctance to discuss unfairness; conversely, without the initiative and guidance of formal associations, individuals in informal meetings are discouraged from instituting collective deliberations. In light of this, this section investigates in detail how utilitarian liberalism is confirmed by practices in individualist solutions—in other words, how ideas and practices are mutually reinforced.

Given the absence of a public method of deliberating and acting in concert within civil society, and the fact that agents rarely refer to the courts, Americans in the automotive parts market depend on individual resolution and power. Without active efforts to create the public realm on the part of associations under the influence of utilitarian liberalism, the specific contractors in conflict rarely choose the collective solution. The reason for suppliers' reluctance to hammer out a collective solution is primarily that the risk and burden assumed by each supplier in the absence of associations' initiative are too large, larger than the benefits. Despite numerous social networks, American suppliers in the automotive parts market have not created social adjustments because few people want to talk about their own unfair cases in the public sphere. When I asked why they did not discuss such unfairness in formal meetings, most suppliers retorted, "Who dares to speak such things?" It is very difficult to appoint a representative who can address such unfair behaviors in a public way.

If associations are unwilling to initiate public deliberation, informal discussions among suppliers are unlikely to contribute to the development of a public way of building fair norms. Although American suppliers meet with other suppliers in numerous informal settings, such as golf clubs and trade fairs, they are very cautious of other suppliers because other suppliers might take advantage of any shared information.[107] In these informal meetings, some suppliers complain of so-called unfair behavior, although only rarely. If a supplier complains of unfair behavior, surrounding suppliers might console the supplier by showing pity. But most of the American suppliers that I interviewed believed that complaints in informal meetings did not provide any solutions, particularly in situations in which formal associations do not initiate a public way of adjudication. While associations are discouraged from organizing public deliberation by members' reluctance to participate in the meetings, suppliers in the U.S. automotive parts market are also discouraged from discussing their own experiences of so-called unfair cases because associations do not initiate and guide the public deliberation of fair governance. Initiative might be needed from either side.

In the absence of horizontal coordination and deliberation among suppliers, powerful customers easily take advantage of their powerless suppliers. American suppliers do not know how other suppliers respond to so-called unfair pressure and treatment. The information that a supplier has about competitors is public knowledge available to anyone through newspapers and journals—where they operate, the price of competitors, whether they are unionized.[108] But suppliers also gain information about their competitors in the same market segment through their own customers. According to consulting company researchers who studied the process of price reduction in the U.S. in 1997 and 1999, suppliers did not know how many discounts customers requested from competitors and what price cuts the competitors gave to their customers.[109] Almost all American suppliers who did find out about competitors' offers to customers were surprised. Some suppliers were shocked, believing they had given too much to their customers, compared with their competitors. In the absence of public deliberation, in which agents criticize unfair behavior and justify their policies, American customers easily abuse the unclear governance of long-term and collaborative contracts in the individual, dyadic relation between two contractors.

In the individual, dyadic relationship, American suppliers have little choice but to tolerate unfairness or increase their own leverage in the market. The easy way to increase leverage is to consolidate their market by buying out other companies in the market. Adversarial acquisitions among suppliers contribute to the atrophy of horizontal relationships. Adversarial acquisitions, the lack of horizontal relationships, and the absence of public deliberation tend to reinforce one another.

The conception of prevalent fairness is constituted in the process of adjudication of conflicts. In the process of solving conflicts in individual, dyadic relations, and in the absence of public deliberation, the criteria for governing conflicts are more likely to be set by powerful customers, and fair criteria become more extremely formal because the rarity of adjustments among agents reduces the common ground as neutral criteria in adjudicating conflicts. Because there is little possibility for collective adjustment of fair norms, American suppliers tend to accept customers' opportunistic behavior as it is, although that behavior may be distasteful. In addition, even the power-driven conception of formal fairness is justified by the utilitarian liberal conception of justice in the market. A president of a supplier association describes the prevalent way of responding to so-called unfair treatment: "[T]hey [unfair behaviors] have been in the industry for many years; many people say, 'if you can't stand the heat, get out of the kitchen.'"[110] Americans in the automotive part market believe that the rules set by the powerful customers are given; if you don't like them, you are free to leave. Although the freedom to exit is limited in the real market, power-driven rules are justified by utilitarian liberalism— any result in the market is fair if an action is made by free choice. American suppliers have come to believe their customers' rules are fair insofar as they treat all competing suppliers equally. Under this extreme type of formal fairness—no matter how customers behave, they are fair if they treat competitors equally—American suppliers are less likely than ever to deliberate customers' prevalent opportunistic behavior in the public realm. Although the extreme type of formal fairness grows out of the individual way of adjudicating conflicts, it reinforces the individual way.

To sum up, contrary to prevalent beliefs, long-term contracts have not generated stable and trustful relationships. On the contrary, due to their incompleteness, long-term contracts open new possibilities for powerful contractors to abuse unclear governance. In particular, the American automotive parts market suffers from rancorous conflicts and distrustful relationships in long-term and collaborative contracts. The reason for the failure to establish fair partnerships in the U.S. is due neither to sparse associations, nor to traditional norms and liberal laws about contracts and contractual relations.

The main reason for power-driven formal fairness and distrustful relationships in the U.S. market is mainly the individual, dyadic way of conflict adjudication. Although Americans in the automotive parts market have no fewer associations and social networks than Germans do, they have not organized a public way of deliberation in which agents criticize opportunistic behavior and deliberate fair norms collectively. It is not *norms about contracts and contractual relations*, but *norms about norm-creation*, particularly utilitarian liberalism, that have influenced the way agents recognize problems and address conflicts. Although so-called unfair cases are prevalent society-wide, Americans in the automotive parts market, under the influence of the utilitarian liberal idea of the public/private dichotomy, have not recognized the problems as a public issue. In the absence of associations' initiation of public deliberation, agents prefer individual solutions, which in turn discourage associations from organizing public deliberation. Thus, initiation from either side is needed for the establishment of public deliberation. In this sense, the new, untraditional experiment of publicly mediated coordination matters, although it is still in an early stage of evolution. The attempts at publicly mediated coordination show not only that utilitarian liberalism is not an unreflective norm about norm-creation, but also that the possibility for American fair partnerships remains open. Nevertheless, the utilitarian liberal model still prevails and is reinforced by the practices of individual solution, such as adversarial acquisition. In the absence of a public way of deliberating fair norms, American suppliers tend to confirm the extremely formal rules set by powerful customers. The extreme type of formal fairness in the U.S. automotive parts market both derives from and reinforces the individual, dyadic method of adjudicating conflicts.

Notes

1. For the various tests of quality including the J. D. Power survey, see Eric Mayne, Tom Murphy, and Drew Winter, "The Quality Crunch," *Ward's Auto World* 37, no. 7 (July 2001): 32–37; "Why Toyota Wins Such High Marks on Quality Surveys," *The Wall Street Journal*, 15 March 2001, A1; "Quality of U.S. Cars Improving Sharply," *Chicago Sun-Times*, 19 March 2001, 2.

2. In the first half of 2001, American automakers slashed production by 10 percent, while BMW and Honda increased production. In the light vehicles segment, the sales of American vehicle manufacturers fell drastically in the first half of 2001—by 17.7 percent for Dodge, 17.9 percent for Lincoln-Mercury, 16.4 percent for Buick, and 25.8 percent for Cadillac. In the small car segment, Chrysler sales shrank by 13.1 percent; GM and Ford slipped more than 3 percent. In luxury car sales, American Lincoln is still problematic. GM's Buick, Cadillac, Pontiac, and Saturn, Ford's Mercury, and Chrysler's Dodge and Jeep are the worst-performing brands so far in 2001. Some of them are precarious in holding brand names. Sales of minivans, a key money-making segment for U.S. automakers, also fell by 21.8 percent. "Who's Next?" *Ward's Auto World* (May 2001): 32; "Detroit Is in Trouble," *Ward's Auto World* (May 2001): 9, 32, 34–36.

3. "Quality: Adage of 'You Get What You Pay For' Holds," *Automotive NewsWire*, 23 July 2001; "Suppliers Skimping on Quality," *Grand Rapids Press*, 25 July 2001, A12.

4. "Quality: Adage of 'You Get What You Pay For' Holds," *Automotive Newswire*, 23 July 2001.

5. Jeffrey K. Liker and Yen-Chun Wu, "Japanese Automakers, U.S. Suppliers and Supply-Chain Superiority," *Sloan Management Review* 42, no. 1 (2000): 83–88.

6. Susan Helper, "Supplier Relations and Technical Change: Theory and Application to the US Automobile Industry" (Ph.D. diss., Harvard University, 1987); idem, "How Much Has Really Changed between U.S. Automakers and Their Suppliers?" *Sloan Management Review* 32, no. 4 (summer 1991): 15–28; Susan Helper and Mari Sako, "Supplier Relations in Japan and the United States: Are They Converging?" *Sloan Management Review* 36, no. 3 (spring 1995): 77–84; Toshihiro Nishiguchi, "Fairness, Rationality and Integration: Success Factors towards a New Organization Model," (Working Paper, International Motor Vehicle Program, MIT, Cambridge, Mass., 1992); Jeffrey Dyer, Dong Sung Cho, and Wujin Chu, "Strategic Supplier Segmentation: The Next 'Best Practice' in Supply Chain Management," *California Management Review* 40, no. 2 (1998): 57–77; OSAT and A. T. Kearney, Inc., *The 21st Century Supply Chain: The Changing Roles, Responsibilities and Relationships in the Automotive Industry* (Southfield, Michigan: A.T. Kearney, Inc., 1996); Ulrich Jürgens, "Communication and Cooperation in the New Product and Process Development Networks: An International Comparison of Country- and Industry-Specific Patterns," in Ulrich Jürgens, ed., *New Product Development and Production Networks: Global Industrial Experience* (Heidelberg: Springer-Verlag, 2000), 107–148; Rati Apana Chotangada, "Governance Systems That Facilitate Innovation: Changing Perspectives of Supplier Customer Relationships. The Case of The Automobile Industry" (Ph.D. diss., University of Cincinnati, 2000); Michael Maloni, "Influences of Power upon Supply Chain Relationships: An Analysis of the Automotive Industry" (Ph.D. diss., Ohio State University, 1997); Janet L. Hartley, "Collaborative Value Analysis: Experiences from the Automotive Industry," *The Journal of Supply Chain Management* 36, no. 4 (fall 2000): 27–32; Ward's Auto World, *Ward's Auto World 22nd Supply Survey*, Supplement to *Ward's Auto World* (August 2000).

7. "Risky Business in Detroit," *Industry Week*, 4 March 1991.

8. Charles W. Hill, "National Institutional Structures, Transaction Cost Economizing and Competitive Advantage: The Case of Japan," *Organization Science* 6, no. 1 (1995): 119–131; Dyer, Cho, and Chu, "Strategic Supplier Segmentation," 57–67; Peter Lawrence, *Managers and Management in West Germany* (London: Croom Helm, 1980); Peter Lawrence, Barbara Senior, and David Smith, "The Anglo-American Contrast: A New Look" (paper presented at Annual Conference of Association of International Business, London, 1998); Geert Hofstede, *Cultures Consequences* (Beverly Hills: Sage Publication, 1980).

9. Michael E. Porter, "Capital Disadvantage: America's Failing Capital Investment System," *Harvard Business Review* 70, no. 5 (1992): 65–82; J. Rogers Hollingsworth, "The Institutional Embeddedness of American Capitalism," in Colin Crouch and Wolfgang Streeck, eds., *Political Economy of Modern Capitalism* (London: Sage Publications, 1997), 133–147; "The Logic of Coordinating American Manufacturing Sectors," in J. L. Campbell, J. R. Hollingsworth, and L. N. Lindberg, eds., *Governance of the American Economy* (New York: Cambridge University Press, 1991), 35–73; John Zysman, *Governments, Markets and Growth* (Ithaca: Cornell University, 1983).

10. Charles F. Sabel, "Ungoverned Production: An American View of the Novel Universalism of Japanese Production Methods and Their Awkward Fit with Current Forms of Corporate Governance" (paper prepared for presentation at the Conference on Socio-Economic Systems of the Twenty-First Century, Tokyo, 1996).

11. See for associationalism, Benri Asanuma, "Manufacturer-Supplier Relationships in Japan and the Concept of Relation-Specific Skill," *Journal of Japanese and International Economics* 3, no. 1 (1989): 1–30; M. Gerlach, *Alliance Capitalism: The Social Organization of Japanese Business* (Berkeley: University of California Press, 1992); Naoki Tabeta, "The Kigyo Keiretsu Organization and Opportunism in the Japanese Automobile Manufacturing Industry," *Asia Pacific Journal of Management* 15, no. 1 (1998): 1–18; Hollingsworth, "The Logic of Coordinating American Manufacturing Sectors," 35–73; Leonard H. Lynn

and Timothy J. McKeown, *Organizing Business: Trade Associations in America and Japan* (Washington, D.C.: American Enterprise Institute for Public Policy Research, 1988); Hiroaki Yamazaki and Matao Miyamoto, eds., *Trade Associations in Business History* (Tokyo: University of Tokyo Press, 1988).

12. James Bamford, "Driving America to Tiers," *Financial World* 163, no. 23 (8 November 1994): 24–27.

13. Jeffrey H. Dyer, "How Chrysler Created an American Keiretsu," *Harvard Business Review* 74, no. 4 (July–August 1996): 43–46.

14. Dyer, "How Chrysler Created an American Keiretsu," 53–54.

15. Interview with A13 on 2 December 1999; interview with A30 on 21 January 2000.

16. Chrysler's SCORE program is a voluntary program in which a supplier suggests a way to reduce costs and work together with Chrysler. The number of participants in SCORE increased dramatically, from 67 percent of appropriated suppliers in 1994 to 91 percent in 1996. In order for suppliers to easily make proposals, Chrysler helped them, providing them with the capability to submit their proposals online and check the status of a given proposal. The average processing time for the proposal has dropped from 199 days in 1993 to 89 in 1996. See Kevin R. Fitzgerald, "Show Suppliers the Money!" *Purchasing* 123, no. 2 (14 August 1997): 40–47.

17. Alex Taylor and Robert A. Miller, "The Auto Industry Meets the New Economy," *Fortune* 130, no. 5 (5 September 1994): 52–57.

18. It was confirmed through interviews that most suppliers believe that Chrysler keeps their information confidential. One supplier said that a team from Chrysler had transferred information from the company to competitors. But even the interviewee of the supplier company agreed that suppliers have some protection from Chrysler. Interview with A12 on 1 December 1999.

19. "Risky Business in Detroit," *Industry Week*, 4 March 1991.

20. Interviews with A30 and A31 on 21 January 2000; interview with A22 on 9 December 1999. See also Dyer, "How Chrysler Created an American Keiretsu," 42, 52.

21. There are some exceptions. I met with a Ford supplier and a GM supplier, who have very long-term business relationships. They have trust in their customers. But normally GM, Ford, and first-tier suppliers disregard the history of relationships.

22. Chrysler initiated the "resident engineers" program, under which the supplier's engineers worked together with Chrysler's engineers. The number of resident engineers increased from 30 in 1989 to 600 in 1996. See "Suppliers on Board," *Ward's Auto World* 32, no. 7 (July 1996): 63–66. The Chrysler teams visit suppliers when suppliers ask them to. The number of visits fell in the late 1990s, as suppliers became more efficient.

23. See "Still Riding High," *Ward's Auto World* 30, no. 12 (December 1994): 51; "Show Suppliers the Money," *Purchasing* 123, no. 2 (14 August 1997): 40–47. A supplier's SCORE figure is considered for its performance rating; its proportion increased from 8 percent of its overall rating in 1994 to 15 percent in 1995. Unlike other suppliers, Chrysler's suppliers improved their margins. See Dyer, "How Chrysler Created an American Keiretsu," 54.

24. "Chrysler Cuts $ 1Billion in Manufacturing Costs," *Industrial Distribution* 85, no. 9 (September 1996): 17.

25. "Focusing on Steps for Success," *Industry Week*, 4 November 1991, 19; "Chrysler Cuts $ 1 Billion in Manufacturing Costs," *Industrial Distribution* 85, no. 9 (September 1996): 17.

26. For the growth of Chrysler's performance, see Jeffrey H. Dyer, "How Supplier Partnership Helped Revive Chrysler," *Harvard Business Review* 74, no. 4 (July/August 1996): 46–47; "Lean Manufacturing Systems Have Big Payoff," *Purchasing* 123, no. 1 (17 July 1997): 221–222; "Following Chrysler," *Economist*, 23 April 1994, 66–67.

27. With trust, suppliers could increase the dedicated assets to serve Chrysler's need. For example, at Chrysler's plant in Belvidere, Illinois, where the Neon is assembled, the distance of shipment from suppliers to the Chrysler plant drops by 43 percent. The average distance of shipment has shrunk by 26 miles.

28. Description of problems in Chrysler's supplier relations is mainly based on Tom Stallkamp's presentation for the First North American Symposium on supply chain management in Atlanta in March 1998. "Captain America," *Supply Management* 3, no. 9 (23 April 1998): 22–25.

29. "Chrysler Wants QS 9000 Standards for All Suppliers," *Purchasing* 120, no. 1 (11 January 1996): 68–69.

30. In the face of financial crisis, Chrysler made efforts to recover. Chrysler's plan for recovery was: (a) reducing material costs by 15 percent by the end of 2002—suppliers were to reduce the price by 5 percent directly, and then another 10 percent was to be cut by collaborative work between Chrysler teams and suppliers in 2001–2002; (b) reducing its workforce by 26,000, or 20 percent, within three years; and (c) closing plants by 2003. "DaimlerChrysler Is Not Alone," *Ward's Auto World* 37, no. 7 (July 2001): 47–48; "Schrempp's Last Chance," *Automotive Business* (March/April 2001): 33–34; "Schrempp Promises Improved Chrysler, Even in Slowdown," *Wall Street Journal*, 12 March 2001, A16.

31. "How Chrysler Will Cut Costs," *Purchasing* 130, no. 3 (8 February 2001): 32.

32. Ward's Auto World, *Ward's Auto Word 23rd Supplier Survey*, Supplement to *Ward's Auto World* (August 2001).

33. "How Chrysler Will Cut Costs," *Purchasing* 130, no. 3 (8 February 2001): 30–32. Chrysler's chief of purchasing Thomas W. Sidlik said that "Instead of using this incremental approach [by the cooperative way], the new initiative is asking for a 5 percent reduction in prices for 2001." Chrysler chief operations officer Wolfgang Bernhard said similarly that "this is a major cornerstone of the turnaround; we need results fast."

34. One of the main reasons for Chrysler's crisis was that the synergy effects that the former Chrysler managers promised before the merger in 1998 had not materialized. When Daimler and Chrysler fused in 1998, it was expected that $3 billion would be saved via common development and purchasing. But chief Jürgen Schrempp decided in September 1999 that Chrysler should remain a separate business due to cultural differences between the two organizations. As the international competition became much tougher and foreign automakers encroached on the Americans' flag-sections, Chrysler launched a redevelopment of the Chrysler PT Cruiser before the model fully realized economic value by its sales. For the old models, Chrysler maintained market shares by giving rebates, losing the margin. "Schrempp's Last Chance," *Automotive Business* (March/April 2001): 35; "An riesige Fusionsvorteile glaubt wohl kaum noch jemand," *FAZ*, 9 October 2000, 24; "Daimler-Chrysler plant Verhandlungen zum Arbeitsplatzabbau in Amerika," *FAZ*, 23 November 2000, 21.

35. "Exclusive Interview: Thomas Stallkamp," *Purchasing* 130, no. 5 (8 March 2001): 42.

36. Japanese transplants in the U.S. still maintain trustful relationships with suppliers and top ranking in quality evaluation and sales. The reason for the Japanese transplants' trustful relationships is mainly that Japanese automakers, particularly Toyota, have engineering edges compared with American automakers—Japanese automakers cultivate cutting-edge methods of engineering and quality management in Japan and apply them to the management of suppliers in the U.S. American suppliers are very much interested in Japanese automakers' engineering. Furthermore, Japanese automakers put great energy into teaching U.S. suppliers, using the method of strict standardization of simple parts for quality management. The case of Japanese transplants shows that distrust and unfair regimes need not be the destiny of U.S. markets, and that fair partnerships in the U.S. are still an open possibility.

37. "GM's Lopez to Accelerate Cost-Cutting," *Wall Street Journal*, 30 September 1992, A5.

38. "GM's Lopez Shakes Up Supplier," *St. Louis Post*, 4 October 1992, E1; "GM Supplier Plants Targeted for Overhaul by Spanish Experts," *The Grand Rapids Press*, 4 October 1992, D. 2; "GM's Lopez to Accelerate Cost-Cutting," *Wall Street Journal*, 30 September 1992, A5.

39. Interview with A13 on 2 December 1999; interview with A19 on 8 December 1999; interview with A23 on 9 December 1999; interview with A26 on 5 January 2000.

40. Interview with A19 on 8 December 1999.
41. "Balking U.S. Automotive Suppliers Talk of Giving Up Business with Car Maker," *Wall Street Journal*, 2 November 1992, A6.
42. "Low Marks: GM Doesn't Make the Grade in Survey of its Suppliers," *Chicago Tribune*, 5 September 1993, 7; "How Many Parts Makers Can Stomach the Lopez Diet?" *Business Week*, 28 June 1993, 45–46; "Mr. Lopez's Many Parts," *The Economist*, 29 May 1993, 73.
43. E-mail interview with US50 on 23 November 1999.
44. These kinds of confidential problems are so frequent that I heard of many cases through interviews. For the above case, particularly, Interviews with A20 and A21 on 8 December 1999; interview with A22 on 9 December 1999; interview with A23 on 9 December 1999.
45. Liker and Wu, "Japanese Automakers, U.S. Suppliers and Supply-Chain Superiority," 88.
46. Interview with A19 on 8 December 1999; interview with A23 on 9 December 1999; interview with A24 on 17 December 1999; interview with A26 on 5 January 2000; interview with A30 on 21 January 2000. Many other empirical studies confirm my findings about how Japanese transplants cultivated close and trustful relationships with American suppliers. See John Paul MacDuffie and Susan Helper, "Creating Lean Suppliers: Diffusing Lean Production Through the Supply Chain," *California Management Review* 39, no. 4 (1997): 118–151; Dave Nelson, Rick Mayo, and Patricia E. Moody, *Powered by Honda: Developing Excellence in the Global Enterprise* (New York: John Wiley & Sons, 1998).
47. "Low Marks: GM Doesn't Make the Grade in Survey of Its Suppliers," *Chicago Tribune*, 5 September 1993, 7; "Balking U.S. Automotive Suppliers Talk of Giving Up Business with Car Maker," *Wall Street Journal*, 2 November 1992, A6; "How Many Parts Makers Can Stomach the Lopez Diet?" *Business Week*, 28 June 1993, 45–46; "Suppliers Fear Tight GM Fist Won't Open Up," *Crain's Cleveland Business*, 22 March 1992, 3.
48. E-mail interview with US38 on 15 November 1999. I met several suppliers who reported to me that GM has disregarded signed contracts to get a better price. See also "Is Harold Kutner GM's Comeback Kid?" *Purchasing* 121, no. 2 (15 August 1996): 40–47; "Suppliers Fear Tight GM Fist Won't Open Up," *Crain's Cleveland Business*, 22 March 1992, 3.
49. GM buyers still engage in so-called unfair behavior. For example, one supplier could not compete well on only a price basis, so the supplier offered GM some ideas on how to manufacture the components with better quality and lower costs. GM used the ideas, but did not award the supplier with the project. The supplier is now reluctant to give new ideas to GM. Many suppliers also mentioned asymmetry and unfairness in exchanges of information between suppliers and GM.
50. "Blitzkrieg!," *Ward's Auto World* 30, no. 9 (September 1994): 23–24.
51. This is a famous story published by Mary Walton. She spent two years with Ford's Taurus team, chronicled in *Car: A Drama of the American Workplace* (New York: W. W. Norton, 1997).
52. Interview with A22 on 9 December 1999; interview with A29 on 11 January 2000.
53. Interview with A23 on 9 December 1999.
54. "Hagenlocker: Ford 2000 On Target," *Ward's Auto World* 31, no. 12 (December 1995): 46–48; "Man with Drive: Mazzorin Challenges Suppliers to Keep Up," *Ward's Auto World* 31, no. 12 (December 1995): 48–50; "Ford Looks for a Few Good Global Suppliers," *Purchasing* 120, no. 11 (11 July 1996) 108–109; "Manufacturing Revolution Underway in Brazil," *Ward's Auto World* 34, no. 8 (August 1998): 30–34; "Ford Stresses Value Analysis to Lower Cost," *Purchasing* 120, no. 3 (7 March 1996): 54–56.
55. Interview with A29 on 11 January 2000.
56. During the summer of 1999, IRN, Inc., located in Grand Rapids, Michigan, conducted a survey on price reduction requests among American suppliers. They sent questionnaires to 926 companies and received 370 surveys from 128 suppliers, a response rate of 14 percent. See IRN, Inc., "News & Views from IRN," (IRN Newsletter, November/December 1999): 1–4; idem, *The Dynamics of Price Reduction Requests Highlights of a Supplier Survey*, Research Report, IRN, Inc., Grand Rapids, Michigan, 1999.
57. OSAT and Kearney, Inc., *The 21st Century Supply Chain*.

58. IRN, Inc., *The Dynamics of Price Reduction Requests Highlights of a Supplier Survey;* "News & Views from IRN," 1–4.

59. Ward's Auto World, *Ward's Auto World 22nd Supplier Survey*, Supplement to *Ward's Auto World* (August 2000); Andreas Bartelt, "Vertrauen in Zulieferbeziehungen der Automobilindustrie: Ergebnisse einer empirischen Untersuchung" (Julius-Maximilians-Universität, Würzburg, Lehrstuhl für Betriebswirtschaftslehr, 2000). See also IKB Deutsche Industriebank, "Automobilzulieferer 1996: Differenzierte Ertragsergebnisse," *IKB Branchenbericht* (December 1997); idem, "1997—ein erfolgreiches Jahr für die deutschen Automobilzulieferer," *IKB Branchenbericht* (December 1998); idem, "Die Automobilzulieferer 1998—Kräftiges Umsatzwachstum, differenzierte Ertragsentwicklung," *IKB Branchenbericht* (December 1999).

60. According to *Ward's Auto World's* twenty-third survey in 2001, more than half of the suppliers agree that the high-tier suppliers passed Chrysler's price cut to the lower-tier suppliers. Only 23.5 percent of respondents denied that they pressed sub-tier suppliers as much as Chrysler did. See "WAW 23rd Annual Supplier Survey," *Ward's Auto World*, August 2001.

61. "Cost Cuts Rattle Supply Chain," *Automotive News*, 20 August 2001, 1–2.

62. Interview with OESA (Original Equipment Supplier Association) on 1 August 2001.

63. Dennis L. Marler, "The Post Japanese Model of Automotive Component Supply: Selected North American Case Studies," (IMVP International Policy Forum, MIT, 1989); Ward's Auto World, *Ward's Auto World 22nd Supplier Survey*, 16; "Risky Business in Detroit," *Industry Week*, 4 March 1991.

64. Laura M. Birou and Stanley E. Fawcett, "Supplier Involvement in Integrated Product Development: A Comparison of US and European Practices," *International Journal of Physical Distribution & Logistics Management* 24, no. 5 (1994): 4–14. The sample of the survey includes not only the automobile industry but also other industries. For the strategies of German automotive parts suppliers, see also table 9, "Competition Strategy Following the Size of Company," in chapter 3 of this book. German suppliers are less likely to put a priority on price leadership; they focus more on innovation and quality.

65. Gunter Lay and Werner Wallmeier, "Stand und Entwicklungstendenzen der Produktionsmodernisierung" (Research Paper of Production Innovation Improvement, Fraunhofer Institut für Systemtechnik und Innovationsforschung, 1999), 27.

66. "Quality: Adage of 'You Get What You Pay for' Holds," *Automotive Newswire*, 23 July 2001; "Suppliers Skimping on Quality," *Grand Rapids Press*, 25 July 2001, A12.

67. Hartley, "Collaborative Value Analysis," 27–32.

68. Marler, "The Post Japanese Model of Automotive Component Supply" (Policy Forum Paper, IMVP, MIT, Cambridge, Mass., 1989); "Sourcing Scramble," *Ward's Auto World* 32, no. 7 (July 1996): 33–35.

69. PricewaterhouseCoopers, "Global Automotive Deal Survey 1998" (Research Report, PricewaterhouseCoopers, 1999).

70. Interview with A22 on 9 December 1999; interview with A26 on 5 January 2000; interview with A30 on 21 January 2000.

71. Ward's Auto World, *Ward's Auto World's 22nd Supplier Survey*, 18–19.

72. OSAT and A.T. Kearney, *The 21st Century Supply Chain*, 28.

73. Robert Putnam, *Making Democracy Work* (Princeton: Princeton University Press, 1993); idem, *Bowling Alone: The Collapse and Revival of American Community* (New York: Simon & Schuster, 2000).

74. See Hollingsworth, "The Logic of Coordinating American Manufacturing Sectors," 35–73; Lynn and McKeown, *Organizing Business*; Yamazaki and Miyamoto, *Trade Associations in Business History*.

75. See Weddle's Automotive Association from http://www.weddles.com/associations/results.cfm?Industry=9; The Internet's Largest Automotive Directory <http://www.autoguide.net/clubs/associations.shtml>; also see "Mutual Interests," *Ward's Auto World* 35, no. 7 (July 1999): 65.

76. Interview with OESA on 1 August 2001; see also "Suppliers Unite for a Strong Voice," *Ward's Auto World* 34, no. 9 (September 1998): 68; "MEMA Forms Automotive Original Equipment Supplier Association," *PR Newswire*, 5 August 1998, 1; "Mutual Interests" 35, no. 7 *Ward's Auto World* (July 1999): 65; "New OE Suppliers Group Has Budget, Big Dreams," *Automotive News*, 10 August 1998, 51.

77. Peter Hall and David Soskice, introduction to *Varieties of Capitalism* (New York: Oxford University Press, 2001).

78. For the emergence of new social networks in the U.S., see Paul Osterman, Thomas A. Kochan, Richard Locke, and Michael J. Piore, *Working in America: A Blueprint for the New Labor Market* (Cambridge, Mass.: MIT Press, 2001); Charles F. Sabel, "Experimental Regionalism and the Dilemma of Regional Economic Policy" (paper prepared for presentation at the Conference on Socio-Economic Systems of Japan, the United States, the United Kingdom, Germany, and France, Tokyo, 1996); Christoph Scherrer, "Governance of the Automobile Industry: The Transformation of Labor and Supplier Relations," in Campbell, Hollingsworth, and Lindberg, *Governance of the American Economy*, 209–235. In addition, my account of associations and new social networks is based on my own interviews, and I am also indebted to professor Gary Herrigel's empirical research.

79. I am indebted to professor Gary Herrigel for this example.

80. For the support of public authorities in the U.S., see Osterman et al., *Working in America*, 141–143, 153.

81. There was much debate over how to organize and fund the training program. State Senator Richard Luft strongly opposed funding the program, saying, "I don't think any corporation should be in the position of administering state funds." He believes that public funds should not support specific private companies. The manager of DCCA, Lori Clark, explained why they chose this strategy: "Caterpillar and Deere were able to very easily identify suppliers that needed help." The UAW also opposed the program. Jim O'Connor, a service representative of UAW, argues that "In allocating money for Caterpillar to spend on its suppliers, the end effect is that work they're currently doing at $17 an hour is going to be performed by folks in non-union shops at $5 to $7 an hour." See "DCCA Training Plan Aims Small," *Crain's Chicago Business* 15, no. 48 (30 November 1992): 3.

82. Interview with TMA on 6 August 2001.

83. For the history of association development in the U.S., see George P. Lamb and Carrington Shields, *Trade Association, Law and Practice* (Boston: Little, Brown and Company, 1971), chap. 1; Louis Galambos, "The American Trade Association Movement Revisited," in Yamazaki and Miyamoto, *Trade Associations in Business History*, 121–138; Udo Staber and Howard Aldrich, "Trade Association Stability and Public Policy," in Richard H. Hall and Robert E. Quinn, eds., *Organizational Theory and Public Policy* (London: Sage Publications, 1983), 163–178; Udo Hermann Staber, "The Organizational Properties of Trade Associations" (Ph.D. diss., Cornell University, 1982); Lynn and McKeown, *Organizing Business: Trade Associations in America and Japan*.

84. Interview with TMA on 6 August 2001.

85. See Lynn and McKeown, *Organizing Business*; Robert H. Salisbury, "Why No Corporatism in America?" in Philippe C. Schmitter and Gerhard Lehmbruch, eds., *Trends Toward Corporatist Intermediation* (London: Sage Publications, 1979), 213–230; Phyllis S. McGrath, *Redefining Corporate-Federal Relations* (New York: The Conference Board, 1979), 79–80.

86. Utilitarian liberalism refers to a strain of liberalism in which the assumptions of utilitarianism and neoclassical economics dominate. Utilitarian liberalism is differentiated from the Kantian strain of liberalism in that utilitarian liberalism is an economist model of liberalism or market liberalism. Utilitarian liberalism assumes that a society is constituted of rational individuals and their voluntary relations on one hand, and the public state on the other. See Jeff Weintraub, "The Theory and Politics of the Public/Private Distinction," in Jeff Weintraub and Krishan Kumar, eds., *Public and Private in Thought and Practice* (Chicago: University of Chicago Press, 1997).

87. Interview with A4 on 18 November 1999; interview with A11 on 30 November 1999; interview with A13 on 2 December 1999. In addition, E-mail interviews with US16 on 3 November 1999; e-mail interview with US56 on 2 December 1999.

88. Suppliers in my interviews report that there are advantages and disadvantages with "snapshot" meetings. For example, when a new buyer comes to a supplier, he or she does not know anything about what the supplier said previously. The supplier can take advantage of the new buyer's ignorance. If the supplier made a mistake in the past, the supplier can hide it. The disadvantage is that a new buyer doesn't know about a supplier's specialty and sets new rules. Interview with A23 on 9 December 1999; interview with A13 on 1 December 1999.

89. Interview with G20 on 23 September 1999.

90. Interview with A4 on 18 November 1999; interview with OESA on 1 August 2001.

91. Ward's Auto World, *Ward's Auto World 22nd Supplier Survey*, 18; interview with A4 on 18 November 1999; interview with A19 on 8 December 1999; interview with OESA on 1 August 2001.

92. German companies in the automotive (parts) industry do not have the personal bonus system. They usually have a general bonus oriented toward department or team achievement.

93. Steven Wayne Casper, "The Legal Framework for Corporate Governance: The Influence of Contract Law on Company Strategies in Germany and the United States," in Hall and Soskice, *Varieties of Capitalism*, 387–416; idem, "Reconfiguring Institutions: The Political Economy of Legal Development in Germany and the United States" (Ph.D. diss., Cornell University, 1997).

94. Louis Galambos, "The American Trade Association Movement Revisited."

95. Interview with OESA on 1 August 2001.

96. Galambos, "The American Trade Association Movement Revisited," 123. Despite antitrust laws, associations in the U.S. have flourished. The number of trade associations increased from 2,895 in 1970 to 3,622 in 1984, when local, state, and regional-level associations were not counted. See Richard S. Tedlow, "Trade Associations and Public Relations," in Yamazaki and Miyamoto, *Trade Associations in Business History*, 140.

97. Scherrer, "Governance of The Automobile Industry," 225; Galambos, "The American Trade Association Movement Revisited," 126–131.

98. The study, titled the "Global Competition Review," which asked more than 800 companies and lawyers to complete a survey in order to evaluate 24 authorities for market competition on all continents except Africa, reports that the German Cartel Office received a five-star grade. The German Cartel Office was evaluated as excellent in their ability to struggle against the cartel and to control fusion, although it scored low in the area of flexibility. See "Ein Lob für die Leistung des deutschen Kartellamts," *FAZ*, 27 April 2000, 21; "Dann wird es bei uns eben keine Lenkungsfertigung mehr geben," *FAZ*, 24 May 1994, 25.

99. A president of an automotive supplier association says, "We are not afraid of antitrust law. We are not allowed to align ourselves to fix the price on a specific product. But, we can act together to improve business practices; our association can recommend 'the code of conduct.'" Interview with TMA on 6 August 2001.

100. E-mail interview with AIAG on 22 December 1999; e-mail interview with AIAG on 12 January 2000; e-mail interview with AIAG on 3 December 1999.

101. For different ideas of the liberal conception of "public/private," see Weintraub and Kumar, *Public and Private in Thought and Practice*; James Meadowcroft, ed., *The Liberal Political Tradition: Contemporary Reappraisals* (Cheltenham: Edward Elgar, 1996).

102. Interview with A18 on 7 December 1999; interview with A19 on 8 December 1999; e-mail interview with US63 on 22 December 1999.

103. Interview with OESA on 1 August 2001. See also "Suppliers Unite for a Strong Voice," *Ward's Auto World* 34, no. 9 (September 1998): 68; "MEMA Forms Automotive Original Equipment Supplier Association," *PR Newswire*, 5 August 1998, 1; "Mutual Interests,"

Ward's Auto World 35, no. 7 (July 1999): 65; "New OE Suppliers Group Has Budget, Big Dreams," *Automotive News*, 10 August 1998, 51.

104. The discussion of the way in which the OESA deals with issues is based on my personal interview with OESA on 1 August 2001.

105. See Scherrer, "Governance of the Automobile Industry," 213–214.

106. I am grateful to Professor Gary Herrigel for this story of the WMDC. See also Josh Whitford and Jonathan Zeitlin, "Governing Decentralized Production: Institutions, Public Policy, and the Prospects for Inter-Firm Collaboration in US Manufacturing" (research paper presented at meetings of the Society for the Advancement of Socio-Economics, Minneapolis MN, June 2002).

107. Interview with A26 on 5 January 2000; interview with A7 on 22 November 1999; interview with A11 on 30 November 1999; interview with A18 on 7 December 1999; interview with A23 on 9 December 1999.

108. Interview with A11 on 30 November 1999; interview with A13 on 2 December 1999.

109. Interview with A9 on 24 November 1999; interview with A13 on 2 December 1999.

110. Interview with A30 on 21 January 2000.

Chapter Three

TRANSFORMATION IN THE GERMAN SUPPLIER MARKET

As chapter 1 of this book reveals, U.S. markets still suffer from distrust due to the unclear governance of the new markets, while Germans have established fair partnerships in a similar type of long-term and collaborative market, which, contrary to rigid institutionalist expectation, have been successfully adopted by both Germans and Americans in the automotive industries. Another notable point is that fair partnerships prevail in German markets regardless of tier position and power, while in the U.S. automotive parts market, the relationships between first-tier suppliers and sub-tier suppliers are as confrontational and distrustful as those between automakers and first-tier suppliers.

The German automotive (parts) industry has successfully overcome the structural crisis of the first half of the 1990s by developing society-wide trustful cooperation. After recovering from the crisis of 1992 and 1993, German automakers set new sales records every year from 1997 to 1999. At the end of the 1990s, when international competition in the automobile industry occurred between all lean producers, Americans suffered from a drop in sales due to quality problems mainly resulting from pathologies of distrustful relationships with suppliers, while Germans in the automotive (parts) industry achieved great success in the market, having established trustful cooperation with suppliers. Despite the gloomy expectations of the early 1990s, German suppliers stand as the worldwide benchmark for the development of system competence and radical measures of cost reduction and high innovation.[1] Contrary to predictions based on power approaches, the German automotive industry successfully recovered, not by exploiting suppliers, but by developing trustful cooperation with them.[2]

Why have Germans successfully built flexible and trustful cooperation? How have Germans tempered customers' opportunism and unfair behavior, which had prevailed in the first half of the 1990s? How have fair norms and trustful relationships been established in German markets? How have German suppliers developed solidarity among themselves?

The reason that German suppliers and automakers were able to build fair and trustful partnerships while American suppliers did not is not that German suppliers are large and powerful. On the contrary, most German suppliers are small- and medium-sized companies; in fact, they are normally much smaller than American companies. Many experts, basing their expectations on power approaches, thought in the early 1990s that only a few big suppliers would survive and develop long-term and trustful relationships, while small suppliers would fail under pressure from high-tier suppliers as well as automakers; however, German sub-tier suppliers have improved their competitiveness and developed relationships with their customers. Power approaches fail to explain why German suppliers have developed trustful relationships throughout the supply chain while Americans have not.

Many institutionalists identify different institutional environments to explain the divergence of national political economies. In particular, institutionalists of Comparative Institutional Advantages, such as Hall, Soskice, Casper, and Vitols, who mainly rely on the German model, argue that the German model of political economy based on corporatist coordination and a patient financial system persisted even in the 1990s, thanks to its comparative institutional advantages. However, the institutionalist explanation does not account for the fact that Germans undertook significant changes in their production and market systems, loosening traditional corporatist coordination and dissolving traditional ties between banks and industrial manufacturers, rather than taking advantage of corporatist institutional advantages. In the early 1990s, almost all agreed that the German economy needed restructuring; the crisis was not just cyclical, despite the later arguments of some institutionalists such as Carlin and Soskice (1997) and Vitols (2000).[3] Institutionalists of Comparative Institutional Advantages argue that the German model of high-quality incremental innovation, based on professional specialization and corporatist supporting institutions, is strongly competitive in medium technology sectors such as the machine tool and automobile industries. However, the crisis in the first half of the 1990s occurred in these very sectors, the flagship industries that represented the German model. Contrary to the arguments of the Comparative Institutional Advantage theorists, the advantages of a nation's institutions did not translate well across the different conditions of international market competition. The traditional craft-based German system of production and the supporting corporatist institutions that had been praised for high competitiveness even at high wages turned out to be too rigid to compete in the turbulent conditions of international markets in the 1990s. Centralized coordination of vocational training proved too inflexible to keep pace with the rapid changes in technology and the volatile demands of the market. The traditional strategy of upskilling based on narrowly defined vocational orientation did not provide companies with sufficient solutions to the crisis of the German political economy in the 1990s. As chapter 1 of this book has already shown, the deployment of skilled workers changed from being based on a vocation-orientated principle to utilizing a more cross-functional and inter-vocational collaborative model, while the vocational training itself changed from narrow specialism to a more broad generalism without sacrificing the quality of skill. Furthermore, with the adoption of decentralized lean production, centralized corporatist coordination of working conditions and wages has been replaced by decentralized pacts at the plant level (*Verbetrieblichung von Regelungskompetenz*).

Meanwhile, many institutionalists also emphasized bank-based long-term financial resources (versus American short-termism based on the stock market) for long-term and trustful relationships, arguing that American companies subject to the short-term whims of shareholders would not build long-term contractual relations, while Germans could more easily develop long-term relations because of their bank-based financial system.[4] On the other hand, some institutionalists, such as Markovits and Streeck, emphasize German corporate governance, particularly co-determination (*Mitbestimmung*), to explain the long-term cooperation of German companies. Large German companies are required by German corporate law to build a dual board structure consisting of managing board and a supervisory board. The elected worker representatives on the supervisory board have rights of information and veto on certain issues by constituting half of the seats on the supervisory board. The institutionalists believe the workers' influence on decision making dampens the shareholder values.[5]

As has already been examined, however, American boards of directors became insiders instead of outsiders who represent only shareholders, which did not deter the development of Japanese-style supplier relations. Institutionalists also fail to explain why Germans were able to transform their supplier relations from traditional short-term contractual relations to long-term ones, even in the ironic situation in which large German companies had begun to adopt the shareholder value system and German managers of customer companies had begun to orient themselves toward a shareholder value system.[6] Furthermore, a recent empirical study reveals that legal co-determination has had no negative effect on shareholder wealth; the existence of co-determination does not dampen the shareholders' value because the institutions can be operated in many different ways.[7] Although some institutionalists focus on the works councils that they believe suppress the whims of shareholders, as we shall see later, the works council of Volkswagen, one of the strongest in Germany, supported Lopez's confrontational model in the crisis of the early 1990s, having compared the inefficiency of the existing model to the alternative of the Lopez model.

On the other hand, as has already been examined, legal systems and norms about contracts and contractual relations do not explain the dynamic process of norm-creation in a novel context related to the division of labor, contrary to the arguments of institutionalists such as Casper (1997; 2001) and Teubner (2001).[8] It was not until the 1990s that Germans began to favor long-term and closely interactive contracts, a development that occurred even later than it had in the U.S. In contrast to Casper's explanation, even regulatory courts in Germany have difficulty in controlling price-driven, opportunistic behavior in the market. In addition, contrary to the institutionalist emphasis on German communitarian culture (versus American individualism) or social networks of associations, the German conception of substantive fairness and trustful market regime in the 1990s was neither inherited from traditional norms about contractual relations nor predetermined by social networks of associations.[9] In the first half of the 1990s, the relationships between automakers and suppliers in the German automotive parts market were very similar to those in the U.S. supplier market. Contrary to the cultural hypothesis, many empirical studies reveal that German "communitarianism" did not deter strong self-interest-oriented conflicts in the early 1990s; the German automotive parts market also suffered from unfair behavior by powerful customers.[10] For example, in an empirical study by Mittelstandsinstituts Niedersachsen based on 437 suppliers, 87.7 percent of German suppliers argued in the early 1990s that they felt discriminated against and pressed by their powerful customers. In addition, 84 percent of suppliers held that they had had to concede to unfair requests by customers.[11] Despite the existence of so-called regulatory law and communitarian culture, German markets suffered from unfair behavior by powerful parties, as did their American counterparts in the late 1980s and the first half of the 1990s.

Culture itself was undergoing changes. Many cultural changes occurred in German management in the 1980s and 1990s while the German economy was restructuring itself during a time of crisis. Many culturalists argue that a strong tradition of *Technik* and weak business thinking in Germany accounted for a lowered sensitivity to costs and managers' long-term cooperative commitments, while business thinking in the U.S. created short-termism.[12] But in the sense of education and recruitment, business courses in Germany increased dramatically. As Porter observed, the grip of *Technik* on German management loosened up at the end of the 1980s, when financially trained executives took the helm in more companies. Lawrence and Edwards themselves also argue that "Graduates [of business schools] began to impact on German business life."[13] German managers became more cost-conscious.

More importantly, the traditional norms about contracts and contractual relations did not work for the new long-term and closely interactive markets in the 1990s. Regarding the confrontational situation of the early 1990s, a chief of a supplier company said that "The consensus on business norms in the automobile parts markets was to a high degree endangered."[14] Particularly, the traditional norm of fairness, such as *Leben und leben lassen* (Live and let live) no longer worked in the new collaborative market, in which automakers and suppliers could not survive by only single, in-house efforts (*Einzelkämpferdasein*); the survival of both parties depended on collaboration through the sharing of information.[15] The introduction of new collaborative markets under international competition required the creation of new norms about contracts and contractual relations.

New conceptions of fair norms and trustful partnerships in the German supplier market of the 1990s were not naturally given by traditional norms about contracts and contractual relations, but resulted from a painful and complicated norm-creating process in which agents confronted each other and participated in the formation of new norms. The reason that the German supplier market built fair and trustful cooperation while the American market did not is found in the different ways in which agents deliberate conflicts and understand politics. Unlike American suppliers, who tried to solve conflicts with their customers in a bilateral relation, German suppliers discussed unfair problems in the civic public realm. The differences between the American and German supplier markets lie not in the suppliers' affiliation in associations, but in their different ways of interacting in the associations, particularly deliberating and acting in the social networks.

In the process of investigating why and how Germans have developed society-wide fair partnerships in the automotive parts market, the next section of this book highlights the development of the relationships between automakers and suppliers; then the reasons German suppliers developed solidarity will be studied; finally, the kinds of effects the social adjustments created will be examined.

Automakers and Suppliers in the German Market

The establishment of fair partnerships in Germany was a process by which big customers changed their rationality of economic efficiency from a confrontational model to flexible cooperation for development as well as for production. The changes of idea (*Umdenken*) arose not only out of reinterpretations of market conditions, but also out of the conflict-laden interactions between automakers and suppliers. Even in the same culture and institutions, agents developed different models for market governance. In particular, in the early 1990s, there were two different models of relationships between automakers and suppliers. One was confrontational, focusing on price cuts by taking advantage of incomplete contracts and unclear governance. Suppliers were asked by this type of automaker or higher-tier supplier to reduce prices even after the suppliers had utilized all possible cost-saving methods. The other model was cooperative: automakers and suppliers tried to form cooperative relationships in many dimensions, such as logistics, quality management, and development. This customer group allowed suppliers to claim "the right to profit."[16] BMW and Mercedes belonged to the cooperative group. Volkswagen, Audi, and Opel (the GM subsidiary in Germany) were in the confrontational group, although Volkswagen and Audi improved their relationships in the second half of the 1990s. Many surveys revealed that German suppliers gave VW and Audi the worst grade, while Mercedes and BMW received the best grade.[17]

Furthermore, it was through a confrontational and painful process that German suppliers established their own fair-partnership alternative to the confrontational model. At the early stage of transformation toward long-term and collaborative markets, German suppliers opposed the form of the collaborative market itself. In the process of the conflict-laden transformation, German suppliers elaborated their alternative, based on their cooperative experiences with BMW and Mercedes. It is noteworthy that German suppliers succeeded in spreading the fair model throughout society while American suppliers failed to further develop the fair partnerships of Chrysler as a society-wide norm. Before investigating the roots of such differences, this section delves into what kinds of models automakers developed in the early stages of transformation; in particular, the next step is to explore the general overview of the process of contentious transformation before probing the different variations automakers developed.

The establishment of fair and trustful relationships between automakers and suppliers was not a naturally given process but a conflict-laden one in which agents searched for alternatives and redefined their own relations. In the late 1980s and early 1990s, the conflicts between automakers and suppliers revealed that the traditional norms about contracts and contractual relations did not work any longer. German suppliers and many automotive experts opposed the adoption of the new methods of the collaborative markets, such as just-in-time and total quality management, by defining the new form of collaborative markets as abuse of power from the perspective of traditional market governance. The confrontational line in the late 1980s and early 1990s was not over what kinds of collaborative markets should be adopted, but over whether to adopt the new collaborative markets in the first place. In particular, under the traditional norms of fairness for market governance, German suppliers believed that the new form of collaborative markets was unfair in that it transferred many responsibilities to suppliers. By contrast, automakers argued the necessity of new collaborative relations because of tough international competition and the problem of the existing German model under so-called "lean debate."[18]

To the suppliers, the adoption of new collaborative markets meant breaking down the traditional cozy relationships. Until the late 1980s, German automakers and suppliers set price by the "thumb calculation." Accustomed to the advantages of high-class market segments, German automakers were not very sensitive to prices of parts. In the mid 1980s, German suppliers had explicitly higher profit rates than did automakers.[19] In the early 1990s, when over-engineering and rigidity resulted from the existing German model of production and market coordination, Germans needed to rationalize their interfirm relations. Automakers initiated the organizational reform by requesting that suppliers improve their competence as collaborative partners, and reformulated the way of setting prices by pressing down prices of parts. It was Opel purchasing chief Jose Ignacio Arriotua Lopez who initiated the shock of transformation to the new markets in 1987. Many suppliers complained of Lopez's relentless policy, saying that "we are totally open to blackmail. Many suppliers deliver already under the cost limit."[20]

German automakers at first wanted to distance themselves from Lopez's brisk course. They waited to see the results of the conflicts before choosing their own course. As economic prospects became gloomy and international competition became tougher in the early 1990s, German automakers also began to take part in the painful breakdown of traditional interfirm relations. However, until the early 1990s, most German suppliers were not ready to become development partners for a new collaborative market; few suppliers developed design capacity. Although the focal point of early restructuring was so-called "just-in-time" delivery in the early 1990s, only 5 to 10 percent of components and parts were delivered by way of just-in-time delivery.[21] The exchange of information between automakers and suppliers was rare (*zufällig*) in the early 1990s; at this time, German suppliers were just at the inception of structural rationalization.[22]

In the early 1990s, most suppliers contested not what kind of collaborative relations were required for just-in-time delivery and how to establish it, but whether to establish collaborative relations. Most suppliers complained of the just-in-time delivery system itself. Until the late 1980s, German companies were a single fighter (*Einzelkämpferdasein*) in the market in the sense that they mainly focused on in-house rationalization, independent of customers. In this sense, just-in-time delivery would interfere in the autonomy of production in a supplier company. For example, when a bumper maker adopted the just-in-time system in the early 1990s, the number of bumpers, the deadline, and the way the bumpers should be produced became dependent on the automaker.[23] German suppliers and workers believed this to constitute discrimination by market power (*Nachfragmacht*). Another point of confrontation between automakers and suppliers was "open information of costs" (*gläsernen Taschen*). In the full-fledged collaborative markets at the end of 1990s, automakers and suppliers shared their know-how and costs in order to review together new possibilities for improvement of products, cost structure, and production. But earlier in the 1990s, German suppliers were very suspicious of the concept of open information itself, although the use of open information for collaboration could lead to a trustful partnership, as the "open information of costs" policy (*gläsernen*

Taschen) between BMW and its suppliers showed.[24] Suppliers' resistance to the new form of collaborative market was based on the traditional way of thinking about interfirm governance.

Traditionally, production was organized only by in-house people. The transactions in the market served only to transfer the finished product based on each agent's own cost calculation, which was hidden from the trading partner in order to secure a better position in the market. Under the traditional system of independent operation and distant market relations, the fair norm for the governance of transactions in the market was *Leben und leben lassen,* which, as previously noted, refers to the idea that an agent should not interfere in the way of production or the transactions with the agent's contract partner. From the perspective of this traditional norm, the automakers' requests for just-in-time delivery and open information for collaboration were seen as an unfair and restriction of supplier freedom in the market.[25]

In addition, the adoption of the new collaborative relation itself meant an increase in the burdens on suppliers. For example, German suppliers complained that the just-in-time delivery system was a way to transfer the cost of inventory.[26] Because few German suppliers had integrated quality management in the process of production in the early 1990s, the automakers' request for high quality meant to suppliers an increase in quality inspectors. In particular, under the peculiarity of the German legal system's governance of liability, acceptance of "exit inspection" by suppliers instead of "entrance inspection" by customers meant higher insurance costs for suppliers.[27] Furthermore, the newly adopted policy of "target costing" and customers' abuse of unclear governance broke down the traditional cozy relationships.[28]

At the inception of the transformation toward a new form of collaborative market, German suppliers rejected the collaborative market itself by confusing a form of collaborative market with unfair governance of collaborative markets. But the direct resistance against new collaborative policies, such as just-in-time delivery, open information, and cost reduction, did not provide any solutions to the conflicts. In particular, once numerous international studies had revealed the backwardness of German (supplier) productivity, German suppliers could not achieve legitimacy by claiming that they had improved productivity more than automakers in the last decade, or by employing the strategy of demystification of Japanese lean production.[29] For example, according to the research of McKinsey, the productivity of German suppliers, measured by value-creation per working time, was significantly lower than that of American suppliers as well as the Japanese.[30] In quality ratings, German suppliers also received low grades in the early 1990s. The number of defective parts was 2.5 times lower in Japanese companies than in German companies.[31] In a survey by A. T. Kearney that compared top suppliers from Germany, Spain, and England, German suppliers received a low grade for productivity.[32]

German suppliers could hardly avoid restructuring and developing a collaborative form of market relations for their own survival in global competition. They came to recognize that neither "soft trust" between automakers and suppliers nor the rigid stability based on traditional distant market relations would give any solution in the market. It was in the mid 1990s that German suppliers made tremendous efforts to restructure their production and market relations.[33] German suppliers improved their competitiveness through the optimization of the production process and, at the same time, developed their competence as development partners for collaboration with customers. The way of restructuring was mainly through suppliers' changes of ideas on economic rationality (*Umdenken*)—the flexible innovation of German suppliers hinged on their active strategy of customer orientation, which will be illustrated later.[34] It is noteworthy that most German suppliers began to recognize cooperation with customers as one of the most important measures for improvement of competitiveness around 1994 and 1995.[35]

More importantly, German suppliers established their alternative (fair and trustful cooperation) to the automakers' confrontational model in the process of criticizing unfair behavior. Once suppliers adopted a new form of collaborative market, they searched for an alternative way of governing the collaborative market. Due to the efforts of suppliers and social agents like associations, the number of unfair cases began to taper off in 1995. According to the research of Gernot Diehlmann, whose empirical basis is from 1994 to January 1996, the risks of customers taking advantage of suppliers' new technologies and information were relatively small.[36] Many people, such as Hans Dieter Oelkers, general manager of Wirtschaftsverband Stahlverformung (Trade Association of Steel Forging), admitted in 1995 that the outstandingly unfair cases had become rare.[37] The two studies conducted by the Forschungstelle Automobilwirtschaft (FAW) of the Universität Bamberg (Research Center of Automobile Economics in Bamberg University) in 1993 and 1998 reveal that the number of unfair cases decreased clearly in 1998, while confidential problems prevailed in 1993. As analyzed in chapter 1 of this book, almost all in the German automotive community agree that the relationships between automakers and suppliers have improved even though price pressure has increased.

German automakers could not continuously disregard the fair rules set by suppliers and social agents. Once fair rules for the collaborative relations were established in a public way, the transgression of such rules lost legitimacy. The use of "bare power without legitimacy" deterred the voluntary cooperation of suppliers that was needed to develop high special capability. In the process of deliberation in the public realm, German automakers had the burden of justifying their positions. Leading up to an examination of how German suppliers and social agents developed fair rules and solidarity among suppliers in a public way, the next subsection studies in detail different strategies of automakers and how they turned toward cooperation. The different models provided Germans with a new repertoire for building alternatives in the new market.

The Cooperative Way

In the late 1980s and early 1990s, Mercedes and BMW were suffering from severe competition in global markets. Particularly, Mercedes, in 1993, suffered from deficits due to the structural rigidity of its huge in-house production and traditional methods of supplier management. In the crisis of the early 1990s, and against the background of the so-called lean debate, the two automakers reorganized relations not only in-house but also with their external suppliers. The economic crisis did not generate a confrontational model automatically. Mercedes and BMW developed more cooperative relationships with suppliers. Although their programs, like Mercedes' Tandem in the early period of transformation toward a long-term and collaborative market, were just a "communication arrangement," rather than cooperation for development, the cooperative spirit of Mercedes and BMW was an important resource to German suppliers, with which they could further develop an alternative model to the confrontational policies. This section illuminates how BMW and Mercedes developed a cooperative policy even during the crisis.

BMW (Bayerischen Motoren Werke). BMW introduced collaborative relations with suppliers earlier than any other automaker in Germany. In the 1980s, BMW had already initiated flexible cooperation with suppliers, reducing its in-house production by about 30 percent. Sabel, Kern, and Herrigel call BMW's supplier management an archetype of "system integrator."[38] BMW divided a vehicle into forty modules such as gear, cockpit, door, and the like; then it developed so-called simultaneous engineering with its suppliers. For example, to develop a module of a cockpit consisting of dashboard, instrument panel, air conditioner, and navigation system, BMW calls many different component suppliers, such as electronic and plastic parts suppliers; then they discuss not only technology but also cost reduction. Suppliers participate in the very early stages of development with BMW. Subdepartments under the purchasing department and R&D division, such as those concerned with the power train and engine, discuss with corresponding suppliers how to develop each part.[39] BMW provided German suppliers with a model of a collaborative market as well as fair partnerships, based on which German suppliers could elaborate their own alternative of fair partnership in protesting VW's confrontational model in the first half of the 1990s.

The reason for the early development of collaboration at BMW is first that BMW developed a strategy by believing that the development of technology was too rapid for a company to follow.[40] This contrasts with Mercedes' internalization of technology by prioritizing its development.

Whereas Mercedes aimed at the domination of technology by building technology centers in-house until the late 1980s, BMW maintained only small parts in-house, believing that huge in-house production might cause rigidity; also, being a small corporation, they lacked such capacity. Actually, BMW did not have much in-house knowledge of electronics. For development of their navigation system, BMW had to cooperate with electronics suppliers. This type of collaboration led to BMW recognizing in the late 1980s that many innovations came from external suppliers and that it needed close cooperation with suppliers to innovate new technology and constantly improve products and production.

In the roundtable discussion of simultaneous engineering, BMW and suppliers emphasized a open information of costs (*gläsernen Taschen*).[41] Actually, German suppliers in the early 1990s criticized automakers' request for the transparent exchange of information because they worried about customers' abuse of proprietary information. But the transparent exchange of information within BMW did not cause any complaints; in fact, BMW's policy of transparent exchange of information was frequently mentioned as an example of partnership with suppliers. The problem was not whether to adopt collaborative markets, but how to govern the risks and benefits of collaborative markets. BMW was able to establish trustful cooperation in the policy of transparent exchange of information because, as the chief of BMW purchasing in my interview argued, "It was a matter of fairness." First, BMW is very careful not to steal supplier's know-how. The chief of BMW purchasing emphasized that if BMW takes the know-how of a supplier and gives it to a competitor in order to get a cheaper price, the exchange of information will not be transparent any more.

BMW is also concerned with the fair distribution of risks, responsibilities, and benefits in collaborative market relations. Like other automakers in Germany, BMW makes long-term contracts in which prices are renegotiated yearly considering technological changes. The difference between BMW and other automakers in the first half of the 1990s lay not in short-term versus long-term contracts, but in its way of doing business in long-term contractual relations. The target price is not dictated unilaterally but is the result of a process in which BMW and suppliers consider together the changes of design and technology. Although there is no fixed rate for division of benefits (such as 50:50), BMW and suppliers try to create agreement after analyzing the calculations of both sides. Few suppliers report that BMW dictates prices or revises them unilaterally without considering the supplier's conditions, as VW did in the early 1990s. In addition, BMW tries to pay for good quality. For example, if a development project is given up by BMW in the middle of the process, or if a project is not realized, BMW pays for the costs of development directly and, in most cases, gives the suppliers future business for another project.

BMW also works toward a fair distribution of responsibilities and a fair exchange of commitments. German suppliers appreciate BMW's openness and commitment in collaborative work. A supplier reports the behavior of BMW in collaboration: "BMW people suggest their own ideas and discuss with suppliers in depth how to develop a new technology. BMW spends time and money to get deep understanding."[42] Another supplier holds that "BMW and Daimler have better understanding of suppliers' conditions. Daimler and BMW accept earlier and better what a supplier says."[43] Many German suppliers in my interviews contrast BMW with unfair automakers.

Sharing responsibilities and risks with suppliers and working together are basic principles at BMW. For example, when the practice of entrance inspection by a customer was under transformation toward exit inspection by suppliers, causing an abundance of burdens on suppliers, BMW behaved differently from other automakers in distributing the risks and costs. Although BMW also changed to exit inspection, BMW assisted suppliers in improving quality management by working together and dispatching BMW's own quality engineers to supplier plants. By contrast, other automakers, such as VW and Audi, simply transferred risks and burdens to suppliers, providing little assistance. VW and Audi neither considered the specific conditions of suppliers nor incorporated quality management into the production process in the early 1990s. BMW and its suppliers, however, incorporated their own quality management into the flexible development and production process.[44]

The BMW cooperative model provided an example of fair partnership in which German suppliers had been able to develop a fair-cooperation alternative to the unfair and confrontational model in a new form of long-term and collaborative market. For example, after approximately forty German suppliers revolted against automakers' unfair behaviors in 1992, the cooperative model of BMW was referred to by both parties' representatives in the process of forming the Non-Binding Recommendations for General Business Conditions (*Leitfaden für Zusammenarbeit*) in the German Automobile Association (VDA).

Mercedes-Benz (Daimler-Benz). Daimler-Benz developed a collaborative parts market later than other German automakers.[45] It was during the hard times of the first half of the 1990s that Daimler-Benz changed its supplier relations. Until the late 1980s, Daimler-Benz continued to pursue vertical integration rather than collaborative relations with external suppliers. Daimler-Benz's response to the risks of fluctuating international markets in the 1980s was to reduce the proportion of automobile production and to increase the proportion of public contracts, such those with as MTU, Dornier, AEG, and MBB. Daimler-Benz aimed at building a technical center through internalization of technology, rather than relying on external suppliers to develop complicated quality. The strategy of internalizing technical sources deterred Daimler-Benz from changing toward a new form of collaborative market with external suppliers.[46] But against the background of lean debate and Daimler's deficit in the first half of the

1990s, Daimler-Benz not only reformed its own internal structure by dismantling its hierarchy and adopting a process-oriented team structure, it also realigned its relations with suppliers.[47]

Economic loss does not always lead automakers to a confrontational policy. It was when Daimler-Benz lost a record DM 2.8 billion in 1993 that Daimler developed a cooperative program called Tandem. The cooperative policy was adopted primarily because Daimler-Benz had reinterpreted the meaning of its relations with suppliers. In the past, Daimler had regarded suppliers as just a buffer or cushion (*verlängerte Werkbank*) against fluctuations in the business cycle. Until the early 1990s, Mercedes engineers developed almost all blueprints and distributed the task-note (*Lastenheft*) to many suppliers at the same time. Although Mercedes searched for the lowest price, price negotiation was not so tough until the late 1980s because Mercedes was less sensitive to price due to low competition in their market segment of high-class cars.[48] But in the 1990s, the development of technology in various areas becomes too rapid for Daimler's in-house capability to catch up. As they wanted to be at the forefront of technology for high-quality cars, Mercedes (Daimler's automobile section) had to respond flexibly to the changes in technology. For example, about 1,800 components were changed in the production of the E-class car between 1995 and 1998 in order to maintain a technological edge.[49] This flexible capability to keep pace with rapid developments in technology is possible only through cooperation with suppliers. Mercedes recognized that it is impossible as well as ineffective to try to maintain technological sources in-house; suppliers are important sources for efficient production and innovation.

But Mercedes did not adopt a cooperative model immediately. In the early stage of the crisis, when Daimler was suffering from large deficits, Mercedes held to the traditional view of the role of suppliers and pressed them to cut prices. But after reflection upon the negative effects of the confrontational model, Mercedes began to adopt trustful cooperation with suppliers. In the early 1990s, Mercedes waited to gauge the success of the confrontational policy of the Lopez model; then, a short time after observing how the open confrontation between suppliers and VW was detrimental to flexible cooperation with each other, Mercedes moved toward a more cooperative policy as an alternative to confrontation. Mercedes recognized that confrontation might cost the company an abundance of benefits, not only to its own reputation but also to the generation of suppliers' voluntary cooperation, which would be an important source for Mercedes' innovation.

At the inception of cooperation in 1993, the Tandem program was a mere communication arrangement rather than a method of collaboration for development. But many suppliers appreciated the efforts of Mercedes. The reason the automaker received extensive voluntary cooperation from suppliers was not simply that suppliers were proud of giving their ideas to Mercedes, a symbol of high technology—suppliers believed that being a supplier to Mercedes was a kind of certificate of the high quality of their products[50]—but also that Mercedes and BMW were trying to develop an alternative to VW's confrontational policy in a situation in which suppliers and social agents eagerly searched for an alternative logic to the confrontational necessity.[51] The extensive support of suppliers accelerated the development of a cooperative policy at both Mercedes and BMW. Later, Mercedes further developed the Tandem program to include cooperation for technological innovation. The difference between Mercedes' Tandem and Chrysler's SCORE program is that the SCORE program focuses on cost-saving in existing products, while the full-fledged Tandem focuses on future products, for example, on new technology and savings in the development process.[52]

For the further development of trustful cooperation, Mercedes was also concerned with fairness. Like BMW, Mercedes did not take advantage of suppliers' know-how and cost information. Mercedes paid for the supplier's development efforts. A small supplier with about fifty workers reported that Mercedes paid for the development costs immediately if his firm did not get business for serial production or if the project failed to materialize.[53] The mutuality of information exchange created trustful cooperation between Mercedes and suppliers. Many suppliers appreciate that Mercedes gives information and ideas to suppliers. By working together, suppliers and Mercedes find a better solution for cost reduction and improvement of quality.

The benefits were divided fairly.[54] Although the division of direct benefits is not exactly 50:50 between Mercedes and a supplier, suppliers believe that it is fair because Mercedes helps them to be competitive in the market. A supplier holds, after evaluating its collaboration with Mercedes, that "Mercedes is fair although Mercedes also cuts prices because we worked together and made the part cheaper through working together."[55] By working together, suppliers gain benefits in the development of specialty and quality of products, which improves their market position. The target price of a product in the negotiation between Mercedes and suppliers is a goal set by both sides within an acceptable range.[56] The calculation starts with current prices of parts and benchmarking in comparison with other automakers' cars; then Mercedes adds more to the price, reflecting suppliers' innovation and special technology, with the aim of striking a balance between price and quality.[57]

Since 1995, the Tandem program has clearly served as a fair and cooperative alternative to the unfair and confrontational model. In a 1995 survey by the FAW institute of Bamberg University, Mercedes was rated highest by suppliers as well as dealers. VW and Audi received the worst score, demonstrating that their confrontational policy, which had been based on the necessity of economic efficiency, had lost legitimacy now that suppliers and social agents had developed a fair alternative model through public deliberation. Awareness of the cooperative methods of Mercedes and BMW strengthened suppliers' demands for fair and cooperative governance.

The Confrontational Way: Volkswagen Konzerne

Volkswagen created a typical confrontational model in the early 1990s by adopting GM's Lopez model, taking advantage of incomplete governance by engaging in opportunistic behavior such as arbitrary revision of contracts and violation of confidentiality. A more important aspect is that many other customers in the German markets imitated VW's way of doing business in the crisis of the first half of the 1990s. VW's confrontational policies and its radical departure from traditional markets gained legitimacy among many Germans in the early 1990s, because the inefficiency of the traditional form of market relations and production system did not provide a solution. VW's adjustment was a test case for the possibility of the development of German partnerships (*Testfall für die deutsche Industrie*).[58]

However, VW Konzerne turned toward fair partnership, as epitomized by Mercedes' Tandem program, at the end of the 1990s. In the second half of the 1990s, when suppliers and social agents began to differentiate the new form of collaborative market from the confrontational model of governance by developing fair partnerships as an alternative to the confrontational way in the new markets, VW's policy in collaborative markets lost legitimacy. In view of the alternative of fair partnerships, VW could not continuously disregard the society-wide shared criteria of fair norms if it was to use suppliers' voluntary cooperation for technical innovation and high quality. This section illustrates how VW adopted the confrontational model in the early 1990s and why VW then changed its confrontational policy to fair partnerships with suppliers in the second half of the 1990s.

It was during the economic crisis of 1992 and 1993 that VW adopted its confrontational policy, although it should be noted that economic crisis does not always lead to a confrontational policy. When the business cycle of the automobile industry plunged in the second half of 1992 after a long period of upswing beginning in 1983, Volkswagen suffered from a huge deficit of DM 1.94 billion.[59] After the special boom resulting from reunification ended in 1992, the crisis revealed VW's structural weakness of low productivity and less competence for profitability. VW chief Ferdinand Piech held in the early 1990s that VW productivity was backward by 30 percent in comparison with the Japanese. Although the VW production system was praised in the 1980s as a German model of production based on professional specialization, the traditional method made it almost impossible to catch up with competitors.[60] Because of its strong works council, VW could not easily choose the American-style solution of massive layoffs. Another easy more feasible method of cost reduction was confrontation with suppliers: VW asked suppliers for a massive price cut immediately. Audi (VW's high-class car sector) met with supplier resistance by requesting a massive price cut in 1992, before GM purchasing chief Jose Ignacio Lopez de Arriortua moved to VW.

It was Lopez who carried out relentless and systematic rationalization.[61] Lopez reorganized the traditional departmental structure in favor of team orientation, attacking bureaucratic inertia and middle management, which he called a paralyzed layer (*Lähmschicht*).[62] At the same time, Lopez restructured relations with suppliers to create a new form of market.

Traditionally, VW was different from Opel in dealing with its suppliers. Price setting was based on the so-called thumb calculation, in which suppliers had a great deal of room in which to maneuver. But the traditional relations between VW and suppliers were characterized by little exchange of information, much idleness (*Eitelkeit*), and plenty of indolence (*Bequemlichkeit*). It took a long time to develop a part, so the costs were very high. The work in the development of parts was double- and triple-engineered. Alongside with other German automakers, until the late 1980s, VW was not so sensitive to price. But as competitors, like the Japanese automakers, developed products in less time and at lower costs, VW could not compete with them by maintaining traditional market relations with suppliers.

The works council of VW, one of the strongest in Germany, did not derail Lopez's confrontational policy, although many institutionalists expected that the peculiar German corporate governance, i.e., the strong works councils, would generate long-termism or cooperative culture.[63] According to the prevalent view of institutionalists, co-determination (*Mitbestimmung*), in which works councils strongly influence the decision making of German corporations by constituting the half-seats of the supervisory board independent of management boards, dampens the short-termism of shareholders' value; thus, it contributes to the establishment of long-term cooperation.[64] But in a situation in which there seemed few alternatives to the traditional inefficiency of VW in the crisis of 1993, the VW works council supported Lopez's confrontational model instead of deterring it. VW employees had more to gain than to fear from the nomination of Lopez. The director of the VW Konzerne works council, Klus Volker, said that Lopez would be able to break away the crusted bureaucratic structure of VW.[65] The people of the works council supported Lopez's confrontational policy, worrying instead about their job security in the economic crisis.

Lopez adopted the new form of Japanese-style collaborative works with suppliers, but the governance of collaborative markets was adversarial. The Lopez team was sent to suppliers to impose rationalization, and at the same time, they requested a huge, unorthodox price cut. Lopez's purchasing and production teams generated distrust among suppliers by taking advantage of incomplete contracts and uncertain rules for collaboration. A supplier characterizes the situation: "The contract, which we made together, did not have worth anymore. We had to renegotiate the contract. It was unfair." Lopez's teams demanded cost reductions by frequently changing the conditions of the existing contract (*nachträglich*).[66] In the process of collaborative work, the Lopez team took advantage of suppliers' proprietary information.[67] The Lopez team also assisted suppliers in the process of rationalization, but the team requested price reductions greater than the supplier's savings. Moreover, the Lopez team did not consider the supplier's conditions of production. Hubertus Benteler, chief of a supplier company in Paderborn, maintained that "we need time for cost reductions but Lopez wants to have it always immediately."[68] Lopez's teams were concerned more with taking profits away from suppliers than with increasing the common pie through collaboration.

In the second half of the 1990s, VW slowly changed its confrontational model to cooperative relationships with suppliers. Although the Lopez approach had saved a huge amount of money,[69] it was abandoned after Lopez left VW in 1996. Francisco Garcia Sanz, the director of VW group purchasing who took over Lopez's position and brought an end to the Lopez policy, admitted in December 1997 that VW used to be "not an easy customer and sometimes uncomfortable."[70] When queried directly in my interviews, almost all German suppliers agreed that VW does not use the Lopez model any more ("Lopez model ist schon vorbei").[71]

German suppliers in my interviews reported the changes in VW as follows: "Now, the style is not so unfair as in 1993. The people [of VW] are thinking of partnership although they are still powerful"; "VW also has improved the relationships with suppliers. They follow DC's Tandem"; "Volkswagen group is also beginning the partnership recently. Volkswagen also tries to see the entire process, not the unit of product, and attempts to reduce the price through working together with suppliers."[72] VW reoriented its policy away from the unfair and confrontational model to fair partnerships with suppliers. Why did VW change the policy when the Lopez model had brought large savings? The reason is first that VW began to be concerned with quality. As a chief of VW purchasing teams responded when I asked why VW changed the policy: "One thing I would like to say: we are now concerned with cars of a high class. We have Lamborghini, Rolls-Royce and Bentley. VW is now changing to a 'technology group.'"[73] This answer may not be sufficient, considering that those high-class cars were not main concerns for Volkswagen AG, and that the policy of fair partnerships is also carried out for the mass-car sectors. An important factor is that VW needed more and more suppliers' cooperation, even for mass cars. As the chief of VW purchasing teams put it: "What we need is cooperation in the development. It is not possible to be the first one in the technology in the market by simply having numerous suppliers for each part. Therefore, we want to be more attractive to our suppliers to let them give us their latest development. We need a new philosophy to be more attractive to suppliers."[74] VW needed suppliers' voluntary cooperation to keep pace with the rapidly changing technology. The reason VW wanted trustful cooperation with German suppliers is that it had come to recognize through its own experiences that the cheapest supplier is not always the best. In the mid 1990s, VW, like other large German customers, rushed to foreign suppliers in low-wage countries. Sometimes the German supplier's know-how was transferred to the foreign suppliers in order to get a better price, which brought criticism from German suppliers. But VW, alongside other German customers, experienced many problems, such as quality issues, in dealing with the cheapest foreign suppliers. These events led customers to turn their business back to the old suppliers.[75] By 1997, VW maintained plenty of German suppliers. For example, VW outsourced 60 to 65 percent of total car value for the Golf model, and the rate for other car models in 1997 was similar. Eighty percent of the VW suppliers were German, while 15 to 18 percent came from the rest of Europe.[76]

Having experimented with cheap foreign suppliers and borne the costs of the subsequent quality problems, customers came to recognize that a relatively expensive but competent supplier could bring bigger benefits through small but frequent improvement of quality and cost reduction in the process of close collaboration for development as well as production. The benefits from collaboration with German suppliers became greater as German suppliers improved their development capability as well as their competence for quality production in the mid 1990s. According to the chief of VW purchasing: "It is really a short-term idea to choose the cheaper supplier. The supplier might bring the product in about 4DM cheaper. It is very nice! But we will not have a headlamp in a next project because the producer with very low level of price is normally not able to develop the products VW requested."[77] VW could hardly disregard the German suppliers, who had improved their competence as special problem solvers rather than simple traditional parts suppliers.[78] VW began to recognize that collaborative work with competitive suppliers brings much greater benefits than simply choosing the cheapest one in the market.

But perhaps the most important reason for the policy makeover was that VW had difficulty generating voluntary cooperation from German suppliers, who protested against VW's unfair policies. The Lopez teams' unfair behavior aroused an abundance of criticism not just from suppliers but also from trade unions, associations, and politicians. For example, Sigrid Skarpelis-Sperk, an economic politician in the Social Democratic Party (SPD), called a hearing in the Bundestag criticizing automakers' abuse of power.[79] IG Metall stipulated six conditions for partnership after criticizing automakers' unfairness.[80] Numerous supplier trade associations, such as foundry and forging and die-casting industry associations, accused German automakers of unfair behaviors. The supplier trade associations built a confederation called the *Arbeitsgemeinschaft Zulieferindustrie* (ArGeZ) to organize their opposition power against automakers. The ArGeZ, the VDA (German Automobile Association), and the BDI (German Industry Association) tried to deter unfair behaviors by mediating both sides of conflicts or protesting the actions of a specific customer and publishing the unfair cases.

VW could not disregard public criticism continuously because VW was also concerned with its own reputation. VW had to justify its policy or mitigate the confrontation. For example, the VW supervisory board considered sending Lopez to the Seat of Spain in order to avoid bad publicity from tough relationships with suppliers and legal conflicts about industrial espionage with GM.[81] The Lower Saxony government, which owns 20 percent of VW shares and 40 percent of its voting capital, tried to mitigate conflicts between VW and suppliers. The Lower Saxony government organized conferences for peaceful adjustment in which representatives of management, unions, and academic institutions participated. VW chief Ferdinand Pïech and purchasing director Lopez had to justify their policy in these meetings.[82] For example, in May 1993, VW's Pïech and Lopez, the VDA president, and the representatives of the supplier industry met at the initiative of Gerhard Schröder, then president of Lower Saxony and a VW supervisory member. In this meeting, Lopez was berated for his relentless purchasing policies. Supplier representatives held that German suppliers had already improved productivity more than automakers had. VW chief Pïech repeatedly promised that "We request from our suppliers no more than we ask from our own plants."[83] Pïech and Lopez also emphasized international competition and the backwardness of German production as their justification. VW bore the burden of justifying its position in front of the public through numerous meetings, a process quite different from the U.S. scenario.

Following these meetings, VW had increased difficulty initiating voluntary cooperation with German suppliers. VW's justification based on economic necessity became less effective once suppliers and social agents had articulated fair partnership as a feasible alternative to unfair confrontation in the collaborative market. From the second half of 1992 to early 1994, when German automakers and suppliers were in the middle of an economic crisis, VW's justification for its tough policies, which emphasized economic necessity, tough international competition, and the backwardness of German productivity, was relatively effective.[84] In the face of numerous international studies revealing the backwardness of German suppliers' productivity, suppliers admitted that they needed restructuring. German suppliers complained of Lopez's relentless pressure, but they admitted that they needed Lopez to overcome the crisis of the German automobile industry. German suppliers did not believe that the old entrenched bureaucratic structure of VW, which Lopez and Pïech were dismantling, could be helpful for the German automobile (parts) industry. According to consulting company Weirauch & Partner's survey of 364 managers in German auto supplier companies, 95 percent of managers of VW supplier companies and 84 percent of managers of non-VW supplier companies evaluated Lopez as "a top manager with capability to execute reform" (*durchsetzungsfähigen Spitzenmanager*); 58 percent of VW suppliers and 72 percent of non-VW suppliers believed that without Lopez, the VW bureaucratic mentality (*VW-Beamtenmentalität*) would take over. Although they complained about Lopez's relentless policies, suppliers did not believe that Lopez should retreat. In the crisis of the early 1990s, German suppliers needed Lopez's talent for breaking through the crisis, even though they disliked him.[85]

However, as suppliers slowly overcame the crisis by restructuring their organization in the mid 1990s, VW's continuing justification based on the backwardness of German productivity became less effective. First of all, as German suppliers who had rejected the new form of collaborative market at the inception of transformation developed an alternative to the Lopez model in the new form of collaborative markets, "German suppliers slowly started to show less respect to the 'relentless' [Lopez]," as a headline in a main German daily newspaper (*Frankfurter Allgemeine Zeitung*) put it in 1995. A description of a public meeting between Lopez and suppliers indicates clearly how much difficulty Lopez faced in arousing voluntary cooperation from suppliers.

His English is hard to understand, and his German is as good as not. In whole and fragmented, Spanish-sounding sentences are shot forward. ... Ignacio Lopez, executive for Production and Purchasing of Volkswagen AG, was instructing the chiefs of 300 automotive suppliers in Frankfurt that they have no ground for optimism. ... Again and again he warns of the Japanese capability for restructuring and the fast growing states in the Asian-Pacific Rim. "Always the same" groaned many men in the hall in lowered voices. "The crisis is not fate but a challenge," Lopez preaches and tells the suppliers what they have to do; ... "the total value-creation chain should be considered"; ... "The solution to the cost crisis lies in the collaboration [*Zusammenarbeit*] between automakers and suppliers." Lopez swore to the patiently listening people: "They will kill us if we are not together." "They" are the Asians. What Lopez means by collaboration [*Zusammenarbeit*] is this: from the [normal market] price that the customer is ready to pay, a certain amount is subtracted; a third of the [subtracted] amount will go to the suppliers as a "fair benefit,"; two-thirds goes to the customer as added value. ... What is normally left after subtracting a certain amount is actually the bare costs needed for the total production process. With the bare costs, suppliers must operate. Here the suppliers become restless [*unruhig*]: "What is a fair benefit at all, Mr. Lopez?," asks a supplier. "What does VW do anyway?" asks another. "Must the suppliers alone solve all the problems in the auto industry?" The 300 guests applaud; the mood escalates. Lopez pacifies them by referring to the improvement process in VW's own house and admits that theoretically all tiers in the value creation chain have to aim at the same profit in the end. "Everything is blah, blah [*Alles Blabla*]," a listener whispers to his neighbor. One man stands up and asks whether it is true or not that VW has had bad experiences with certain foreign suppliers and is now paying German suppliers [*Anbietern*] all of the price again, only to get satisfactory parts. He does not receive any real answer from Lopez. ... Another director of a supplier company dares to show with the microphone his disappointment and advises Lopez: "Before you arouse the enthusiasm of your customers, you had better first arouse your partners—your suppliers."[86]

VW could hardly generate cooperation from suppliers by disregarding the fair rules that suppliers had established in the public realm. If there were no socially shared fair rules, powerful automakers like VW could easily carry out opportunistic policies, taking advantage of competition among suppliers as has already been seen in the American case. But unlike the American automotive parts market, in which associations regard the automakers' unfair behaviors as private issues and suppliers try to solve the problems in an individual, dyadic relation with a customer, German suppliers and associations have established an alternative of fair rules by the process in which they criticized unfair behaviors and deliberated solutions in numerous formal and informal meetings, which will be investigated later in detail. In the public realm, customers have the burden of justifying their behavior. VW had to generate cooperation by embracing society-wide norms or else lose legitimacy.

Relationships between Suppliers

Reluctant to pursue adversarial American-style relationships between suppliers, German suppliers have developed fair partnerships and solidarity among themselves. In the American market, first-tier suppliers such as Delphi, Lear, and Navistar transfer their burdens directly to sub-tier suppliers, and unfair treatment and pressure pass all the way down through the supplier chain. By contrast, German first-tier suppliers do not confront their sub-tier suppliers in the same way as they are treated by automakers. In my mini-survey, as has already been shown, almost all American sub-tier suppliers (90 percent) agreed that the unfair buck was passed down through the supplier chain. By contrast, most German sub-tier suppliers (89 percent) maintained that first-tier suppliers did not confront them. Many other surveys in Germany, such as those conducted by Andreas Bartelt (2000) and Lay and Wallmeier (1999), also confirm my finding that higher-tier and sub-tier suppliers in the German markets have developed trustful cooperation.[87] When automakers pressed prices down significantly in the crisis of 1993, many first-tier suppliers in Germany tried to find another, more cooperative way of reducing costs. A German supplier describes the situation of the crisis: "At that time, there was more combining feeling [we-feeling] among suppliers against Lopez. For example, the customer people [first-tier suppliers] said to us, 'We have problems, as everybody knows. We have to work somehow. How can we?' At that time we were more cooperative, to meet the pressure together."[88] As was shown in chapter 1 of this book, German suppliers have developed solidarity and fair partnerships among themselves regardless of power and tier position, contrary to the expectations of power theorists.

Why and how have German suppliers developed fair cooperation among themselves? Why have German high-tier suppliers not damaged relationships with sub-tier suppliers by easily transferring unfair treatment and pressure down the supply chain, as their American counterparts have? The reason for fair cooperation among German suppliers is not that German suppliers lacked a tier structure like the Americans'; although they are less strictly pyramidal than Japanese relations, German relations between suppliers did become closer to the pyramidal tier structure. Perhaps the main reason for society-wide fair partnerships among suppliers is that German suppliers struggle against unfair behavior by big customers in the public realm. In a later section, the process of the public way of social adjustment will be delved into in detail. In this section, an investigation is made as to why and how German suppliers have developed solidarity and fair partnerships among themselves. In particular, the strategies of German suppliers in the automotive parts markets will be highlighted in order to show their method of responding to the customers' unfair and tough pressure, which differs from that of their American counterparts.

The reason for trustful cooperation among German suppliers is first that their strategies for the development of semi-assembled systems increased complementarity among themselves. While strategies of volume orientation and quick growth by acquisition prevailed among the Americans suppliers, German suppliers did not tend to use either of these tactics. In the U.S. supplier market, quick growth by acquisition and volume orientation caused an overlapping of suppliers' products and specialties that deterred trustful cooperation among suppliers. By contrast, specialty orientation and less quick growth in German supplier society contributed to cooperation among suppliers due to their complementarity of specialty. Why are German suppliers more likely to focus on their small specialty than Americans? Why are German suppliers less likely to grow quickly by acquisition or merger? The reasons for low levels of quick growth by acquisition will be addressed first.

In order to meet complicated tasks and develop the semi-assembled systems that automakers request in the new collaborative market, German suppliers are more likely to use collaboration between small companies. PricewaterhouseCoopers' Global Automotive Deal Survey 1998 reveals that although there was a trend of merger and acquisitions, the frequency and volume of these between German companies were far below the level of American companies. In these acquisition deals, American companies accounted for 56.6 percent (180 deals) of the world's automotive supplier deals; deals by Germans made up 6.9 percent of the total. American companies are used to antagonistic takeovers, accomplished against the will of the existing management because of their stock market system. A study of all industries conducted by J. P. Morgan confirms that German companies are less likely to choose the strategy of hostile takeover. According to J. P. Morgan, there have been 222 hostile takeovers in Europe since 1990; only four of these takeover deals involved German companies, while most involved British companies, which engaged in 148 hostile bids.[89] The financial system of stock markets in the U.S. and the U.K. facilitated antagonistic takeovers, whereas the German financial system, based on banks, tended to discourage them. In particular, co-determination (*Mitbetstimmung*) as a peculiarity of German corporate governance tended to deter antagonistic takeovers by potential predators, although contrary to institutionalist explanation, co-determination and the patient financial system alone did not generate long-term and trustful relationships with suppliers, as has already been investigated.

In addition, most small- and medium-sized supplier companies in Germany are less oriented to a simple expansion policy because they are, in most cases, family-owned. Under family ownership, German suppliers are very cautious about simply expanding the size of company because they are averse to dependence on banks and other financial institutions.[90] Furthermore, most family owners of small- and medium-sized companies in Germany do not easily sell or buy out their own companies because they have strong emotional attachments to them. In a given region, the company often has long been identified with the family itself in the sense of social reputation and status. An owner of a small company remarked, "Everyone in this region knows who I am. Through several generations, my family is the company. The company does not mean just money or profit. The company also means my family."[91] The owners of German supplier companies under family ownership are less likely to sell the company and move to another place than are Americans under the stock-market system.

Although German suppliers outsourced their production to foreign countries very aggressively in the globalizing 1990s due to high costs of production in Germany, they did not give up domestic production in Germany. According to a survey by the *Wirtschaftsverband Stahlverformung* (Trade Association of Steel Forging) in 1996, about 75 percent of German suppliers confirmed that globalization contributed to the security of domestic employment.[92] To ratchet up competitiveness without depending on great financial power or opting for quick expansion through acquisition, German suppliers had to find another strategy, which was in most cases to improve their quality, productivity, and innovative power by focusing on a small core-specialty area. In addition, German suppliers made use of the synergic effects of intercompany collaboration instead of mergers or acquisitions. The strategy of focusing on small core specialties and using intercompany collaboration contributed to the growth of complementarity between suppliers in the German markets; thus, these strategies were more likely to contribute to the establishment of trustful cooperation among German suppliers than among their American counterparts.

Furthermore, because Germany has the highest labor and production costs, German suppliers compete with foreign competitors in low-wage countries not in the areas of price competition or economies of scale, but in differentiation of products, better quality, and innovative products. As is demonstrated in table 9, German suppliers at the turn of the century focused on improvement of quality, innovation, and product flexibility, rather than price leadership. Even small companies in the German automotive parts market prioritized quality, innovation, and product differentiation over price leadership.

TABLE 9 Competition Strategy Following the Size of Company

	Automobile Suppliers with			
	below 100 Employees (n=19)	100 to 499 Employees (n=26)	500 and More Employees (n=20)	P[1]
Factor for competition (without multiple entry)				
Price	5.3%	7.7%	20.0%	.278
Quality	52.6%	42.3%	20.0%	.100
Innovation	15.8%	23.1%	35.0%	.381
Punctuality of delivery	10.5%	7.7%	0.0%	.371
Product flexibility	10.5%	19.2%	25.5%	.516
Service	5.3%	0.0%	0.0%	.303

[1]Test on the sameness of mean with the one factor ANOVA. Significant on the 5% level.
Source: Lay and Wallmeier (1999b: 27).

This does not mean, however, that German companies persist in their traditional production system as institutionalist explanation holds. On the contrary, in the new environment of international competition, in which foreign lean producers in Japan and the U.S. can produce more flexibly than German companies based on professional specialization, German companies have had to restructure their production and market systems. Actually, until the late 1980s, as chapter 1 of this book reveals, few suppliers developed collaborative market relations in Germany. Many suppliers were not open to discussing their problems in the associations because they worried about leaking information about their specialties. A chief of a supplier industry association describes clearly the different mood during the 1980s and the 1990s: "In the past, they [suppliers] were closed, just focusing on their secret know-how, worrying that somebody else might steal the know-how; today the mood has changed. They are more open and look around."[93] German suppliers changed their attitude in the same associations, seeking and developing new cross-functional collaboration. In order to compete with lean producers and low-wage–based foreign producers, Germans in the automotive industry had to reorganize their traditional methods of skill formation and skill deployment in the production process, which in turn caused changes in traditional corporatist institutions, to be examined later. German suppliers' strategies of high quality and product differentiation had to be pursued under a new type of production and market system completely different from the past craft system and distant markets, contrary to the institutionalist explanation. Although the advanced training system for highly skilled labor continues to be utilized and emphasized, high-skilled labors are organized under the priority of cross-functional teams in the entire process of value creation.

In order to do this, German suppliers first improved their competence as development partners or special problem solvers for the collaborative market, while at the same time undertaking massive restructuring of their production process throughout the 1990s, as will be highlighted later. Traditionally, German suppliers were called "expanded working places" (*verlängerte Werkbänke*). Few suppliers had independent development capacity; most produced the simple parts developed by customers, serving as a buffer zone for fluctuations in the automobile business. Except in the cases of several large companies like Bosch, suppliers invested very little capital in development, as little as 1 percent of their turnover.[94] They were production specialists, not developers. But as table 10 shows, German suppliers spent plenty of capital to improve their competence as development partners.

TABLE 10 Investment in the German Automotive Industry (investment % of turnover)

	1993	1994	1995	1996	1997	1998	1999
Small supplier[1]	—	5.9	6.3	6.5	6.7	8.9	9.8
Middle supplier[2]	—	4.2	5.9	6.6	7.2	9.9	8.1
Big supplier[3]	—	4.3	4.8	6.9	6.8	5.5	5.0
Average for Supplier		4.9	5.5	6.7	6.8	7.2	6.7
Automakers[4]	—	4.1	4.2	5.2	5.6	5.4	5.1

[1]Turnover of less than DM 50 Million.
[2]Turnover between DM 50 and 100 Million.
[3]Turnover of more than DM 100 Million.
[4]Mercedes-Benz is excluded from 1997 data.
Source: My own calculation based on *IKB Branchenbericht* from 1997 to 1999.

At the end of the 1990s, 80 percent of small suppliers had the capacity for their own product development, as did 92 percent of medium-sized suppliers and 94.7 percent of big suppliers. A notable point is not just that German suppliers improved their competence as development partners in a short time, but also that even small suppliers developed the competence to be development partners.[95] The prevalent view that only system suppliers would prosper with their development capacity while small suppliers would suffer is too simple an idea. Small companies were able to improve their competence as development partners by reducing their focal areas. Traditionally, German suppliers developed a strategy of diversification of products in order to hedge their market fluctuation. But in the 1990s, in order to improve their competence with relatively little capital, German small suppliers focused on a small area by reducing the size of their company or their product ranges.[96] By concentrating on a small, core specialty, they were able to increase their competence for development and innovation, resulting in more complicated and value-added products.[97]

The strong concentration on specialty in Germany facilitated horizontal cooperation through mutual complementarity. This is in contrast to the case in the U.S., where it is easy to find that system suppliers and components suppliers in collaborative work are very cautious of sharing information in light of the overlapping of their products. German suppliers are less likely to overlap with each other, thanks to their specialty orientation. In Germany there are few suppliers that produce a whole system. A relatively large component supplier coordinates with other component suppliers for, say, a sealing system, whereas American automakers buy a total sealing system from one system supplier. In most cases, a German system supplier is just an integrator of component suppliers while maintaining its core specialty.[98]

However, the concentration on small specialty areas does not mean confinement to a narrow specialty. On the contrary, German suppliers developed cross-functional teams and collaborative market relations in order to overcome the rigidity of the traditional craft system. Traditionally, German suppliers, who focused on a narrow specialty based on the craft system, did not consider the technical connection between their products and other parts that automakers purchased. The traditional craft-based system hindered cross-functional communication and collaborative work. What German companies made tremendous efforts toward in the 1990s was reorganization of this craft-based system into cross-functional teams and collaborative market systems. In a collaborative market, German suppliers came to consider the technical connections and side effects among different parts.

Reflection on the rigidity of narrow-minded specialty turned German suppliers toward more proactive, close interaction with others in order to improve their flexible innovation. German suppliers came to recognize that the collaborative markets are very important for their innovation.[99] Although some suppliers suffered from unfair treatment such as the leaking of confidential information by customers, they were very proactive in maintaining close interactions with customers and other suppliers, instead of retreating to independent rationalization in-house as they had in the past. For example, one exhaust system supplier, whose chief had protested unfair cases in a public meeting, did not distance itself from close interactions with customers because the supplier could not be at the forefront of innovation in the absence of closely interactive relations with customers as well as their own suppliers. As an employee of the system supplier put it, "If this firm alone develops a new product and puts the patent on it, the product is very safe, but the product might not be fit for the customer's demand."[100] Many suppliers in my interviews reported a similar strategy: "Keeping a current confidentiality and patent is very passive. Opening and working together is the best and a very active policy to keep ahead in the current trend of technology and production efficiency."[101] It was through close connection with customers as well as with neighboring suppliers that German suppliers developed strong innovation of products and production regardless of their position in the supplier chain.[102] The strategy of flexible innovation through close interaction with customers as well as their own suppliers is more likely to involve German suppliers in the governance of relationships.

The strategies of German suppliers—concentration on small specialties instead of quick expansion by acquisition, product differentiation and flexible innovation instead of price leadership or volume orientation, reflection upon rigidity of traditional craft-based systems and narrow-minded specialties, and flexible innovation through close interaction with others—contributed to the development of fair partnerships in the German automotive parts market. In particular, as German sub-tier suppliers develop their high competence as development partners, it becomes more costly to lose the benefits resulting from close interactions with them. Without close and flexible cooperation with sub-tier suppliers, a system supplier is more likely to lag in quality and technology in its own market.[103]

However, the relatively high complementarity that stems from German suppliers' concentration on their specialties might not be sufficient to explain the fair partnerships between suppliers. For example, although Ymos AG had successfully developed a new door module for Daimler's Smart car by collaborating with other suppliers, as Gerhard Krischer, chief of Ymos AG, emphasized, they needed clearer fair rules for governance of the relationships. The closer the relations between companies, the more the new norms of fairness are needed.[104] Collaborative works themselves do not generate fair norms, as was shown in the investigation of American supplier relations in chapter 2 of this book. Agents must expend effort to make new rules. In this sense, it is noteworthy that German suppliers have developed their own fair norms for governance of the new collaborative markets through a process of protesting unfair customers in numerous meetings. German first-tier suppliers could hardly generate voluntary cooperation from sub-tier suppliers by overruling the socially shared norms. In the situation of high complementarity in which first-tier suppliers need sub-tier suppliers' assistance for flexible application engineering, losing legitimacy through unfair behavior can damage their competitiveness in the markets.

It is more noteworthy that German high-tier suppliers could not reasonably violate the fair criteria that they themselves had set in the process of criticizing automakers' unfairness in formal or informal meetings, an effect that can be termed "self-binding by self-legislation." In the first half of the 1990s, when automakers treated suppliers in an unfair way, German suppliers organized criticism against automakers in the public realm. In this process, suppliers felt solidarity against automakers; in addition, they developed their own fair criteria for governance of long-term and collaborative markets. In other words, the process of criticizing unfairness in the public sphere was also the process of expressing and building self-criteria. If a supplier criticized customers' unfair behavior in the public sphere, the supplier could hardly impose the same unfairness on its sub-tier suppliers.

This logic is born out in practice. In particular cases in which a first-tier supplier behaves in an unfair way, the sub-tier suppliers sometimes notify an automaker of the unfairness of the first-tier supplier who has accused the automaker of unfairness; or, an association of sub-tier suppliers reports the unfairness to the German Automobile Association (VDA), the forum where the first-tier supplier accused the automaker of unfair behavior. The effect of self-binding by self-legislation will be considered in depth in the next section which discusses social adjustment.

Social Adjustment in the German Automotive Parts Market

Although German automakers needed collaboration from highly competent suppliers, as the former, American case shows, powerful automakers might have continuously executed their own rules in individual, dyadic relations if there had not been massive efforts by German suppliers and social agents to protest against unfair behavior and to establish alternatives in the public realm. Although German suppliers have a relatively strong complementarity in comparison with American suppliers, system suppliers might have easily passed their pressure on to sub-tier suppliers, taking advantage of competition among them, if there had not been solidarity generated by suppliers in the process of struggling against automakers' unfair behavior in the public realm. This section explores how German suppliers and social agents established an alternative of fair rules, in particular the manner in which the public way of deliberating conflicts affects governance and the conception of fairness.

The different practices of adjudicating conflicts have led to differences between the American and German market regimes. German suppliers established fair partnerships as an alternative to a confrontational model in the process of publicly criticizing automakers' unfair behavior. If automakers and system suppliers were to generate voluntary cooperation from suppliers, they could not continuously disregard socially shared criteria of fairness. In the process of struggling against automakers' unfairness, German suppliers have formed a common front against unfairness. The solidarity of sharing common criteria for fairness makes it difficult for

German first-tier suppliers to violate fair norms, mainly because they would be reluctant to contradict their own criteria in public view. Before the public way of adjudicating conflicts and the manner in which it affects governance are highlighted, the next subsection will investigate the social fabric that might influence the establishment of stable communities.

Social Fabric

Relatively long-term personal relationships in a small society contribute to stable observance of social norms not simply because the long-term relationships might increase future benefits, but also because familiarity in a small and densely constituted community facilitates the sharing of common norms and makes social reprimands possible. If a small community has an abundance of benefits from socialized capital and common activities, agents are less likely to defect, considering the benefits from the utilization of socialized capital. Furthermore, social networks provide agents with basic connections through which they can develop the civic public realm for collective deliberation. This does not mean that the dense networks of German associations generated civic norms. As has already been examined in chapter 2 of this book, contrary to institutionalist explanation, the new norms of the 1990s were developed neither by the corporatist resolution nor by regulatory courts in Germany. By contrast, the traditional structure of centralized corporatist institutions did change. True, there is little change in formal institutions such as co-determination and centralized corporatist coordination, but the scope of institutional coverage, the way of working, and the role of German institutions in the economic system, at the practical level, have changed.

This section focuses on the changes in the social fabric. A market society is not fixed, but is constantly changing due to agents' reflection on the rationality of the current organization. For example, in U.S. markets, the introduction of a cross-functional training system contributed to the instability of personal relationships between buyers and vendors. This subsection explores how German agents in the automotive parts market reorganized the construction of their society in the process of restructuring during the 1990s, and what effects the changed organization had on the establishment of stable norms.

Traditionally, people in German companies had long-term personal relationships, which were cultivated by the peculiar German training system called the "dual system."[105] Normally, German skilled workers must complete a three-year vocational training course (*Berufausbildung*) before being employed. Trainees must complete an apprenticeship within a company while at the same time receiving formal schooling at a public vocational school (*Berufschule*). This dual system of vocational training, along with the highly tracked and standardized education system, results in Germans getting jobs very closely related to their educational backgrounds.

For example, approximately 80 percent of those who complete an apprenticeship find a job in the occupational field in which they are trained. Twelve years after leaving school, approximately 60 percent of apprentices still work in the same occupational field. By contrast, five years after leaving school, approximately 70 percent of Americans work at jobs without any formal skill requirements.[106] Because of the high cost of long-term apprenticeship and the tracked German education system, few people give up their current specialty to move to another. Moreover, skill in a specialized area is not just a technical matter but is closely related to social status. People in a specialized area have long-term personal relationships because they rarely move to a different specialty. This dual system was, until the late 1980s, praised as an instrument for producing highly skilled labor.

As has already been discussed, the crisis of the craft system–based German model in competition with lean producers in the early 1990s revealed that the traditional craft-based production system needed restructuring. To increase flexibility, German companies reorganized their vocational training system, moving toward more generalism in the skill formation; they also adopted a cross-functional team structure in the sense of skill deployment, as their American counterparts did in the 1990s. In addition, contrary to the arguments of Comparative Institutional Advantage theorists, Germans began to deconstruct their centralized corporatist coordination, rather than enjoying the advantages resulting from the corporatist institutions. As Germans adopted cross-functional teams and closely interactive supplier relations in the 1990s, the traditional centralized corporatist coordination of wages, working conditions, and skill formation was undergoing transformation toward "decentralization" or "de-standardization" by way of such practices as company- or plant-level pacts and organization-based training (learning by doing).

For example, according to studies by the Economic and Social Science Institute (Wirtschafts- und Sozialwissenschaftliches Institut: WSI), the usage of opening clauses by German companies increased from 10 percent in 1994 to 22 percent in 1999. The usage of hardship clauses, which allow a company to diverge from the collective standard under certain conditions with the support of both trade unions and employer associations, also increased to 28 percent in East Germany during this period. About 15 percent of German companies simply breach the valid collective agreements, thereby engaging in unregulated decentralization. The Works Council Survey 1999/2000, conducted by the WSI, suggested that there might be additional cases of unknown "unregulated contravention," considering that the works councils have difficulty declaring their plants' contravention of collective agreements.[107] In particular, small- and medium-sized companies, which account for two-thirds of total employees in Germany, increasingly tend to exit from collective agreements. In a survey conducted by the Association of Medium-Sized Companies, one-third of West German companies do not strictly follow the collective agreements.[108] In 1997, only 14.4

percent of West German plants and 12.3 percent of East German plants were covered by valid collective agreements as well as works councils. Additionally, 29.5 percent of the West German plants and 46 percent of the East German plants had neither a works council nor a collective agreement. Plant-level bargaining replaced centralized sectoral bargaining, as 46 percent of large German companies negotiated company-level pacts.[109] As German companies began to doubt the suitability of corporatist collective agreements in the 1990s, the density of employer associations declined significantly, from 59 percent in 1980 to 35 percent in 1998; in similar fashion, trade union density also declined significantly in the last decade, from 32.3 percent in 1991 to 21.3 percent in 2000.[110] Once centralized corporatist coordination of working conditions and wages was replaced by decentralized pacts at the plant level (*Verbetrieblichung von Regelungskompetenz*), corporatist institutions no longer provided either egalitarian wage structure or a linear wage increase. The "social peace" role of traditional corporatist industrial relations has been undermined, mainly by a weakening of labor in its power relations with capital and by high unemployment. Works councils have also changed their main role: once the protectors of standards of collective agreements, they now function largely as consultants, engaging in telephone consulting, conducting seminars on specific issues, and providing honorary recommendations.

More importantly, the traditional methods of skill formation and deployment of skills in production, realized by centralized corporatist institutions, were undergoing transformation, contrary to the institutionalist explanation. While the theorists of Comparative Institutional Advantage argue otherwise, Germans did indeed change their appreciation of corporatist institutional advantages. German employers began to doubt the effectiveness of the corporatist solution—that is, centralized corporatist coordination of deep skilling for its craft production system. The vocational training system in Germany, a dual system of practical training at a company and theoretical education at school, had been realized by centralized corporatist coordination among labor, capital, and the state. But as German managers became more sensitive to costs and to the pressure of cost reduction, and as German employers began to see vocational training as a cost factor rather than a strategy of investing in human capital for long-term benefits, the vocational training system began to change. Training contracts for apprenticeships decreased dramatically, dropping by half between 1987 and 1995. For example, in metalworking industries, the number of apprenticeship contracts declined from 51,637 in 1987 to only 27,490 in 1993. More importantly, employers and industrial experts in Germany began to question the suitability of the traditional corporatist coordination of skill formation within the new system of flexible lean production. The rapid changes in technology rendered formally defined occupations obsolete, and adjusting to new problems in the process of cross-functional collaboration took time. To increase workers' competence for cross-functional collaboration, Germans reformed their vocational training, revising more than 100 regulations on the curricula and procedures of vocational training and creating about twenty six new vocations. At the same time, German companies began to focus on retraining and organization-based training (learning by doing) instead of basic vocational training.[111] As the production system moved from its traditional vocation-oriented basis toward a cross-functional team structure, vocational training tended to shift from traditional specialization to flexibilization through de-specialization or generalism (*Flexibilisierung des Arbeitskräftepotentials durch berufliche Entspezialisierung*), although the qualification levels of skilled workers were not reduced.[112]

However, these changes in traditional practices and institutions do not mean convergence toward the American model or convergence toward the best practices, contrary to neoliberal expectation. These German cross-functional teams do not exactly mirror the American or Japanese cross-functional teams, although the restructuring of German industry was inspired by the foreign models of Japanese and American lean production. American companies developed a complete team structure, while many German companies created a dual structure of functional departments and process-oriented teams. The German version is a kind of creative imitation based on reflection on their own institutions.

The effects of cross-functional teams upon the social fabric differ from those produced in the U.S. Although Germans companies have adopted cross-functional teams, German people in German companies maintain relatively long personal customer-supplier relationships in comparison with those in American companies, mainly because of the differing forms of newly created cross-functional organization. As chapter 2 of this book reveals, the adoption of cross-functional teams in the U.S. has generated instability in personal relationships between buyers and vendors. By adopting a cross-functional training system, American companies circulate their people across different functional areas. In the past, people in American companies moved within a functional department, climbing up the ladder of hierarchy within the department. But since American companies adopted cross-functional team structure in the 1990s, the standard is now for newcomers in a company to move among the different departments during the several years of their training. Due to this cross-functional training system and high turnover, American suppliers see frequent changes of trading partners; American companies circulate their people so often that trading partners rarely have time to develop stable personal relationships.

By contrast, German companies do not circulate their people as frequently as Americans do, although they have also successfully adopted cross-functional teams. The reason for the relatively stable personal relationships in Germany is not the persistence of the old pattern of the craft system, but the peculiar form of the metrics structure that has resulted from various experiments of restructuring. This particular form of the German cross-functional team is rooted neither in the persistence of the traditional path of the vocation-oriented production system, nor in an exact convergence toward an ideal method of production. In an early stage of restructuring, some German companies adopted a complete team structure to overcome the problems of traditional vocational and functional departments. But under the complete team structure, people in a small team were overburdened with several projects, and they had problems coordinating priority among different projects.[113] The result was that people in different teams were performing the same job twice. Furthermore, different teams duplicated each other's efforts because the capability of a specialty was dispersed to small teams.[114]

Now, the ongoing efforts to reduce redundancy have produced a new, dual structure incorporating both teams and departments. German companies under the new system still maintain vocational and functional departments to accumulate and coordinate specialties. But the departments in this new dual structure are not the same as those within a structure of complete departments. "In the past, the departments were a kind of kingdom. Recently, the project teams have sovereignty," said a director of marketing and public relation in a large supplier company.[115] Although departments still exist, the process-oriented teams are at the center of organizing jobs for a project. A team recruits people from departments as the teamwork proceeds. Departments serve the operation of a team, and people are educated to fulfill the team's work.[116] Due to this dual system, people in German companies are more likely to move within departments rather than across departments. Career movement in Germany is still closely related to educational background.

In addition to the circulation of people in a company, the different structures of the cross-functional teams in the U.S. and German markets create different kinds of solidarity and identity among people. American automakers develop a complete team structure based on a car model. Competition in a U.S. company occurs between different platform teams based on car models. By contrast, under the dual system of teams and departments in German companies, competition occurs between different specialties. For example, the electronics department in a German company addresses only electronic parts but for different car models (e.g., E- and S-class cars at Mercedes), while mechanical departments address each mechanical part for various cars. People in different specialties, including suppliers, compete with one another for importance and influence in making a car, considering the target costs. For example, the design of parts, procedure of jobs, and location of parts can change the costs. The competition between different specialties in Germany creates strong identity and solidarity among people within a special area, including suppliers. A chief of the Mercedes purchasing team clearly describes the identity of people in the same specialty:

For example, the mechnical [engine] guys and electronic guys are very different people. They have their own style. They sometimes have difficulty in
understanding each other. But, within their Fachbereich, they have a strong solidarity. They are proud of their products. Mercedes engineers in a department
and their direct suppliers know each other very well because they are in the
same mindset.[117]

The people in the same special area, including suppliers, have relatively
strong solidarity among themselves, although recent vocational training
has encouraged more generalism.[118]

Due to the differing circulation of people and the different structure of
organization, personal relationships in the German auto industry are relatively longer and more stable than those in the U.S. In my interview, the
chief of BMW purchasing said that "[s]ome people in the seating-devel-
opment section of R&D department have about 20 years' contact with
suppliers. It is not so exceptional. The relationships with suppliers in personal contact are very stable."[119] This is not just BMW's story. A chief of a
purchasing team at VW remarked on the same topic: "[People] stay for a
longer time in the same department because they have to accumulate their
knowledge and very specific know-how."[120] Many German suppliers
report that they have been in contact with most of their customers for five
to ten years, and that they will meet with a buyer again in the future. Inci-
dentally, German suppliers complain that they have difficulty developing
long-term personal relationships with American customers.

Another reason for the stable personal relationships in Germany is that
in German companies, buyers receive no personal bonus based on individual achievements of price cuts. It is more important for buyers seeking
promotion in German companies to develop ties with a reliable, high-
quality supplier.[121] In contrast, American buyers often want to reduce
prices during short-term contact in order to get personal bonuses.

Yet another interesting thread in the weaving of the social fabric is the
fact that Germans have built new social networks in addition to their existing social networks of associations. Based on their strategies, such as a hes-
itancy to quickly expand, concentration on a small specialty, and flexible
innovation through close interactions with others, Germans built new social
networks in order to restructure their organizations. In the early 1990s,
when the traditional craft system revealed its rigidity and automakers
requested many organizational reforms to overcome the structural crisis,
German suppliers suffered not just from a limitation of financial resources,
but also from the problem of deciding how to overcome the structural crisis. In this situation, they tried to develop collective solutions by building
social networks. Many social agents such as associations and regional governments facilitated the development of voluntary collaborative activities
among suppliers, organizing many automotive "Initiatives" in each *Land*
(state). For example, the VIA (Verbundinitiativ Automobil NRW) was established in Nordrheinwestfalen; the Gemeinschaftsinitiative Wirtschaft und

Politik in Baden-Württemberg; the MOBIL in Hessen; BAIKA in Bayern; the Zulieferer-Initiative-Lean in Niedersachsen; the Automobil-Zulieferinitiative in Rheinland-Pfalz.[122] In these Initiatives in the German automotive industry, suppliers worked together first for organizational reforms such as team structure and total quality management; then they directed their efforts at facilitating collaboration for development. The VIA is worth examining as a typical example of the Initiatives.

The VIA in Nordrheinwestfalen represents a typical horizontal cooperation among suppliers.[123] At first, the VIA was initiated by a small working circle (*Arbeitskreis*) consisting of ten small- and medium-sized auto suppliers in the areas of Sauerland, Siegerland, and Bergisches Land. The cooperative project was further developed at the end of 1993 through the encouragement of the Nordrheinwestfalen economics minister. The advisory board (*Beirat*) of the VIA is constituted of representatives of all automakers as well as of suppliers, industry and commerce chambers, economic associations, trade unions, and banks. The everyday management of coordinating common projects is conducted by a consulting company called Agiplan AG.

The main job of the Initiative was to build supplier networks for horizontal cooperation to perform the complicated tasks requested by customers. The Initiative encouraged suppliers not only to restructure their organization but also to develop suppliers' competence, whereby the maker of a single part might move on to a more complicated component or system supplier through horizontal cooperation. For example, six auto suppliers from Nordrheinwestfalen cooperated on the development of a system. It was clear that the more rapid innovation and more complicated systems requested by automakers could hardly be realized by a small supplier alone. For the development of a lock system, the six suppliers, including a lock component maker, a special switch maker, and a sheet metal supplier, cooperated to develop a complicated lock system. The cooperative project was supported by VW and BMW and helped along by the consulting company Agiplan AG. After Agiplan AG informed suppliers about the VIA program, suppliers in the region submitted 190 projects, in which 720 companies participated until 1996. The cooperating suppliers could receive 50 percent of the financial support for their projects from the regional government. Participants in the projects could save costs by 20 to 35 percent. Actually, the lifespan of the VIA, originally set at five years, was extended further owing to its success.

In Bavaria, the BAIKA (Bayerischen Innovations- und Kooperationsinitiative- Automobilzulieferindustrie) was also initiated by many regional working circles (*Arbeitkreise*) under the leadership of Bayern Innovative GmbH in Nuremberg.[124] At the beginning, the eight regional *Arbeitkreise*— Augsburg, Bayreuth, Aschaffenburg, Ingolstadt, Nuremberg, Regensburg, Rosenheim, and Würzburg/Schweinfurt—were arranged to recognize concrete innovations and cooperation interests of the participant companies in the spheres of development, qualification, and information rationalization. Of the more than 700 companies that took part in the BAIKA programs, 230 companies delivered detailed information on their experiences and future goals. Through numerous workshops, suppliers came together to deliberate together their common problems, such as organizational reform, total quality management, and globalization. Meanwhile, twelve regional collaborative clusters were established. The activities of the clusters ranged from collaboration for purchasing common facilities to the analysis of experiences and collaborative development of products. Under the BAIKA's active involvement, about fifty collaboration projects for development of products had been launched by 1999. BAIKA managed to improve the competitiveness of suppliers through cooperation and network building.

These collaborative efforts and the support of social agents enabled German suppliers to carry out organizational reform in a very short time; in addition, they built more dense social networks. But a more important aspect of their establishment is that Germans have deliberated not only economic efficiency but also politics of market governance, unlike their American counterparts. A supplier who participated in the BAIKA evaluated the Initiative: "Such meetings [in BAIKA] are very important to us. We get new ideas of markets and trends in technology. And we find our sub-suppliers and customers there. We meet our current customers and suppliers in the meetings of the BAIKA. Yes, we also discuss the unfair behavior."[125] Considering that Americans in the automotive parts market have also developed many social networks but have failed to establish fair norms, the social networks might not be sufficient for the development of fair governance. The difference between the U.S. and German markets lies not in whether there are social networks, but in the ways of deliberating norms and understanding politics in the similar "physical" space that their social networks provide. The next section explores how Germans deliberate their conflicts and norms in the civic public realm.

The Public Way of Creation of Fair Norms

Long-term personal relationships and a closely knit community may not be sufficient for the establishment of fair partnerships in a collaborative market. Personal relationships may have a positive effect on the cultivation of stable relationships between companies, but as one empirical study reveals, agents in both U.S. and German companies are more likely to act based on the strategy and vision of their companies than on their personal relationships.[126] As we have seen, Americans in the market have developed dense social networks but have failed to establish society-wide fair norms for governance of long-term and collaborative markets. Dense networks may facilitate the consolidation of social norms, but they do not automatically generate civic norms. This was demonstrated in the 1990s, when the traditional regime of market governance ceased to work and agents in the U.S. and German markets had to build new ethical codes. Facing similar problems concerning the unclear governance of new, long-term, collaborative markets, Germans in the automotive parts market successfully established fair partnerships while their American counterparts did not, even given the latter's dense social networks. What really distinguishes the U.S. from German markets is the way that agents interact in social networks, in other words, *the different manners of adjudicating conflicts and deliberating norms*. This section investigates how Germans in the automotive parts market established the alternative of fair rules, particularly the manner in which the public way of deliberation affects governance and the conceptions of fairness.

The central reason for the difference in market regimes is that Germans in the automotive parts market created a distinctively public way of confrontation and deliberation, unlike their American counterparts. It was the suppliers' collective resistance against automakers in 1992 that first aroused the attention of the automotive industry community and initiated a public way of deliberation for the governance of the new collaborative markets.[127] German suppliers' complaints, which were on the rise, due to automakers' new requests for price cuts and new tasks intended for a collaborative market, exploded in 1992 when Audi requested an unconventional price cut of 5 to 10 percent, along with many organizational reforms. About forty suppliers held a meeting in Baden-Baden, directly opposing the automaker's new purchasing policies. The forty suppliers, all members of the German Automobile Association (VDA), in which there are about 350 first-tier suppliers, protested against not only the price pressure but also the "open information of costs" policy (*gläsernen Taschen*) for collaborative work, both considered unfair from the perspective of the traditional criteria of market governance. The rebel group threatened to build a new organization separate from the existing VDA. As one newspaper described it, "The tone between *mittelständischen* [small- and mid-sized] suppliers and their powerful customers became increasingly tougher and tougher."[128] Although the suppliers' revolt against automakers in 1992 did not provide a clear alternative to the automakers' confrontational model in a collaborative market, it was sufficient to arouse public attention and to initiate a public method of conflict adjustments.

The VDA, many social organizations, and local governments, tried to mitigate the most severe conflicts in numerous meetings. These efforts created a public method of deliberation in which agents could elaborate and justify their own criteria for a new policy. Major German newspapers and magazines criticized automakers' unfair cases. The Lower Saxony government, which holds 20 percent of share values and 40 percent of voting rights in VW, opened many public meetings between automakers, particularly VW representatives, and suppliers.[129] The SPD-Bundestag faction organized a meeting for discussing unfair cases and called a hearing in the congress to criticize automakers' abuse of power.[130] Trade unions, including IG Metall and IG Chemie, organized their own positions against automakers' confrontational policies.[131] Not only the German Industry Association (Der Bundesverband der Deutschen Industrie: BDI) but also many supplier associations, such as forging and die-casting industry associations, organized public discussions in which participants tried to build fair criteria for governance.

But the primary location of conflict adjustment after the open revolt in 1992 was the VDA, where the two sides, automakers and suppliers, confronted each other directly. The VDA tried to mitigate the conflicts by organizing such meetings as a "conversation for peace" (*Friedensgesprächen*) and a "supplier day" (*Zulieferertag*). In these meetings, suppliers articulated their opinions on fair governance by sharing their experiences of unfairness. For example, in a "supplier day" meeting, Hubert Stärker, chief of Zeuna-Stärker GmbH, a supplier company, reproached German automakers for exporting the intellectual property (*das geistige Eigentum*) of German suppliers to foreign competitors in low-wage countries. After Stärker's presentation, the rest of the suppliers also reported similar unfair experiences.[132] The representatives of suppliers held meetings independent of automakers in order to articulate their opinions, then took memoranda to automakers and developed mutual adjustments with them.

This process of adjustments between automakers and suppliers has paralleled the VDA's organizational changes. Traditionally, there were no special departments for suppliers in the VDA. A supplier reported to me in an interview, "In the past, the VDA was an association for car makers, not for the suppliers, but today there are many meetings constituted by both sides, automakers and suppliers."[133] After the strike of German suppliers, the VDA developed many channels for suppliers' independent voices. For example, it collected suppliers' complaints through committees such as the Fairness Committee (*Fairnessrat*). The Fairness Committee ensured that both the automakers and big suppliers observed fair rules.[134] The Fairness Committee addressed especially bad cases of unfairness and kept accusers anonymous to protect them from retaliation by the accused. Suppliers notified the *Fairnessrat* of unfair experiences, for instance, with an automaker that revised the contract arbitrarily. The *Fairnessrat*'s involvement encouraged the automaker to correct its policy. If a customer did not correct its behavior, the VDA published an account of the customer's behavior in the newspaper. Later, the top-level meetings constituted of the chief executives (CEOs) of automaker and supplier companies, gradually replaced the jobs of the *Fairnessrat*.[135] In the CEO meetings, automakers and suppliers discussed the problems of fair rules. The discussion was published, making it available to all of the members. Confrontation and adjustments in the VDA initiated the public way in which suppliers could develop socially shared criteria for fair rules.

Through confrontation and adjustments in numerous meetings, the VDA established basic rules for fair governance. The suppliers and automakers in the VDA created the Guidelines for Collaborative Works between Automakers and Suppliers (*Leitfaden für die Zusammenarbeit zwischen den Automobilherstellern und ihren Zulieferern*) in 1992. At their inception, the VDA-*Leitfaden* (Guidelines) had many limitations. They described only the basic spirit for cooperation, and there remained an abundance of issues to clarify further; thus, there was much room for different interpretations of fairness for cooperation.[136] The VDA-Guidelines were not so effective as one might expect not simply because Opel (GM) and Ford did not participate, but more importantly, because suppliers themselves did not establish clearly their own alternative to the automakers' requests to restructure and adopt collaborative markets. Suppliers at that time tended to oppose the collaborative market itself. Nevertheless, the social adjustments in the VDA were important in the sense that the VDA-Guidelines assured the Federal Cartel Office (Bundeskartellamt) of the abuse of automakers' power (*Nachfragmacht*); more importantly, they initiated a public process for creating fair norms.

The confrontation between automakers and suppliers in the early period of transformation toward a new market concerned not the kinds of governance that were called for in collaborative markets, but the confrontation between old norms of fairness and the necessity of new collaborative markets. In the crisis of the early 1990s, automakers proposed a new form of collaborative market by emphasizing international competition and the necessity of structural reform, whereas suppliers opposed collaborative markets by regarding the automakers' attempts to adopt new relations as unfair interference in their independent operations. Facing tough international competition and structural crisis in 1992 and 1993, however, most suppliers could not avoid the necessity of organizational reform. After numerous international studies had revealed the backwardness of German suppliers' productivity, they came to recognize that the traditional norm of *Leben und leben lassen* did not work any more; they needed new market relations. This is why early industry frameworks such as the VDA guidelines were less effective. Once they accepted the necessity of restructuring toward the new form of market relations, German suppliers clearly developed an alternative for market governance by contesting market rationality.

Another formal space for the establishment of fair rules was the Federal Association of German Industry (Der Bundesverband der Deutschen Industrie: BDI). As a top organization of industry associations, the BDI attracts sufficient public attention; furthermore, the authority of its decisions is highly respected. Like the VDA, the BDI continuously organized public meetings through which it tried to set fair rules corresponding to each topic as different issues arose. The *BDI-Arbeitkreis*, called *Zulieferfragen* (Supply Questions), by organizing numerous meetings proportionally constituted of suppliers and automakers, set the Fair Quality Management Agreement (*faire Qualitätssicherungsvereinbarungen*) in 1992; it also addressed the revision of contracts in 1993.[137] In 1994, the BDI developed further the Guiding Rules for Supplier Relations (*Leitsätze für Zulieferbeziehungen*) under consensus between big customers and suppliers. The Guiding Rules were important in the sense that they showed that the old form of contractual relations no longer worked, as a daily newspaper put it ("Die alten Verträge reichen nicht aus").[138]

The guidelines (BDI-*Leitsätze* and VDA-*Leitfaden*) have been continuously elaborated by various industry associations to which member suppliers report their unfair cases. In particular, the six different trade associations—the Foundry Association (Deutscher Gießereiverband e.V.: DGV), the Trade Association of Iron, Plate, Metal Industries (Wirtschaftsverband Eisen, Blech und Metall verarbeitende Industrie e.V: EBM), the General Association of Synthetic Industry (Gesamtverband kunststoffverarbeitende Industrie e.V: GKV), the Rubber Association (Wirtscahftsverband der deutschen Kautschukindustrie: W.d.K.), the Trade Association of Metal Industry (Wirtschaftsvereiningung Metalle e.V: WVM), and the Steel Forging Association (Wirtschaftsverband Stahlumformung e.V.: WSU)—founded a confederation called the Working Community of Supplier Industry (Arbeitsgemeinschaft Zulieferindustrie: ArGeZ) in 1993.[139] The purpose of the ArGeZ foundation was the formation of a power bloc to counter the automakers (*Gegenmacht über Autohersteller*).[140] The ArGeZ collaborated with the BDI and the VDA not only to develop fair rules, but also to promote the policing of opportunism in daily practices.[141] The ArGeZ has continuously maintained public attention by meeting with politicians at the federal as well as the state level, by publishing reports of unfairness, and by organizing forums such as the meeting in the Hannover Messe (Hanover Trade Fair) every year in which unfair cases are presented and discussed.[142] The ArGeZ, whose members are small- and medium-sized companies (about 8,000 companies), elaborated fair rules, proposing more than 100 detailed fair norms on very controversial points such as confidentiality, liability, insurance, costs for machine tools, supplementary price changes, and the like. The ArGeZ's fair rules gained public legitimacy not just through confirmation by the Federal Cartel Office, which published the ArGeZ's detailed fair rules as announcement no. 151/99 in the Federal Law Gazette (*Bundesanzeiger*), but also through public meetings such as the annual *Hannover Messe*.[143]

The fact that German associations have developed fair rules in the public realm does not mean that the centralized corporatism of associations brought about paralegal resolutions. Casper (1997; 2001) argues that German courts were able to utilize the rules; thus, powerful customers were prohibited from behaving opportunistically. But on the contrary, as a chief of the ArGeZ admitted in an interview with me, the industry norms developed by associations could not be adopted by the courts, being still too unclear for the courts to use. The chief of the ArGeZ argued that the fair norms did not have immediate effects on the stabilization of market relations, as they would have if the courts had executed them.[144] The BDI also admitted that it was hard for a third party to define fairness in detailed cases. For example, the BDI-*Leitsätze* and the ArGeZ rules say that unilateral revision of price during the term of a contract is unfair. But it is hard for courts to detect illegality in a revision. In some cases, suppliers believe the revision of prices is fair, while in others, they believe it unfair to stick to the existing terms. In addition, few suppliers sue their customers when they are unfair. Fair norms are important not because they enable the courts to govern the unfair cases, but because the norms provide the minimum criteria as reference points that agents can use to govern their relations or mobilize social reproaches; more importantly, as shall be examined later, the democratic participatory processes generate the social forces or solidarity needed to police unfairness for self-governance in civil society.

The primary significance of fair norms is that those articulated by formal associations such as the BDI and the VDA provide an legitimate alternative to the confrontational model. Particularly weighty are the fair rules developed by the BDI and the ArGeZ, because they have received confirmation by the Federal Cartel Office. As a chief of the Steel Forging Industry Association points out, "This [fair rule] is not legally binding but it is a very strong recommendation; the agreement has a quite strong authority."[145] The decision by the BDI and the agreements between associations do not produce instant effects as would a decision by a court, which would enforce the decision immediately. But the legitimate fair rules developed by the BDI and the VDA are hard for a single company to transgress without losing legitimacy.[146] When legitimate fair rules exist, powerful customers have the burden of justifying themselves when suppliers report their unfair behavior.

In addition, fair norms consist not just of written clauses; they also encompass the establishment of another convincing model of market rationality as an alternative to the confrontational model of the collaborative market. German suppliers tried to differentiate the virtuous effects of fair cooperation from the vicious cycle of the confrontational model. They emphasized that without fair norms such as confidentiality, customers would not get deep information of suppliers' know-how. The relentless pressure on price would exhaust the suppliers' innovative competence; thus, it would diminish the automobile's quality and innovation by the automakers themselves: in the long run, suppliers concluded, the confrontational policy would weaken the automakers' competitiveness. As German suppliers established their competence as development partners in the mid 1990s, fair partnerships became more convincing than the confrontational model. As a chief of a supplier industry association says: "Customers are convinced that they will never succeed when they are fighting with suppliers. Even big customers cannot disregard the criteria formed by social adjustments and discussions; if they disregard it continuously, they will lose legitimacy and face conflicts or solve the conflicts only by power, but it can hurt the big company's own interest and market competitiveness."[147] When there is a socially shared alternative of fair norms and customers have to justify their purchasing conditions in front of a vigilant public, bare power loses legitimacy and rarely generates voluntary cooperation by suppliers. In the existence of an alternative type of efficient way, the simple emphasis on the necessity of restructuring for a new form of collaborative market, like the Lopez model, loses its legitimacy. German suppliers slowly achieved legitimacy for their alternative of fair partnership as they developed competence as collaborative partners around the mid 1990s.

Nevertheless, the most important point in the process of forming fair rules is the participatory process itself, in which agents in the markets express their own rules and build social forces for self-governance in civil society. The democratic participatory process includes not only collaboration between associations at the macro level, but also the process of articulating the opinions and policing unfairness at the micro level. It is also the route by which a supplier carries out the fair rules recommended by its association. First, in everyday life at the micro level, suppliers report unfair cases and consult their trade association. When a supplier receives a new purchasing condition, the company consults its association. In the ArGeZ, for example, there are about 400 legal experts. After consulting with the association, the supplier justifies its position based on the fair rules recommended by the association. German suppliers normally follow the recommendation of the association, not only because they believe it is too risky not to follow the recommendation, but also because non-observation sometimes brings social reproach in a small society.[148]

The process of articulation of fair norms oscillates between the micro and the macro level. The experiences at the micro level are first shared by members of an association. In each trade association, people exchange their experiences and discuss solutions in working groups. Then the association brings its collected data and opinions to a central association, e.g., a national forging association, and the ArGeZ meetings. The ArGeZ, the VDA, and the BDI share the data and collaborate in order to elaborate fair norms and execute them at the macro level. After rules are formulated at the macro level, suppliers in each association discuss the recommendations again. This is the feedback process.

These kinds of meetings for deliberation of fair norms are not confined to the six ArGeZ member industries. There are numerous formal and informal meetings for discussion of unfair cases. In this democratic participatory process of public deliberation, the formal and informal meetings mutually reinforce each other for the development of fair partnerships. The formal arrangements are important in the sense that the fair rules articulated by formal associations provide reference points with which agents in the informal meetings execute their fair partnerships flexibly or police unfairness. As the American case in chapter 2 of this book reveals, in the absence of the articulation of fair rules by formal associations, private discussions in the informal meetings fail to develop society-wide guidelines and dissipate collective efforts to address conflicts.

While formal meetings between associations in the German markets articulate and provide the basic frameworks and directions of fair norms in a society, informal meetings such as informal working circles and bar meetings (*Stammtisch*) not only provide the formal organizations with rich resources for articulation of norms, but also facilitate the saturation of norms in every corner of a society.[149] The fair model articulated by formal associations helps suppliers in informal relations to be more proactive in building fair cooperation.[150] For example, when one supplier received unfair pressure from a customer, the supplier at first had informal meetings with that customer's other suppliers. Then the suppliers resisted the customer explicitly and implicitly, while at the same time suggesting to the customer a cooperative way to reduce costs.[151] In another case, German suppliers invited an automaker's purchasing teams to informal meetings in which they asked what the automaker's policies were in the purchasing process. The informally teamed-up suppliers negotiated general conditions with the automaker in order to improve their position.[152] Faced with proactive suppliers, customers tended to move toward a cooperative way not only because the customers had to justify their behavior, but also because they came to know that the voluntary cooperation of competent suppliers could bring bigger benefits than those obtained with bare power without legitimacy.

The democratic participatory process matters for the formation of society-wide fair partnerships not simply because it creates an alternative to the confrontational model, but, more importantly, because the participatory process of the formation of fair norms is the process of the formation of solidarity to police unfairness and execute fair norms. In particular, the participatory processes in numerous formal and informal meetings are the processes of legislating self-norms. The fair rules that German suppliers set by criticizing customers' unfair behavior are hard for suppliers themselves to transgress in front of the public. For example, a chief of a supplier company explains why suppliers tended to observe the fair rules after describing numerous meetings for discussion of unfair experiences:

> If somebody expresses his personal opinion in a meeting [for the discussion of unfair experiences] by saying "the proposal might be right, but I have a different opinion; so, I will do in a different way," and he behaves in a way different than the general guideline; then, almost all members agree that such behavior is acceptable because all members understand what the situation is. But, what is not acceptable is that somebody behaves in a different way from what he said. If a supplier does not observe the rules after he agreed on the proposal for the general conditions in the process of discussion, then the supplier will lose his or her face among members.[153]

The participatory way through numerous formal and informal meetings makes it possible for agents in the German markets to express their own criteria; thus, the rules they are bound to observe are their own.

The effects of self-binding by self-legislation in the democratic participatory process also contribute to the formation of solidarity among suppliers themselves, particularly between first-tier suppliers and sub-tier suppliers. For example, one supplier, a member of the Bayern Metal Association (VBM), told me in an interview: "In the VBM, there are not just first-tier suppliers, but also second-, third-tier suppliers. While they discuss unfair behaviors, first-suppliers had difficulty in treating sub-tier suppliers in an similarly unfair way as they criticized in the protest against automakers."[154] The democratic participatory process in public deliberation is different from the notification of rules in a top-down way because the participatory process creates the effect of self-binding by self-legislation. This is one of main reasons that German first-tier suppliers developed fair partnerships among themselves. This is also in contrast to their American counterparts, who easily transferred the pressures initiated by automakers to sub-tier suppliers in dyadic relations without considering burdens of justification before the public. A manager of a big first-tier supplier company, a member of the VDA in Germany, also mentions the difficulty of treating sub-tier suppliers in an unfair way: "He [chief of this firm] is one of representatives for suppliers in the VDA. You could imagine that he argues fairness for German suppliers in the VDA. It is impossible that the representative of German suppliers treats them in an unfair way while speaking fairness against automakers."[155] In the process of criticizing unfair behavior and expressing their own criteria of fair governance, Germans suppliers expanded their solidarity for fair norms because they themselves could not violate their own rules expressed in the public realm.

In this sense, the activities of the ArGeZ are very important in the formation of society-wide fair partnerships not just because the ArGeZ increased the public sphere, but, more importantly, because their protest against unfairness enabled the first-tier suppliers of the VDA to reflect on their relative position in the entire supply chain. The members of the ArGeZ are in most cases sub-tier suppliers, while the suppliers affiliated with the VDA are first-tier suppliers. Because the members of the ArGeZ work together with suppliers of the VDA by taking part in the Fairness Committee of the VDA or by protesting against unfair customers, the first-tier suppliers of the VDA cannot treat their sub-tier suppliers in the same unfair way that they criticized in the protest against automakers. If not for the activities of the ArGeZ, the first-tier suppliers of the VDA might have easily passed unfair pressure to sub-tier suppliers by allying with automakers of the VDA.

Similarly, other supplier associations also developed mutual understandings and solidarity in the process of protest against automakers' unfair behavior. For instance, in the early 1990s, when suppliers complained that just-in-time delivery meant that automakers would transfer responsibility by changing entrance inspection by customers (*Wareneingangskontrolle*) to exit inspection by suppliers, first-tier suppliers gave more tolerance to their own sub-tier suppliers. The Electronic Association (ZVEI) and the Machine Tool Association (VDMA) did not force their sub-tier suppliers to accept the exit inspection. The reason these associations delayed adopting a policy of exit inspection or of helping suppliers transition to exit inspection is that they too were criticizing automakers' unfair behavior.[156] The public method of establishing fair norms makes it easier for agents to reflect on their own relative position in the entire society and develop solidarity amongst the tiers of supply.

Finally, it is noteworthy that while Germans in the automotive parts market do not hesitate to discuss in the public realm anything that they have experienced commonly, this cannot be said of their American counterparts. Americans in the automotive parts market hesitate to address such unfair cases in their associations because they believe, under the influence of utilitarian liberalism, that such cases are a private matter between two contractors in the market, and moreover that all things in the market are private except the legal rules. American associations address neutral issues, that is, non-political and technical items. By contrast, Germans in the automotive parts market believe that they can discuss anything common to themselves because common concerns are beyond competition. A German supplier points out very clearly what German suppliers believe about public issues:

> The relations with customers are confidential to some extent. It [the confidential part] is not an issue to discuss in the VDA and anywhere. But, when you face something which does not belong to the confidential items, for example, if you receive a letter which a customer sent to all the suppliers asking for a price cut, why should you not discuss the contents of the letter with other suppliers? It is nothing specific to just between you and your customer. That contains something general to all the suppliers.[157]

Germans in the automotive parts market discuss anything that they hold in common with their competition in formal and informal meetings. This German conception of the public sphere contrasts with the American conception of the public, which has been confirmed and justified through agents' practices in the U.S. automotive parts market. The American conception of the public realm refers to the government, while the German conception means neither the governmental nor the private realm (family or intimate relationships). The American method of market governance is close to the regime of utilitarian liberalism, while the German way of market governance is an alternative type of liberal regime that owes its vigor to Tocqueville's conception of political society or Hannah Arendt's conception of the public realm.

The civic public realm as a liberal-regime alternative to utilitarian liberalism enriches the common ground among members in a society by allowing agents to deliberate and act in concert through democratic participation. Actually the conception of fairness in the German automotive parts market is much richer than that of the American market. The conception of fairness in the American supplier market is an extreme form of formal justice; the formal rules are not universally valid precepts developed by reason, but a consequence of everyday adjustments in individual, dyadic deliberation, the extremely power-dominant form of justice. American suppliers do not necessarily believe arbitrary revision of contracts and confidentiality problems to be unfair; instead, they believe that such cases are given conditions. The customer-made rules, although they may be distasteful, can appear fair to American suppliers insofar as they apply to all suppliers equally. This formal and power-based conception of fairness in the American automotive supplier markets is a consequence of processes of conflict adjudication in which agents try to solve conflicts in dyadic relation between two differently empowered contractors rather than in a public way.

By contrast, the rich conception of fairness in the German automotive parts market has produced a wealth of fair norms for governance of long-term and collaborative markets. German suppliers expect customers to respect not just formal rules such as observation of confidentiality, but also many substantive criteria such as reciprocity in exchange of information, commensurate sharing of benefits, and appropriate exchange between quality and price.[158] The reason for the establishment of such richer norms of fairness in the German supplier market is that agents in the market share their common experiences and develop common ground for governance by adjusting their personal indignation and partial views of fairness in a public way. The public way in which agents deliberate social norms is more likely to create the expectation of substantive fairness.

It was through the public way of deliberating norms and adjudicating conflicts that Germans in the automotive parts market established society-wide fair partnerships and a workable conception of substantive fairness in the new form of long-term and collaborative contractual relations in the 1990s. In numerous formal and informal meetings, German suppliers criticized customers' unfair behavior, and, at the same time, they established their own alternative model of fair cooperation in response to the confrontational model that had prevailed in the new collaborative market. In the process of deliberating fair norms, powerful customers had the burden of justifying their policies in front of a vigilant public. Once there existed a legitimate and feasible alternative of fair cooperation, the behavior of disregarding socially shared fair norms could hardly generate voluntary cooperation from suppliers. In particular, as German suppliers improved their competence as development partners, German automakers came to recognize that voluntary cooperation by competent suppliers generated greater benefits than the use of bare power without legitimacy. In a parallel development, German suppliers were able to increase solidarity among themselves through their participation in the process of public deliberation. The process of criticizing unfair behavior in numerous formal and informal meetings was a process of expressing self-rules. The self-rules expressed in the public realm were hard to violate in front of the public. Thus, German first-tier suppliers who criticized automakers' unfair behavior in the public space could not impose on their sub-tier suppliers the same unfairness that they had criticized in the process of protest against customers' behavior. The formal associations set the basic frameworks and direction of common norms, while the informal meetings not only provided rich resources for the articulation of norms, but also made easier the distribution of norms to the entire society.

Notes

1. Hans Seifert, chief of Boston Consulting, expected in the early 1990s that half of the jobs in the German automotive supplier industry would disappear by 2000 due to the pressure of world competition and low productivity by German suppliers. For gloomy expectations about German suppliers in the early 1990s, see "Hoher Stellenabbau bei Automobilzulieferern," *Frankfurter Allgemeine Zeitung* (hereafter, *FAZ*), 1 March 1994, 17. For the successful story of German suppliers at the end of the 1990s, see "Perspecktiven der Zulieferindustrie," *FAZ*, 14 September 1999, B1.
2. Many institutionalists and power theorists expected the recovery of the German automobile industry to proceed as follows: German automakers would externalize costs of production to suppliers in order to increase competitiveness. The reason for this expectation was that experts believed German automakers could not reduce workers' wages due to the strength of trade unions. See Bob Hancke, "Vorsprung aber nicht länger (nur) durch Technik: Die schnelle Anpassung der deutschen Automobilindustrie an neue internationale Wettbewerbsbedingungen," in Frieder Nashold, David Soskice, Bob Hancke, and Ulrich Jürgens, eds., *Ökonomische Leistungsfähigkeit und institutionelle Innovation: Das deutsche Produktions- und Politikregime im globalen Wettbewerb* (Berlin: WZB-Jahrbuch, 1997), 214 and 230. But at the end of the 1990s, Minister of Economics Günter Rexrodt correctly pointed out fair relations and fair cooperation to explain the successful development of the automobile industry. See "Erfolgereich im globalen Wettbewerb," *FAZ*, 8 September 1997, B2.
3. Sigurt Vitols, "Globalization: A Fundamental Change to the German Model?" in Richard Stubbs and Geoffrey R. D. Underhill, eds., *Political Economy and the Changing Global Order* (Oxford: Oxford University Press, 2000), 373–381; Wendy Carlin and David Soskice, "Shocks to the System: The German Political Economy under Stress," *National Institute Economic Review* 59, no. 159 (January 1997): 57–76.
4. This argument, based on the financial system, prevails throughout almost all institutionalist writings. See in particular Michael E. Porter, "Capital Disadvantage: America's Failing Capital Investment System," *Harvard Business Review* 70, no. 5 (1992): 65–82; Ronald Dore, *Stock Market Capitalism: Welfare Capitalism—Japan and Germany versus the Anglo-Saxons* (New York: Oxford University Press, 2000); Richard Deeg, "Banks and Industrial Finance in the 1990s," *Industry and Innovation* 4, no. 1 (1997): 53–74; Vitols, "Globalization," 373–381.

5. See Wolfgang Streeck, "Works Councils in Western Europe: Cooperation through Representation," in Joel Rogers and Wolfgang Streeck, eds., *Works Councils: Consultation, Representation and Cooperation in Industrial Relations* (Chicago: University of Chicago Press, 1995), 313–348; Andrei S. Markovits, ed., *Political Economy of West Germany: The Model of Deutschland* (New York: Praeger, 1982); G. Leminsky, *Bewährungsproben für ein Management des Wandels: Gewerkschaftliche Politik zwischen Globalisierungsfalle und Sozialstaatsabbau* (Berlin: Sigma, 1998).

6. Through the 1990s, German companies moved more and more toward shareholding value orientation. First, the shares in the stock market increased rapidly from 1.7 percent to 11.9 percent for external financing in 1998. More importantly, the orientation toward a shareholding value system has been adopted by managers. In the 1990s, German managers began to implement shareholder value. For example, German managers implemented new devices to evaluate management performance such as new controlling systems, stock options, and stock market listings of company divisions. See Ulrich Jürgens, Katrin Naumann, and Joachim Rupp, "Shareholder Value in an Adverse Environment: the German Case," *Economy & Society* 29, no. 1 (2000): 54–79.

7. Jürgens, Naumann, and Rupp, "Shareholder Value in an Adverse Environment," 63–65.

8. Steven Wayne Casper, "Reconfiguring Institutions: The Political Economy of Legal Development in Germany and the United States" (Ph.D. diss., Cornell University, 1997); idem, "The Legal Framework for Corporate Governance: The Influence of Contract Law on Company Strategies in Germany and the United States," in Peter Hall and David Soskice, eds., *Varieties of Capitalism* (New York: Oxford University Press, 2001), 387–416; Gunther Teubner, "Legal Irritants: How Unifying Law Ends Up in New Divergences," in Hall and Soskice, *Varieties of Capitalism,* 417–441.

9. Many cultural and institutional theorists compare Anglo-Saxon individualism to German communitarianism. German culture was also supported by the dense social networks of associations. See Christel Lane, "The Social Constitution of Supplier Relations in Britain and Germany," in Richard Whitley and Peer Hall Kristensen, eds., *The Changing European Firm: Limits to Convergence* (London: Routledge, 1996); Dore, *Stock Market Capitalism: Welfare Capitalism;* Geert Hofstede, *Cultures Consequences* (Beverly Hills: Sage, 1980); Peter Lawrence, *Managers and Management in West Germany* (London: Croom Helm, 1980); Lawrence, *Issues in European Business* (London: Macmillan, 1998).

10. Numerous articles and books on the German automotive supplier markets described such unfair behavior and conflicts in the early 1990s. See Hendrik Heinze, "Ein Virtuell-flexibles zuliefermodell—Neue Positionen für Automobilzulieferunternehmen" (Ph.D. diss., St. Gallen University, 1996), 105–109; "Schlechte Noten für Volkswagen," *Blick durch die Wirtschaft,* 12 September 1995, 7; Manfred Deiß and Volker Döhl, eds., *Vernetzte Produktion: Automobilzulieferer zwischen Kontrolle und Autonomie* (Frankfurt: Campus Verlag, 1992); Hans Gerhard Mendius and Ulrike Wendeling-Schröder, eds., *Zulieferer im Netz—Zwischen Abhängigkeit und Partnerschaft: Neustrukturierung der Logistik am Beispiel der Autombilzulieferung* (Cologne: Bund-Verlag GmbH, 1991); Markus Pohlmann, Maja Apelt, Karsten Buroh, and Henning Martens, *Industrielle Netzwerke: Antagonistische Kooperationen an der Schnittstelle Beschaffung-Zulieferung* (Munich: Rainer Hampp Verlag, 1995), 134–167.

11. Eberhard Hamer, "Zuliefererdiskriminierung: Machtwirtschaft statt Marktwirtschaft?" in Mendius and Wendeling-Schröder, *Zulieferer im Netz,* 75–76.

12. Lawrence, *Managers and Management in West Germany;* Peter Lawrence, Barbara Senior, and David Smith, "The Anglo-American Contrast: A New Look" (paper presented at annual conference of Association of International Business, London, City University, 1998); Hofstede, *Cultures Consequences.*

13. Michael Porter, *The Competitive Advantage of Nations* (New York: Free Press, 1990), 717; Peter Lawrence and Vincent Edwards, *Management in Western Europe* (New York: St. Martin's Press, 2000), 106.

14. "Autoindustrie gefährdet industriellen Konsens," *Handelsblatt,* 25/26 June 1993, 19.

15. *Leben und leben lassen* means literally "to live and let live." This refers to the idea that people should allow other people to live in their own ways as they themselves want to live, based on their own freedom. In other words, people should not interfere in the affairs of others. This norm is based on the classical market relations. Each agent in the market calculates her or his costs of input and margins. Hiding the information of real costs and demanding power, they compromise at a price assuming that the price is satisfactory to the trading partner; otherwise the trading partner will exit the deal. It matters to this concept of fairness whether there is sufficient freedom to exit and search for another deal. But this norm does not fit the situation in which trading partners have to increase their common pie by sharing information and working together. See "Autohersteller brauchen die Zulieferer," *FAZ*, 5 March 1993, 15.

16. "Zulieferer brauchen Gewinne für investitionen," *Süddeutsche Zeitung*, 16 September 1994, 29.

17. According to a survey by *Forschungsstelle Automobilwirtschaft* (FAW) of Bamberg in 1995, presented in Internationale Automobil-Ausstellung (IAA)'95, Volkswagen, Audi, and Ford received the worst rating from German suppliers. Mercedes rated best not only by suppliers but also by dealers. See "Schlechte Noten für Volkswagen," *Blick durch die Wirtsachft*, 12 September 1995, 7. A survey by Scientific Consulting in early 1995 also revealed a similar evaluation by suppliers. According to the survey, the favorite customers with whom German automotive suppliers want to work are BMW, Mercedes, and Porsche. German suppliers complained that they had difficulty in working with VW and two American companies (Opel and Ford). See Scientific Consulting, "Restrukturierungstrends in der deutschen Automobilzulieferindustrie im internationalen Vergleich" (Research Report of Scientific Consulting, Cologne, 1995); "Jeder zweite Autozulieferer geht ins Ausland," *Süddeutsche Zeitung*, 6 July 1995, 20.

18. When P. James Womack, Daniel T. Jones, and Daniel Roos, *The Machine That Changed the World: The Story of Lean Production* (New York: HarperPerennial, 1990) was published in 1990, German automotive experts began to devote attention to Japanese flexible lean production. The book revealed the backwardness of European automakers' productivity in comparison with international competitors, particularly Japanese automakers. This book stirred an abundance of debate in German society, so-called "lean debate," on whether or how German industries could adopt the Japanese lean production system.

19. Dirk Riesselmann, "Entwicklung der Automobilzulieferindustrie: Strukturen, Lieferantentypen und Erfolg" (Ph.D. diss., Universität Bundesweher, Hamburg, 1998), 51–52.

20. Frank Andreas Linden and Karl Heinrich Rüssmann, "Faust im Nacken," *Manager Magazin* 8 (1988): 99.

21. Daniel Goeudevert, "Die Rolle der Zulieferindustrie angesichts der weltweiten Wettbewerbsverschärfung," in Mendius and Wendeling-Schröder, *Zulieferer im Netz*, 102.

22. "Schlechte Noten für Zulieferer," *Süddeutsche Zeitung*, 2 November 1993, 29; "Niedersachsen fördert Fahrzeug-Zulieferer," *FAZ*, 1 September 1994, 12.

23. "Zulieferern sitzt die Zeit im Nacken," *VDI nachrichten*, 8 November 1991, 12.

24. BMW's "open information of costs" policy was not criticized. On the contrary, it facilitated very trustful cooperation with suppliers. This showed another type of collaborative market. See "Hersteller und Zulieferer müssen die Japaner gemeinsam kontern," *Handelsblatt*, 27 February 1992, 15.

25. Hamer, "Zuliefererdiskriminierung: Machtwirtschaft statt Marktwirtschaft?" 65–79.

26. Manfred Holzhauser, "Der Wind bläst gewaltig ins Gesicht," in Mendius and Wendeling-Schröder, *Zulieferer im Netz*, 117–122.

27. Referring to the German legal system, suppliers and automakers contested whether to use entrance inspection or exit inspection. According to German laws such as Bürgerlichen Gesetzbuch (BGB), Handelsgesetzbuch (HGB), the Gesetz zur Regelung des Rechtes der Allgemeinen Geschäftsbedingungen (AGB-Gesetz), and the Entscheidungen des Bundesgerichtshofes (BGH), customers should do entrance inspection (*Wareneingangskontrolle*). §377 HGB requires customers to prove the products immediately

upon entrance (*Wareneingangskontrolle*). After this process of proof, the buyer loses the right of refusal of defects. This clause can be changed only in an individual contract between two specific transaction partners. But if the general form of contract generated by a company rejects entrance inspection and at the same time specifies the recall right for defects, it is not effective (BGH VIII ZR 149/90 vom 19.6. 1991). The introduction of just-in-time delivery made it impossible for customers to conduct the entrance inspection. The transformation to exit inspection put a large burden on suppliers, not just because they needed to undertake a high level of quality management, but also because they took on increased liability risks. See Bernhard Nagel, Birgit Rieß, and Gisela Theis, *Der Lieferant on Line: Just-in-Time Produktion und Mitbestimmung in der Automobilindustrie* (Baden-Baden: Nomos Verlagsgesellschaft, 1990); J. Ensthaler, A. Füssler, and D. Nuissl, *Juristische Aspekte des Qualitätsmanagements* (Berlin: Springer-Verlag, 1997); Steven Casper and Bob Hancke, "Global Quality Norms with National Production Regimes: ISO 9000 Standards in the French and German Car Industries," *Organization Studies* 20, no. 6 (1999): 961–985.

28. See Holzhauser, "Der Wind bläst uns gewaltig ins Gesicht," 117–122; Oliver Friedmann, *Target Costing in der Produktentwicklung am Beispiel eines Automobilzulieferers: Ein methodisch-empirischer Ansatz zur zielkostenorientierten Produktentwicklung* (Frankfurt am Main: Peter Lang GmbH, 1997), 102–103, 115–116.

29. The de-mystification of Japanese production was carried out by trade unions as well as social scientists and some automotive suppliers. Trade unions were worried about the collapse of supplier companies, which meant loss of jobs. In addition, the simple transfer of costs to suppliers, many people believed, would result in the deterioration of working conditions at supplier companies, and ultimately, worse conditions in supplier companies would have wave effects on other industries. See Klaus Zwickel, ed., *Vorbild Japan? Stärken und Schwächen der Industriestandorte Deutschland und Japan* (Frankfurt am Main: Otto Brenner Stiftung, 1996); Werner Neugebauer, "Gewerkschaftliche Ansatzpunkte zur Verbesserung der Arbeitnehmervertretung bei Automobilzulieferern und -herstellern in Bayern," in Mendius and Wendeling-Schröder, *Zulieferer im Netz*, 178; "Hoffnung auf mehr Mitbestimmung," *Blick durch die Wirtschat*, 13 January 1993, 7.

30. This research is based on 100 German suppliers, 163 Japanese suppliers, and 132 American suppliers. See Heinze, "Ein virtuell-flexibles Zuliefermodel," 98–99.

31. This is based on MIT research and quoted in many German books and articles. See Womack, Jones, and Roos, *The Machine That Changed the World*, 96ff.; Marcus Reeg, *Liefer- und Lieistungsbeziehungen in der deutschen Automobilindustrie: Strukturelle Veränderungen aus unternehmerischer und wirtschaftspolitischer Sicht* (Berlin: Duncker & Humbolt, 1998), 104.

32. Walter Hillebrand and Frank A. Linden, "Noch einmal mit Gefühl" *Manager Magazin* (March 1993): 103.

33. According to the research of IG Metall (a trade union), only 4 percent of employees in the automotive industry in 1990 participated in group work. The figure grew rapidly after the crises of 1992 and 1993, with 9 percent of automotive employees in 1993 and 22 percent in 1994 took part in team work. See Michael Schumann, "The German Automobile Industry in Transition," *Economic and Labour Relations Review* 8, no. 2 (1997): 230–231. Riesselmann, "Entwicklung der Automobilzulieferindustrie," 156–157. There are also several studies that show the development of restructuring in German companies. See Stefan Zischka, "Gestaltung der Kunden- und Marketorientierung und Anwendung des Quality Function Deployment in Entwicklungsprojekten der deutschen Automobilzulieferindustrie: Ergebnisse einer Umfrage," (Institute Newsletter on Quality Management, Institut für Qualitätsicherung, Hanover University, 1998); Gunter Lay and Werner Wallmeier, "Stand und Entwicklungstendenzen der Produktionsmodernisierung" (Research Paper of Production Innovation Improvement, Fraunhofer Institut für Systemtechnik und Innovationsforschung, Karlsruhe, 1999).

34. For the German suppliers' strategies, see Riesselmann, "Entwicklung der Automobilzulieferindustrie"; Horst Wildemann, *Entwicklungs- und Vertriebsnetzwerke in der Zulieferindustrie*

(Munich: Transfer-Centrum GmbH, 1998); Gunter Lay and Werner Wallmeier, "Auto-mobilzulieferer—Quo vadis? Strategien, Produktionsstrukturen und Leistungsindik-atoren der Automobilzulieferindustrie Deutschlands" (Memorandum of Production Innovation Improvement, Fraunhofer Institut für Systemtechnik und Innovations-forschung, Karlsruhe, 1999); Lay and Wallmeier, "Stand und Entwicklungstendenzen der Produktionsmodernisierung."

35. See Risselmann, "Entwicklung der Automobilzulieferindustrie," 157–160.

36. Gernot Diehlmann, *Vorentwicklungsmanagement in der Automobilzulieferindustrie: Konzep-tionelle Grundlagen und empirische Untersuchung zur erfolgsorientierten Gestaltung der Vorentwicklung in Automobilzulieferunternehmen* (Frankfurt am Main: Peter Lang GmbH, 1998), 208, 224–225.

37. For many industrialists' and industrial experts' evaluation of the relaxing of tension between automakers and suppliers, see "Nur Wenige Firmen schaffen Sprung zum A-Lieferanten," *Handelsblatt*, 8 March 1995, 35; "Die Zulieferer befürchten bereits die nächste Rezession," *FAZ*, 8 April 1995, 16; "Autozulieferer denkt an leichte Presier-höhung," *Handelsblatt*, 3 May 1995, 23; "Zulieferer können nicht aufatmen," *Süddeutsche Zietung*, 9/10 September 1995, 21.

38. According to Sabel, Kern, and Herrigel, there are two types of flexible production sys-tems. One bases its flexibility on internal decentralization, with which a big company coordinates its internal parts; GM belongs to this type. The other is "system integrator," which develops flexible cooperation with external suppliers. See Charles F. Sabel, Horst Kern, and Gary Herrigel, "Collaborative Manufacturing: New Supplier Relations in the Automobile Industry and the Redefinition of the Industrial Corporation" (IMVP International Policy Forum, May 1989). See also Hillebrand and Linden, "Noch einmal mit Gefühl," *Manager Magazin* (March 1993): 100–110; idem, "Die Jagd ist auf," *Manager Magazin* (December 1993): 128–142.

39. The story about BMW is mainly based on my personal interviews with the company.

40. Interview with BMW purchasing chief on 18 May 2000 in Munich.

41. "Hersteller und Zulieferer müssen die Japaner gemeinsam kontern," *Handelsblatt*, 27 February 1992, 15.

42. Interview with G11 on 17 September 1999.

43. Interview with G44 on 5 May 2000.

44. See Steven Wayne Casper, "How Public Law Influences Decentralized Supplier Network Organization in Germany: The Cases of BMW and Audi," (Discussion Paper FS I 95-314, Wissenschaftszentrum Berlin für Sozialforschung, Berlin, 1995); idem, "Nationale Insti-tutionengefüge und innovative Industrieorganisation: Zulieferbeziehungen in Deutsch-land," in Naschold, Soskice, Hancke, and Jürgens, *Ökonomische Leistungsfähigkeit und institutionelle Innovation*, 235–250; interview with BMW. Later, other German automak-ers adopted this policy; interviews with Mercedes.

45. Daimler-Benz refers to the corporation name while Mercedes refers to the automobile section of the corporation. In this book, they have the same connotation in the absence of special mention. The story of Daimler-Benz in this book relies mainly on my personal interviews with the Mercedes purchasing team. I had interviews with Mercedes several times: 8 September 1999; 13 September 1999; 16 September 1999.

46. Sabel, Kern, and Herrigel, "Collaborative Manufacturing," 22; interview with G49 on 11 May 2000.

47. Mercedes reduced the level of in-house production by up to 30 percent in the A Class pro-duction and up to 15 percent in the production of a small mass car called Smart. See "C-Change at Mercedes," *Marketing Week*, 2 July 1993, 28–31; "Mercedes Trims Production Costs with 'Baby Benz,'" *Wall Street Journal*, 23 April 1993; "Mit leeren Händen," *Manager Magazin* (September 1993): 37–51; "Smart Project May Make Daimler Smarter," *Automotive News*, 22 April 1996, 19; "Swatchmobile Gets Name, Price," *Wall Street Journal*, 18 May 1995, A13; "Mercedes-Benz C-Class Suppliers," *Automotive News-Europe*, 3 July 2000, 23; "Strategic Outsoucring: It's Your Move," *Datamation* 44, no. 2 (February 1998): 32–41.

48. "Gemeinsam strampeln sie auf dem Tandem," *FAZ*, 11 September 1993, 16.

49. *Tandem Journal* (Daimler 1999).

50. Interview with G4 on 10 September 1999.

51. "Geminsam strampeln sie auf dem Tandem," *FAZ*, 11 September 1993, 16; "Autohersteller brauchen die Zulieferer," *FAZ*, 6 March 1993, 15.

52. "Daimler-Chrysler bündelt Einkauf," *Handelsblatt*, 16 February 1999, 19.

53. Interview with G49 on 11 May 2000.

54. Interviews with G5 on 10 September 1999; interview with G6 on 13 September 1999; interview with G16 on 21 September 1999; interview with G29 on 12 April 2000; interview with Mercedes on 8 September 1999.

55. Interview with G6 on 13 September 1999.

56. Interview with G4 on 10 September 1999.

57. Interview with Mercedes on 13 September 1999.

58. For the Volkswagen Konzern, I conducted several interviews, not only with Volkswagen in Wolfsburg but also with Audi in Ingolstadt. The story of VW in this book mainly relies on my personal interviews. Interview with Audi on 19 May 2000; interviews with VW on 7 June and 22 June 2000.

59. Hartmut Berg and Jens Müller, "The Volkswagen AG and Its Suppliers in the Region of Hannover: Adjustment Requirements and Regional Economic Policy" (Discussion Paper in Political Economy, no. 65, Dortmund University, 1995), 10–11.

60. Bruno Cattero, *Lavorare alla Fiat: Arbeit bei VW: Technologie, Arbeit und soziale Regulierung in der Automobilindustrie* (Münster: Westfälisches Dampfboot, 1998); idem, "Beruf und Berufsausbildung—Mythen und Widersprüche im 'deutschen Modell,'" in Bruno Cattero, ed., *Modell Deutschland, Modell Europa, Problems Perspectiven. Europa- und Nordamerika-Studien* (Opladen: Leske + Budrich, 1998): 225–246; "Endlich wieder ein Wagen für das Volk," *Handelsblatt*, 3 August 1993, 13.

61. Jose Ignacio Lopez de Arriortua was born in Basque Spain. His numerous nicknames, such as "Working Animal" (*Arbeitstier*), "Cost Presser" (*Kostendrücker*), and "Merciless Guy" (*der Gnadenlose*), characterize Lopez's style of business. In 1987, he became a purchasing chief of Opel, the GM subsidiary in Germany, where he was nickname of "Grand Inquisitor" (*Grossinquisitor*) because he pressed suppliers under his interrogation. In 1988, he became the chief of all European purchasing at Opel; he then moved to Detroit, where he was called "Revolutionary Rescuer" (*revolutionärer Sanierer*). In 1993 Lopez moved to VW, even though GM offered Lopez the entire American business. See "Der VW-Aufsichtrat stimmt Veränderungen im Vorstand zu," *FAZ*, 17 March 1993, 18.

62. "Die Mitarbeiter bekommen 'leuchtende Augen' oder sie legen sich quer," *Handelsblatt*, 30/31 July 1993, 3.

63. Works councils (*Betriebsräte*) in large German companies are stronger than in any other country because works councils participate in the supervisory board with management due to the legality of co-determination (*Mitbestimmung*). VW management had to compromise with its works council; otherwise, even the chief would be forced to leave VW. For example, Rudolf Leiding, who introduced the Golf (one of VW's best-selling cars), had to step down in 1975 due to confrontation with the works council. Toni Schuücker and Carl Hahn, Leiding's successors, did not dare to confront the works council, which burdened VW with high over-employment and high wages. See Berg and Müller, "The Volkswagen AG and Its Suppliers in the Region of Hanover," 9.

64. Markovits, *Political Economy of West Germany*; Streeck, "Works Councils in Western Europe," 313–348; Carlin and Soskice, "Shocks to the System," 57–76; Leminsky, *Bewährungsproben für ein Management des Wandels*.

65. "Das Führungsgremium bei Volkswagen ist nun komplett," *FAZ*, 18 March 1993, 18.

66. Interview with G9 on 15 September 1999; "Lopez und die Folgen für Volkswagen," *Süddeutsche Zeitung*, 22 July 1993, 18.

67. Interview with G17 on 21 September 1999.

68. "Zulieferer: Auf Sparkurs," *VDI nachrichten*, 16 July 1993, 8.

69. Lopez aimed at saving DM 12 billion within 5 years. Within one year, VW claimed in 1993, it could cut production costs by 10.2 percent to DM 1.6 billion. See "Künftig nur noch zwölf Stunden für ein Auto," *VDI nachrichten*, 1 April 1994, 6; "Bei VW geht es spanisch zu," *Die Welt*, 25 March 1993, 1.
70. "Volkswagen has 5 key priorities for suppliers," *Automotive News*, 8 December 1997.
71. I explicitly asked about 33 suppliers whether VW still uses the Lopez model; 32 suppliers answered clearly that VW does not use the Lopez model any more, while one supplier said that it remains in some parts.
72. Interview with G6 on 13 September 1999; interview with G7 on 14 September 1999; interview with G9 on 15 September 1999; interview with G15 on 21 September 1999; interview with G16 on 21 September 1999; interview with G31 on 13 April 2000; interview with G42 on 2 May 2000.
73. Interview with VW on 7 June 2000.
74. Ibid.
75. "Die deutsche Zulieferindustrie fühlt sich benachteiligt," *FAZ*, 25 April 1994, 21.
76. "Volkswagen has 5 Key Priorities for Suppliers," *Automotive News*, 8 December 1997, F16.
77. Interview with VW on 7 June 2000.
78. "Die Anbindugn der Zulieferer wird immer enger," *VDI nachrichten*, 15 April 1994, 5.
79. "SPD prangert 'Faustrecht' der Autohersteller an," *Handelsblatt*, 7 July 1993, 16.
80. IG Metall was worried that automakers' unfair pressure might cause high unemployment in the parts industries and might deteriorate working conditions in general. See Siegfried Roth, "Autombilhersteller und ihre Zulieferer in Deutschland und Japan," in Zwickel, *Vorbild Japan?* 175–205; Thomas Klebe and Siegfried Roth, "Autonome Zulieferer oder Diktat der Marktmacht?" in Mendius and Wendeling-Schröder, *Zulieferer im Netz*, 180–199.
81. "Vorest kein Ende der Ermittlungen," *Handelsblatt*, 25 May 1994, 2.
82. Berg and Müller, "The Volkswagen AG and Its Suppliers in the Regioin of Hannover," 23–38.
83. This was an indication of mitigation in the early 1990s. Piech used this justification for the first half of the 1990s. See "Endlich wieder ein Wagen für das Volk," *Handelsblatt*, 3 August 1993, 14; "Mit VW durch dick und dünn gehen," *Süddeutsche Zeitung*, 17 May 1993, 28.
84. See Lopez, "Herausforderungen und Chancen in der europäischen Automobilindustrie," in Mendius and Wendeling-Schröder, *Zulieferer im Netz*, 89–98; Daniel Goeudevert, "Die Rolle der Zulieferindustrie angesichts der Weltweiten Wettewerbsverschärfung," in *Zulieferer im Netz*, 99–110.
85. "Zulieferer: Lopez schadet VW nicht," *FAZ*, 3 September 1993, 18; "Why Did GM and VW Think One Man Vital to Their Businesses?" *Management Today*, 1 November 1993, 16–17.
86. "Was ist ein fairer Gewinn, Herr Lopez," *Frankfurter Allgemeine Zeitung (FAZ)*, 18 February 1995 (translation mine).
87. See Andreas Bartelt, "Vertrauen in Zulieferbeziehungen der Automobilindustrie: Ergebnisse einer empirischen Untersuchung" (Research Paper, Julius-Maximilians-Universität Würzburg, Lehrstuhl für Betriebswirtschaftslehre und Marketing, 2000); Lay and Wallmeier, "Stand und Entwicklungstendenzen der Produktionsmodernisierung." German sub-tier suppliers did not have lower profits and turnover than the first-tier suppliers. See also IKB Deutsche Industriebank, "Automobilzulieferer 1996: Differenzierte Ertragsergebnisse," *IKB Branchenbericht* (December 1997); idem, "1997—ein erfolgreiches Jahr für die deutschen Automobilzulieferer," *IKB Branchenbericht* (December 1998); idem, "Die Automobilzulieferer 1998—Kräftiges Umsatzwachstum, differenzierte Ertragsentwicklung," *IKB Branchenbericht* (December 1999).
88. Interview with G33 on 17 April 2000. There are many remarks similar to this story: Interview with G14 on 20 September 1999; interview with G16 on 21 September 1999; interview with G51 on 12 May 2000.
89. See Jürgens, Neumann, and Rupp, "Shareholder Value in an Adverse Environment: The German Case," 72.

90. Interview with G22 on 21 March 2000; interview with G24 on 3 April 2000.
91. Interview with G22 on 21 March 2000.
92. "Zulieferer engagieren sich im Ausland," *Handelsblatt*, 6/7 September 1996, 19.
93. Interview with a chief of Arbeitsgemeinschaft Zulieferindustrie (ArGeZ) on 23 June 2000. See also Linden and Rüsslmann, "Die Faust im Nacken," 88–109.
94. Lay and Wallmeier, "Stand und Entwicklungstendenzen der Produktionsmodernisierung," 25; Linden and Rüsslmann, "Die Faust im Nacken," 88–109.
95. See Lay and Wallmeier, "Stand und Entwicklungstendenzen der Produktionsmodernisierung," 25; Gernot Diehlmann, *Vorentwicklungsmanagement in der Automobilzulieferindustrie: Konzeptionelle Grundlagen und empirische Untersuchung zur erfolgsorientierten Gestaltung der Vorentwicklung in Automobilzulieferunternehmen* (Frankfurt am Main: Peter Lang GmbH, 1998), 221–223, 260–261.
96. Interview with G17 on 21 September 1999. For example, an aluminum die-cast parts supplier with 155 workers made 200 or 300 parts in the past. But recently this firm concentrates on several special parts to increase their specialty.
97. Interview with G24 on 3 April 2000. Many other suppliers also outlined a similar strategy: Interview with G3 on 9 September 1999; interview with G5 on 10 September 1999; interview with G11 on 17 September 1999; interview with G31 on 13 April 2000.
98. In addition, German automakers themselves are very careful to organize the suppliers so as to prevent overlap in a project. Sometimes automakers divide participants in a more detailed way, or they organize the meeting in a sequential way, depending on the situation. Interview with G36 on 20 April 2000; interview with G48 on 10 May 2000; interview with G52 on 15 May 2000; interview with G54 on 23 May 2000.
99. Interview with G35 on 19 April 2000.
100. Interview with G32 on 14 April 2000.
101. Interview with G23 on 31 March 2000. I heard a similar story in other interviews. Interview with G1 on 7 September 1999; interview with G3 on 9 September 1999; interview with G4 on 10 September 1999.
102. Diehlmann, *Vorentwicklungsmanagement in der Autombilzulieferindustrie*, 250–251; IKB Deutschindustriebank, "1997—ein erfolgreiches Jahr für die deutschen Automobilzulieferer," 2. According to Wildemann's research, conducted in 1995, German suppliers are very customer-oriented; they spend 42 percent of their budget for R&D in a specific customer-oriented development. See Horst Wildemann, *Entwicklungs-, und Vertriebsnetzwerke in der Zulieferindustrie*, 74.
103. Interview with G19 on 19 September 1999; interview with G28 on 7 April 2000.
104. "Kooperation mit Haken und Ösen," *Handelsblatt*, 3 September 1996, 15; "Türmodule direct aus Band geliefert," *Handelsblatt*, 27 March 1996, 25.
105. See Thomas Hinz, "Vocational Training and Job Mobility in Comparative Perspective," in Pepper D. Culpepper and David Finegold, eds., *The German Skills Machine* (New York: Berghahn Books, 1999), 159–188; Wolfgang Littek and Ulrich Heisig, "Taylorism Never Got Hold of Skilled White-Collar Work in Germany," in Wolfgang Littek and Tony Charles, eds., *The New Division of Labour: Emerging Forms of Work Organization in International Perspective* (Berlin: Wlafter de Gruyter, 1995), 373–396.
106. Hinz, "Vocational Training and Job Mobility in Comparative Perspective," 165–170.
107. Reinhard Bispinck, "Betrieblich Interessenvertretung, Entgelt und Tarifpolitik," *WSI Mittelungen* 54, no. 2 (2001); Anke Hassel, "The Erosion of the German System of Industrial Relations," *British Journal of Industrial Relations* 37, no. 3 (1999): 483–505.
108. Hassel, "The Erosion of the German System of Industrial Relations," 498–499; Heinze Tüsselmann and Arne Heise, "The German Model of Industrial Relations at the Crossroads: Past, Present and Future," *Industrial Relations Journal* 31, no. 3 (2000): 162–176.
109. Hassel, "The Erosion of the German System of Industrial Relations," 494, 487.
110. Bernhard Ebbinghaus, "Dinosaurier der Dienstleistungsgesellschaft? Der Mitgliederschwund deutscher Gewerkschaften im historischen und internationalen Vergleich" (MPIfG Working Paper 02/3, Max-Planck-Institut für Gesellschaftsforschung, March

2002); Michael Fichter, "Trade Union Members: A Vanishing Species in Post-Unification Germany?" *German Studies Review* 20, no. 1 (1997): 83–104.

111. In the early 1990s, expenditure on retraining (DM 36 billion) exceeded the costs of basic vocational training (DM 30 billion) for the first time. See Hermann Schmidt, "The Impact of Globalization on Vocational Training and Continuing Education," in Dieter Dettke, ed., *The Challenge of Globalization for Germany's Social Democracy: A Policy Agenda for the Twenty-First Century* (New York: Berghahn Books, 1998); Karin Wagner, "The German Apprenticeship System under Strain," in Culpepper and Finegold, *The German Skills Machine*, 66; Martin Baethge, Volker Baethge-Kinsky, and Peter Kupka, "Facharbeit—Auslaufmodel oder neue Perspektive?" *SOFI-Mitteilungen* 26 (1998): 81–98.

112. Schmidt, "The Impact of Globalization on Vocational Training and Continuing Education," 220; Baethge, Baethge-Kinsky, and Kupka, "Facharbeit—Auslaufmodell oder neue Perspektive?" 82–85, 91–92.

113. Interview with G26 on 5 April 2000; interview with G27 on 6 April 2000; interview with G45 on 8 May 2000.

114. Interview with G40 on 27 April 2000; interview with G45 on 8 May 2000.

115. Interview with G26 on 5 April 2000.

116. This system is prevalent not just in German automakers but in supplier companies. All of the German automakers (Mercedes, BMW, VW, and Audi) and suppliers I visited work under this dual structure of team and departments.

117. Interview with Mercedes on 16 September 1999.

118. Interview with G10 on 15 September 1999; interview with G11 on 17 September 1999; interview with G19 on 22 September 1999.

119. Interview with BMW on 18 May 2000.

120. Interview with VW on 22 June 2000.

121. Interview with G27 on 6 April 2000.

122. Siegfried Roth, "Kooperationsnetzwerke: Gewerkschaftliche Aktivitäten in der Automobil-und Zulieferindustrie," *Industrielle Beziehungen* 1, no. 4 (1994): 382–383; "Von internationaler Bedeutung," *FAZ*, 12 September 1995, B3; interview with Automobil-Zulieferinitiative Rheinland-Pfalz on 6 June 2000.

123. Eckhard Hermann, "Nordrheinwestfälisches Verbundprojekt (VIA) als Beispiel unternehmerischer Partnershchaften in der Automobilzulieferindustrie," in Udo Winand and Klaus Nathusius, eds., *Unternehmensnetzwerke und virtuelle Organizationen* (Stuttgart: Schaeffer-Poeschel Verlag, 1998), 54–56; Klaus Nathusius, "Partnerschaften und Wertschöpfung in der Automobilindustrie," in Winand and Nathusius, *Unternehmensnetzwerke und virtuelle Organizationen*, 44–58; Iris Bender, *Struktureller Wandel in der Automobilindustrie und die Einfluss strategischen Industrie- und Handelspolitik* (Frankfurt am Main: Peter Lang GmbH, 1996), 233ff.; "Zulieferer sollen künftig intensiver kooperien," *Handelsblatt*, 15 February 1994, 14; "Durch Kooperation fit für Markt," *Handelsblatt*, 13 September 1995, 28; "Landeskasse hilft dem Mittelstand," *Handelsblatt*, 25 March 1997; "Newcomer bündeln Kräfte," *FAZ*, 14 September 1999, B11.

124. Interview with G30 on 13 April 2000; interview with G31 on 13 April 2000; interview with G45 on 8 May 2000; "Konzentration in der Autoindustrie führt zu Konsequenzen bei Zulieferern," *Blick durch die Wirtschaft*, 11 May 1998, 1; "Bayern antwortet auf Globaliesierung," *FAZ*, 14 September 1999, B11.

125. Interview with G31 on 13 April 2000.

126. See Stephan Schrader and Henrik Sattler, "Zwischenbetriebliche Kooperation: Informaler Informationsaustausch in den USA und Deutschland," *Die Betriebswirtschaft* (DBW) 53, no. 5 (1993).

127. See Walter Hillebrand and Frank A. Linden, "Noch einmal mit Gefühl," *Manager Magazin* (March 1993): 100–110; idem, "Die Jagd ist auf," *Manager Magazin* (December 1993): 128–142; "Gereizte Stimmung bei den Zulieferern der Autoindustrie," *FAZ*, 7 December 1992, 18; "Teves: Böse Überraschung im kommenden Jahr," *FAZ*, 15 December 1992, 20; "Automobilhersteller verlangen harte Preiszugeständnisse," *VDI nachrichten*, 23 April 1993, 10.

128. "Autohersteller brauchen die Zulieferer," *FAZ*, 6 March 1993, 15.
129. "Schröder: Wir wollen die VW-Standorte stärken," *FAZ*, 27 August 1993, 15.
130. "SPD pranger 'Faustrecht' der Autohersteller an," *Handelsblatt*, 7 July 1993, 16.
131. "Kunststoffverband: Pkw-Hersteller missbrauchen eindeutig ihre Marktmacht," *Handelsblatt*, 15 April 1993, 15.
132. "Die Zulieferer fürchten um ihr geistiges Eigentum," *FAZ*, 15 Sep. 1993, 18.
133. Interview with G44 on 5 May 2000.
134. Interview with VDA on 22 September 1999; interview with ArGeZ on 23 June 2000; "Fair geht vor," *Handelsblatt*, 9 June 1994, 12; "Der VDA will das geistige Eigentum der Zulieferer besser schützen," *FAZ*, 9 June 1994, 16.
135. Interview with VDA on 22 September 1999.
136. Interview with BMW chief of purchasing on 18 May 2000.
137. "Partnerschaft drückt sich in fairen Abkommen aus," *Handelsblatt*, 2 September 1992, B2.
138. See "Nicht Preisdiktat, sondern gemeinsamer Kostenplan," *Handelsblatt*, 19 July 1993, 3; "Die Zahl der Zulieferer wird radikal reduziert," *Handelsblatt*, 26 July 1993, 4; "Die alten Verträge reichen nicht aus," *Handelsblatt*, 18/19 November 1994, 6.
139. Initially, when ArGeZ was founded, seven trade associations made up the confederation. The association not counted in the above is *Wirtschaftsvereinigung Ziehereien und kaltwalzwerke e.V.* (Z+K).
140. Interview with ArGeZ on 23 June 2000.
141. Interview with ArGeZ; Theodor L. Tutmann, "Wertschöpfung durch Wertschätzung," *Beschaffung aktuell* 4 (1995): 30–34; "Die Mittelständler wehren sich gegen Machtmißbrauch," *Handelsblatt*, 26/27 November 1993, 18; "Autozulieferer verlangen faire Verträge," *FAZ*, 1 July 2000, 43.
142. "Die deutsche Zulieferindustrie fühlt sich benachteiligt," *FAZ*, 25 April 1994, 21; "Mittelständische Unternehmer wollen den konzernen endlich Paraoli bieten," *Handelsblatt*, 26 April 1994, 17; "Schmiedeindustrie steht wieder unter Dampf," *Handelsblatt*, 23/24 September 1994, 23; "Von Fairness hält Industrie nicht viel," *Handelsblatt*, 7/8 April 1995, 20.
143. For ArGeZ's fair rules, see ArGeZ (Arbeitsgemeinschaft Zulieferindustrie), "Die Fairneßregeln von BDI und VDA in der Praxis," (Document of the ArGeZ, 1995); idem, "Grundzüge von Entwicklungsvereinbarungen: Bausteine und Erläuterungen" (Document of ArGeZ-Arbeitskreis, 1996); idem, "Kooperationsmodelle im Zulieferbereich" (Supplier Forum of ArGeZ, Frankfurt am Main, 29 October 1997); "Nachfragemacht und Vertragsgestaltung in Industrie und Handel," (Supplier Forum of ArGeZ, Swissötel Düsseldorf, 11 November 1998) "Konditionenempfehlung der ArGeZ: Klauseln zur vertraglichen Gestaltung partnerschaftlicher Lieferbeziehungen" (Full Text of Publication in the Federal Law Gazette, No. 245, 28 December 1999).
144. Interview with ArGeZ on 23 June 2000.
145. Interview with ArGeZ on 23 June 2000.
146. For the comparison between the VDA-*Leitfaden* in 1992 and the BDI-*Leitsätze* in 1994, see ArGeZ, "Die Fairneßregeln von BDI und VDA in der Praxis."
147. Interview with ArGeZ on 23 June 2000.
148. Interview with G24 on 3 April 2000; interview with G27 on 6 April 2000.
149. There are three to five fairs (*Messen*) for each special trade sector, at which agents talk about customers' behavior. Interview with G14 on 20 September 1999; interview with G17 on 21 September 1999; interview with G19 on 22 September 1999.
150. Interview with G9 on 15 September 1999; interview with G14 on 20 September 1999; interview with G45 on 8 May 2000.
151. Interview with G45 on 8 May 2000.
152. Interview with G50 on 11 May 2000.
153. Interview with G37 on 25 April 2000.
154. Interview with G31 on 13 April 2000.
155. Interview with G26 on 5 April 2000.

156. Later suppliers began to adopt exit inspection, but they had few problems because suppliers got ISO norms and were relieved of high insurance under the agreement between the insurance association and industry associations, and also because they had improved their quality management tremendously. For the favorable conditions of ZVEI and VDMA, see Casper, "Nationale Institutionengefüge und innovative Industrieorganization," 235–250.

157. Interview with G44 on 5 May 2000. Many other suppliers describe the public sphere in a similar way. Interview with G45 on 8 May 2000; interview with G50 on 11 May 2000; interview with G55 on 24 May 2000.

158. The fair distribution of benefits does not mean a precisely even division of benefits between automakers and suppliers. Suppliers in many cases admit the relative power asymmetry and believe fair even distribution of 40:60, considering the heavy pressure of other customers. Interview with G26 on 5 April 2000; interview with G15 on 21 September 1999; interview with G35 on 19 April 2000; interview with G37 on 25 April 2000; interview with G41 on 28 April 2000.

CONCLUSION

The recent transformation in advanced market societies under global-ization challenges existing theoretical frameworks. The path dependency of institutionalism and the neoliberal universal relevancy of market rationality cannot adequately explain the dynamic process of the transformation. Contrary to the institutionalist argument of path-dependent national patterns, national economies such as the U.S. and German market societies underwent a strikingly similar pattern of adjustments under tough international competition, instituting deintegration, creating contractual relations, adopting flexible lean production systems, and developing collaborative market relations. But the convergent pattern of market relations does not confirm the rejuvenation of market liberalism based on the neoclassical market. The new form of long-term and collaborative markets, adopted by both the U.S. and German markets, leaves room for new divergence due to their unclear governance. As this book has revealed, however, different market regimes are constituted not by prior norms or institutional arrangements concerning contracts and contractual relations, but rather by the ongoing politics of problem-solving practices. This conclusion highlights the theoretical implications for the constitution of market regimes, reconceptualizing the market and politics.

Traditionally, market liberalism has paralleled the development of the market in modern history. As Weintraub says, "Liberalism is the philosophy of civil society," reduced to the contractual relations in the market.[1] Contracts and contract law are key features of liberal theories of justice, as P. S. Atiyah explains: autonomous individuals choose to impose obligations on themselves by an exercise of free will. However, the market in the last decades of the twentieth century did not confirm the rejuvenation of market liberalism. This ironic consequence led to reflection upon the fundamental principles of the neoliberal paradigm based on neoclassical economics. This book contests the universal relevancy of the neoclassical market rationality and the neoliberal conception of justice. In particular, this book argues that

Notes for this section are on page 205.

market regimes are contextualized based on the division of labor, and more importantly, that they are constituted by the manners in which agents deliberate market rationality and fairness for market governance.

Market regimes are governed neither by universal justice, nor by the apparent single necessity of market rationality. Market liberals (or neoliberals), basing their theories on neoclassical economics, emphasize the universal relevance of market rationality beyond politics and a strictly market-based conception of justice. The neoliberal paradigm of the market is based on the assumption that voluntary exchange for self-interest maximization is the most efficient way. The so-called perfect competition in an ideal market provides guidelines for the best efficiency. To the extent that customs or politics constrains free exchange, the market becomes less efficient. Therefore, politics, social identity, and morality should only minimally intrude on market processes. Justice in the neoliberal market is founded upon the fundamental principles of right and wrong deduced from natural reason beyond division of labor, which can be applied to any case regardless of the particularity of groups. Market liberals believe that justice is beyond the division of labor; it is constituted by an abstraction of universal personhood and the principle of individual freedom.[2] Liberal justice is based on the fundamental principle of individual free will; all rights and duties arise exclusively from independent and voluntary will. In the neoliberal paradigm, so long as one has a well-functioning market in which agents express their individual free will, its outcomes will necessarily be just, regardless of substantive issues. Market liberals believe that societies will converge toward the most efficient form of market liberalism, represented empirically by the American-led form of neoclassical market, as the state retreats and globalization progresses.

However, as this book has shown, the market is governed neither by universal justice, nor by the apparent single necessity of market rationality as the neoliberal paradigm assumes. Market regimes are relativized by the division of labor. The new markets that emerged through deintegrating existing hierarchical governance of bureaucratic corporations in both the U.S. and Germany represent a reorganization of the existing neoclassical, distant markets into long-term, collaborative markets as the rationality of the division of labor was reconstituted. In the era of mass production and extreme separation between conception (by customer) and execution (by supplier), simple tasks and homogeneous products produced by standardization enabled the neoclassical markets to work; in the traditional markets, the customer could easily switch vendors in a short period without attention to their history of relationships and identity. But in the new long-term and collaborative markets, the focus is on agents' commitments and willingness to cooperate instead of anonymous relations, in order to achieve the benefits of flexible, collaborative engineering.

More fundamentally, on the contrary to the market liberals' assumption, an ideal type of market rationality is not the apparent single necessity for economic efficiency in the market. Market liberals argue that the market based on anonymity principle, free of any constraints such as customs and politics, is the best way for economic efficiency. In this paradigm, politics is outside the market; politics and justice are in opposition to the economic efficiency. But politics is not outside the market. The reason for the existence of politics in the market is based on the fact that an ideal type of market rationality is not the apparent single necessity that the neoliberal paradigm assumes. Rather, multiple types of market rationality are in play, as are the politics that constitute them. In the sense of Weber's ideal type, there are many different ideal types of rationality for economic efficiency.[3] For example, from the viewpoint of the production process, standardization is rational, whereas from the perspective of product innovation, standardization becomes burdensome. When the focus is on transaction costs, vertical integration might be rational, but when the focus is on flexible innovation of products and production, vertical integration can be suboptimal. From the viewpoint of economies of scale, volume orientation may be the best strategy, but when it comes to economies of scope, it can be suboptimal. To secure the easy mobility of contractual relations, short-term contracts based on the anonymity principle may be most desirable, but from the perspective of flexible application engineering, they can be less so. Contrary to the neoliberal belief that market rationality is independent of politics, market society is constituted by contests and conflicts between different perspectives, not between well-understood and misunderstood rationality.

In the same vein of *politics among multiple rationalities*, this book has contradicted the rigid path dependency of institutionalism and has argued for the agents' reflexivity. Although institutionalists are rightly concerned with the varieties of market regimes and contextualized market rationalities, they fail to explain how a new social order emerges, departing from the traditional pattern of production and market regimes. Agents' perspectives of economic rationality, under which they interpret institutional constraints or benefits, are neither fixed nor constantly the same, contrary to institutionalist explanation. For example, Germans in the 1990s began to doubt the comparative institutional advantages of their traditional corporatist coordination, although strictly vocation-oriented skill formation and skill deployment, supported by centralized corporatist institutions, had been praised until the 1980s. In the 1990s, when the German model of production and market systems suffered in international competition with more flexible lean producers, Germans could not stick to the old rationality of their institutional advantages, contrary to the arguments of the institutionalists of Comparative Institutional Advantages. Instead, they deconstructed the centralized corporatist coordination toward decentralization and reorganized their vocation-oriented skill formation and skill deployment toward de-specialized generalism and cross-functional deployment of skills. As the processes of transformation in the U.S. and Germany show, even under the same national institutions and culture, agents retaining different perspectives of economic rationality contested the interpretation of institutional advantages, developing different strategies.

It is not only market rationality that is constituted by the politics of multiple rationalities, but the norms of fairness as well. The market in which agents pursue self-interests inherently contains various conflicts and opportunism; thus, it needs neutral rules to adjudicate conflicts for its proper functioning. To secure orderly interactions in the market, agents in the market have to justify why one agent is allotted more than another. To adjudicate conflicts, a market society needs fair criteria. Contrary to the arguments of power approaches, market regimes differ tremendously in the sense of how an authority of justice is legitimated and on what basis it is justified. Bad governance of a market can cause not just instability of the market but also economic pathologies. In particular, the new form of long-term and closely interactive markets needs more stable and trustful relationships; contrary to the prevalent belief, it has generated more difficulty in governing due to its incomplete contracts and unclear governance in the distribution of risks and benefits.

Fair rules in the market refer to impartial criteria as references to rule. But the impartial rules or fair governance in a market do not need to be neoliberal formal justice, which is driven by abstract natural reason, and is free from the politics of interpreting everyday indignation. From the perspective of impartiality, fair rules such as a fair wage, a just price, and a fair exchange prevail, as opposed to exploitation and opportunism. Although the Golden Rule of fairness (reciprocity) prevails across societies, the meaning and forms of reciprocity are different. For example, unethical behaviors such as dishonesty and hiding information are legitimate in the neoclassical market, insofar as the behavior does not violate formal law. By contrast, in a society in which subordinate and superior relationships are emphasized, or in which agents in markets collaborate with one another, hiding information might be unfair. New problems related to the constitution of market rationality and the division of labor constantly challenge the existing justice of the market. In this sense, fairness in a market society that works for conflict resolution is not deduced by natural reason across societies or beyond politics.

The multiple instances of fair norms about contracts and contractual relations does not mean that norms of fairness are predetermined by nationally particular cultures. As has already been stated, fair norms about contracts and contractual relations are constantly constituted in novel contexts in which new problems emerge from the contests among multiple rationalities. Many institutionalists and culturalists fail to explain how new norms are constituted. Many culuralists and institutionalists focus on the ad hoc process of the emergence of social norms and argue for a locked-in pattern of norms about contracts and contractual relations produced by a small historical event or an isomorphic process of internalizing norms among agents in different societies. For example, some institutionalists argue that the Bismarckian laws of works councils were crucial to the formation of a peculiar German market capitalism that persists until now; others hold that the early historical choice about the role of the state in the U.S. shaped the peculiarity of American free market. Ronald Dore and Charles W. Hill argue that the cultural heritage developed during the Tokugawa era in Japan generates trustful norms for cooperative teams, while the culture of individualism in the U.S. market causes adversarial and short-term contracts.

However, impartial fairness or common grounds as guidelines for adjudication are not predetermined by prior norms about contracts and contractual relations. Existing norms and institutions are continuously contested and reinterpreted. It was not until World War II that Japanese firms developed collaborative markets. Large corporations in the U.S., like Chrysler and the Japanese transplants, developed fair partnerships under the so-called self-interest–oriented culture. As a new division of labor or a new market rationality emerges, societies face new problems for governance. In particular, the new form of closely interactive markets generates new problems for governance, such as how to distribute risks, responsibilities, and benefits. As this book has shown, agents in the new markets urgently need new criteria of market governance because the traditional norms about contracts and contractual relations, based on autonomous operation, do not work for governance of collaborative work. According to institutionalist approaches, cultures exist external to agents, and thus agents internalize the norms through sanctions and incentives; otherwise, cultures are unreflective cognitive frameworks. The former approach is in the tradition of Parsons, while the latter is the approach of new institutionalists such as DiMaggio and Powell.[4] But both institutionalist approaches fail to explain how meanings of social norms and cultures are reconstituted in different contexts. They fail to explain that cultures and new norms about contracts and contractual relations are continuously constituted and sustained by the practices of reflexive agents.

The agents' reflexivity and their proactive constitution of market rationality and fairness do not mean that institutions are not important in constituting the market regime. Quite to the contrary, in practice, institutions are "objective" conditions that play an important role in generating motives for reflexivity. The objective conditions and results of practices engender a tension between habitus (internally represented institutions) and practices. In this sense, habitus is not taken for granted or unreflective, as new institutionalists assume. In addition, in the process of norm-creation and constitution of the market regime, institutions provide agents with a repertoire of alternatives, or they influence agents by offering incentives that favor specific actions, although their constraints are not comprehensive. What this book has contested is not the fact that institutions influence agents' activities, but the rigid view of path-dependent institutionalism that disregards agents' reflexivity. In other words, this book has opposed the rigid view that norms and institutional arrangements about contracts and contractual relations have constant meaning and characteristics, independent of agents' reflection and reinterpretation.

How are fair norms and regimes created and, more importantly, sustained? Fair rules in the market should be continuously reconstituted by politics, continuously redefining opportunism. This book argues that fair norms arise out of indignation in the face of unfairness in everyday life in advance of the exercise of natural reason or what Rawls calls "considered conviction." Paul Ricoeur clearly explains the first step in the formation of justice:

> I deliberately speak of the unjust before the just—just as Plato and Aristotle do so often, and so intentionally. Was not our first entry into the region of lawfulness marked by the cry: "that's not fair"? This is a cry of indignation, one whose perspicacity is sometimes confusing when measured against the yardstick of our adult hesitations when summoned to pronounce in positive terms upon the justice or fairness of something. Indignation, in the face of injustice, comes far in advance of what John Rawls calls "considered convictions," whose clash no theory of justice can deny or refuse to consider.[5]

Indignation in the face of unfairness provides rich resources and reference points for building an authentic sense of justice. The motives of indignation include both formal and substantive aspects of justice, such as betrayed promises, disproportionate retributions, and unequal shares. Agents in a society constitute fair norms by differentiating fair from opportunistic behavior in the process of everyday practices. This process of differentiating fair from unfair or opportunistic behavior in everyday practices contradicts the justice deduced by abstract natural reason, which is beyond the everyday politics of the formation of fair norms. The sense of unfairness or definition of opportunism is subject to the issues that arise out of different forms of division of labor and the contest of rationality related to division of labor.

This does not mean that indignation is sufficient for the formation of an authentic sense of fairness. Indignation might be based on personal preferences; it cannot substitute for legitimate criteria of adjudication of conflicts. For example, Americans as well as Germans in the automotive parts market were angry at powerful parties' opportunistic behavior, such as abusing proprietary information, engaging in an asymmetric exchange of information, arbitrary revision of agreements, and leveraging unreasonable pressure for price cuts. But this indignation in the U.S. and Germany did not necessarily generate workable fairness in the market. In the U.S., agents' indignation dissipated in the absence of mutual adjustments in the civic public realm, while indignation in Germany enabled substantive fairness to work. Indignation is not sufficient for the formation of an authentic sense of fairness, one that is workable in adjudicating conflicts, because fair norms must be impartial. A judgment, whether it occurs in a court or in private relations, does not work as a fair criterion insofar as it is based on personal preferences or partiality. Impartiality emerges from reciprocal recognition: we cannot expect others to respect our interests unless we respect theirs. This reciprocal recognition comes out of an imaginative or hypothetical situation. But the hypothetical situation should not be always the same one that neoliberals assume in the abstract bargaining model or ahistorical personhood. Agents can build hypothetical situations by reflecting on current conflicts. The elements of hypothetical situations are not immutable but dependent on the context of conflicts. Agents develop different types of hypothetical situations; they can adjust to one another by judging the substantive issues based on formal criteria or by evaluating formal criteria based on substantive justice.

In this sense, the manner in which agents deliberate conflicts is important for the constitution of fair norms and formation of fair regimes. In the process of constituting impartial and common grounds, different conceptions of fairness and different market regimes, this book has argued, result from different kinds of problem-solving practices in a novel context of problems, that is, the manner in which agents organize deliberation of conflicts and new solutions (public vs. individual, dyadic ways). The public method of deliberating fair norms and adjudicating conflicts in the German automotive parts market fostered the establishment of substantive fairness and society-wide fair partnerships. In contrast, the individual, dyadic way of deliberation in the U.S. automotive parts market produced fair norms based on an extreme form of formal fairness; distrust and cynicism dominated long-term contractual relations.

In the process of deliberating conflicts and fair norms in the public realm, powerful parties in the German market had the burden of justifying their own position; later, they had difficulty violating their own norms. Agents' reflexivity upon fair norms does not mean that agents can do anything. To the contrary, agents are constrained by the ways of organizing deliberation. Deliberation in the public realm helped agents in the German market to reflect on their relative position; having acquired sensitivity to others' criteria of fair norms, agents were less likely to fall into partial preferences. In addition, democratic participation in the public realm was also the process of legislating self-rules. The process in which German suppliers criticized their customers' unfair behavior in the public realm was at the same time that of expressing their own criteria for fair governance. Democratic participation in public deliberation is needed for mutual adjustments in order to create impartial grounds; but more importantly, the democratic participatory process is also the process in which agents generate self-governance by legislating self-norms. In dealing with their own suppliers, German first-tier suppliers could rarely violate their own criteria of fairness in the public eye. This is why German suppliers have developed fair partnerships between suppliers through the entire supplier chain.

By contrast, in the absence of mutual adjustments in the civic public realm, Americans' indignation remains at a personal level, which, in turn, has facilitated the prevalence of abstract formal justice. The isolated dyadic relations between two parties to a contract in the U.S. market have deterred the establishment of society-wide fair partnerships. This does not mean that Americans failed to establish fair partnerships because they do not have sufficient associations in society. Contrary to Robert Putnam's expectation, Americans in the automotive parts market have sufficient associational networks for a public realm if they should intend to organize public deliberation. The problem is that American associations do not address so-called unfair behavior in the public realm, despite having sufficient networks. To return to Robert Putnam's metaphor, Americans in the automotive parts market are bowling together, but they do not talk about politics within their community.

In the absence of democratic participation in public deliberation of conflicts, Americans in the automotive parts market have had little chance to reflect on their position and to relativize their partial views. Powerful customers are less burdened with justifying their position in the public realm. Unconcerned with violating self-rules or society-wide fair rules, first-tier suppliers in the American market easily choose the option of transferring burdens all the way down through the supplier chain. Because the powerful customer can easily set rules for governance unilaterally in dyadic relations, the fair norms in the U.S. market have resulted in an extreme form of formal justice—it is fair only if a customer treats all suppliers in the same way, whether or not the customer's behavior is unethical and distasteful. It is noteworthy that this extremely formal justice is constituted in the process of deliberating conflicts in individual, dyadic relations, instead of being predetermined by cultural heritage or created by abstract natural reason. In the early stage of transformation toward collaborative markets, Americans in the automotive parts market also had expectations of substantive justice regarding the distribution of risks and responsibility, but their individual, dyadic method of deliberating conflicts forced agents to adopt this extreme form of fairness rather than creating rich resources of fair norms by adjusting various partial views of what is fair.

Different types of market regimes can be contested. The civic liberal regime characteristic of the German case is an alternative to the utilitarian liberal regime. Under the utilitarian liberal dichotomy of public/private, American associations efface the civic public realm in which agents could, if they chose, deliberate their common activities and act in concert. Although some Americans in the market have contested utilitarian liberalism by creating new publicly mediated institutions and deliberating the code of conduct in the market, the utilitarian liberal model of deliberating conflicts and norm-creation still prevails, reinforced by agents' practices. In practice, the utilitarian liberal distinction between public and private refers to the distinction between governmental and non-governmental sectors. By defining the common ground as only the governmental area, this utilitarian liberal paradigm excludes the civic public realm that is neither the government nor households (nor intimate relations), in which individuals can deliberate and adjust their conflicts. Agents in U.S. market society believe that politics should occur only in the public defined by utilitarian liberalism, that is, in the administrative government and its jurisdiction. These extreme formal criteria of justice for market governance grow out of the individual, dyadic way of deliberating conflicts; furthermore, the formal justice is reinforced by the individual process of problem solving in the market.

As an alternative to the utilitarian liberal regime, this book posits a civic liberal model based on the German case. Germans in the automotive parts market discuss, debate, and deliberate their prevalent unfair cases in formal as well as informal meetings. Germans in the market believe that they can address unethical issues because they are prevalent throughout society. Through deliberation and adjustments of different partial views in the public realm, Germans have created a rich common ground that includes not only formal rules but also substantive criteria for governance of collaborative markets. Civic liberalism has been rediscovered by Tocqueville's conception of "political society," Hannah Arendt's conception of the "public realm," and Habermas's conception of the "public sphere." This public space (*öffentliche Raum*), constituted by neither government nor private households, stems from Aristotle. The politics of Aristotle refer to the process by which members of community deliberate common issues and make decisions, that is, their participation in collective self-determination. Germans in the automotive parts market have developed collective self-government and self-determination through this public deliberation.

This book's key conclusion is that this public method of deliberation is more likely to activate substantive fair norms and the stability of fair partnerships than isolated, dyadic methods. In an attempt to activate the public realm for democratic and active participation, utilitarian liberalism can be an obstacle. Civic liberalism, on the other hand, should be encouraged in order to develop rich fair norms and society-wide fair partnerships.

Notes

1. Jeff Weintraub, "The Theory and Politics of the Public/Private Distinction," in Jeff Weintraub and Krishan Kumar, eds., *Public and Private in Thought and Practice* (Chicago: University of Chicago Press, 1997), 13.
2. David P. Levine, "Justice and Economic Democracy," *Review of Political Economy* 10, no. 3 (1998): 343–363.
3. The conception of ideal type refers to neither the accumulation and combination of empirical data nor the consensus of agents with diverse motives in the real world; rather, it is an analytical tool that is produced through an analytical accentuation of certain elements of reality.
4. See note 24 in the introduction of this book.
5. Paul Ricoeur, *The Just*, trans. David Pellauer (Chicago: University of Chicago Press, 2000), x.

APPENDIX

This book tests for non-response bias by comparing the responses to the first survey and the responses to the second, follow-up survey. After receiving responses in the first comprehensive mail survey, I sent the same questionnaires to the non-respondents of the first survey, 200 randomly selected suppliers in each country. In order to test for non-response bias, I tested the difference of means between the participants of the first survey (First Group) and the participants of the second, follow-up survey (Follow-Up Group), assuming that the Follow-Up Group might have more in common with those who did not respond at all than the First Group. The test shows no significant differences between the First Group and the Follow-Up Group at all variables used in this paper at the significance level of 0.1.

Test for Non-Response Bias

In the United States

Variables	t-test for Equality of Means		
	Mean Difference	t	Sig. (2-tailed)
Possibility of customer abuse	-.13	-.536	.595
Openness and transparency	.21	1.147	.257
Violation of confidentiality	-.13	-.572	.570
Abuse of information	.07	.306	.761
Disregarding contracts	.06	.282	.779
Asymmetry, (a) s-c info	.06	.382	.704
Asymmetry, (b) c-s info	-.21	-1.306	.196
Price pressure	-.16	-.822	.415
General appreciation of fairness	-.19	-1.053	.298

Note: N: First Group = 139; Follow-up Group = 34.

In Germany

Variables	t-test for Equality of Means		
	Mean Difference	t	Sig. (2-tailed)
Possibility of customer abuse	-.13	-.536	.595
Possibility of Customer Abuse	.07	.397	.698
Openness and Transparency	-.06	-.406	.686
Violation of Confidentiality	.07	.345	.731
Abuse of Information	-.03	-.174	.863
Disregarding Contracts	-.09	-.504	.616
Asymmetry, a) s-c info	.13	1.028	.308
Asymmetry, b) c-s info	.14	.936	.353
Price Pressure	-.06	-.279	.781
General Appreciation of Fairness	-.10	-.763	.448

Note: N: First Group = 109; Follow-up Group = 38.

BIBLIOGRAPHY

Primary sources are recordings of interviews and the mail survey. Main secondary sources are newspapers and magazines. German sources are *Börsen Zeitung, Deutsche Presse-Agentur, Deutsche Verkehrszeitung, Frankfurter Allgemeine Zeitung (FAZ), Handelsblatt, Süddeutsche Zeitung.* U.S. secondary sources are *Automotive Industries, Purchasing, Ward's Auto World.*

Interview sources and secondary sources from newspapers are not enumerated in this bibliography, but are noted in the footnotes. Primary evidence is personal interviews with main figures in the U.S. and German automotive parts markets. I also conducted interviews via e-mail. "Interview with G" in the footnotes refers to an interview with a German supplier, while "Interview with A" refers to an interview with a U.S. supplier. "E-mail interview" refers to an interview conducted by e-mail. I differentiated personal interview from e-mail interview by writing "e-mail interview with US" (versus "interview with A") and "e-mail interview with D" (versus "interview with G").

Abernathy, William J., Kim B. Clark, and Alan M. Kantrow. "The New Industrial Competition." *Harvard Business Review* 59, no. 5 (1981): 68–81.

Adler, Paul S., Thomas A. Kochan, John Paul MacDuffie, Frits K. Pil, and Saul Rubinstein. "United States: Variations on a Theme." In *After Lean Production: Evolving Employment Practices in the World Auto Industry,* edited by Thomas A. Kochan et al., 61–84. Ithaca: Cornell University Press, 1997.

Aigner, Jürgen, and Wilfried Kuckelkorn. "Die weltweite Verflechtung konzerneigener und selbständiger Lieferbetriebe im Hause Ford." In *Zulieferer im Netz,* edited by Hans Gerhard Mendius and Ulrike Wendeling-Schröder, 131–140. Cologne: Bund-Verlag GmbH, 1991.

Albert, Michel. *Capitalism versus Capitalism.* New York: Four Walls Eight Windows, 1993.

Allen, Christopher S. "Institutions Challenged: German Unification, Policy Errors, and the 'Siren Song' of Deregulation." In *Negotiating the New Germany: Can Social Partnership Survive?* edited by Lowell Turner, 139–156. Ithaca: ILR Press, an imprint of Cornell University Press, 1997.

Altmann, Norbert. "Japanisierung der Interessenvertretung bei systemischer Rationalisierung?" In *Vernetzte Produktion: Automobilzulieferer zwischen Kontrolle und Autonomie,* edited by Manfred Deiß and Volker Döhl, 81–105. Frankfurt: Campus Verlag, 1992.

Altmann, Norbert, and Dieter Sauer, eds. *Systemische Rationalisierung und Zulieferindustrie: Sozialwissenschaftliche Aspekte zwischenbetrieblicher Arbeitsteilung.* Frankfurt: Campus Verlag, 1989.

Andrews, David M. "Capital Mobility and State Autonomy: Toward a Structural Theory of International Monetary Relations." *International Studies Quarterly* 38, no. 2 (1994): 193–218.

Arendt, Hannah. *The Human Condition.* Chicago: University of Chicago Press, 1958.

ArGeZ (Arbeitsgemeinschaft Zulieferindustrie). "Der Zulieferer als Entwicklungspartner—Chancen und Risken." Supplier Forum of ArGeZ, Hagen, 9 November 1995.

———. "Die Fairneßregeln von BDI und VDA in der Praxis." Document of ArGeZ, 1995.

———. "Grundzüge von Entwicklungsvereinbarungen: Bausteine und Erläuterungen." Document of ArGeZ-Arbeitkreis, 1996.

———. "Die Globalisierung der Zuliefermärkte." Supplier Forum of ArGeZ, Maritim Hotel, Cologne, 2 October 1996.

———. "Kooperationsmodelle im Zulieferbereich." Supplier Forum of ArGeZ, Frankfurt am Main, 29 October 1997.

———. "Nachfragemacht und Vertragsgestaltung in Industrie und Handel." Supplier Forum of ArGeZ, Swissôtel Düsseldorf, 11 November 1998.

———. "Konditionenempfehlung der ArGeZ: Klauseln zur vertraglichen Gestaltung partnerschaftlicher Lieferbeziehungen." Full Text of Publication in the Federal Law Gazette, No. 245, 28 December 1999.

———. "Zulieferindustrie im 21. Jahrhundert." Supplier Forum of ArGeZ, Düsseldorf, 27 January 2000.

Arrighetti, Alessandro, Reinhard Bachmann, and Simon Deakin. "Contract Law, Social Norms and Inter-Firm Cooperation." *Cambridge Journal of Economics* 21, no. 2 (1997): 171–195.

Asanuma, Benri. "Japanese Manufacturer-Supplier Relationships in International Perspective: The Automobile Case." Working Paper No. 8, Faculty of Economics, Kyoto University, 1988.

———. "Manufacturer-Supplier Relationships in Japan and the Concept of Relation-Specific Skill." *Journal of Japanese and International Economics* 3, no. 1 (1989): 1–30.

Atiyah, P. S. *The Rise and Fall of Freedom of Contract.* Oxford: Clarendon Press, 1979.

———. "Contract as Promise." *Harvard Law Review* 95, no. 2 (1981): 509–528.

———. *An Introduction to the Law of Contract.* 4th ed. Oxford: Clarendon Press, 1989.

Audi. "Purchasing Process of VW Group." Document of Audi, 2000.

Automotive Associations. Motor Source Guide, 2001.

Baethge, Martin, Volker Baethge-Kinsky, and Peter Kupka. "Facharbeit—Auslaufmodel oder neue Perspektive?" *SOFI-Mitteilungen* 26 (May 1998): 81–98.

Baily, M. N., and H. Gerbach. "Efficiency in Manufacturing and the Need for Global Competition." Brookings Papers on Economic Activity: Microeconomics, 1995, 307–358.

Ballew, Paul D., and Robert H. Schnorbus. "Realignment in the Auto Supplier Industry: the Rippling Effects of Big Three Restructuring." *Economic Perspectives* 18, no. 1 (1994): 2–9.

Bamford, James. "Driving America to Tiers." *Financial World* 163, no. 23 (8 November 1994): 24–27.

Bartelt, Andreas. "Vertrauen in Zulieferbeziehungen der Automobilindustrie: Ergebnisse einer empirischen Untersuchung." Summary of Research Paper, Julius-Maximilians-Universität Würzburg, Lehrstuhl für Betriebswirtschaftslehre und Marketing, 2000.

———. "Vertrauen in Zuliefernetzwerken der Automobilindustrie: Eine theoretische und empirische Analyse." Ph.D. diss., Julius-Maximilians-Universität, Würzburg, 2000.

BDI (Bundesverband der Deutschen Industrie e. V.). "BDI-Grundsätze des Leistungswettbewerbs im Zulieferwesen fortgeschrieben." Document of BDI, 1993.

———. "Leitsäte für Zulieferbeziehungen." BDI Publication, No. 279 (1994).

Beale, Hugh, and Tony Dugdale. "Contracts Between Businessmen: Planning and The Use of Contractual Remedies." *British Journal of Law and Society* 2 (summer 1975): 45-60.

Beatson, Jack, and Daniel Friedmann. "From 'Classical' to Modern Contract Law." In *Good Faith and Fault in Contract Law*, edited by Jack and Beatson and Daniel Friedmann, 3–21. Oxford: Clarendon Press, 1995.

Beatson, Jack, and Daniel Friedmann, eds. *Good Faith and Fault in Contract Law*. Oxford: Clarendon Press, 1995.

Becker, Gary S., and George J. Stigler. "Law Enforcement, Malfeasance, and Compensation of Enforcers." *The Journal of Legal Studies* 3, no. 1 (1974): 1–18.

Bender, Iris. *Struktureller Wandel in der Automobilindustrie und der Einfluß strategischer Industrie- und Handelspolitik*. Frankfurt am Main: Peter Lang GmbH, 1996.

Bennett, Jr., Robert B. "Just-In-Time Purchasing and the Problem of Consequential Damages." *Uniform Commercial Code Law Journal* 26 (spring 1994): 332–358.

Bensaou, M. "Interorganizational Cooperation: The Role of Information Technology: An Empirical Comparison of US and Japanese Supplier Relations." Working Paper in the INSEAD Working Paper Series, 1993.

———. "Portfolios of Buyer-Supplier Relationships." *Sloan Management Review* 40, no. 4 (summer 1999): 35-44.

Berg, Hartmut, and Jens Müller. "The Volkswagen AG and Its Suppliers in the Region of Hannover: Adjustment Requirements and Regional Economic Policy." Discussion Paper in Political Economy, no. 65, Dortmund University, 1995.

Berg, Peter, Eileen Appelbaum, Thomas Bailey, and Arne Kalleberg. "The Performance Effects of Modular Production in the Apparel Industry." *Industrial Relations* 35, no. 3 (1995): 356–373.

Berger, Suzanne, and Ronald Dore, eds. *National Diversity and Global Capitalism*. Ithaca: Cornell University, 1996.

Bernheim, B. Douglas, and Debraj Ray. "Collective Dynamic Consistency in Repeated Games." *Games and Economic Behavior* 1, no. 4 (1989): 295–326.

Bieber, Daniel, and Dieter Sauer. "Kontrolle is gut! Ist Vertrauen besser? Autonomie und Beherrschung in Abnehmer-Zulieferbeziehungen." In *Zulieferer im Netz*, edited by Hans Gerhard Mendius and Ulrike Wendeling-Schröder, 228–254. Cologne: Bund-Verlag GmbH, 1991.

Birou, Laura M., and Stanley E. Fawcett. "Supplier Involvement in Integrated Product Development: A Comparison of US and European Practices." *International Journal of Physical Distribution & Logistics Management* 24, no. 5 (1994): 4–14.

Bispinck, Reinhard. "Betrieblich Interessenvertretung, Entgelt und Tarifpolitik." *WSI Mittelungen* 54, no. 2 (2001).

Blenkhorn, D. L., and A. H. Noori. "What It Takes to Supply Japanese OEMs." *Industrial Marketing Management* 19, no. 1 (1991): 21–30.

BMW. *Process Future: BMW and Their Suppliers*. BMW Process Consulting, 1998.

Boaz, David, and Edward H. Crane, eds. *Market Liberalism: A Paradigm for the 21st Century*. Washington, D.C.: Cato Institute, 1993.

Bochum, Ulrich, and Heinz-Rudolf Meissner. "Entwicklungstendenzen in der Automobilzulieferindustrie: Logistik, Just-in-time und die Zukunftsperspektiven einer angebundenen Branche." Research Community for International Economics, Structure and Technology Politics, FAST-Study, no. 91988.

Bogdan, Michael. *Comparative Law*. Deventer: Kluwer, 1994.

Botschen, Günther, and Markus Webhofer. "Mehr Bürokratie statt Wettbewerbsvorsprung." *Absatzwirtschaft* 2 (1997): 70–73.

Bourdieu, Pierre. *The Logic of Practice*. Stanford, Calif.: Stanford University Press, 1992.

———. *Outline of a Theory of Practice*. Cambridge: Cambridge University Press, 1998.

Boyer, Robert. "The Convergence Hypothesis Revisited: Globalization but Still the Century of Nations?" In *National Diversity and Global Capitalism*, edited by Suzanne Berger and Ronald Dore, 29–59. Ithaca: Cornell University Press, 1996.

———. "Will the Japanese and the German Innovation Systems Cope with the Challenges of the 21st Century?" Economic Research Center Discussion Paper, School of Economics, Nagoya University, 1999.

Boyer, Robert, and Daniel Drache, eds. *States Against Markets: The Limits of Globalization*. London: Routledge, 1996.

Bryan, Lowell, and Diana Farrell. *Market Unbound: Unleashing Global Capitalism.* New York: John Wiley & Sons, 1996.

Burchell, Brendan, and Frank Wilkinson. "Trust, Business Relationships and the Contractual Environment." *Cambridge Journal of Economics* 21, no. 2 (1997): 217–237.

Calamari, John D., and Joseph M. Perillo. *The Law of Contracts.* 3rd ed. St. Paul, Minn.: West Publication, 1987.

Callahan, Thomas, J. "Comparisons of the Competitive Position of Canadian, Mexican, and U.S. Suppliers." *The Journal of Supply Chain Management* 36, no. 4 (fall 2000): 43–54.

Camilleri, Joseph A., and Jim Falk. *The End of Sovereignty? The Politics of a Shrinking and Fragmenting World.* Brookfield, Vt.: Edward Elgar, 1992.

Campbell, David, and Donald Harris. "Flexibility in Long-Term Contractual Relationships: The Role of Cooperation." *Journal of Law and Society* 20, no. 2 (1993): 166–191.

Campbell, John L., J. Rogers Hollingsworth, and Leon N. Lindberg, eds. *Governance of the American Economy.* New York: Cambridge University Press, 1991.

Carlin, Wendy, and David Soskice. "Shocks to the System: The German Political Economy under Stress." *National Institute Economic Review* 59, no. 159 (January 1997): 57–76.

Carr, Amelia S., and Larry R. Smeltzer. "The Relationship of Strategic Purchasing to Supply Chain Management." *European Journal of Purchasing & Supply Management* 5 (1999): 43–51.

Carr, Christopher. "Productivity and Skills in Vehicle Component Manufacturers in Britain, Germany and the USA and Japan." *National Institute Economic Review* no. 139 (February 1992): 97–87.

Casper, Steven Wayne. "How Public Law Influences Decentralized Supplier Network Organization in Germany: The Cases of BMW and Audi." Discussion paper FS I 95-314, Wissenschaftszentrum Berlin für Sozialforschung, Berlin, 1995.

———. "Reconfiguring Institutions: The Political Economy of Legal Development in Germany and the United States." Ph.D. diss., Cornell University, 1997.

———. "Nationale Institutionengefüge und innovative Industrieorganisation: Zulieferbeziehungen in Deutschland." In *Ökonomische Leistungsfähigkeit und institutionelle Innovation: Das deutsche Produktions- und Politikregime im globalen Wettbewerb,* edited by Frieder Naschold, David Soskice, Bob Hancke, and Ulrich Jürgens, 235–250. WZB-Jahrbuch, 1997.

———. "High Technology Governance and Institutional Adaptiveness." Discussion Paper FS I 99-307, Wissenschaftszentrum Berlin für Sozialforschung, 1999.

———. "The Legal Framework for Corporate Governance: The Influence of Contract Law on Company Strategies in Germany and the United States." In *Varieties of Capitalism: The Institutional Foundations of Comparative Advantage,* edited by Peter Hall and David Soskice, 387–416. New York: Oxford University Press, 2001.

Casper, Steven Wayne, and Bob Hancke. "Global Quality Norms within National Production Regimes: ISO 9000 Standards in the French and German Car Industries." *Organization Studies* 20, no. 6 (1999): 961–985.

Cattero, Bruno. *Lavorare alla Fiat: Arbeiten bei VW: Technologie, Arbeit und soziale Regulierung in der Automobilindustrie.* Münster: Westfälisches Dampfboot, 1998.

———. "Beruf und Berufausbildung—Mythen und Widersprüche im 'deutschen Modell.'" In *Modell Deutschland, Modell Europa, Problems Perspectiven,* edited by Bruno Cattero, 225–246. Opladen: Leske + Budrich, 1998.

Cattero, Bruno, ed. *Modell Deutschland, Modell Europa, Problems Perspectiven.* Europa- und Nordamerika-Studien. Opladen: Leske + Budrich, 1998.

Charny, David. "Nonlegal Sanctions in Commercial Relationships." *Harvard Law Review* 104, no. 2 (1990): 373–467.

———. "Illusions of A Spontaneous Order: 'Norms' in Contractual Relations." *University of Pennsylvania Law Review* 144, no. 5 (1996): 1841–1858.

Chirinko, Robert S., and Julie Ann Elston. "Finance, Control and Profitability: An Evaluation of German Bank Influence." Faculty Research Paper no. 9940, University of Central Florida, 1999.

Choi, Thomas Y. "Comparison of Quality Management Practices: Across the Supply Chain and Industries." *The Journal of Supply Chain Management* 35, no. 1 (winter 1999): 20–27.

Chotangada, Rati Apana. "Governance Systems That Facilitate Innovation: Changing Perspectives of Supplier Customer Relationships. The Case of The Automotive Industry." Ph.D. diss., University of Cincinnati, 2000.

Clark, K. B. "Project Scope and Project Performance: The Effect of Parts Strategy and Supplier Involvement on Product Development." *Management Science* 35, no. 10 (1989): 1247–1263.

Clune, William H. "Unreasonableness and Alienation in the Continuing Relationships of Welfare State Bureaucracy: From Regulatory Complexity to Economic Democracy." *Wisconsin Law Review* 1985, no. 2 (1985): 707–740.

Cohen, Morris R. "The Basis of Contract." *Harvard Law Review* 46, no. 4 (1933): 553–92.

Cohen, Stephen. *Modern Capitalist Planning.* Berkeley: University of California Press, 1977.

Cole, Robert. "U.S. Quality Improvement in the Auto Industry: Close but No Cigar." *California Management Review* 32, no. 4 (summer 1990): 71–85.

Cole, Robert E., and Taizo Yakushiji. "The American and Japanese Auto Industries in Transition." Report of the Joint US-Japan Automotive Study, Center for Japanese Studies, University of Michigan, Ann Arbor, 1984.

Cooter, Robert D. "Decentralized Law for a Complex Economy: The Structural Approach to Adjudicating the New Law Merchant." *University of Pennsylvania Law Review* 144, no. 5 (1996): 1643–1696.

Cooter, Robert, and Thomas Ulen. *Law and Economics.* Reading, MA: HarperCollins, 1988.

Cox, Andrew. *State, Finance and Industry: A Comparative Analysis of Post-War Trends in Six Advanced Industrial Economies.* Sussex: Wheatsheaf Books, 1986.

Crouch, Colin, and Wolfgang Streeck. "Introduction: The Future of Capitalist Diversity." In *Political Economy of Modern Capitalism: Mapping Convergence and Diversity*, edited by Colin Crouch and Wolfgang Streeck, 1–18. London: Sage Publications, 1997.

Crouch, Colin, and Wolfgang Streeck, eds. *Political Economy of Modern Capitalism: Mapping Convergence and Diversity.* London: Sage Publications, 1997.

Culpepper, Pepper D. "Still a Model for the Industrialized Countries?" In *The German Skills Machine: Sustaining Comparative Advantage in a Global Economy*, edited by Pepper D. Culpepper and David Finegold, 1–34. New York: Berghahn Books, 1999.

Cusumano, Michael A. "The Limits of 'Lean.'" *Sloan Management Review* 35, no. 4 (summer 1994): 27–32.

Cusumano, Michael A., and Akira Takeishi. "Supplier Relations and Management: A Survey of Japanese, Japanese-Transplant, and U.S. Auto Plants." *Strategic Management Journal* 12, no. 7 (October 1991): 563–588.

Daimler-Benz AG. *Das Großunternehmen und der indstrielle Mittelstand: Eine Untersuchung über die klein- und mittelbetrieblichen Zulieferer der Daimler-Benz AG.* Stuttgart-Untertürkheim: Daimler-Benz AG, 1962.

D'Alessio, Nestor, and Herbert Oberbeck. "Ist das deutsche Modelle der 'corporate governance' am Ende?" In *Modell Deutschland, Modell Europa, Problems Perspectiven*, edited by Bruno Cattero, 99–116. Opladen: Leske + Budrich, 1998.

Deakin, Simon, Christel Lane, and Frank Wilkinson. "Trust or Law? Towards an Integrated Theory of Contractual Relations between Firms." *Journal of Law and Society* 21, no. 3 (1994): 329–349.

Deakin, Simon, and Jonathan Michie, eds. *Contracts, Cooperation, and Competition: Studies in Economics, Management, and Law.* Oxford: Oxford University Press, 1997.

———. "Contracts and Competition: An Introduction." *Cambridge Journal of Economics* 21, no. 2 (1997): 121–125.

Deeg, Richard. "Banks and Industrial Finance in the 1990s." *Industry and Innovation* 4, no. 1 (1997): 53–74.

Deiß, Manfred, and Volker Döhl, eds. *Vernetze Produktion: Automobilzulieferer zwischen Kontrolle und Autonomie.* Frankfurt: Campus Verlag, 1992.

"Deutsche Raus." *Manager Magazin* (September 1993): 8–11.

Diehlmann, Gernot. *Vorentwicklungsmanagement in der Automobilzulieferindustrie: Konzeptionelle Grundlagen und empirische Untersuchung zur erfolgsorientierten Gestaltung der Vorentwicklung in Automobilzulieferunternehmen*. Frankfurt am Main: Peter Lang GmbH, 1998.

Diener, Wolfe W., and Stefan Dransmann. "Unternehmenspartnerschaften in der Automobilzulieferindustrie: Ergebnisse einer empirischen Untersuchung." In *Unternehmensnetzwerke und virtuelle Organizationen*, edited by Udo Winand and Klaus Nathusius, 11–31. Stuttgart: Schaeffer-Poeschel Verlag, 1998.

DiMaggio, Paul J. "Culture and Economy." In *The Handbook of Economic Sociology*, edited by Neil J. Smelser and Richard Swedberg, 27–57. Princeton: Princeton University Press, 1994.

DiMaggio, Paul J., and Walter W. Powell. "The Iron Cage Revisited: Institutional Isomorphism and Collective Rationality in Organizational Fields." *American Sociological Review* 48, no. 2 (1983): 147–160.

————. Introduction to *The New Institutionalism in Organization Analysis*. Chicago: The University of Chicago Press, 1991, 1–38.

D'Iribarne, Philippe. "A Check to Enlightened Capitalism." In *Political Economy of Modern Capitalism: Mapping Convergence and Diversity*, edited by Colin Crouch and Wolfgang Streeck, 161–172. London: Sage Publications, 1997.

Döhl, Volker, and Manfred Deiß. "Von der Lieferbeziehung zum Produktionsnetzwerk-Internationale Tendenzen in der Reorganisatioin der zwischenbetrieblichen Arbeitsteilung." In *Vernetzte Produktion: Automobilzulieferer zwischen Kontrolle und Autonomie*, edited by Manfred Deiß and Volker Döhl, 5–48. Frankfurt: Campus Verlag, 1992.

Doleschal, Reinhard. "Just-in-time-Strategien und betriebliche Interessenvertretung in Automobil-Zulieferbetrieben." In *Systemische Rationalisierung und Zulieferindustrie*, edited by Nobert Altmann and Dieter Sauer, 155–205. Frankfurt: Campus Verlag, 1989.

————. "Daten und Trends der bundesdeutschen Automobil-Zulieferindustrie." In *Zulieferer im Netz*, edited by Hans Gerhard Mendius and Ulrike Wendeling-Schröder, 35–60. Cologne: Bund-Verlag GmbH, 1991.

Döring, Kurt. "Die ungleichen Partner." *Zeit*, 9 April 1965.

Dore, Ronald. *Taking Japan Seriously*. Stanford, Calif.: Stanford University Press, 1987.

————. "The Distinctiveness of Japan." In *Political Economy of Modern Capitalism: Mapping Convergence & Diversity*, edited by Colin Crouch and Wolfgang Streeck, 19–32. London: Sage Publications, 1997.

————. *Stock Market Capitalism: Welfare Capitalism—Japan and Germany versus the Anglo-Saxons*. New York: Oxford University Press, 2000.

Drucker, Peter. *The Concept of the Corporation*. New York: John Day Company, 1946.

Dyer, Jeffrey H. "How Supplier Partnerships Helped Revive Chrysler." *Harvard Business Review* 74, no. 4 (July–August): 46–47.

————. "How Chrysler Created an American Keiretsu." *Harvard Business Review* 74, no. 4 (July–August 1996): 42–56.

————. "Specialized Supplier Networks as a Source of Competitive Advantage: Evidence from the Auto Industry." *Strategic Management Journal* 17, no. 4 (1996): 271–291.

Dyer, Jeffrey H., Dong Sung Cho, and Wujin Chu. "Strategic Supplier Segmentation: The Next 'Best Practice' in Supply Chain Management." *California Management Review* 40, no. 2 (1998): 57–77.

Dyer, Jeffrey H., and W. G. Ouchi. "Japanese-Style Partnerships: Giving Companies a Competitive Edge." *Sloan Management Review* 35, no. 1 (fall 1993): 51–63.

Ebbinghaus, Bernhard. "Dinosaurier der Dienstleistungsgesellschaft? Der Mitgliederschwund deutscher Gewerkschaften im historischen und internationalen Vergleich." MPIfG Working Paper 02/3, Max-Planck-Institut für Gesellschaftsforschung, March 2002.

Eberwein, Wilhelm, and Jochen Tholen. *Euro-Manager or Splendid Isolation? International Management—An Anglo-German Comparison*. Berlin: Walter de Gruyter, 1993.

Ebke, Werner F., and Bettina M. Steinhauer. "The Doctrine of Good Faith in German Contract Law." In *Good Faith and Fault in Contract Law*, edited by Jack Beatson and Daniel Friedmann, 171–190. Oxford: Oxford Clarendon Press, 1995.

Eisenberg, Melvin. "The Bargain Principle and Its Limits." *Harvard Law Review* 95, no. 4 (1982): 741–801.

Eisenhardt, K. M., and B. N. Tabrizi. "Accelerating Adaptive Process: Product Innovation in the Global Computer Industry." *Administrative Science Quarterly* 40, no. 1 (1995): 84–110.

Endres, Egon, and Theo Wehner. "Frictions in the New Division of Labor: Cooperation between Producers and Suppliers in the German Automobile Industry." In *The New Division of Labor: Emerging forms of Work Organization in International Perspective*, edited by Wolfgang Littek and Tony Charles, 457–472. Berlin: Walter de Gruyter, 1995.

Engelskirchen, Heinz-Peter. "Zukunft der Region—Bericht über die Strukturkonferenz der IG Metall, Bonn im März 1990." In *Zulieferer im Netz—Zwischen Abhängigkeit und Partnerschaft*, edited by Hans Gerhard Mendius and Ulrike Wendeling-Schröder. Cologne: Bund-Verlag GmbH, 1991.

Ensthaler, J., A. Füssler, and D. Nuissl. *Juristische Aspekte des Qualitätsmanagements*. Berlin: Springer-Verlag, 1997.

Epstein, Ralph. *The Automobile Industry*. Chicago: A.W. Saw Company, 1928.

Farber, Daniel A. "Contract Law and Modern Economic Theory." *Northwestern University Law Review* 78, no. 2 (1983): 303–339.

Farnsworth, E. Allan. "Good Faith in Contract Performance." In *Good Faith and Fault in Contract Law*, edited by Jack Beatson and Daniel Friedmann, 153–170. Oxford: Clarendon Press, 1995.

Farrell, Joseph, and Eric Maskin. "Renegotiation in Repeated Games." *Games and Economic Behavior* 1, no. 4 (1989): 327–360.

Fichter, Michael. "Unions in the New Länder: Evidence for the Urgency of Reform." In *Negotiating the New Germany: Can Social Partnership Survive?* edited by Lowell Turner, 87–112. Ithaca: ILR Press, an imprint of Cornell University Press. 1997.

———. "Trade Union Members: A Vanishing Species in Post-Unification Germany?" *German Studies Review* 20, no. 1 (1997): 83–104.

Fieten, Robert. *So überleben Automobilzulieferer in schwierigen Zeiten*. Eschborn: Rationalisierung-Kuratorium der Deutschen Wirtschaft (RKW) e.V., 1995.

Fieten, Robert, Werner Friedrich, and Bernhard Lageman. *Globalisierung der Märkte: Herausforderung und Optionen für kleine und mittlere Unternehmen, insbesondere für Zulieferer*. Stuttgart: Schaeffer-Poeschel Verlag, 1997.

Finegold, David, and Karin Wagner. "The German Skill-Creation System and Team-Based Production: Competitive Asset or Liability?" In *The German Skills Machine: Sustaining Comparative Advantage in a Global Economy*, edited by Pepper D. Culpepper and David Finegold, 115–155. New York: Berghahn Books, 1999.

Fitzgerald, Kevin R. "Show Suppliers the Money!" *Purchasing* 123, no. 2 (14 August 1997): 40–47.

Fligstein, Neil. *The Transformation of Corporate Control*. Cambridge, Mass.: Harvard University Press, 1990.

Florida, Richard, and Martin Kenney. "Transplanted Organizations: The Transfer of Japanese Industrial Organization to the US." *American Sociological Review* 56, no. 3 (June 1991): 381–398.

FPN Arbeitsforschung + Raumentwicklung. *Lean Production in der Automobilindustrie und die Lage der Zulieferer: Eine Untersuchung in Südniedersachsen/Nordhessen im Auftrag des RKW*. Kassel: Jenior und Pressler, 1992.

Fried, Charles. *Contract as Promise: A Theory of Contractual Obligation*. Cambridge, MA: Harvard University Press, 1981.

Friedman, Thomas L. *The Luxus and The Olive Tree*. New York: Farrar Straus Giroux, 1999.

Gaiser, Anja Sofia. *Die rechtliche Problematik der Erstbemusterungspraxis in der Automobilindustrie*. Berlin: Duncker & Humbolt, 1997.

Galambos, Louis. *Competition and Cooperation: The Emergence of a National Trade Association.* Baltimore: Johns Hopkins University Press, 1966.

———. "The American Trade Association Movement Revisited." In *Trade Associations in Business History,* edited by Hiroaki Yamazaki and Matao Miyamoto, 121–138. Tokyo, Japan: University of Tokyo Press, 1988.

Gamble, Andrew. *The Free Economy and the Strong State.* 2nd ed. Basingstoke: Macmillan, 1994.

Gandenberger, Otto. *Die Ausschreibung.* Heidelberg: Quelle & Meyer, 1961.

Garrett, Geoffrey. *Partisan Politics in the Global Economy.* New York: Cambridge University Press, 1998.

Geck, Hinrich-Mattias, and Günther Petry. *Nachfragermacht gegenüber Zulieferern: Eine Untersuchung am Beispiel der Automobil- und der elektro-technischen Industrie.* Cologne: Carl Heymanns Verlag KG, 1983.

Genter, Andreas. *Entwurf einer Kennzahlensystems zur Effektivitäts- und Effizienzsteigerung von Entwicklungsprojekten, dargestellt am Beispiel der Entwicklungs- und Anlaufphase in der Automobilindustrie.* Munich: Franz Vahlen, 1994.

Gerlach, M. *Alliance Capitalism: The Social Organization of Japanese Business.* Berkeley: University of California Press, 1992.

Gill, Stephen R., and David Law. "Global Hegemony and the Structural Power of Capital." *International Studies Quarterly* 33, no. 4 (1989): 475–499.

Glendon, Ann, Michael W. Gordon, and Christopher Osakwe. *Comparative Legal Traditions.* St Paul, Minn.: West, 1994.

Goetz, Charles J., and Robert E. Scott. "Enforcing Promises: An Examination of the Basis of Contract." *Yale Law Journal* 89, no. 7 (1980): 1261–1322.

Goeudevert, Daniel. "Die Rolle der Zulieferindustrie angesichts der weltweiten Wettbewerbsverschärfung." In *Zulieferer im Netz,* edited by Hans Gerhard Mendius and Ulrike Wendeling-Schröder, 99–110. Cologne: Bund-Verlag GmbH, 1991.

Goldberg, Victor P. "Toward an Expanded Economic Theory of Contract." *Journal of Economic Issues* 10, no. 1 (1976): 45–61.

———. "Price Adjustment in Long-term Contracts." *Wisconsin Law Review* 1985, no. 3 (1985): 527–544.

Gordon, Robert W. "Macaulay, MacNeil and the Discovery of Solidarity and Power in Contract Law." *Wisconsin Law Review* 1985, no. 3 (1985): 565–580.

Grabowski, Hans, and Kerstin Geiger, eds. *Neue Wege zur Produktentwicklung.* Stuttgart: Raabe Verlag, 1997.

Green, David. *The New Right.* Brighton: Wheatsheaf, 1987.

Griffin, Susan Osborn. "Two Hypotheses Accounting for the Different Levels of Vertical Integration in the U.S. and Japanese Auto Industries." Ph.D. diss., Emory University, 1994.

Haddad, Carol J. "Involving Manufacturing Employees in the Early Stages of Product Development: A Case Study from the U.S. Automobile Industry." In *New Product Development and Production Networks: Global Industrial Experience,* edited by Ulrich Jürgens, 289–312. Heidelberg: Springer Verlag, 2000.

Hadfield, Gillian K. "Problematic Relations: Franchising and the Law of Incomplete Contracts." *Stanford Law Review* 42, no. 4 (1990): 927–992.

Hake, Bruno, and Philip M. Lynch. *The Market for Automotive Parts in Germany, France, and Italy.* Michigan International Commerce Reports. Number 2. Ann Arbor: University of Michigan, 1970.

Hall, Peter A. "The Political Economy of Adjustment in Germany." In *Ökonomische Leistungsfähigkeit und institutionelle Innovation: Das deutsche Produktions- und Politikregime im globalen Wettbewerb,* edited by Frieder Naschold et al., 293–317. Berlin: Ed Sigma, 1997.

Hall, Peter A., and David Soskice, eds. *Varieties of Capitalism: The Institutional Foundations of Comparative Advantage.* New York: Oxford University Press, 2001.

———. "An Introduction to Varieties of Capitalism." In *Varieties of Capitalism,* edited by Peter A. Hall and David Soskice, 1–68. New York: Oxford University Press, 2001.

Hall, Richard H., and Robert E. Quinn, eds. *Organization Theory and Public Policy*. Beverly Hills, Calif.: Sage Publications, 1983.

Hamer, Eberhard. "Zuliefererdiskriminierung: Machtwirtschaft statt Marktwirtschaft?" In *Zulieferer im Netz*, edited by Hans Gerhard Mendius and Ulrike Wendeling-Schröder, 65–79. Cologne: Bund-Verlag GmbH, 1991.

Hammes, Michael. *Die Gestaltung der Leistungstiefe im Spannungsfeld von Unternehmensstrategie und staatlicher Wettbewerbspolitik*. Aachen: Verlag Shaker, 1994.

Hancke, Bob. "Vorsprung, aber nicht länger (nur) durch Technik: Die schnelle Anpassung der deutschen Automobilindustrie an neue internationale Wettbewerbsbedingungen." In *Ökonomische Leistungsfähigkeit und institutionelle Innovation: Das deutsche Produktions- und Politikregime im globalen Wettbewerb*, edited by Frieder Naschold, David Soskice, Bob Hancke, and Ulrich Jürgens, 213–234. Berlin: WZB-Jahrbuch, 1997.

Hancke, Bob, and Helen Callaghan. "Systemwettbewerb order—komplementarität? Deutsche und Amerikanishe Institutionen und Innovationsstrategien im Globalisierungszeitalter." Wissenschaftzentrum Berlin für Sozialforschung, February 1999.

Hanke, Jürgen. *Hybride Koordinations-strukturen: Liefer- und Leistungsbeziehungen kleiner und mittlerer Unternehmen der Automobilzulieferindustrie*. Cologne: Verlag Josef Eul, 1993.

Hardin, Russell. "Magic on the Frontier: The Norm of Efficiency." *University of Pennsylvania Law Review* 144, no. 5 (1996): 1987–2020.

Hart, Oliver. "An Economist's Perspective on the Theory of the Firm." *Columbia Law Review* 89, no. 7 (Nov. 1989): 1757–1774.

———. *Firms, Contracts and Financial Structure*. Oxford: Clarendon Press, 1995.

Hartley, Janet L. "Collaborative Value Analysis: Experiences from the Automotive Industry." *The Journal of Supply Chain Management* 36, no. 4 (fall 2000): 27–32.

Hassel, Anke. "The Erosion of the German System of Industrial Relations." *British Journal of Industrial Relations* 37, no. 3 (1999): 483–505.

Hawley, Ellis W. *The New Deal and the Problem of Monopoly*. Princeton: Princeton University Press, 1966.

Hayek, Friedrich A. *Individualism and Economic Order*. London: Routledge & Kegan Paul Ltd., 1949.

———. *New Studies in Philosophy, Politics, Economics and the History of Ideas*. London: Routledge & Kegan Paul Ltd., [1968] 1985.

———. *Law, Legislation and Liberty. Volume 1. Rules and Order*. Chicago: University of Chicago Press, 1973.

———. *Law, Legislation and Liberty. Volume 2. The Mirage of Social Justice*. Chicago: University of Chicago Press, 1976.

Hecker, Erich. "Neue Abhängigkeiten—neue Belastungen." In *Zulieferer im Netz*, edited by Hans Gerhard Mendius and Ulrike Wendeling-Schröder, 113–116. Cologne: Bund-Verlag GmbH, 1991.

Heinze, Hendrik. "Ein virtuell-flexibles Zuliefermodell—Neue Positionen für Automobilzulieferunternehmen." Ph.D. diss., St. Gallen University, 1996.

Helmholz, Richard. "Continental Law and Common Law: Historical Strangers of Companions." *Duke Law Journal* 39 (December 1990): 1207–1268.

Helper, Susan, R. "Supplier Relations and Technical Change: Theory and Application to the US Automobile Industry." Ph.D. diss., Harvard University, 1987.

———. "Supplier Relations at a Crossroads: Results of Survey Research in the U.S. Automobile Industry." Working Paper Number 89-26, Boston University School of Management, 1989.

———. "How Much Has Really Changed between U.S. Automakers and Their Suppliers?" *Sloan Management Review* 32, no. 4 (summer 1991): 15–28.

———. "Strategy and Irreversibility in Supplier Relations: The Case of the U.S. Automobile Industry." *Business History Review* 65, no. 4 (winter 1991): 781–824.

———. "Supplier Relations and Adoption of New Technology: Results of Survey Research in the U.S. Auto Industry." National Bureau of Economic Research (NBER) Working Paper Series 5278 (September 1995).

Helper, Susan R., and David Hochfelder. "Japanese-Style Supplier Relationships in the American Auto Industry." In *Beyond The Firm: Business Groups in International and Historical Perspective*, edited by Takao Shiba and Masahiro Shimotani, 187–214. Oxford: Oxford University Press, 1997.

Helper, Susan R., and Mari Sako. "Supplier Relations in Japan and the United States: Are They Converging?" *Sloan Management Review* 36, no. 3 (spring 1995): 77–84.

Hempfling-Wendelken, Martina. *Vertikale Beziehungsstrukturen in der deutschen Automobilindustrie: Theoretischer Aufbau von zwischenbetrieblichen Beziehungsumstern und empirische Ergebnisse zu Beurteilungsverfahren*. Frankfurt am Main: Peter Lang GmbH, 1997.

Hermann, Eckhard. "Nordrheinwestfälisches Verbundprojekt (VIA) als Beispiel unternehmerischer Partnerschaften in der Automobilzulieferindustrie." In *Unternehmensnetzwerke und virtuelle Organizationen*, edited by Udo Winand and Klaus Nathusius. Stuttgart: Schaeffer-Poeschel Verlag, 1998.

Herrigel, Gary. "Industrial Order and the Politics of Industrial Change." In *Industry and Politics in West Germany*, edited by P. Katzenstein, 185–220. Ithaca: Cornell University Press, 1989.

———. *Industrial Constructions: The Sources of German Industrial Power*. New York: Cambridge University Press, 1996.

———. "The Limits of German Manufacturing Flexibility." In *Negotiating The New Germany: Can Social Partnership Survive?* edited by Lowell Turner, 177–205. Ithaca: ILR Press, an imprint of Cornell University Press, 1997.

———. "American Occupation, Market Order, and Democracy: Reconfiguring the Steel Industry in Japan and Germany after the Second World War." In *Americanization and Its Limits: Reworking US Technology and Management in Post-War Europe and Japan*, edited by Jonathan Zeitlin and Gary Herrigel, 340–399. Oxford: Oxford University Press, 2001.

———. "Varieties of Collective Regeneration: Comparisons of the German, Japanese and American Steel Industries since the Mid 1970s." Research Paper, University of Chicago, 2002.

Herrigel, Gary, and Charles F. Sabel. "Craft Production in Crisis: Industrial Restructuring in Germany during the 1990s." In *The German Skills Machine: Sustaining Comparative Advantage in a Global Economy*, edited by Pepper D. Culpepper and David Finegold, 77–114. New York: Berghahn Books, 1999.

Herzog, Martin. "Lieferantenbewertung und Qualitätsmanagement-Systeme in der Automobilindustrie." In *Strukturwandel mitgestalten*, edited by Wolfgang Meinig and Heike Mallad, 145–156. Bamberg: FAW Verlag, 1997.

Hill, Charles W. "National Institutional Structures, Transaction Cost Economizing and Competitive Advantage: The Case of Japan." *Organization Science* 6, no. 1 (1995): 119–131.

Hillebrand, Walter, and Frank A. Linden. "Noch einmal mit Gefühl." *Manager Magazin* (March 1993): 100–110.

———. "Die Jagd ist auf." *Manager Magazin* (December 1993): 128–142.

Hinz, Thomas. "Vocational Training and Job Mobility in Comparative Perspective." In *The German Skills Machine: Sustaining Comparative Advantage in a Global Economy*, edited by Pepper D. Culpepper and David Finegold, 159–188. New York: Berghahn Books, 1999.

Hirsch-Kreinsen, Hartmut. "The Machine Tool Industry: New Market Challenges and the Crises of the Traditional German Pattern Innovation." In *New Product Development and Production Networks*, edited by Ulrich Jürgens, 55–66. Berlin: Springer Verlag, 2000.

Hirsch, Paul M., and Michael Lounsbury. "Ending the Family Quarrel: Toward a Reconciliation of 'Old' and 'New' Institutionalism." *American Behavioral Scientist* 40, no. 4 (1997): 406–418.

Hodgson, Geoffrey M. "The Return of Institutional Economics." In *The Handbook of Economic Sociology*, edited by Neil J. Smelser and Richard Swedberg, 58–76. Princeton: Princeton University Press, 1994.

Hofstede, Geert. *Cultures Consequences*. Beverly Hills, Calif.: Sage Publications, 1980.

Hollingsworth, J. Rogers. "The Logic of Coordinating American Manufacturing Sectors" In *Governance of the American Economy*, edited by John L. Campbell, J. Rogers Hollingsworth, and Leon N. Lindberg, 35–73. New York: Cambridge University Press, 1991.

———. "The Institutional Embeddedness of American Capitalism." In *Political Economy of Modern Capitalism*, edited by Colin Crouch and Wolfgang Streeck, 133–147. London: Sage Publications, 1997.

———. "Continuities and Changes in Social Systems of Production: The Cases of Japan, Germany and The United States." In *Contemporary Capitalism*, edited by J. Rogers Hollingsworth and Robert Boyer, 265–310. Cambridge: Cambridge University Press, 1997.

Hollingsworth, J. Rogers, and Robert Boyer, eds. *Contemporary Capitalism: The Embeddedness of Institutions*. Cambridge: Cambridge University Press, 1997.

———. "Coordination of Economic Actors and Social Systems of Production." In *Contemporary Capitalism*, edited by J. Rogers Hollingsworth and Robert Boyer, 1–47. Cambridge: Cambridge University Press, 1997.

Hollingsworth, J. Rogers, and Leon N. Lindberg. "The Governance of the American Economy: The Role of Markets, Clans, Hierarchies and Associative Behavior." In *Private Interest Governance: Beyond Market and State*, edited by Philippe C. Schmitter and Wolfgang Streeck, 221–254. London: Sage Publications, 1985.

Hollingsworth, J. Rogers, Philippe C. Schmitter, and Wolfgang Streeck, eds. *Governing Capitalist Economies: Performance and Control of Economic Sectors*. New York: Oxford University Press, 1994.

Holzhauser, Manfred. "Der Wind bläst uns gewaltig ins Gesicht." In *Zulieferer im Netz*, edited by Hans Gerhard Mendius and Ulrike Wendeling-Schröder, 117–122. Cologne: Bund-Verlag GmbH, 1991.

Homburg, Christian, and Vallendar Jan Becker. "Zertifizierung von Qualitätssicherungssystemen nach den Qualitätssicherungsnormen DIN ISO 9000ff.: Eine kritische Beurteilung." *Wirtschaftswissenschaftliches Stadium*, no. 9 (September 1996).

Hopfeld, Karlheinz. "Gewerkschaftliche Interessenvertretung in einer klein- und mittelbetrieblich geprägten Zulieferregion." In *Zulieferer im Netz*, edited by Hans Gerhard Mendius and Ulrike Wendeling-Schröder, 145–156. Cologne: Bund-Verlag GmbH, 1991.

Hübner, Thomas. "Vertikale Integration in der Automobilindustrie—Anreizsystem und wettbewerbspolitische Beurteilung." Ph.D. diss., Berlin Technology University, 1987.

Hutzel, Jürgen W. *Große und kleine Zulieferer: Eine Untersuchung zur Nachfragermacht industrieller Abnehmer*. Stuttgart: Sprint-Druck GmbH, 1981.

Iber-Schade, Annerose. "Auswirkungen des Strukturwandels in der Automobilindustrie auf Kfz-Zuliefererunternehmen." In *Strukturpolitische Probleme der Automobil-Industrie unter dem Aspekt des Wettbewerbs*, edited by Burkhardt Röper, 95–127. Berlin: Duncker & Humbolt GmbH, 1985.

Iffland, Klaus. "Innovationsmanagement und Globalisierung—Der Einkauf im Wandel." In *Strukturwandel mitgestalten*, edited by Wolfgang Meinig and Heike Mallad, 119–144. Bamberg, Germany: FAW Verlag, 1997.

IHK (Industrie- und Handelskammer Aschaffenburg). "Protokoll zum ersten Workshop im BAIKA-Projekt in der Wirtschaftsregion Unterfranken." Conference Paper of IHK Aschaffenburg, 1998.

IKB Deutsche Industriebank. "Automobilzulieferer 1996: Differenzierte Ertragsergebnisse." *IKB Branchenbericht* (December 1997).

———. "1997—ein erfolgreiches Jahr für die deutschen Automobilzulieferer." *IKB Branchenbericht* (December 1998).

———. "Die Automobilzulieferer 1998—Kräftiges Umsatzwachstum, differenzierte Ertragsentwicklung." *IKB Branchenbericht* (December 1999).

IRN, Inc. "News & Views from IRN." IRN, Inc. Newsletter, November/December 1999.

———. *The Dynamics of Price Reduction Requests Highlights of a Supplier Survey*. Research Report, Grand Rapids, Mich., 1999.

Jenkins, Davis, and Richard Florida. "Work System Innovation among Japanese Transplants in the United States." In *Remade in America: Transplanting and Transforming Japanese Management Systems*, edited by Jeffrey K. Liker, W. Mark Fruin, and Paul S. Adler, 331–360. New York: Oxford University Press, 1999.

Joerges, Christian. "Relational Contract Theory in a Comparative Perspective: Tensions between Contract and Antitrust Law Principles in the Assessment of Contract Relations between Automobile Manufacturers and Their Dealers in Germany." *Wisconsin Law Review* 1985, no. 3 (1985): 581–614.

Johnson, Chalmers. *MITI and the Japanese Miracle: The Growth of Industrial Policy, 1925–1975.* Stanford, Calif.: Stanford University Press, 1982.

Johnston, Russel, and Paul R. Lawrence. "Beyond Vertical Integration—The Rise of the Value-Adding Partnership." *Harvard Business Review* 66, no. 4 (1988): 94–101.

Jürgens, Ulrich. "Germany: Implementing Lean Production." In *After Lean Production: Evolving Employment Practices in the World Auto Industry*, edited by Thomas A. Kochan, Russel D. Lansbury, and John Paul MacDuffie, 109–116. Ithaca: ILR Press, 1997.

———. "Transformation and Mutual Interaction of the Japanese, American and German Production Regimes in the 1990s." Paper presented at the Conference of "Germany and Japan in the 21st Century: Strengths Turning into Weaknesses?" Max-Planck-Institut für Gesellschaftsforschung and Japanisch-Deutsches Zentrum Berlin, Berlin, 22–24 January 1998.

———. "Anticipating Problems with Manufacturing during the Product Development Process." In *Automation in Automotive Industries: Recent Developments*, edited by Anna Comacchio, Giuseppe Volpato, and Arnaldo Camuffo, 74–91. Berlin: Springer Verlag, 1999.

———. "Communication and Cooperation in the New Product and Process Development Networks—an International Comparison of Country- and Industry-Specific Patterns." In *New Product Development and Production Networks: Global Industrial Experience*, edited by Ulrich Jürgens, 107–148. Berlin: Springer Verlag, 2000.

———. "Toward New Product and Process Development Networks: The Case of the German Car Industry." In *New Product Development and Production Networks: Global Industrial Experience*, edited by Ulrich Jürgens, 259–288. Berlin: Springer Verlag, 2000.

Jürgens, Ulrich, and Inge Lippert. "Schnittstellen des deutschen Produktionsregimes: Innovationshemmnisse im Produktentstehungsprozess." In *Ökonomische Leistungsfähigkeit und institutionelle Innovation: Das deutsche Produktions- und Politikregime im globalen Wettbewerb*, edited by Frieder Naschold et al., 65–94. WZB-Jahrbuch. Berlin: Sigma, 1997.

Jürgens, Ulrich, Katrin Naumann, and Joachim Rupp. "Shareholder Value in an Adverse Environment: The German Case." *Economy & Society* 29, no. 1 (2000): 54–79.

Jürgens, Ulrich, and Werner Reutter. "Verringerung der Fertigungstiefe und betriebliche Interessenvertretung in der deutschen Automobilindustrie." In *Systemische Rationalisierung und Zulieferindustrie*, edited by Norbert Altmann and Dieter Sauer, 119–154. Frankfurt: Campus Verlag, 1989.

Kaiser, Kurt. *Vor- und Zulieferungen des Metall Verarbeitenden Handwerks an die Industrie im Regierungsbezirk Düsseldorf.* Rheinisch-Westfälisches Institut für Wirtschaftsforschung. Schriftenreihe, Neue Folge 22, Essen, 1964.

Kamath, Rajan R., and Jeffrey. K. Liker. "A Second Look at Japanese Product Development." *Harvard Business Review* 72, no. 6 (1994): 154–170.

Kelley, John L. *Bringing The Market Back In: The Political Revitalization of Market Liberalism.* New York: New York University Press, 1997.

Kenney, Martin. "Transplantation? A Comparison of Japanese Television Assembly Plants in Japan and the United States." In *Remade in America: Transplanting and Transforming Japanese Management Systems*, edited by Jeffrey K. Liker, W. Mark Fruin, and Paul S. Adler, 256–293. New York: Oxford University Press, 1999.

Kenney, Martin, and Richard Florida. "Beyond Mass Production: Production and the Labor Process in Japan." *Politics & Society* 16, no. 1 (March 1988): 121–158.

Kern, Horst, and Charles F. Sabel. "Verblaßte Tugend: Die Krise des deutschen Produktionsmodells." *Soziale Welt.* Special Edition: Umbrüche gesellschaftlicher Arbeit (1993): 605–624.

Kern, Horst, and Michael Schumann. *Ende der Arbeitsteilung?* Munich: Beck, 1984.

———. "Kontinuität oder Pfadwechsel? Das deutsche Productionsmodell am Scheideweg." In *Modell Deutschland, Modell Europa, Problems Perspectiven*, edited by Bruno Cattero, 85–97. Opladen: Leske+Budrich, 1998.

Kitschelt, Herbert, Peter Lange, Gary Marks, and John D. Stephens, eds. *Continuity and Change in Contemporary Capitalism.* Cambridge: Cambridge University Press, 1999.

Klebe, Thomas, and Siegfried Roth. "Autonome Zulieferer oder Diktat der Marktmacht?" In *Zulieferer im Netz*, edited by Hans Gerhard Mendius and Ulrike Wendeling-Schröder, 180–199. Cologne: Bund-Verlag, 1991.

Klein, Benjamin, Robert G. Crawford, and Armen A. Alchian. "Vertical Integration, Appropriable Rents, and the Competitive Contracting Process." *Journal of Law and Economics* 21, no. 2 (1978): 297–326.

Klier, Thomas H. "How Lean Manufacturing Changes the Way We Understand the Manufacturing Sector." *Economic Perspectives* 17, no. 3 (1993): 2–9.

———. "The Impact of Lean Manufacturing on Sourcing Relationships." *Economic Perspectives* 18, no. 4 (1994): 8–18.

———. "The Geography of Lean Manufacturing: Recent Evidence from the U.S. Industry." *Economic Perspectives* 19, no. 6 (1995): 2–16.

Klinger, K. "Zulieferungen und Zulieferer in betriebswirtschaftlicher Sicht." *Der Betrieb* 12, no. 45 (1959): 1229–1232.

Knight, Frank H. *Risk, Uncertainty and Profit.* Chicago: University of Chicago Press, [1921] 1971.

Koch, Wolfgang, and Peter Strutynski. *Bedeutung, Probleme und Perspektiven der hessischen Automobilzuliefer.* Eschborn: Rationalisierung-Kuratorium der Deutschen Wirtschaft e.V., 1996.

Kochan, Thomas A., Russell D. Lansbury, and John Paul MacDuffie, eds. *After Lean Production: Evolving Employment Practices in the World Auto Industry.* Ithaca: Cornell University Press, 1997.

Kronman, Anthony T. "Contract Law and the State of Nature." *Journal of Law, Economics and Organization* 1, no. 1 (1985): 5–32.

Kronman, Anthony T., and Richard A. Posner, eds. *The Economics of Contract Law.* Boston and Toronto: Little, Brown and Company, 1979.

Küpper, Georg. "Mißbräuchliche Ausübung von Nachfragemacht, insbesondere Lösung des sog. Roß und Reiter-Problems." *Betriebs-Berater.* Special Edition, no. 22 (1997): 1105–1115.

Laleike, Klaus. "Struktur und Wettbewerbsprobleme der Kraftfahrzeug—Teil-Wirtschaft." Ph.D. diss., Rheinisch-Westfälischen Technischen Hochschule Aachen, 1965.

Lamb, George P., and Carrington Shields. *Trade Association, Law and Practice.* Boston: Little, Brown and Company, 1971.

Lamming, Richard. "The Post Japanese Model for International Automotive Component Supply." Working Paper, International Motor Vehicle Program (IMVP), MIT, Cambridge, Mass., September 1988.

———. "The International Automotive Components Industry: The Next 'Best Practice' for Suppliers." Policy Forum Paper, IMVP, MIT, Cambridge, Mass., 1989.

———. "Japanese Supply Chain Relationships in Recession." *Long Range Planning* 33, no. 6 (2000): 757–778.

Lane, Christel. *Industry and Society in Europe: Stability and Change in Britain, Germany and France.* Aldershot, UK: Edward Elgar, 1995.

———. "The Social Constitution of Supplier Relations in Britain and Germany." In *The Changing European Firm: Limits to Convergence*, edited by Richard Whitley and Peer Hull Kristensen. London: Routledge, 1996.

————. "The Social Regulation of Inter-firm Relations in Britain and Germany: Market Rules, Legal Norms and Technical Standards." *Cambridge Journal of Economics* 21, no. 2 (1997): 197–216.

Lane, Christel, and Reinhard Bachmann. "The Social Constitution of Trust: Supplier Relations in Britain and Germany" *Organization Studies* 17, no. 3 (1996): 365–395.

————. "Cooperation in Inter-Firm Relations in Britain and Germany: the Role of Social Institutions." *The British Journal of Sociology* 48, no. 2 (1997).

Lane, Christel, and Reinhard Bachmann, eds. *Trust Within and Between Organizations: Conceptual Issues and Empirical Applications.* Oxford: Oxford University of Press, 1998.

Lange, Thomas, and J. R. Shackleton. *The Political Economy of German Unification.* Oxford: Berghahn Books, 1998.

Langlois, Richard N., and Paul L. Robertson. "Explaining Vertical Integration: Lessons from the American Automobile Industry." *The Journal of Economic History* 49, no. 2 (1989): 365–375.

Lauk, Kurt J. "Germany at the Crossroads: On the Efficiency of the German Economy." *DAEDALUS* 123, no. 1 (January 1994): 57–83.

Laux, James M. *The European Automobile Industry.* New York: Twayne Publishers, 1992.

Lawrence, Peter. *Managers and Management in West Germany.* London: Croom Helm, 1980.

————. *Issues in European Business.* London: Macmillan, 1998.

Lawrence, Peter, Barbara Senior, and David Smith. "The Anglo-American Contrast: A New Look." Paper presented at annual conference of Association of International Business, City University, London, 1998.

Lawrence, Peter, and Vincent Edwards. *Management in Western Europe.* New York: St. Martin's Press, 2000.

Lay, Gunter, and Werner Wallmeier. "Automobilzulieferer—Quo vadis? Strategien, Produktionsstrukturen und Leistungsindikatoren der Automobilzulieferindustrie Deutschlands." Memorandum of Production Innovation Improvement, Fraunhofer Institut für Systemtechnik und Innovationsforschung, Karlsruhe, Germany, 1999.

————. "Stand und Entwicklungstendenzen der Produktionsmodernisierung." Research Paper of Production Innovation Improvement, Fraunhofer Institut für Systemtechnik und Innovationsforschung, Karlsruhe, Germany, 1999.

Legrand, Pierre. "European Legal Systems Are Not Converging." *International Comparative Law Quarterly* 45, no. 1 (1996): 52–81.

————. "Against a European Civil Code." *Modern Law Review* 60, no. 1 (1997): 44–63.

Lehndorff, Steffen. *Zeitnot und Zeitsouveränität in der just-in-time Fabrik: Arbeitszeitorganisation und Arbeitsbedingungen in der europäischen Automobilzulieferindustrie.* Munich: Rainer Hampp Verlag, 1997.

Leminsky, G. *Bewährungsproben für ein Management des Wandels: Gewerkschaftliche Politik zwischen Globalisierungsfalle und Sozialstaatsabbau.* Berlin: Sigma, 1998.

Lester, Richard K. *The Productive Edge: How U.S. Industries Are Pointing the Way to a New Era of Economic Growth.* New York: W.W. Norton & Company, 1998.

Levine, David P. "Justice and Economic Democracy." *Review of Political Economy* 10, no. 3 (1998): 343–363.

Lewis, Richard. "Contracts Between Businessmen: Reform of the Law of Firm Offers and an Empirical Study of Tendering Practices in the Building Industry." *Journal of Law and Society* 9, no. 2 (1982): 153–175.

Liker, Jeffrey K., Rajan R. Kamath, S. Nazli Wasti, and Mitsuo Nagamachi. "Supplier Involvement in Automotive Component Design: Are There Really Large US–Japan Differences?" *Research Policy* 25, no. 1 (1996): 59–89.

Liker, Jeffrey K., W. Mark Fruin, and Paul S. Adler, eds. *Remade in America: Transplanting and Transforming Japanese Management Systems.* New York: Oxford University Press, 1999.

Liker, Jeffrey K., and Yen-Chun Wu. "Japanese Automakers, U.S. Suppliers and Supply-Chain Superiority." *Sloan Management Review* 42, no. 1 (2000): 81–93.

Lilliecreutz, Johan. "Orchestrating Resources Base, Role, and Position: A Supplier's Strategy in Buyer-Dominated Relationships." *European Journal of Purchasing & Supply Management* 4, no. 2–3 (1998): 73–85.

Lindbeck, Assar. "Overcoming the Obstacles to Successful Performance of the Western Economics." *Business Economics* 15, no. 4 (1980).

Linden, Frank Andreas, and Karl Heinrich Rüssmann. "Die Faust im Nacken." *Manger Magazin* 8 (1988): 88–109.

Lippert, Inge. "Reorganizing Process Chains in the German and American Machine Tool Industry." In *New Product Development and Production Networks*, edited by Ulrich Jürgens, 149–180. Berlin: Springer Verlag, 2000.

Littek, Wolfgang, and Ulrich Heisig. "Taylorism Never Got Hold of Skilled White-Collar Work in Germany." In *The New Division of Labour: Emerging Forms of Work Organization in International Perspective*, edited by Wolfgang Littek and Tony Charles, 373–396. Berlin: Walfter de Gruyter, 1995.

Livermore, John. "Exemption Clauses in Inter-Business Contracts." *The Journal of Business Law* (March 1986): 90–102.

Lopez, Jose Ignacio Arriortua. "Herausforderungen und Chancen in der europäischen Automobilindustrie." In *Zulieferer im Netz*, edited by Hans Gerhard Mendius and Ulrike Wendeling-Schröder, 89–98. Cologne: Bund-Verlag GmbH, 1991.

Lowry, S. Todd. "Bargain and Contract Theory in Law and Economics." *Journal of Economic Issues* 10, no. 1 (1976): 1–22.

Luria, Daniel. "Why Markets Tolerate Mediocre Manufacturing." *Challenge* 39, no. 4 (July–August 1996): 11–16.

Lynn, Leonard, H., and Timothy J. McKeown. *Organizing Business: Trade Associations in America and Japan.* Washington, D.C.: American Enterprise Institute for Public Policy Research, 1988.

Lyons, Bruce, and Judith Mehta. "Private Sector Business Contracts: The Text Between the Lines." In *Contract, Cooperation, and Competition*, edited by Simon Deakin and Jonathan Michie, 43–66. Oxford: Oxford University Press, 1997.

Lyons, Thomas F., A. Richard Krachenberg, and John W. Henke, Jr. "Mixed Motive Marriages: What's Next for Buyer-Supplier Relations?" *Sloan Management Review* 31 (spring 1990): 29–36.

Macaulay, Stewart. "Non-Contractual Relations in Business: A Preliminary Study." *American Sociological Review* 28 (February 1963): 55–67.

MacDuffie, John Paul, and Susan Helper. "Creating Lean Suppliers: Diffusing Lean Production Through the Supply Chain." *California Management Review* 39, no. 4 (1997): 118–151.

MacDuffie, John Paul, and Frits K. Pil. "Changes in Auto Industry Employment Practices: An International Overview." In *After Lean Production: Evolving Employment Practices in the World Auto Industry*, edited by Thomas A. Kochan et al., 9–42. Ithaca: Cornell University Press, 1997.

Macneil, Ian R. "The Many Futures of Contracts." *Southern California Law Review* 47, no. 3 (1974): 691–816.

———. "Contracts: Adjustment of Long-Term Economic Relations under Classical, Neoclassical, and Relational Contract Law." *Northwestern University Law Review* 72, no. 6 (January/February 1978): 854–905.

———. *The New Social Contract: An Inquiry into Modern Contractual Relations.* New Haven: Yale University Press, 1980.

———. "Values in Contract: Internal and External." *Northwestern University Law Review* 78, no. 2 (1983): 340–418.

———. "Relational Contract: What We Do and Do Not Know." *Wisconsin Law Review* 1985, no. 2 (1985): 483–526.

Maher, Maria E. "Transaction Cost Economics and Contractual Relations." *Cambridge Journal of Economics* 21, no. 2 (1997): 147–170.

Maloni, Michael. "Influences of Power upon Supply Chain Relationships: An Analysis of the Automotive Industry." Ph.D. diss., Ohio State University, 1997.

Marahrens, Norbert. *Struktur und Angebot von Klein- und Mittelbetrieben im Zulieferbereich.* Göttingen: Verlag Otto Schwartz & Co., 1973.

Markovits, Andrei S., ed. *Political Economy of West Germany: The Model of Deutschland.* New York: Prager, 1982.

Marler, Dennis L. "The Post Japanese Model of Automotive Component Supply: Selected North American Case Studies." Policy Forum Paper, IMVP, MIT, Cambridge, Mass., 1989.

Markesinis, Basil S. "Learning from Europe and Learning in Europe." In *The Gradual Convergence: Foreign Ideas, Foreign Influences, and English Law on the Eve of the 21st Century,* edited by Basil S. Markesinis, 1–32. Oxford: Oxford University Press, 1994.

Mayne, Eric, Tom Murphy, and Drew Winter. "The Quality Crunch." *Ward's Auto World* 37, no. 7 (July 2001): 32–37

McGrath, Phyllis S. *Redefining Corporate-Federal Relations.* New York: The Conference Board, 1979.

McKenzie, Richard B., and Dwight R. Lee. *Quicksilver Capital: How the Rapid Movement of Wealth Has Changed the World.* New York: The Free Press, 1991.

Meadowcroft, James, ed. *The Liberal Political Tradition: Contemporary Reappraisals.* Cheltenham, UK: Edward Elgar, 1996.

Meinig, Wolfgang, and Heike Mallad, eds. *Strukturwandel mitgestalten: Rahmenbedingungen und Zukunftsperspektiven für Automobilhersteller, Importeure, Zulieferer und Handel. Drittes Automobilwirtschaftleches Symposium.* Bamberg: FAW Verlag, 1997.

Meißner, Heinz-Rudolf, Klaus Peter Kisker, Ulrich Bochum, and Jörg Assmann. *Die Teil und die Herrschaft: Die Reorganisation der Automobilproduktion und der Zulieferbeziehungen.* Berlin: Sigma, 1994.

Mendius, Hans Gerhard. "Das Kfz-Gewerbe als externer Vertriebssektor im Kontext neuer Rationalisierungsstrategien der Automobilindustrie." In *Vernetzte Produktion: Automobilzulieferer zwischen Kontrolle und Autonomie,* edited by Manfred Deiß and Volker Döhl, 141–176. Frankfurt: Campus Verlag, 1992.

Mendius, Hans Gerhard, and Ulrike Wendeling-Schröder, eds. *Zulieferer im Netz—Zwischen Abhängigkeit und Partnerschaft: Neustrukturierung der Logistik am Beispiel der Automobilzulieferung.* Cologne: Bund-Verlag GmbH, 1991.

———. "Einleitung: Im Netzwerk der Zuliefer-Abnehmer-Beziehungen in der Automobilindustrie." In *Zulieferer im Netz,* edited by Hans Gerhard Mendius and Ulrike Wendeling-Schröder, 11–32. Cologne: Bund-Verlag GmbH, 1991.

Mendius, Hans Gerhard, and Stefanie Weimer. "Betriebsübergreifende Zusammenarbeit bei der Delegschaftsqualifizierung in kleinen Zulieferunternehmen." In *Zulieferer im Netz,* edited by Hans Gerhard Mendius and Ulrike Wendeling-Schröder, 274–303. Cologne: Bund-Verlag, 1991.

Meyer, Arnoud de. "Product Development in the Textile Machinery Industry." In *Managing Product Development,* edited by Toshihiro Nishiguchi, 280–292. New York: Oxford University Press, 1996.

Meyer, Margit, and Andreas Bartelt. "Ökonomische Analyse von Vertrauen in Zuliefernetzwerken der Automobilindustrie." Working Paper, Business and Marketing, Bavaria Julius-Maximilians University, Würzburg, 1999.

Miller, Gary J. *Managerial Dilemmas: The Political Economy of Hierarchy.* Cambridge: Cambridge University Press, 1995.

Monopolkommission. *Mißbräuche der Nachfragemacht und Möglichkeiten zu ihrer Kontrolle im Rahmen des Gesetzes gegen Wettbewerbsbeschränkungen.* Baden-Baden: Nomos Verlagsgesellschaft, 1979.

Monteverde, Kirk, and David J. Teece. "Supplier Switching Costs and Vertical Integration in the Automobile Industry." *The Bell Journal of Economics* 19, no. 1 (1982): 206–213.

Morrow, James D. *Game Theory for Political Scientists.* Princeton: Princeton University Press, 1994

Moses, Jonathan W. "Abdication from National Policy Autonomy: What's Left to Leave?" *Politics & Society* 22, no. 2 (1994): 125–148.

Mudambi, Ram, and Susan Helper. "The 'Close but Adversarial' Model of Supplier Relations in the U.S. Auto Industry." *Strategic Management Journal* 19, no. 8 (1998): 775–792.

Mudambi, Ram, and Martin Ricketts, eds. *The Organization of the Firm: International Business Perspectives.* London: Routledge, 1998.

Nagel, Bernhard, Birgit Rieß, and Gisela Theis. *Der Lieferant on Line: Just-in-Time Produktion und Mitbestimmung in der Automobilindustrie.* Baden-Baden: Nomos Verlagsgesellschaft, 1990.

Nakamura, Masao, Sadao Sakakibara, and Roger G. Schroeder. "Just-in-Time and Other Manufacturing Practices: Implications for U.S. Manufacturing Performance." In *Remade in America,* edited by Jeffrey K. Liker, W. Mark Fruin, and Paul S. Adler, 361–384. New York: Oxford University Press, 1999.

Naschold, Frieder. "Ökonomische Leistungsfähigkeit und institutionelle Innovation—Das deutsche Produktions- und Politik-regime im globalen Wettbewerb." In *Ökonomische Leistungsfähigkeit und institutionelle Innovation,* edited by Frieder Naschold et al., 19–62 Berlin: Sigma, 1997.

Naschold, Frieder, David Soskice, Bob Hancke, and Ulrich Jürgens, eds. *Ökonomische Leistungsfähigkeit und institutionelle Innovation: Das deutsche Produktions- und Politikregime im globalen Wettbewerb.* WZB-Jahrbuch, Berlin: Sigma, 1997.

Naschold, Frieder, and David Soskice. "Zur Bedeutung der Institutionen in der Wirtschaftsentwicklung." In *Ökonomische Leistungsfähigkeit und institutionelle Innovation,* edited by Frieder Naschold et al., 9–18. Berlin: Sigma, 1997.

Nathusius, Klaus. "Partnerschaften und Wertschöpfung in der Automobilindustrie." In *Unternehmensnetzwerke und virtuelle Organizationen,* edited by Udo Winand and Klaus Nathusius. Stuttgart: Schaeffer-Poeschel Verlag, 1998.

Necker, Tyll. "Der Automobilstandort Deutschland zur Jahrtausendwende." In *Strukturwandel mitgestalten,* edited by Wolfgang Meinig and Heike Mallad, 71–81. Bamberg: FAW Verlag, 1997.

Nee, Victor. "Sources of the New Institutionalism." In *The New Institutionalism in Sociology,* edited by Mary C. Brinton and Victor Nee, 1–16. New York: Russell Sage Foundation, 1998.

Nelson, Dave, Rick Mayo, and Patricia E. Moody. *Powered by Honda: Developing Excellence in the Global Enterprise.* New York: John Wiley & Sons, 1998.

Neugebauer, Werner. "Gewerkschaftliche Ansatzpunkte zur Verbesserung der Arbeitnehmervertretung bei Automobilzulieferern und –herstellern in Bayern." In *Zulieferer im Netz,* edited by Hans Gerhard Mendius and Ulrike Wendeling-Schröder, 169–179. Cologne: Bund-Verlag, 1991.

Neumann, Horst. *Mythos Japan: Unternehmensvergleich zur Wettbewerbsstärke der deutschen und japanischen Automobilindustrie.* Berlin: Ed Sigma, 1996.

Nishiguchi, Toshihiro. "Fairness, Rationality and Integration: Success Factors towards a New Organizational Model." Working Paper, International Motor Vehicle Program (IMVP), MIT, Cambridge, Mass., 1992.

———. *Strategic Industrial Sourcing: The Japanese Advantage.* New York: Oxford University Press, 1994.

North, D. C. *Structure and Change in Economic History.* New York: W.W. Norton & Company, 1981.

———. *Institutions, Institutional Change and Economic Performance.* Cambridge, UK: Cambridge University Press, 1990.

Novak, Sharon, and Steven D. Eppinger. "Sourcing By Design: Product Complexity and the Supply Chain." *Management Science* 47, no. 1 (2001): 189–204.

Oberhauser, Ann. "Manufacturer and Supplier Relations in the United States Automobile Industry." Paper presented to the 10th Annual Applied Geography Conference, Oak Ridge, Tenn., 14–17 October 1987.

O'Brien, Richard. *Global Financial Integration: The End of Geography.* London: Printer, 1992.

OESA (Original Equipment Suppliers Association). "Highlights of OESA 2000—Value Added Services and Activities." Document of OESA, 2001.

———. "The North American Automotive Industry: Strategies for Competing." Management Briefing Seminars, University of Michigan, Traverse City, Mich., 7 August 2001.

Ohmae, Kenichi. *The Borderless World: Power and Strategy in the Interlinked Economy.* New York: Harper Business, 1991.

———. *The End of the Nation State.* New York: Free Press, 1995.

———. *The Invisible Continent: Four Strategic Imperatives of the New Economy.* New York: HarperCollins, 2000.

Okamoto, Yumiko. "Multinationals, Production Efficiency and Spillover Effects: The Case of the U.S. Auto Parts Industry." *Weltwirtschaftliches Archiv* 135, no. 2 (1999): 241–260.

Okamuro, Hiroyuki. "Changing Subcontracting Relations and Risk-Sharing in Japan: An Econometric Analysis of the Automobile Industry." *Hitotsubashi Journal of Economics* 36 (1995): 207–218.

Oliver, Nick, and Barry Wilkinson. *The Japanization of British Industry.* New York: Basil Blackwell, 1988.

Olson, Mancur. *The Rise and Decline of Nations.* New Haven: Yale University Press, 1982.

Orru, Marco, Nicole Woosley Biggart, and Gary G. Hamilton. *The Economic Organization of East Asian Capitalism.* Thousand Oaks, Calif.: Sage Publications, 1997.

OSAT, and A. T. Kearney, Inc. *The 21st Century Supply Chain: The Changing Roles, Responsibilities and Relationships in the Automotive Industry.* Southfield, Michigan: A.T. Kearney, Inc., 1996.

Osterman, Paul, Thomas A. Kochan, Richard Locke, and Michael J. Piore. *Working in America: A Blueprint for the New Labor Market.* Cambridge, Mass.: MIT Press, 2001.

Ouchi, William G. "Markets, Bureaucracies, and Clans." *Administrative Science Quarterly* 25, no. 1 (1980): 129–141.

Parks, Kent. "Automotive Parts Industry Study." Small Business and Technology Development Center (SBTDC), University of North Carolina, 1999.

Peters, B. Guy. *Institutional Theory in Political Science: The New Institutionalism.* New York: Printer, 1999.

Peters, Jürgen. "Supplier and Buyer Market Power, Appropriability, and Innovation Activities: Evidence for the German Automobile Industry." Discussion Paper, no. 173, Institut für Volkswirtschaftslehre, Augsburg University, 1998.

———. *Technolgische Spillovers zwischen Zulieferer und Abnehmer: Eine Spieltheoretische Analyse mit einer empirischen Studie für die deutsche Automobilindustrie.* Heidelberg: Physica-Verlag, 1999.

———. "Buyer Market Power and Innovative Activities." *Review of Industrial Organization* 16, no. 1 (2000): 13–38.

Peters, Jürgen, and Wolfgang Becker. "Hochschulkooperationen und betriebliche Innovationsaktivitäten: Ergebnisse aus der deutschen Automobilzulieferindustrie." Discussion Paper, no 178, Institut für Volkswirtschaftslehre, Augsburg University, 1998.

Petzold, Inge. "Die Zulieferindustrie: Eine Betriebswirtschaftliche Untersuchung unter Besonderer Berücksichtigung der industriellen Zulieferbetriebe zur Automobilindustrie." Ph.D. diss., Wirtschaftswissenschaft, Düsseldorf, 1968.

Pierenkemper, Toni. "Trade Associations in Germany in the Late Nineteenth and Early Twentieth Centuries." In *Trade Associations in Business History*, edited by Hiroaki Yamazaki and Matao Miyamoto, 233–268. Tokyo: University of Tokyo Press, 1988.

Pildes, Richard H. "The Destruction of Social Capital Through Law." *University of Pennsylvania Law Review* 144, no. 5 (1996): 2055–2077.

Piore, Michael J., and Charles F. Sabel. *The Second Industrial Divide.* New York: Basic Books, 1984.

Pohlmann, Markus. "Antagoistische Kooperation und distributive Macht: Anmerkungen zur Produktion in Netzwerken." *Soziale Welt: Zeitschrift fuer sozialwissenschaftliche Forschung und Praxis* 47, no. 1 (1996): 44–67.

Pohlmann, Markus, Maja Apelt, and Henning Martens. "Autonomie und Abhängigkeit—Die Voraussetzungen der kooperation an der Schnittstelle Beschaffung-Zulieferung." In *Vernetzte Produktion: Automobilzulieferer zwischen Kontrolle und Autonomie*, edited by Manfred Deiß and Volker Döhl, 177–208. Frankfurt: Campus Verlag, 1992.

Pohlmann, Markus, Maja Apelt, Karsten Buroh, and Henning Martens. *Industrielle Netzwerke: Antagonistische Kooperationen an der Schnittstelle Beschaffung-Zulieferung*. Munich and Mering: Rainer Hampp Verlag, 1995.

Porter, Michael E. *Cases in Competitive Strategy*. New York: Free Press, 1983.

———. *The Competitive Advantage of Nations*. New York: Free Press, 1990.

———. "Capital Disadvantage: America's Failing Capital Investment System." *Harvard Business Review* 70, no. 5 (1992): 65–82

Posner, Eric A. "Law, Economics, and Inefficient Norms." *University of Pennsylvania Law Review* 144, no. 5 (1996): 1971–1986.

Posner, Richard A. *Economic Analysis of Law*. 4th ed. Boston: Little, Brown and Company, 1992.

Powell, Walter W. "Neither Market Nor Hierarchy: Network Forms of Organization." *Research in Organization Behavior* 12 (1990): 295–336.

Powell, Walter W., and Peter Brantley. "Magic Bullets and Patent Wars: New Product Development and the Evolution of the Biotechnology Industry." In *Managing Product Development*, edited by Toshihiro Nishiguchi, 233–260. New York: Oxford University Press, 1996.

Powell, Walter W., Kenneth W. Koput, and Laurel Smith-Doerr. "Interorganizational Collaboration and the Locus of Innovation: Networks of Learning in Biotechnology." *Administrative Science Quarterly* 41 (1996): 116–145.

PricewaterhouseCoopers. "Global Automotive Deal Survey 1998." Research Report, PricewaterhouseCoopers, 1999.

Putnam, Robert. *Making Democracy Work*. Princeton: Princeton University Press, 1993.

———. *Bowling Alone: The Collapse and Revival of American Community*. New York: Simon & Schuster, 2000.

Pyke, F., and W. Sengenberger, eds. *Industrial Districts and Local Economic Regeneration*. Geneva: International Institute for Labour Studies, 1992.

Rae, John Bell. *American Automobile Manufacturers: The First Forty Years*. Philadelphia: Chilton, 1959.

Reeg, Marcus. *Liefer- und Leistungsbeziehungen in der deutschen Automobilindustrie: Strukturelle Veränderungen aus unternehmerischer und wirtschaftspolitischer Sicht*. Berlin: Duncker & Humbolt, 1998.

Reese, J., and R. Geisel. "JIT Procurement: A Comparison of Current Practices in German Manufacturing Industries." *European Journal of Purchasing & Supply Management* 3, no. 3 (1997): 147–154.

Ricoeur, Paul. *The Just*. Translated by David Pellauer. Chicago: University of Chicago Press, 2000.

Riesselmann, Dirk. "Entwicklung der Automobilzulieferindustrie: Strukturen, Lieferantentypen und Erfolg." Ph.D. diss., Bundeswehr University, Hamburg, 1998.

Roe, Mark J. "Corporate Law and Politics." In *European Economic and Business Law*, edited by Richard M. Buxbaum, Gerard Hertig, Alain Hirsch, and Klaus J. Hopt. Berlin: Walter de Gruyter, 1996.

Roeper, Hans. "Teile- und Montage-Industrie." *Betriebswirtschaftliche Forschung und Praxis* 1, no. 9 (1949): 558–563.

———. "Die Vor-, Zu-, und Unterlieferung." *Betriebswirtschaftliche Forschung und Praxis* 1, no. 7 (1949): 501–503.

Rogers, Joel, and Wolfgang Streeck. *Works Councils: Consultation, Representation and Cooperation in Industrial Relations*. Chicago: University Chicago Press, 1995.

Rommel, Günter, Jürgen Kluge, Rolf-Dieter Kempis, Raimund Diederichs, Felix Brück, and McKinsey & Company, Inc. *Simplicity Wins: How Germany's Mid-Sized Industrial Companies Succeed*. Boston: Harvard Business School Press, 1995.

Roth, Siegfried. "Kooperationsnetzwerke: Gewerkschaftliche Aktivitäten in der Automo-
bil- und Zulieferindustrie." *Industrielle Beziehungen* 1, no. 4 (1994): 374–384.

———. "Automobilhersteller und ihre Zulieferer in Deutschland und Japan." In *Vorbild
Japan? Stärken und Schwächen der Industriestandorte Deutschland und Japan*, edited by
Klaus Zwickel, 175–205. Frankfurt am Main: Otto Brenner Stiftung, 1996.

———. "Germany: Labor's Perspective on Lean Production." In *After Lean Production*,
edited by Thomas A. Kochan, Russel D. Lansbury, and John Paul MacDuffie, 117–136.
Ithaca: ILR Press, 1997.

———. "Aktuelle Lage und Perspektiven der Automobilzulieferindustrie." Information
Seminar Paper, Kolbenschmidt Pierburg AG., Neckarsulm, 14 July 1998.

Sabel, Charles F. "Studied Trust: Building New Forms of Cooperation in a Volatile Economy." In *Industrial Districts and Local Economic Regeneration*, edited by F. Pyke and W.
Sengenberger, 215–250. Geneva: International Institute for Labour Studies, 1992.

———. "A Measure of Federalism: Assessing Manufacturing Technology Centers." Paper
prepared for the workshop Manufacturing Modernization, Atlanta, Ga., September
1994.

———. "Learning by Monitoring: The Institutions of Economic Development." In *The
Handbook of Economic Sociology*, edited by Neil J. Smelser and Richard Swedberg,
137–165. Princeton: Princeton University Press, 1994.

———. "Experimental Regionalism and the Dilemma of Regional Economic Policy." Paper
presented to Conference on Socio-Economic Systems of Japan, the United States, the
United Kingdom, Germany and France, Tokyo, 16 February 1996.

———. "Ungoverned Production: An American View of the Novel Universalism of
Japanese Production Methods and Their Awkward Fit with Current Forms of Corporate Governance." Paper prepared for presentation at the Conference on Socio-Economic Systems of the Twenty-First Century. Tokyo, Japan, 1996.

———. "Constitutional Orders: Trust Building and Response to Change." In *Contemporary
Capitalism: The Embeddedness of Institutions*, edited by J. Rogers Hollingsworth and
Robert Boyer, 154–188. Cambridge: Cambridge University Press, 1997.

Sabel, Charles F., John R. Griffin, and Richard E. Deeg. "Making Money Talk: Towards a
New Debtor Creditor Relation in German Banking." Paper presented at Conference on
Relational Investing, Center for Law and Economic Studies, Columbia University
School of Law, New York, 6–7 May 1993.

Sabel, Charles F., Horst Kern, and Gary Herrigel. "Collaborative Manufacturing: New Supplier Relations in the Automobile Industry and the Redefinition of the Industrial Corporation." Policy Forum Paper, IMVP, MIT, Cambridge, Mass., May 1989.

Sabel, Charles F., and Jonathan Zeitlin. "Stories, Strategies, Structures: Rethinking Historical Alternatives to Mass Production." In *World of Possibilities: Flexibility and Mass Production in Western Industrialization*, edited by Charles F. Sabel and Jonathan Zeitlin, 1–33.
New York: Cambridge University Press, 1997.

Sako, Mari. "Component Supply Structures in Japan: Myths and Reality of Keiretsu Relationships." IMVP, *JAMA Forum* 14, no. 2 (1996): 16–19.

———. "Suppliers' Associations in the Japanese Automobile Industry: Collective Action
for Technology Diffusion." *Cambridge Journal of Economics* 20, no. 6 (1996): 651–671.

Sako, Mari, and Susan Helper. "Determinants of Trust in Supplier Relations: Evidence
From the Automotive Industry in Japan and the United States." *Journal of Economic
Behavior and Organization* 34 (spring 1998): 387–417.

Sako, Mari, Richard Lamming, and Susan R. Helper. "Supplier Relations in the Multinational Automotive Industry." In *The Organization of the Firm: International Business Perspectives*, edited by Ram Mudambi and Martin Ricketts, 178–194. London: Routledge,
1998.

Salisbury, Robert H. "Why No Corporatism in America?" In *Trends Toward Corporatist Intermediation*, edited by Philippe C. Schmitter and Gerhard Lehmbruch, 213–230. London:
Sage Publications, 1979.

Santos, Hermilio. *Industrieverbände und Policy-Netwerke: Die Rolle der Automobilverbände bei der Formulierung von industriepolitischen Massnahmen unter besonderer Berücksichtigung Deutschland und Japans*. Frankfurt am Main: Peter Lang, 1998.

Sauer, Dieter. "Auf dem Weg in die flexible Massenproduktion." In *Vernetzte Produktion: Automobilzulieferer zwischen Kontrolle und Autonomie*, edited by Manfred Deiß and Volker Döhl, 49–80. Frankfurt: Campus Verlag, 1992.

Sauer, Dieter, and Norbert Altmann. "Zwischenbetriebliche Arbeitsteilung als Thema der Industriesoziologie." In *Systemische Rationalisierung und Zulieferindustrie*, edited by Norbert Altmann and Dieter Sauer, 5–28. Frankfurt: Campus Verlag, 1989.

Scherer, F. M. *Industrial Market Structure and Economic Performance*. Chicago: Rand McNally College Publishing Company, 1980.

Scherrer, Christoph. "Umbrüche im Beschaffungswesen der US-Automobilindustrie" In *Systemische Rationalisierung und Zulieferindustrie*, edited by Norbert Altmann and Dieter Sauer, 207–249. Frankfurt: Campus Verlag, 1989.

———. "Governance of the Automobile Industry: The Transformation of Labor and Supplier Relations." In *Governance of the American Economy*, edited by J. L. Campbell, J. R. Hollingsworth, and L. N. Lindberg, 209–235. New York: Cambridge University Press, 1991.

Schindele, Sylvia. "Entwicklungs- und Produktionsverbünde in der deutschen Automobil- und zulieferindustrie unter Berücksichigung des Systemgedankens." Ph.D. diss., Technischen Hochschule Darmstadt, 1996.

Schmidt, Hermann. "The Impact of Globalization on Vocational Training and Continuing Education." In *The Challenge of Globalization for Germany's Social Democracy: A Policy Agenda for the Twenty-First Century*, edited by Dieter Dettke, 218–232. New York: Berghahn Books, 1998.

Schmidt, Morten. "Habitus Revisted." *American Behavioral Scientist* 40, no. 4 (1997): 444–453.

Schmitter, Philippe C. "Levels of Spatial Coordination and The Embeddedness of Institutions." In *Contemporary Capitalism*, edited by J. Rogers Hollingsworth and Robert Boyer, 311–317. Cambridge: Cambridge University Press, 1997.

Schmitter, Philippe C., and Wolfgang Streeck. "The Organization of Business Interests: A Research Design to Study the Associative Action of Business Interests in the Advanced Industrial Societies of Western Europe." Discussion Paper IIM/LMP 81-13, Berlin: Wissenschaftszentrum, 1981.

Schrader, Stephan, and Henrik Sattler. "Zwischenbetriebliche Kooperation: Informaler Informationsaustausch in den USA und Deutschland." *Die Betriebswirtschaft* 53, no. 5 (1993): 589–608.

Schumann, Michael. "The German Automobile Industry in Transition." *Economic and Labour Relations Review* 8, no. 2 (1997): 221–247.

———. "Frißt die Shareholder-Value-Ökonomie die Modernisierung der Arbeit?" In *Arbeit, Gesellschaft, Kritik Orientierungen wider den Zeitgeist*, edited by Hartmut Hirsch-Kreinsen and Harald Wolf, 19–30. Berlin: Sigma, 1998.

Scientific Consulting. "Restrukturierungstrends in der deutschen Automobilzulieferindustrie im internationalen Vergleich." Research Report of Scientific Consulting, Cologne, 1995.

Scruton, Roger. "Public Space and the Classical Vernacular." In *The Public Face of Architecture: Civic Culture and Public Spaces*, edited by Nathan Glazer and Mark Lilla. New York: Free Press, 1987.

Seiffert, Ulrich. "Vom individuellen Erfindertum zur Eskalation des technischen Fortschritts: Worauf muß sich die Automobilwirtschaft gefaßt machen?" In *Strukturwandel mitgestalten*, edited by Wolfgang Meinig and Heike Mallad, 95–117. Bamberg: FAW Verlag, 1997.

Seltzer, Lawrence H. *A Financial History of the American Automobile Industry*. Boston, Mass.: Houghton Mifflin Company, 1928.

Semlinger, Klaus. "Stellung und Probleme kleinbetrieblicher Zulieferer im Verhältnis zu großen Abnehmern." In *Systemische Rationalisierung und Zulieferindustrie*, edited by Norbert Altmann and Dieter Sauer, 89–118. Frankfurt: Campus Verlag, 1989.

———. "New Developments in Subcontracting: Mixing Market and Hierarchy." In *Towards a New Europe? Structural Change in the European Economy*, edited by Ash Amin and Michael Dietrich, 96–115. Brookfield, Vt.: Edward Elgar, 1991.

Senate Fiscal Agency. "Motor Vehicle Industry Trends: U.S. and Michigan." Report Paper for Senate Fiscal Agency, Government Document, Lansing, Mich., 1997.

Simon, Hermann. "Lessons from Germany's Midsize Giants." *Harvard Business Review* 70, no. 2 (1992): 115–123.

Simpson, A. W. B. "Innovation in Nineteenth Century Contract Law." *The Law Quarterly Review* 91, no. 362 (1975): 247–278.

Smith, Adam. *The Wealth of Nations.* Edited by Edwin Cannan. New York: The Modern Library, 1937.

Soskice, David. "Reinterpreting Corporatism and Explaining Unemployment: Coordinated and Non-coordinated Market Economies." In *Labour Relations and Economic Performance*, edited by Renato Brunetta and Carlo Dell' Aringa, 170–211. New York: New York University Press, 1990.

———. "The Institutional Infrastructure for International Competitiveness: A Comparative Analysis of the UK and Germany." In *Economics for New Europe*, edited by Anthony B. Atkinson and Renato Brunetta, 45–66. New York: New York University Press, 1991.

———. "Technologiepolitik, Innovation und nationale Institutionengefüge in Deutschland." In *Ökonomische Leistungsfähigkeit und institutionelle Innovation*, edited by Frieder Naschold et al., 319–348. Berlin: Ed Sigma, 1997.

———. "Divergent Production Regimes: Coordinated and Uncoordinated Market Economies in the 1980s and 1990s." In *Continuity and Change in Contemporary Capitalism*, edited by Herbert Kitschelt et al., 101–134. Cambridge: Cambridge University Press, 1999.

Speidel, Richard E. "Court-Imposed Price Adjustments Under Long-term Supply Contracts." *Northwestern University Law Review* 76, no. 3 (1981): 369–422.

Springer, Roland. *Rückkehr zum Taylorismus? Arbeitspolitik in der Automobilindustrie am Scheideweg.* Frankfurt: Campus Verlag, 1999.

Staber, Udo Hermann. "The Organizational Properties of Trade Associations." Ph.D. diss., Cornell University, 1982.

Staber, Udo, and Howard Aldrich. "Trade Association Stability and Public Policy." In *Organizational Theory and Public Policy*, edited by Richard H. Hall and Robert E. Quinn, 163–178. Beverly Hills, London: Sage Publications, 1983.

Stigler, George J. *The Theory of Price.* New York: Macmillan Company, 1946.

———. "Perfect Competition, Historically Contemplated." *Journal of Political Economy* 65, no. 1 (1957): 1–17.

———. "Competition." In *International Encyclopedia of the Social Science*, edited by David L. Sills, 181–186. New York: Macmillan Company & Free Press, 1968.

Stinchcombe, Arthur L. "On Virtues of the Old Institutionalism." *Annual Review of Sociology* 13 (1997): 1–18.

Strange, Susan. "The Future of Global Capitalism: Or, Will Divergence Persist Forever?" In *Political Economy of Modern Capitalism*, edited by Colin Crouch and Wolfgang Streeck, 182–191. Thousand Oaks, Calif.: Sage Publications, 1997.

———. *The Retreat of the State: The Diffusion of Power in the World Economy.* New York: Cambridge University Press, 1996.

Streeck, Wolfgang. *Social Institutions and Economic Performance.* London: Sage Publications, 1992.

———. "Works Councils in Western Europe: Cooperation through Representation." In *Works Council: Consultation, Representation and Cooperation in Industrial Relations*, edited by Joel Rogers and Wolfgang Streeck, 313–348. Chicago: University of Chicago Press, 1995.

———. "Lean Production in the German Automobile Industry: A Test Case for Convergence Theory." In *National Diversity and Global Capitalism*, edited by Suzanne Berger and Ronal Dore, 138–170. Ithaca: Cornell University Press, 1996.

———. "German Capitalism: Does it Exist? Can It Survive?" In *Political Economy of Modern Capitalism: Mapping Convergence & Diversity*, edited by Colin Crouch and Wolfgang Streeck, 33–54. London: Sage Publications, 1997.

———. "Beneficial Constraint: On the Economic Limits of Relational Voluntarism." In *Contemporary Capitalism*, edited by J. Rogers Hollingsworth and Robert Boyer, 197–219. Cambridge: Cambridge University Press, 1997.

Summers, Lawrence, and Vinod Thomas. "Recent Lessons of Development." *World Bank Research Observer* 8 (1993): 241–254.

Sundhoff, Edmund, and Hermann-Adolf Ihle. *Handwerksbetriebe als Lieferanten von Industrieunternehmungen: Bericht über Durchführung und Ergebnisse einer Untersuchung in Niedersächsischen Betrieben*. Göttingen: Verlag Otto Schwartz, 1964.

Sundhoff, Edmund, and Gerhard Pietsch. *Die Lieferantenstruktur industrieller Großunternehmungen; Bericht über Durchführung und Ergebnisse einer Untersuchung in Niederächsischen Betrieben*. Göttingen: Verlag Otto Schwartz, 1964.

Swedberg, Richard. "Markets as Social Structures." In *The Handbook of Economic Sociology*, edited by Neil J. Smelser and Richard Swedberg, 255–282. Princeton: Princeton University Press, 1994.

Tabeta, Naoki. "The Kigyo Keiretsu Organization and Opportunism in the Japanese Automobile Manufacturing Industry." *Asia Pacific Journal of Management* 15, no. 1 (1998): 1–18.

Taylor III, Alex, and Robert A. Miller. "The Auto Industry Meets the New Economy." *Fortune* 130, no. 5 (5 September 1994): 52–57.

Tedlow, Richard S. "Trade Associations and Public Relations." In *Trade Associations in Business History*, edited by Hiroaki Yamazaki and Matao Miyamoto, 139–172. Tokyo: University of Tokyo Press, 1988.

Teubner, Gunther. "Legal Irritants: How Unifying Law Ends Up in New Divergences." In *Varieties of Capitalism: The Institutional Foundations of Comparative Advantage*, edited by Peter Hall and David Soskice, 417–441. New York: Oxford University Press, 2001.

Thompson, George V. "Inter-Company Technical Standardization in the Early Automobile Industry." *Journal of Economic History* 14 (winter 1954): 1–20.

Tolliday, Steven. "Enterprise and State in the West German Wirtschaftswunder: Volkswagen and the Automobile Industry, 1939–1962." *Business History Review* 69 (autumn 1995): 273–350.

Turner, Lowell. "Unifying Germany: Crisis, Conflict, and Social Partnership in the East." In *Negotiating the New Germany:Can Social Partnership Survive?* edited by Lowell Turner, 113–136. Ithaca: ILR Press, an imprint of Cornell University Press, 1997.

Tüsselmann, Heinze, and Arne Heise. "The German Model of Industrial Relations at the Crossroads: Past, Present and Future." *Industrial Relations Journal* 31, no. 3 (2000): 162–176.

Tutmann, Theodor L. "Wertschöpfung durch Wertschätzung." *Beschaffung aktuell* 4 (1995): 30–34.

Unger, Roberto Mangabeira. *The Critical Legal Studies Movement*. Cambridge, Mass.: Harvard University Press, 1983.

Valazza, Michael J., and Gary G. Wada. "Creating a Successful Partnership with a Contract Manufacturer." *Pharmaceutical Technology* 25 (2001): 36–42.

VIA (Verbundinitiative Automobil NRW). "Leitfaden zur Einführung von Kontinuierlichen Verbesserungsprozessen (KVP) in mittelständischen Unternehmen." Scientific Consulting and Dr. Schulte-Hillen GmbH BDU, 1998.

VDA (Verband Der Automobilindustrie, e.V). "Die deutsche Automobilindustrie und ihre Verbände." Schriftenreihe des VDA No. 9, 1970.

———. "Neue Anstöße für den Strukturwandel in der deutschen Automobilindustrie." Symposium, 25 April 1989.

———. "Leitfaden für die Zusammenarbeit zwischen den Automobilherstellern und ihren Zulieferern." Pamphlet of the VDA, 1992.

———. "Produzieren am Standort Deutschland: Probleme der Automobil-Zulieferindustrie." Pamphlet of the VDA, 1994.

———. *Profitable Waschstumsstrategien in der Automobil-zulieferindustrie.* McKinsey & Company, Inc., Institut für Kraftfahrewesen Aachen (ika) VDA 20, 1999.

Vekas, Lajos. "Contract in a Rapidly Changing Industrial Environment." *Zeitschrift für die gesamte Staatswissenschaft* 152, no. 1 (1996).

Vincent-Jones, Peter. "Contract and Business Transactions: A Socio-Legal Analysis." *Journal of Law and Society* 16, no. 2 (1989): 166–186.

Vitols, Sigurt. "Globalization: A Fundamental Challenge to the German Model?" In *Political Economy and the Changing Global Order,* edited by Richard Stubbs and Geoffrey R.D. Underhill, 373–381. Oxford: Oxford University Press, 2000.

Volkswagen AG. *Qualitätsfähigkeit Lieferanten: Beurteilungsrichtlinie QM-Systemaudit Prozessaudit, Produktaudit.* Volkswagen Pamphlet, Volkswagen AG, January 1997.

———. *Qualitätsmanagementvereinbarungen zwischen dem Volkswagen—Konzern und seinen Lieferanten.* Volkswagen Pamphlet, September 1998.

———. "Der Volkswagen Konzern." Pamphlet of Beschaffung, Volkswagen, 2000.

von Bötticher, Gotthard. "Made in Germany—gestern, heute, morgen? Veränderungespotentiale der Produktionsstufe Mercedes-Benz." In *Strukturwandel mitgestalten,* edited by Wolfgang Meinig and Heike Mallad, 86–93. Bamberg: FAW Verlag, 1997.

von Brunn, Johann Heinrich. *Wettbewerbsproblem der Automobilindustrie.* Cologne: Carl Heymanns Verlag KG, 1979.

von Kubota, Hideo, and Herman Witte. "Strukturvergleich des Zulieferwesens in Japan und in der Bundesrepulbik Deutschland." *Zeitschrift für Betriebswirtschaft* 60, no. 4 (1990): 383–406.

Vorländer, Hans. "Is there a liberal political tradition in Germany?" In *The Liberal Political Tradition,* edited by James Meadowcroft, 101–114. Brookfield, Vt.: Edward Elgar, 1996.

Wagner, Karin. "The German Apprenticeship System under Strain." In *The German Skills Machine: Sustaining Comparative Advantage in a Global Economy,* edited by Pepper D. Culpepper and David Finegold, 37–76. New York: Berghahn Books, 1999.

Wagstaff, I. *Prospects for Europe's Automotive Components Market: Assessment of Original Equipment and Aftermarket Demand by Product to 2000.* London: Economist Intelligence Unit, 1996.

Walton, Mary. *Car: A Drama of the American Workplace.* New York: W. W. Norton and Company, 1997.

Ward's Auto World. *Ward's Auto World 22nd Supplier Survey.* Supplement to *Ward's Auto World* (August 2000).

———. *Ward's Auto World 23rd Supplier Survey.* Supplement to *Ward's Auto World* (August 2001).

Weintraub, Jeff. "The Theory and Politics of the Public/Private Distinction." In *Public and Private in Thought and Practice,* edited by Jeff Weintraub and Krishan Kumar, 1–42. Chicago: University of Chicago Press, 1997.

Weintraub, Jeff, and Krishan Kumar, eds. *Public and Private in Thought and Practice: Perspectives on A Grand Dichotomy.* Chicago: University of Chicago Press, 1997.

Weiss, Linda, and John M. Hobson. *States and Economic Development: A Comparative Historical Analysis.* Oxford: Polity Press, 1995.

Wever, Kirsten S. "Renegotiating the German Model: Labor-Management Relations in the New Germany." In *Negotiating the New Germany,* edited by Lowell Turner, 207–226. Ithaca: ILR Press, an imprint of Cornell University Press, 1997.

Whitford, Josh, and Jonathan Zeitlin. "Governing Decentralized Production: Institutions, Public Policy, and the Prospects for Inter-Firm Collaboration in US Manufacturing." Research Paper presented at meetings of the Society for the Advancement of Socio-Economics, Minneapolis, June 2002.

Whitley, Richard. "The Social Construction of Economic Actors: Institutions and Types of Firm in Europe and Other Market Economies." In *The Changing European Firm*, edited by Richard Whitley and Peer Hull Christensen, 39–66. London: Routledge, 1996.

Whitley, Richard, and Peer Hull Christensen, eds. *The Changing European Firm: Limits to Convergence*. London: Routledge, 1996.

Whittaker, D. H. *Small Firms in the Japanese Economy*. Cambridge: Cambridge University Press, 1997.

Wildemann, Horst. *Die deutsche Zulieferindustire im europäischen Markt—ein Blick die Zukunft: Ergebnisse einer Delphi Studie*. Technische Universität München, 1993.

———. *Entwicklungs- und Vertriebsnetzwerke in der Zulieferindustrie*. Munich: Transfer-Centrum GmbH, 1998.

Williamson, Oliver E. *Markets and Hierarchies: Analysis and Antitrust Implications*. New York: Free Press, 1975.

———. "Transaction-Cost Economics: The Governance of Contractual Relations." *Journal of Law and Economics* 22, no. 2 (1979): 233–261.

———. "The Organization of Work: A Comparative Industrial Assessment." *Journal of Economic Behavior and Organization* 1 (1980): 5–38.

———. *The Economic Institutions of Capitalism*. New York: Free Press, 1985.

———. "Strategizing, Economizing, and Economic Organization." *Strategic Management Journal* 12, special issue (winter 1991): 75–94.

Wisner, Joel D., and Keah Choon Tan. "Supply Chain Management and Its Impact on Purchasing." *The Journal of Supply Chain Management* 36, no. 4 (2000): 33–42.

Womack, James P., Daniel T. Jones, and Daniel Roos. *The Machine That Changed the World: The Story of Lean Production*. New York: Harper Perennial, 1990.

World Bank. *World Development Report: The State in a Changing World*. New York: Oxford University Press, 1997.

Wriston, Walter B. *The Twilight of Sovereignty: How the Information Revolution Is Transforming Our World*. New York: Scribners, 1992.

Wynstra, Finn, Arjan Van Weele, and Mathieu Weggemann. "Managing Supplier Involvement in Product: Three Critical Issues." *European Management Journal* 19, no. 2 (2001): 157–167.

Yamazaki, Hiroaki, and Matao Miyamoto, eds. *Trade Associations in Business History: The International Conference on Business History 14*. Tokyo: University of Tokyo Press, 1988.

Yergin, Daniel, and Joseph Stanislaw. *The Commanding Heights: The Battle Between Government and the Marketplace That Is Remaking the Modern World*. New York: Simon & Schuster, 1998.

Yost, Jeffrey Robert. "Components of the Past and Vehicles of Change: Parts Manufacturers and Supplier Relations in the U.S. Automotive Industry." Ph.D. diss., Case Western Reserve University, 1998.

Zahn, Wolfgang. "Target Costing bei einem Automobilzulieferer: Ein Implementierungsansatz aus Werks-Controlling-Sicht." *Controlling*, no. 3 (1995): 148–153.

Zirger, B. J., and J. L. Hartley. "A Conceptual Model of Product Development Cycle Time." *Journal of Engineering and Technology Management* 11, no. 3– 4 (1994): 229–251.

———. "The Effect of Acceleration Techniques on Product Development Time." *IEEE Transactions on Engineering Management* 43, no. 2 (1996): 143–152.

Zischka, Stefan. "Gestaltung der Kunden- und Marktorientierung und Andwendung des Quality Function Deployment in Entwicklungsprojekten der deutschen Automobilzulieferindustrie: Ergebnisse einer Umfrage." Institute Newsletter on Quality Management, Institut für Qualitätsicherung, Hanover University, 1998.

Zulieferinitiative Rheinland-Pfalz. "Bericht über die Aktivitäten der 'Initiative zur Förderung der rheinland-pfälzischen Automobilzulieferindustrie." Universität Kaiserslautern, Zulieferinitiative Rheinland-Pfalz, 2000.

Zweigert, Konrad, and Hein Kötz. *An Introduction to Comparative Law.* Oxford: Clarendon Press, 1992.

Zwickel, Klaus, ed. *Vorbild Japan? Stärken und Schwächen der Industriestandorte Deutschland und Japan.* Frankfurt am Main: Otto Brenner Stiftung, 1996.

Zwicker, Dieter G. "Trade Associations in Germany and the United States of America—Antitrust Restrictions on the Ability of Trade Associations to Regulate Themselves." *The Antitrust Bulletin* (winter 1984): 775–831.

Zysman, John. *Governments, Markets and Growth.* Ithaca: Cornell University Press, 1983.

INDEX

Note: page references with a *t* indicate a table on the designated page.